Tricks of the Microsoft® Windows Vista™ Masters

J. Peter Bruzzese

CHESHIRE LIBRARIES	
Askews	29-Jun-2007

800 East 96th Street
Indianapolis, Indiana 46240 USA

Tricks of the Microsoft® Windows Vista™ Masters

Copyright © 2007 by Que Publishing

All rights reserved. No part of this book shall be reproduced, stored in a retrieval system, or transmitted by any means, electronic, mechanical, photocopying, recording, or otherwise, without written permission from the publisher. No patent liability is assumed with respect to the use of the information contained herein. Although every precaution has been taken in the preparation of this book, the publisher and author assume no responsibility for errors or omissions. Nor is any liability assumed for damages resulting from the use of the information contained herein.

10-Digit International Standard Book Number: 0-7897-73689-6

13-Digit International Standard Book Number: 978-0-7897-73689-5

Bruzzese, J. Peter.
   Tricks of the Microsoft Windows Vista masters / J. Peter Bruzzese. — 1st ed.
      p. cm.
   ISBN 0-7897-3689-6
   1. Microsoft Windows (Computer file) 2.   Operating systems (Computers)   I. Title.
   QA76.76.063B782157 2007
   005.4'46—dc22

                                                2007012299

Printed in the United States of America

First Printing: May 2007

Trademarks

All terms mentioned in this book that are known to be trademarks or service marks have been appropriately capitalized. Que Publishing cannot attest to the accuracy of this information. Use of a term in this book should not be regarded as affecting the validity of any trademark or service mark.

Warning and Disclaimer

Every effort has been made to make this book as complete and as accurate as possible, but no warranty or fitness is implied. The information provided is on an "as is" basis.

Bulk Sales

Que Publishing offers excellent discounts on this book when ordered in quantity for bulk purchases or special sales. For more information, please contact

    U.S. Corporate and Government Sales
    1-800-382-3419
    corpsales@pearsontechgroup.com

For sales outside of the U.S., please contact

    International Sales
    international@pearsoned.com

ASSOCIATE PUBLISHER
Greg Wiegand

ACQUISITIONS EDITOR
Loretta Yates

DEVELOPMENT EDITOR
Todd Brakke

MANAGING EDITOR
Gina Kanouse

PROJECT EDITOR
George E. Nedeff

COPY EDITOR
Megan Wade

SENIOR INDEXER
Cheryl Lenser

PROOFREADER
Harrison Ridge
Editorial Services

TECHNICAL EDITOR
Terri Stratton

PUBLISHING COORDINATOR
Cindy Teeters

MULTIMEDIA DEVELOPER
Dan Scherf

BOOK DESIGNER
Anne Jones

COMPOSITOR
Jake McFarland

This Book Is Safari Enabled

The Safari, Enabled icon on the cover of your favorite technology book means the book is available through Safari Bookshelf. When you buy this book, you get free access to the online edition for 45 days. Safari Bookshelf is an electronic reference library that lets you easily search thousands of technical books, find code samples, download chapters, and access technical information whenever and wherever you need it.

To gain 45-day Safari Enabled access to this book:

- Go to http://www.quepublishing.com/safarienabled
- Complete the brief registration form
- Enter the coupon code SQG4-HKRF-NP9W-FHF2-QPLY

If you have difficulty registering on Safari Bookshelf or accessing the online edition, please e-mail customer-service@safaribooksonline.com.

Contents at a Glance

	Introduction 1
1	General Tips and Tricks of the Masters 7
2	Mastering the Control Panel 51
3	Mastering Administration 101
4	Security Enhancements 135
5	Disk Configuration and Volume Tricks 181
6	Office 2007 Tricks for Vista Masters 209
7	Master Vista Networking 233
8	System Recovery and Diagnostic Tricks 259
9	Mastering the New Vista Apps 297
10	Group Policy Power 319
	Index 339

Table of Contents

Introduction 1
    Who Are the Vista Masters? 2

1 General Tips and Tricks of the Masters 7
    Where to Begin 7
    The Welcome Center 8
        Altering the Welcome Center 9
        Disabling the Welcome Center 10
    Shortcut Keys 10
        Windows Key Shortcuts 11
        User Logging Shortcuts 12
        Creating Your Own Shortcuts 13
        Beyond Vista Tools 14
    Desktop Customization 15
        Enhance Explorer Performance 15
        Changing the Boot Graphic 16
        Start Menu Configuration 17
        Command Prompt for Administrators 19
        Tweaking the Clock 21
        Vista DPI Scalings 22
        Using Shift to Slow Down Animations 23
    The Windows Sidebar 24
        Group Policy Settings 25
        Creating a Gadget 25
    The Boot Process: From XP to Vista 26
        Booting Up in XP 26
        The Vista Boot Process 27
        Editing the Boot Process 28
        Dual-Booting XP and Vista 31
        Removing Vista from Your Dual-Boot System 32

Contents   **v**

    MSCONFIG: The System Configuration Tool 33
        General 34
        Boot 34
        Services 35
        Startup 35
        Tools 36
        Additional Information 37
    Shortcut Menu: "Shift" Your Shortcuts 37
    Windows Explorer 39
        Saved Searches: What Are They, and How Can You Make Your Own? . . .40
        Enabling the Preview Pane 41
        Improvements to the Explorer UI 42
        Selecting Files with Check Boxes. 42
    Search: The Next Generation 43
        Search Box Tips 44
        Natural Language Search 45
        File List Heading Tips 46
        Beyond the Standard Search: Advanced Search Options 47
        Some Final Search Points: Internet Search, Control Panel Search 48
    Metadata: Organizing Your Documents, Music, and Pictures 49
        How Do You Add Metadata? 49
        Erasing Metadata Before You Share a Document .50

2 Mastering the Control Panel **51**
    Configuring the Control Panel 51
        Expanding Control Panel from the Start Menu 52
        Getting to Applets As Quickly As Possible 53
        Creating a Customized Control Panel Folder 55
    Breaking Down the Control Panel Applets 56
        Add Hardware 56
        AutoPlay 58
        Date and Time 59
        Default Programs 59

Device Manager 60
Folder Options 62
iSCSI Initiator 65
Pen and Input Devices 67
Printers 68
Regional and Language Options 72
Sync Center 74
Text to Speech 75
Windows SideShow 76
Windows Update 76
Color Management 78
What's Coming in the Future? 80
Indexing: Find the Needle in the Haystack 80
Modify Index Options 81
Advanced Index Options 81
Offline Files: Synchronizing Your World 82
How the Synchronization Works 84
Sync Errors, Warnings, and Resolutions 84
Parental Control 85
Manually Configuring the Allow-Block Websites List 87
Power Options: Don't Hibernate, Shutdown, Standby—Just Sleep 89
Disable Hibernation 90
Shortcut Keys to Sleep 91
Configuring Power Options 91
Group Policy Settings 92
Speech Recognition: You Talk, Vista Listens 93
Starting Speech Recognition 94
Start Listening 94
Opening the Speech Reference Card 95
Taking the Speech Tutorial 95
Training Your Computer to Better Understand You 96
Advanced Speech Options 96
Tablet PC: The Flintstones Meet the Jetsons 97

Contents vii

3 Mastering Administration 101
    The Desktop Tech: A Modern-Day Hermes 101
    User Accounts 102
        Literally Creating the Accounts 102
        Using Net User to Create Accounts 104
        Modifying Your User Accounts 105
        Additional Options from the Computer Management Console 108
    Computer Management 109
        Task Scheduler 111
        The Vista Event Viewer 116
        Services and the SC.exe Command 119
    Sharing System Resources 120
        Sharing Files Through the Public Folder 121
        Sharing Any Folder 122
    The System Window 126
        Computer Name 127
        Hardware 128
        Advanced 128
        System Protection 131
        Remote 132
    More Useful Tools 133

4 Security Enhancements 135
    Understanding Vista's "Hidden" Security Features 137
        Address Space Layout Randomization 137
        Windows Service Hardening 137
        Windows Integrity Control 138
        Windows Resource Protection 139
        ACLs Versus Integrity: Who Wins? 141
        Additional Features to Vista Security 141
    User Access Control 142
        How UAC Keeps Track of Privileges 145
        UAC and File and Registry Virtualization 149
        Configuring UAC Settings 150

Internet Explorer Security 153
    Protected Mode 153
    The Phishing Filter 154
    Some Additional IE Security Features 157
CardSpace/InfoCard—Don't Leave Home Without It 159
Windows Defender 161
    SpyNet 162
    Advanced Defender Information 163
    Beyond Windows Defender 166
The Malicious Software Removal Tool—Postinfection Removal 167
Windows Firewall 169
    Windows Firewall (Simple Settings) 170
    Windows Firewall with Advanced Security 172
    Vista Firewall Versus Third-Party Solutions 180

5   Disk Configuration and Volume Tricks 181

Vista File System Review 181
    The Rise and Fall of WinFS 182
    Transactional NTFS and Transactional Registry 184
Disk Management 185
    Disk Terminology Review 186
    Converting a Disk to Dynamic and Back to Basic 188
    Moving Disks Between Systems 189
    Basic Disks/Dynamic Disks—Creating Partitions and Volumes 190
    Disk Repair and Preventative Management 190
Understanding NTFS Permissions 193
    NTFS Permission Settings 194
    Permissions Are Cumulative, Deny Is Unforgiving 196
    Share Permissions Mixing with NTFS 197
EFS and BitLocker 199
    Looking Deeper into EFS 201
    BitLocker Overview 201
    BitLocker Planning and Recovery 202
ReadyDrive 205

Previous Versions 205
 Advanced Configuration Options for Previous Versions 207

6 Office 2007 Tricks for Vista Masters 209

The New Interface 209
 Terminology for Working with the New UI 210
 Customizing Your Interface 211
 The Mini Toolbar 212
Word 2007 213
 Saving Files As PDF (or XPS) 213
 Preparing Your Documents for Distribution 214
 The Document Inspector 215
 Full Screen Reading 216
 The Building Block Organizer 217
 Translation Tools 218
 Using Word 2007 As a Blog Editor 219
Excel 2007 220
 Adding in the Analysis ToolPak Add-in 222
 SmartArt for Excel 2007 224
 Sharing Your Excel Data 224
 Using Google to Share Data 225
 Dragging Tip to Fill Cells Quickly 226
 Conditional Formatting 226
 Going Beyond the Highlights 227
PowerPoint 2007 228
 Working with Themes 229
 Going Beyond the Highlights 229
Outlook 2007 230

7 Master Vista Networking 233

The Network and Sharing Center 233
 The Network Connectivity Status Indicator 234
 The Network Map 235
 Customizing Network Settings 238

Wireless Networking 239
    Getting Connected 240
    Ad-Hoc Wireless Networks 241
    Windows Connect Now 244
Function Discovery 245
Media Sharing with Windows Media Connect 246
    Evolution of Windows Media Connect to Windows Media
        Player Network Sharing Services 246
    Setting Up Media Sharing 247
Network Diagnostics 248
    Initiating a Diagnostic 248
    Command-Line Tools 251
Windows Meeting Space: Virtual Meetings, Real-time Collaboration 253
    People Near Me 253
    Starting Windows Meeting Space 254

8   System Recovery and Diagnostic Tricks 259

Backup and Restore Center 259
    The Backup and Restore Center 260
    Accessing Backups with Virtual PC or Virtual Server 261
    Backup Status and Configuration 263
The System Rating 264
Windows System Assessment Tool 266
Problem Reports and Solutions 267
    What Is Corporate Error Reporting? 268
Reliability and Performance Monitor 270
    Reliability Monitoring 271
    Resource Monitor 272
    Performance Monitor 273
    Data Collector Sets and Reports 276
    System Information Tool 278
    What's New in Task Manager 278
Memory Diagnostics Tool 281

ReadyBoost and SuperFetch 284

    ReadyBoost 284

    SuperFetch 285

    Where Is My Memory? 286

Vista Recovery: Advanced Boot Options, WinRE, and WinPE 288

    Advanced Boot Options in Vista 288

    The Windows Recovery Environment 289

    Windows PE 2.0 290

    The Basic Tools of WinPE 290

    Bootable USB Keys 295

9   Mastering the New Vista Apps 297

Internet Explorer 7 297

    Quick Tabs 298

    Tab Groups: Grouped Favorites and Multiple Home Pages 299

    Increasing the Number of Tabs 300

    Additional IE7 Features 300

Windows Mail 301

    New Features of Windows Mail 301

    Backing Up Your Windows Mail 303

Windows Contacts and Calendar 304

    Windows Contacts 304

    Windows Calendar 305

Windows Photo Gallery 307

Windows Movie Maker 310

Windows Media Player 11 310

Windows Media Center 313

Windows DVD Maker 314

A Few More Media Tips 316

    Volume Control 316

    The Snipping Tool 317

10	**Group Policy Power** **319**

    Group Policy Enhancements 319

        Number of Policies Increased 320

    ADMX Files 321

        A Conversion Tool from ADM to ADMX 324

        The Central Store 324

        Additional Points to Remember 325

    Network Location Awareness 326

    Multiple Local GPOs: Some Animals Are More Equal 327

        Creating These Alternative Policies 328

    New Group Policy Settings 329

        Power Management 330

        Blocking Device Installation 330

        Security Settings with Advanced Firewall 331

        Printer Assignment Based on Location 332

        Controlling Windows Defender Through Group Policy 332

        Delegating Printer Driver Installation to Users 332

        User Account Control 332

        Tablet PC Policies 333

        Wireless and Wired Policies 333

        Windows Error Reporting 334

    Group Policy Tools: Carpenters Have Toolbelts, GP Admins Have
        USB Keychains 335

Index **339**

About the Author

J. Peter Bruzzese is an independent consultant and trainer for a variety of clients, including New Horizons and ONLC.com. Over the past 10 years, Peter has worked for/with Goldman Sachs, CommVault Systems, and Microsoft, to name a few. He focuses on corporate training and has had the privilege of working with some of the best trainers in the business of computer education. In the past he specialized in Active Directory and Exchange instruction, as well as certification training, and holds the following certifications: from Microsoft, MCSA 2000/2003, MCSE NT/2000/2003, and MCT; from Novell, CNA; from Cisco, CCNA; from CIW, CIW Master and CIW Certified Instructor; from Comptia, A+, Network+, and iNET+.

Peter enjoys taking complex technical topics and breaking them down into something easy to understand and enjoyable to learn. This is what he has tried to do in the many books he has authored and coauthored, including *Enterprise Storage Solutions* (written with good friend Chris Wolf), *Exam Cram: Windows 2000 Active Directory* (with Will Willis and David Watts), and *218 MCSA Passport Guide* (with Walter Glenn).

Peter is also a contributor to *Redmond Magazine* and several tech sites. He has spoken on the MCP TechMentor Conferences and is currently a speaker for the TechPartner Conference. He has also created a variety of mini-training clips to assist others in learning more about networking, Office 2007, and Vista (www.cliptraining.com). His belief is that short training sessions in a familiar environment yield greater results.

You can catch up with Peter at jpb@cliptraining.com.

Dedication

This book is dedicated back to the Vista developers, authors, bloggers, and admins who made the book incredibly fun to write.

Acknowledgments

Writing a book about a new operating system, especially a book that tries to present the highest level of experience and knowledge, takes considerable time and effort. You literally have to spend hundreds of hours reading through material to find the "best of the best." That time comes from somewhere (or someone), and so my first thank you goes to my loving and supportive wife Jenny. After 10 years of marriage, I can easily say that being with you is the best decision I've ever made.

I'd also like to show appreciation for my family, who are always supportive. To my parents, Jerry and Marion Bruzzese, who let me build my castles in the sky but make sure my feet are always on the ground. I would also like to thank other family members who have supported me over the years: Jaclyn and Alex, Tom and Kathy, Tim and Jennine, Ron and Alicia, John and Cathie, Earl and Tina, Randy and Lisa, Jeremy and Shannon, Steve and Karla, Helen and little McKayla, and Sarah.

I'd like to thank my research assistant Alan Wright, who truly pushed the boundaries of standard thought to explore every possible feature Vista has to offer. I would like to thank Ronald Barrett and Timothy Duggan of ERE in Manhattan for their support with both the software and hardware needed to make this book come together. As usual, I would like to thank David Solomon for getting me started as an author and for continuing to be a good friend and mentor.

I have many to thank from the technology sector, including authors, instructors, tech bloggers, and in-the-trenches admins. Without your comments, your experiences, your frustrations, your successes, this book would just be another book about how to use Vista, as opposed to a book about how YOU, the Vista Masters, use Vista.

I cannot say enough about the folks at Que. I'd especially like to thank my acquisitions editor Loretta Yates for her patience in working with me and her organizational ability, which helped bring this book together from idea to print. I'd also like to thank my development editor Todd Brakke, who knew the perfect way to take my chapters and adjust them into the "Masters" theme. I'd like to thank my technical editor Terri Stratton, who has an expansive knowledge of Microsoft Vista; George Nedeff, this book's project editor; and Megan Wade, my copy editor, for catching all my typing/grammatical errors. I'd also like to thank Linda Harrison and Cheryl Lenser, who proofread and indexed the book. And a special thanks to the cover designer Anne Jones.

We Want to Hear from You!

As the reader of this book, *you* are our most important critic and commentator. We value your opinion and want to know what we're doing right, what we could do better, what areas you'd like to see us publish in, and any other words of wisdom you're willing to pass our way.

As an associate publisher for Que Publishing, I welcome your comments. You can email or write me directly to let me know what you did or didn't like about this book—as well as what we can do to make our books better.

Please note that I cannot help you with technical problems related to the topic of this book. We do have a User Services group, however, where I will forward specific technical questions related to the book.

When you write, please be sure to include this book's title and author as well as your name, email address, and phone number. I will carefully review your comments and share them with the author and editors who worked on the book.

    Email: feedback@quepublishing.com

    Mail: Greg Wiegand
              Associate Publisher
              Que Publishing
              800 East 96th Street
              Indianapolis, IN 46240 USA

Reader Services

Visit our website and register this book at www.quepublishing.com/register for convenient access to any updates, downloads, or errata that might be available for this book.

Introduction

TRICKS OF THE MICROSOFT WINDOWS MASTERS

"*We learned a lot during the Vista [process]. People can see how we've mixed together our Office talent and Windows talent to get the best of both worlds, and how we're going to do things going forward.*"

—Bill Gates, interview with Steven Levy for *Newsweek* (February 1, 2007)

Did you know that it is often necessary to sift through 250 to 400 tons of rock, gravel, and sand to mine a one carat diamond? And once a diamond is found, it must be cut precisely by a craftsman and polished to bring out the shine we all appreciate. In the case of diamonds, they must be both "discovered in the rough" and "crafted into an object of beauty" before placed before us in a showcase.

The same is true of the gems you'll find within this book. We scoured the earth, sifting from among "masters" of the Vista operating system until we discovered the finest points we could. Then we put them together and shined them up so that you hold in your hands a truly impressive collection. The tips and tricks we've put together include group policy edits, shortcut keys, security settings, and more. We even review some of the more important new features of Vista such as Parental Controls, Windows Meeting Space, and BitLocker technology so you'll be completely up-to-date on all that Vista has to offer.

Sometimes this book contains a tip or trick; sometimes it provides the background material from Microsoft developers on how and why a tool was developed and how it can be used to increase your productivity; and yet other times we simply present the facts of what Vista can do. In the event you buy only one book on Windows Vista, you are holding all you need.

Why sift through 1,500-page volumes on Vista or hundreds of web blogs when we've already done it for you and collected exactly what you're looking for? As you thumb through the Table of Contents, you'll notice that we have grouped our tips and tricks by categories that will make finding what you need easy. Best of all, each point is concise so there is no need to waste valuable time reading through fluff or dull material—only clarity.

All that being said, we truly hope you enjoy the tricks within. It's in no way exhaustive—there are always more gems to be found in the world of Microsoft. But this is as comprehensive a collection of Vista knowledge as you're likely to find in print.

Who Are the Vista Masters?

This book includes many, many quotes and tricks from outside sources. I contacted Microsoft developers, fellow authors and trainers, Internet bloggers, and experts in their fields and asked permission to quote them. Some of the developers at Microsoft even took the time to read portions of the book to confirm its quality and accuracy. To all of them I'd like to say thank you.

Here is a list of the major contributors to the book. There are even more inside:

- Jeff Atwood, a Microsoft Windows developer since 1992, for his tips on the blog site www.codinghorror.com
- Jon Hicks, deputy editor of the *Official Vista Magazine*, along with Paul Douglas, editor of *Vista Magazine* (http://www.windowsvistamagazine.co.uk/)

- Chris Holmes, a Vista blogger and tech guru (along with Dena Reiter and Kristan Kenney) for their tricks and insight at www.chris123nt.com
- Terri Stratton, Microsoft MVP, is the publisher and news editor of "The Tablet PC" website at http://thetabletpc.net/
- Tim Sneath, group manager, client platform evangelism, Microsoft, for his blog site http://blogs.msdn.com/tims/
- Josh Phillips (founder of enthusiast website WindowsConnected.com)
- Long Zheng, one of the most respected Vista bloggers, at http://www.istartedsomething.com
- Tony Campbell, for his great blog site at http://vista.beyondthemanual.com/, as well as his work with Jonathan Hassell on the book *Windows Vista: Beyond the Manual* by Apress
- Alan Wright (technical guru and educator for many years, currently in the Detroit area), for his insight and research on Vista subject matter
- Ronald Barrett, director of information technology at ERE, an accounting and financial services firm in Manhattan, for his years as an IT professional specializing in a variety of fields, including security and Thin Client solutions
- Tim Grey, director of the Professional Photo Community at Microsoft (www.microsoft.com/prophoto/), for his knowledge on color management and digital imaging
- Michael Bourgoin, program manager at Microsoft for the Desktop and Graphics Technologies Color Team, for his in-depth insight into the world of color management
- Joli Ballew, a technology trainer and writer in the Dallas area with more than two dozen books to her credit (www.joliballew.com), for her blogging on Vista subject matter and her contribution to this book with information on parental control and speech recognition; she is also a contributor to the Microsoft Expert Zone at http://www.microsoft.com/windowsxp/expertzone/meetexperts/ballew.mspx
- Michael Howard, Microsoft security developer, for reading over and contributing to the security information in Chapter 4, for his blog site http://blogs.msdn.com/michael_howard/default.aspx, and his books on SDL Lifecycle and his book *Writing Secure Code for Vista*
- Mark Minasi (www.minasi.com) for his newsletters, books, and seminars, which all include his acerbic wit and humor
- Ed Bott, author of the book *Special Edition Using Microsoft Office 2007* (and a list of other titles), for his in-depth coverage of Office and Vista in his books and on his website at www.edbott.com

- Timothy Duggan, network administrator at ERE and co-founder of ClipTraining.com, for his generosity and constant support on this project, as well as his technical knowledge
- John Walkenbach, Excel author, for his book *John Walkenbach's Favorite Excel 2007 Tips and Tricks*
- David Gainer, the group program manager for the Microsoft Excel team, for the team's blog site at http://blogs.msdn.com/excel/default.aspx
- Bill Jelen (www.mrexcel.com), for being an Excel guru and putting out so many books, videos, and clips on how to use Excel to its full extent
- Echo Swinford, for her great website about PowerPoint 2007 (http://www.echosvoice.com/2007.htm) and her latest book, *Fixing PowerPoint Annoyances*
- Bob Kelly, the founder of AppDeploy.com (a resource focused on desktop management products and practices), for his podcasts at http://www.realtime-vista.com/podcast/
- Greg Frost, program manager within the Core Windows Networking division, for his many great articles on the MSDN blog site at http://blogs.msdn.com/wndp/ and his own personal blog site at http://blog.gabefrost.com/
- Mitch Tulloch, president of MTIT Enterprises (http://www.mtit.com), for his many outstanding articles regarding Vista and networking; Mitch is both a scholar and a gentleman, and we thank him for the contributions he has made to this work
- Brien M. Posey (www.brienposey.com), a technical author who has produced thousands of articles, tips, and whitepapers since 1995, for his insight into the future of networking
- James Bannan, technical writer for acpmag.com, for his articles on dual-boot with Vista and media sharing, which can be found on apcmag.com
- Daniel Nerenberg, an MCSA, an MCSE, an MCTS, and a consultant with a Montreal-based IT services firm who is the vice president of the Montreal IT pro user group (http://www.mitpro.ca and www.thelazyadmin.com)
- Bryant Likes, who has been developing applications on the Microsoft platform since 1996 and who currently works as a senior solution developer for Avanade, for his SQLXML blog at http://blogs.sqlxml.org/bryantlikes
- Ben Armstrong, the Virtual Machine Guy and program manager of the Virtual Machine Team at Microsoft (http://blogs.msdn.com/Virtual_PC_Guy/), for the help he has given toward understanding VHD files
- John Kellett (http://www.johnkellett.co.uk), for the information he provides on Performance Monitor
- David Solomon (www.solsem.com), for his incredible coverage of Windows architecture in the book *Microsoft Windows Internals, Fourth Edition*

- Parveen Patel, a developer on the WinRE team blog site (http://blogs.msdn.com/winre/default.aspx), for all the great information he provides on Vista recovery
- Mario Szpuszta, Microsoft developer in Austria (http://blogs.msdn.com/mszCool), for his information on creating a Windows PE disk
- James O' Neil, developer (http://blogs.technet.com/jamesone/default.aspx), for his assistance in creating a bootable USB drive with Windows PE
- Paul McFedries, the president of Logophilia Limited, for his book *Windows Vista Unleashed*
- Darren Mar-Elia, CTO and founder of SDM Software, Inc., a start-up focused on delivering innovative Group Policy management solutions (www.sdmsoftware.com)
- Jakob H. Heidelberg, an MCSE:Security/Messaging, MCDST, MCT, and CCNA who works as a system consultant for Interprise Consulting, a Microsoft Gold Partner based in Denmark, for the information regarding Group Policy changes in Vista http://www.windowsecurity.com/Jakob_H_Heidelberg/
- Derek Melber, the director of education and compliance solutions at DesktopStandard Corp., for his many books and articles over the years, especially those on Group Policy at windowsecurity.com; he is not only an excellent teacher, but I consider it a privilege to call him my friend
- Jeremy Moskowitz (http://www.gpanswers.com), for his Group Policy knowledge and teaching ability; I can honestly say he is one of the best speakers I've had the privilege to listen to, and he has been a good friend, as well. I appreciate knowing and working with him

Chapter 1

GENERAL TIPS AND TRICKS OF THE MASTERS

Where to Begin

If we might take one guess as to why you are reading this book, it's because you are one of millions of people who are daily users of the Windows operating system. Whether you have a love-hate, a love-love, or even a hate-hate relationship with Windows Vista, by virtue of holding this book in your hand, we know you have an interest in . . . mastering this operating system. It's not about working with it, not about getting by with it, not about making money with it (although all three are valid reasons to catch up with Vista and this book will help you accomplish all three of those fine goals). But the main reason you wanted *this* book is because every trick, every tip, every explanation joins you to our world, the Vista Masters.

IN THIS CHAPTER

- Where to Begin
- The Welcome Center
- Shortcut Keys
- Desktop Customization
- The Windows Sidebar
- The Boot Process: From XP to Vista
- MSCONFIG: The System Configuration Tool
- Shortcut Menu: "Shift" Your Shortcuts
- Windows Explorer
- Search: The Next Generation
- Metadata: Organizing Your Documents, Music, and Pictures

While most of this book is broken down into chapters governing specific aspects of the Vista OS, this opening chapter revolves around several subjects that relate more to the startup process and desktop features. You'll learn about the boot process, shortcut keys, the new Windows Explorer features, and the new search options. All these discussions will be to the point and filled with explanations, tips, and tricks to not only educate you on the new features, but also to help you embrace and dominate them.

From here, you'll notice that other chapters discuss Group Policy changes, networking tricks, and so forth. The cool thing about a book like this is you don't have to read it from beginning to end, but can pick it up, start at any heading, read that one section, and get the full sense of the subject.

So, let's get started at the beginning....

The Welcome Center

The first screen you come to when you start Vista the first time (or hundredth if you don't turn this off) is the Welcome Center (see Figure 1.1). The Welcome Center is designed to help beginners work with Vista, providing some basic information about the system they are using. If a user selects the option in the upper-right corner labeled Show More Details, the system settings appear. From the Welcome Center, a user can access the Control Panel, Ease of Access settings, and Personalization settings, and even learn more about new features—its actually both helpful and visually appealing. There is even an option for new users to watch Vista demos. If you are an administrator, you might want to encourage users to take advantage of some of these instructional features.

Scott M. Fulton wrote an article (http://www.tgdaily.com) entitled "Microsoft unconcerned about OEM's Vista antitrust complaint" which says, in part:

> The provision, which was identified as "Welcome Center," is a panel that users see when the operating system is booted for the first time. It was created to comply with directives of the company's antitrust settlement with the government, that the operating system provide equal access to all OEMs who want to install special software packages in order to customize Windows for their customers.

One of the key reasons for the Welcome Center appearing by default is so that Microsoft could comply with the government's request for the OS to provide equal access to all OEMs who want to install software for their customers as part of the antitrust settlement. So, OEMs are entitled to extra information on how to alter the Welcome Center to use it for themselves.

FIGURE 1.1
The Welcome Center meets you at the door when you first start Vista.

Altering the Welcome Center

To customize the Welcome Center, you have to manipulate a file called `Oobe.xml`. More information can be found about this in the Windows Automated Installation Kit (AIK). As noted by John Savill, FAQ Editor, at windowsitpro.com:

 The kit comprises all the elements needed for the automated installation of the Windows Vista OS, including:

- Documentation consisting of whitepapers and compiled HTML that discusses the technologies.

- Microsoft Windows Preinstallation Environment (WinPE), which is the basis for the capture and deployment of Vista.

- The WAIK tools, which by default are installed to C:\Program Files\Windows AIK\ and consist of the Windows System Image Manager to enable the management of answer files to be used for automating installations; tools to manage WinPE instances; and ImageS, which is used to mount and modify the content of Windows Image (WIM) files.

To learn more about creating WinPE instances and using ImageX, turn to Chapter 8, "System Recovery and Diagnostic Tricks."

Disabling the Welcome Center

Fortunately, if you don't like the Welcome Center you can just clear the Run at Startup check box in the bottom-left corner to disable it. There are also extreme approaches to disabling it by a Registry entry. It's totally unnecessary, but very fun to know anyway. This tip was posted at Flexbeta.net by an admin named Gsurface:

Start the Registry Editor by entering `regedit` or `regedt32` in the Search field off the Start orb. Navigate through to the following key: HKEY_CURRENT_USER, Software, Microsoft, Windows, CurrentVersion, Run. Scroll down until you see the key named WelcomeCenter. Delete the key and the Welcome Center will not come back on startup. You might check out the value data on the edit string and notice that it mentions executing `rundll32.exe` and then `oobeflrdr.dll` (literally it says `"rundll32.exe oobefldr.dll,ShowWelcomeCenter"`).

Note that in this tip, OOBE stands for out-of-box experience, which is defined by the user's first contact with a software application. So, in this case, upon startup the `oobefldr.dll` is executed, which is the `.dll` for the Welcome Center.

You could also open a command prompt in elevated Administrative permissions, by going to the Start orb, under All Programs, Accessories, right-click the command prompt and select "Run as Administrator" and run the following command to delete that key:

```
reg delete "HKCR\CLSID\{FD6905CE-952F-41F1-9A6F-135D9C6622CC}"
```

You can also type `reg /?` from the command line to see some of the other options, but we will consider more Registry edits later in the book.

> **NOTE**
> You can also use Group Policies to prevent the Welcome Center from appearing. We discuss Group Policy later in the book, but we won't deny your curiosity or make you go looking for it: User Configuration, Administrative Templates, Windows Components, Windows Explorer, Do not display the Welcome Center at logon.
>
> If you want to prevent the Welcome Center from appearing by using an unattended installation, you can configure the SkipUserOOBE setting in the `Unattend.xml` file.

Shortcut Keys

Shortcuts act as dividers between the masses. Some love clicking their way around an interface, while others love their keyboards. Back in the '90s when the game *Descent* became popular for online play, the guy who tried to fight with the joystick always lost out to the flexible fingers of the keyboard pilot. Speed was always on his side. It's no different today with your operating system. It will always be faster to use your keyboard than to force your hand to reach for the mouse. And if you're not yet a big user of shortcuts, you'll probably be surprised how much a couple of quick keystrokes can accomplish.

Windows Key Shortcuts

If you're an experienced Windows user, you probably already know that you push the Windows Key to bring up the Start menu. But in addition to that, there are a bunch of standard Windows Key shortcuts, the most useful of which are listed in Table 1.1. (Note that this table also includes a couple of shortcuts that don't require the Windows key.)

Table 1.1—Vista Shortcuts using the Windows key

Shortcut Key	Description
⊞+B	Sets focus to first icon in the notification area. You can use arrow keys to move among the icons in the notification area or press Tab to move around on the taskbar.
⊞+D	Show Desktop (without the Sidebar).
⊞+E	Windows Explorer (opens to Computer).
⊞+F	Find Files or Folders (aka Search).
⊞+M	Minimize All windows (Sidebar not included).
⊞+Shift+M	Undo Minimize All Windows.
⊞+R	Open the Run dialog box.
⊞+Tab	3-D Flip (flips you through your applications but with a cool graphic instead of the standard Alt+Tab). Requires the use of the Aero user interface.
⊞+Pause/Break	System Properties.
⊞+F1	Windows Help.
⊞+L	Locks workstation. If the user account has a password, it must be reentered to unlock the system again.
⊞+U	Ease of Access Settings.
⊞+Spacebar	This shows the Sidebar (the Sidebar must be open, but minimized).
Ctrl+⊞+Tab	Brings up Flip-3D, but it will stay on the desktop so you can scroll up, down, left and right.
⊞+T	Allows you to tab between application buttons on the taskbar.
Ctrl+Shift+Esc	Opens Task Manager.
Alt+Tab	Windows Flip. Allows you to choose an open application to switch to by repeatedly pressing the Tab key.

One of our favorite shortcuts comes from Jon Hicks, Deputy Editor of the Official Vista Magazine (http://www.windowsvistamagazine.co.uk/). Jon says:

Here's a neat tip I learned while I was talking to Microsoft last week: keyboard shortcuts for the Quick Launch icons in Vista. You can open any icon in the Quick Launch bar (just to the right of the Start button) by holding down the Windows key and pressing what I'll call the "rank number" of the icon—the number that corresponds to its position in the list. So, in my desktop here, Windows + 1 opens Outlook, Windows + 2 opens Internet Explorer, Windows + 5 opens the Snipping Tool and so on. This means that you can set a really simple keyboard shortcut to any program you want—just right-click the program in the Start Menu and choose Add To Quick Launch, then drag-and-drop it to assign the number you want.

Steve Clayton, Microsoft
http://blogs.msdn.com/stevecla01

This is such a cool little time saver mainly as I am a big user of "show desktop"—Win Key + 1 in this case. If you're running Vista, give it a go. For some additional eye candy, minimize all apps (Win Key + 1 for me) and then hold Ctrl and the scroll wheel on your mouse if you have one. Cool eh?

User Logging Shortcuts

Some keystrokes aren't exactly shortcuts. They are keystrokes to get you where you want to be. For example, to shut down or switch users and so forth, you can use the shortcuts in Table 1.2.

Table 1.2—User Logging Shortcuts

Shortcut	Description
⊞ (and then) three right arrows and Enter	To Shut down
⊞ (and then) three right arrows and U	To Shut down
⊞ (and then) three right arrows and R	To Restart
⊞ (and then) three right arrows and W	To Switch Users
⊞ (and then) one right arrow and Enter	To Sleep

Creating Your Own Shortcuts

With as many shortcut keys as Windows has, there are bound to be some functions you use on a daily basis that don't have a convenient shortcut. Fortunately, you can create your own. Go to the Start orb and find an application for which you want to create

> **NOTE** It might initially look like you aren't able to change the shortcut because nothing happens when you put the cursor in the box, but after you type the keys you want to use for the shortcut, it should update the box.

the shortcut (let's say Notepad, for example). Right-click the application and then select Properties. On the shortcut tab (shown in Figure 1.2), you can select the Shortcut key box and type the shortcut key you want to use to activate the application.

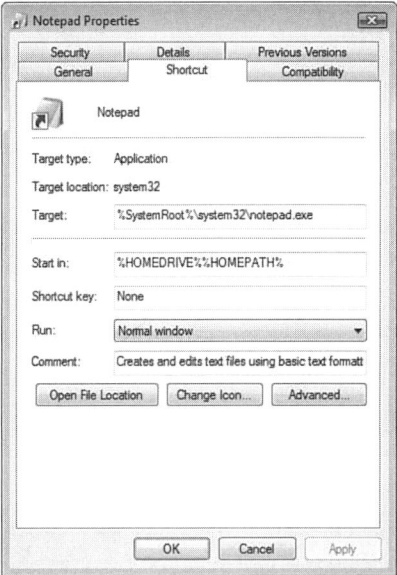

FIGURE 1.2
The Shortcut tab enables you to establish additional shortcut keys.

You might, at times, have difficulties changing these shortcuts depending on how programs are installed on your system or whether you are on a network. This is because Vista's User Account Control (UAC) might stop you from assigning shortcuts to items on the Start menu you didn't personally create. The reason for this is that these items might exist in the All Users folders and you aren't the owner of those programs; therefore, you don't have the right to change the shortcuts for these applications.

Granted, you could disable UAC if you knew how and had the rights. But if you do have the right, there's also a less drastic measure you can take that doesn't compromise your system's security. Open Windows Explorer with your administrative account (click Start, Programs, Accessories, and then right-click Windows Explorer and select Run as Administrator). From here, you can find your way to the Start menu programs, right-click the program, go to Properties, and then change the shortcut from there.

> **NOTE:** The Start menu for all users is located as C:\ProgramData\Microsoft\Windows\Start Menu with the ProgramData folder being hidden by default as a system folder. For the current user you can look under c:\users\<username>\appdata\roaming\microsoft\windows\Start menu.

Another option if you are having problems with shortcuts is to find the executable for the application for which you want to establish the shortcut key. Right-click the application icon, select Send, and then choose the option to send it to the desktop as a shortcut. Because you created this specific shortcut, you can right-click, open its Properties, and then enter whatever shortcut key you like. It's yours so you own it and can work with it without UAC getting involved.

Beyond Vista Tools

There has always been a market for tools that can help you make your working experience more customizable with Windows. In the world of shortcut keys, a great tool we used to work with was WinKey (the latest and final version is 2.8 from Copernic). You can still find this on the Web if you run a search for "winkey."

You can also look for other tools on sites such as download.com and so forth. One nice tool is AutoHotkey (it's a little tricky for newbies in the world of scripting, though). It's a free, open-source utility for Windows that is constantly evolving. Here are some of the self-proclaimed uses from the AutoHotKey website (www.autohotkey.com):

- Automate almost anything by sending keystrokes and mouse clicks. You can write a mouse or keyboard macro by hand or use the macro recorder.
- Create hotkeys for your keyboard, joystick, and mouse. Virtually any key, button, or combination can become a hotkey.
- Expand abbreviations as you type them. For example, typing "btw" can automatically produce "by the way."
- Create custom data entry forms, user interfaces, and menu bars.
- Remap keys and buttons on your keyboard, joystick, and mouse.
- Respond to signals from handheld remote controls via the WinLIRC client script.
- Convert any script into an EXE file that can be run on computers that don't have AutoHotkey installed.

Desktop Customization

For many of us, changing the way Windows looks is part of the fun (and frustration) of using Windows. You want Windows to be a console that meets your needs in the most efficient and visually appealing way possible. Some want big buttons, a pretty ocean background, and happy sounds. Others want to feel like they are on the Starship Enterprise. In either case, users want the look and functionality that makes them happy.

These tips give you a quick lesson on how to configure your system the way you want it.

Enhance Explorer Performance

These are just a few pointers on making your system appear faster. Depending on the hardware you're using when you install Vista, you will see varying degrees of speed. Here are a few ideas to speed things up.

Go into your Advanced System Settings. (Right-click the Computer icon in the Start menu and select Properties. Then click the Advanced Computer Settings link to open the System Properties dialog box.) On the Advanced tab, under Performance, click Settings. The Visual Effects tab opens (see Figure 1.3). From here, you can easily click to have Vista turn all settings on or off for best Performance or best Appearance. Or you can customize this yourself by choosing to disable certain options.

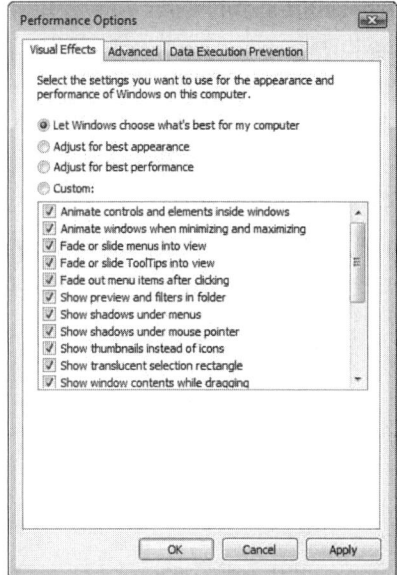

FIGURE 1.3
Making adjustments to your Visual Effects can improve your Vista experience.

Chris Holmes, a Vista blogger and tech guru, along with Dena Reiter and Kristan Kenney, wrote up a bunch of great tips on working with Vista and tweaking the Vista environment, at www.chris123.net.com.

Try turning on/off these options to see how performance improves:

- Fade or Slide Menus into View
- Fade or Slide Tooltips into View
- Fade Out Menu Items after Clicking
- Show Shadows under Menus
- Slide Open Combo Boxes
- Slide Taskbar Buttons
- Use a Background Image for Each Folder Type

Changing the Boot Graphic

Some of us love the Vista boot screens. We love when that little orb appears in the middle of the screen and then the colorful login screen displays. For those who don't love it just the way it is, well, you can actually change it slightly. During boot, behind the scenes is a boot screen that Vista techno-geeks call Aurora. The only difference between it and what you see by default is that, instead of a scrolling bar with a Vista graphic at the beginning of the process, you see a stationary picture with the text "Starting Windows Vista" at the bottom.

Chris Holmes

http://www.windows-now.com/blogs/chris123nt/articles/16664.aspx

If you are tired of the default boot screen in Windows Vista, there is a better looking one hidden away, and it looks like the "Aurora" that everyone has been raving about since Longhorn was in its alpha days.

To enable the "Aurora" boot screen:

1. Press the ⊞ + R combination on your keyboard to display the Run dialog.
2. Type **MSCONFIG.EXE**.
3. If User Account Control prompts you to allow the action, click on "Continue."
4. In the "System Configuration" window, click on the "Boot" tab.

5. Select your Windows Vista installation and under "Boot options", check "No GUI boot."

6. Press OK.

7. In the dialog that appears, check "Don't show this message again", and then click on "Restart."

8. Your computer will now reboot, and you will see the "aurora" boot screen with text that says "Starting Windows Vista."

And if you really like the Aurora boot screen you should also try out the Aurora screensaver.

Start Menu Configuration

If you are reading this book, you probably already know how to configure your own Start menu. So, we are just going to give you a few tips on the how and why of things just in case you missed out on some of the more useful options at your disposal.

First, your Start menu icons are large by default. Although that isn't a bad thing, if you use the smaller ones, you can put twice as many programs on the Start menu without affecting the size of the font.

To make this adjustment, right-click the Start orb and select Properties. Within the Start menu tab, you can select the Customize button next to the Start menu options. You will see a Customize Start menu list; scroll down to the bottom (wisely taking note of other options for future changes) to see that the Use Large Icons box is selected by default (see Figure 1.4). Clear this check box to see the difference. You might also note that this is the same location for choosing your default Internet browser or email program that appears within the Start menu.

Terri Stratton
Microsoft MVP

> While talking about large icons it would be a good chance to talk about changing the size of the desktop icons as well. Right-click the Desktop, Select View then click Classic icons.

You might take note that going into the Properties of the Start menu also gave you the option to go back to the Classic Start menu with your icons on the desktop and the single-pane Start menu options.

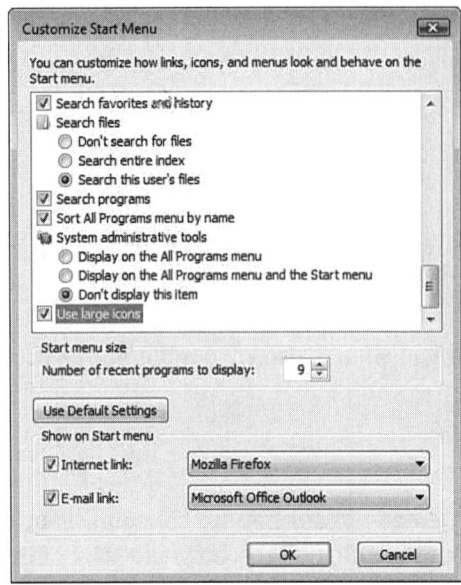

FIGURE 1.4
Advanced customization options for the Vista Start menu.

The Administrative Tools folder can also be put on the Start menu and in the All Programs folder by opening the Customization settings and scrolling down (look right above the Use Large Icons setting). From here, you can make it so that your Administrative Tools are easier to get to (as shown in Figure 1.5).

TIP
In previous versions of Windows, the Run command was immediately accessible from the Start menu. In Vista, you have to click your way to the Accessories folder to find the shortcut icon. Obviously, there's always the ⊞+R shortcut. However, if you like the Run command being located on the Start menu, you can use the same methods mentioned previously to customize your Start menu and return the Run command to its rightful place. (If you use the Classic Start menu mode, the Run command is automatically restored to the Start menu.)

Keep in mind, though, that the Search dialog box in the Start menu acts as an impromptu Run command. Just type the program you are looking for into the Search field and then press Enter.

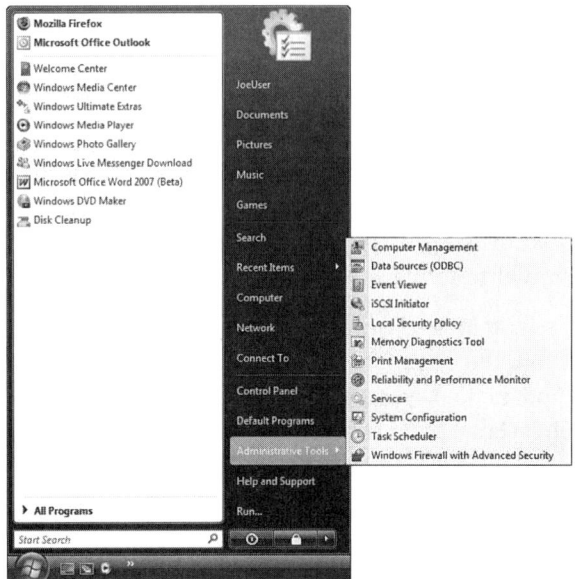

FIGURE 1.5
You need your tools close at hand.

Command Prompt for Administrators

While we are on the subject of configuration, it's important to note that some of your programs will be affected by the new User Account Control (UAC). Because User Account Control restricts a lot of actions that many programs could previously have performed without obstacle, many legacy applications run afoul of these new security measures. Enabling programs to get around these restrictions is easy to do, but you have to make an extra effort to run these tools and applications with administrative credentials. It's not so hard to do. You saw earlier in this chapter that it's a simple matter of right-clicking whichever application or shortcut you want to run and then selecting the Run as Administrator option.

Terri Stratton
Microsoft MVP

Pinning the Command Prompt or any other frequently used program to the Start menu is also an option. It's then quickly available to right-click to run as administrator. It can also be added to the Quick Launch, but most like saving space there for more frequently used programs.

20 Tricks of the Windows Vista Masters

Tim Sneath,
Microsoft Vista Technical Evangelist
http://blogs.msdn.com/tims/ under the heading
from "Windows Vista Secret #10: Open an Elevated Command Prompt in Six Keystrokes"

User Account Control is, as I mentioned in secret #4, an important part of the security protection that Windows Vista offers. For any user with administrative credentials, you can always execute a process with full admin rights by right-clicking on the executable or shortcut and choosing "Run as Administrator."

For myself, I regularly want to open an admin-level command prompt, and it's a distraction to have to move my hands off the keyboard to go through the elevation contortions. So I was delighted to find a little keyboard shortcut for launching an elevated process. Simply press Ctrl+Shift+Enter from the search bar on the Start menu with a selected application, and that triggers elevation.

For example, to launch an elevated command prompt, simply press the Win key; type `cmd`; press Ctrl+Shift+Enter; and then hit Alt+C to confirm the elevation prompt. Six keystrokes to an elevated command prompt!

(Once I've got an elevated command prompt, I always like to execute color 4f as my first input so that this console window is visually differentiated from other non-elevated windows.)

How do you know for sure if your command prompt is elevated or not? Well, after some complaints Microsoft added a note to the top of your command prompt that says "Administrator" if it is elevated. So, if you don't want to change the color you can just look at the title bar. However, here is a tip that came from blogger Josh Phillips (founder of enthusiast website WindowsConnected.com) at http://windowsconnected.com/blogs/joshs_blog/

I am often juggling between a few command prompts at once and glancing at the title bar hasn't been stopping me from using the wrong command prompt from time to time. So here is a quick tip that will add a bigger visual clue to your admin level command windows.

Step 1: Create a batch file using the following and save it to your hard disk.

```
@echo off
pushd %SystemRoot%\System32
set ADMINTEST=~~4uDude.JHP
:START
MD %ADMINTEST% > NUL 2>&1
if exist %SystemRoot%\System32\%ADMINTEST% GOTO ADMIN
```

```
        GOTO END
        :ADMIN
        color 4f
        RD %ADMINTEST%
        :END
        set ADMINTEST=
        popd
```

Basically this batch file is a simple test if you have admin right by trying to create a folder under system32 which a non-admin would not have rights to do. If successful it will change the background color to red. You could do this a number of different ways, but this gives you the concept.

Step 2: Create a string value called "autorun" under HKEY_LOCAL_MACHINE\Software\Microsoft\Command Processor then point it to the file that you created in Step1. This value will run the batch file anytime a command prompt is started and change the color for you.

Tweaking the Clock

Here is one tip for getting a little extra functionality from the Vista clock on the taskbar. As simple as that clock is, many users need to keep track of time in multiple time zones. Fortunately, you can do that right within your taskbar.

Right-click your clock on the taskbar and select Adjust Date/Time. Select the Additional Clocks tab and then determine whether you need one or two additional clocks; then select which names and time zones you require.

The next time you hover your mouse over your time, you will see the other time zones you have configured. This is a great tool for travelers who like to call home or business employees who have offices and clients in other zones.

You could also set up gadgets in the Windows Sidebar to show you multiple times in different zones. You are welcome to choose whichever method you like best.

> **TIP**
> Control the View in the Notification Area. In the bottom-right corner of your screen are several notification icons, including the time, volume, networking, and power options. With additional applications that you install, this area can really grow out of control, but usually you can alter the icons that appear. In XP you could set the notification bar to not show items that were inactive. In Vista you can still do that, but you can also hide the clock, volume, network, and power options. One reason you might decide to hide the clock is that you don't need two clocks on your system. If you have the Windows Sidebar running a clock, you don't need the one at the bottom.

Vista DPI Scalings

Although these options might seem confusing at first, it won't take you long to get used to the new configurations for DPI scalings in Vista. You can open the Control Panel and open the Appearance and Personalization options (then select Personalize), or you can right-click in the middle of your screen and select Personalize.

These settings allow you to configure most aspects of the Windows UI, including your screen background (wallpaper), screensavers, window color schemes, sounds, mouse pointers, themes, and display settings. In addition, here is where you configure your Windows Aero settings if your display adapter (video card) supports it.

One of the more useful settings you can change is the Font DPI settings. If you type `Adjust font size` in the Search box, you will see the link for the DPI Scaling utility shown in Figure 1.6. The default scale is 96 DPI, which might be too small. The second option is 120 DPI, which many users find to be too large. If you click the Custom DPI option, however, you can use the slider to change the font size to something that suits your specific needs.

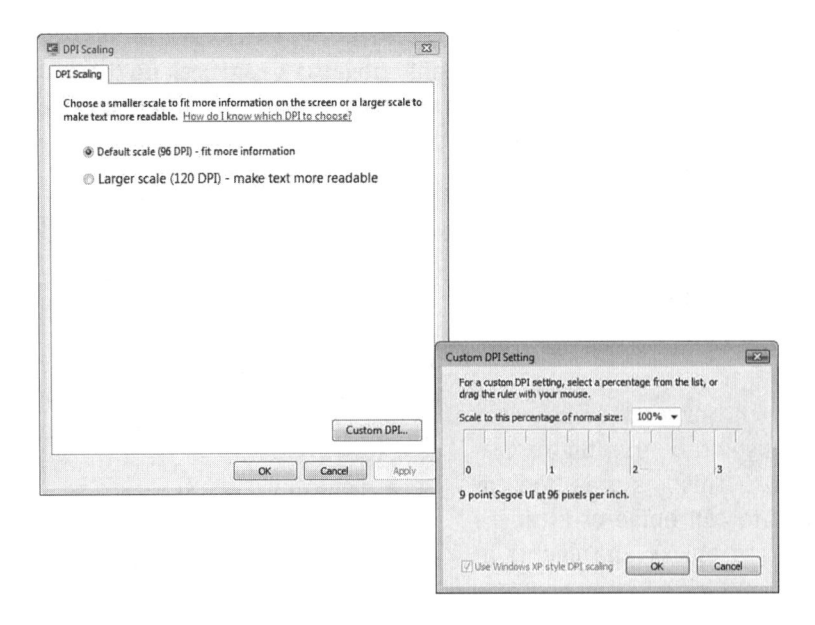

FIGURE 1.6
Adjust your DPI settings to suit your needs.

Long Zheng, one of the web's most respected Vista bloggers wrote at http://www.istartedsomething.com/:

As anyone who uses an ultra-portable laptop would know, reading ultra-minimalistic weblogs with 9px-sized fonts on a high-resolution 1400×1050 display panel spanning an entire 12× is like an everyday blessing for eye-care companies. Now's a good time to invest in the laser eye surgery business.

Whilst desktop monitors have always maintained the adequately readable 96 DPI standard with LCD displays, pixel-density on laptops has reached as high as 144 DPI, and that means smaller interfaces and fonts. But who doesn't want more pixels? The more pixels, the clearer the image.

Windows Vista aims to reduce the negative effects of high-DPI displays by introducing an updated DPI-scaling engine for the desktop compositor. This allows icons, interfaces and text to be scaled bigger to compensate for the extra pixels. In theory, everything should look just as crisp and detailed compared to the default 96 DPI. But in practice, due to lack of vectorized interface elements and icons, it's not perfect.

When you go to change the percentage of DPI the drop down button only allows you to select up to 200%. However, if you move the slider you can go as high as 500% (not recommended, but fun to see). Long Zheng notes that, "Theoretically you would need a 12-inch display with a resolution of 7000×5250 to properly appreciate 480 DPI."

Using Shift to Slow Down Animations

Here is another tip from Chris Holmes: If you are using Windows Aero, you can perform a neat Registry trick to slow down the animations (minimize/maximize) when you hold down the Shift key on your keyboard. But you are going to have to modify the Registry a little.

Not only does this allow you to see the animations a bit clearer but it also leaves Flip 3D on screen when you let go of the Ctrl+WindowsKey+Tab combination. (Normally Flip 3D departs the screen as soon as you let go of the key combo.) Also, whenever you minimize or maximize (or close) a window, if you hold the Shift key down you will see how impressive Vista is in slow-mo. Here's how to do it:

1. Open the Run dialog box (⊞+R), type `regedit.exe`, and then click OK. (If User Account Control prompts you to allow the action, click Continue.)
2. Navigate to HKEY_CURRENT_USER\Software\Microsoft\Windows\DWM.
3. In the right side, right-click an empty space and hover over New; then from the menu that appears, click DWORD (32-bit) Value.
4. Give the new DWORD value a name of `AnimationsShiftKey`.
5. Double-click the DWORD and then give it a value of 1.

24 Tricks of the Windows Vista Masters

6. Click OK and close the Registry Editor.
7. Log off of Windows and then log back on again.
8. Hold the Shift key and minimize or maximize a window. You will notice that the animation is slowed down. To stop this, simply let go of the Shift key on your keyboard.

The Windows Sidebar

It's the first thing you may notice different about Windows Vista when you log in (next to the little round Start orb and the exceptional graphics). We are referring to the Windows Sidebar.

What is the need for the Sidebar? Sometimes you just need a mini set of applications available to you quickly, such as a clock for the time, or a calendar, or a calculator, or a weather report. The Sidebar gives you access to these things by providing mini applications called *gadgets*. The gadgets you immediately see are a clock, a picture viewer (to which you can add your own personal pictures if you don't like the ones Microsoft provides), and news feeds based on RSS.

The tool is easy to use, easy to configure, and easy to turn off (that's your prerogative), as shown in Figure 1.7.

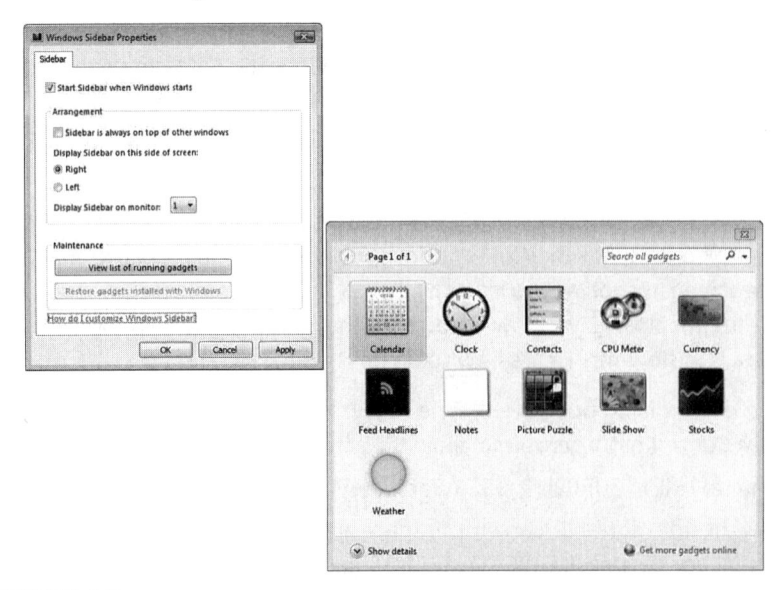

FIGURE 1.7
Windows Sidebar options include changing the location and configuration of the sidebar itself, as well as choosing new gadgets to add.

Group Policy Settings

The Windows Sidebar is neither friend nor foe. It's an option. And it can be disabled. For administrators, the big question might be "how can I disable it throughout my domain?" The two sets of Group Policy settings are the computer level and the user level. Either one works, but disabling the Sidebar at the computer level ensures that all users sitting at the system have the policy applied.

To change the Group Policy for Windows Sidebar, go to the Group Policy Object Editor (using `gpedit.msc` from the Run dialog box). Open either Computer Configuration or User Configuration settings, under Administrative Templates; then, under Windows Components, look for Windows Sidebar. You'll see the following settings:

- **Override the More Gadgets Link**—By default, the Windows Sidebar directs users to the Microsoft-provided gadgets. If you would like your users directed elsewhere, you can establish that change here by enabling the setting and providing the alternative location. If you leave this unconfigured or disable it, users are simply directed to the default site.

- **Turn Off Windows Sidebar**—The Sidebar is turned on by default (unless your hardware cannot support it and then it will be disabled). You can force it to be turned off by configuring this setting in your policies.

- **Disable Unpacking and Installation of Gadgets That Are Not Digitally Signed**—Gadgets can be packaged up as compressed files being signed digitally or not. You can configure this policy setting to ensure that all compressed gadget files will not be unpackaged or installed unless they are digitally signed.

- **Turn Off User Installed Windows Sidebar Gadgets**—No doubt users will want to install gadgets of their own, and many gadgets are being created these days. If that doesn't bother you, you can leave this setting alone. If you don't like the idea of any user being able to add any gadget he chooses, configure this to disable user-installed gadgets.

To turn off the Sidebar for your own personal system, you can always select Control Panel, Appearance and Personalization, Windows Sidebar Properties and then deselect the Start Sidebar when Windows Starts option.

Creating a Gadget

You don't have to settle for the gadgets Microsoft provides. Microsoft fully intends for users and developers to create their own. It's actually not all that difficult if you've ever authored a web page. The Microsoft gadgets website walks you through creating a simple gadget at http://microsoftgadgets.com/Sidebar/DevelopmentOverview.aspx.

You start with a directory you create to hold your files and then an HTML page. Create an XML file for the gadget manifest. You can test the gadget and make revisions as you go. Finally, you can package your gadget as a simple ZIP file (or CAB file) to distribute.

> **TIP**
> Those who really want to develop their own gadgets can refer to the MSDN site regarding various security concerns with gadgets (http://blogs.msdn.com/sidebar/archive/2006/08/31/733880.aspx). Keep in mind that with any gadget you create, if it attempts to access sites that have been prohibited by the Parental Control settings or by Windows Defender settings and so forth, the gadget won't work.

The Boot Process: From XP to Vista

To understand some of the utilities available in Vista, you have to understand some of the in-depth changes that come with Vista. We would love to go straight into a discussion of how the boot process works in Vista and bring you directly up to speed; however, if you never studied the process in earlier versions of Windows, you might not want the 0-60 approach. So, first we are going to discuss how the process worked in XP; then we'll explain the differences in Vista. You'll see that a good discussion of both might even prove helpful when trying to handle dual-boot situations.

Booting Up in XP

The first thing that happens when you turn on your PC is that it goes through a boot process. The computer first does a power-on self test (POST) for itself and then a POST for any adapter card that has its own BIOS (such as a modern video card). Your BIOS then reaches out to read the Master Boot Record (MBR). The MBR is the first sector of your hard disk, which XP created when you installed it. The MBR is preconfigured to read the first sector of the active partition, which contains the pointer code to the Ntldr file (sort of your supervisor for the entire boot process). There are several other boot files that Ntldr now calls upon, such as `ntdetect.com, bootsect.dos` (when you dual boot), and `ntbootdd.sys` (needed for some SCSI adapters).

When Ntldr has control, it starts by considering memory addressing and starting the file system. Then it reads a special file called the `boot.ini` and displays a boot menu. It's that `boot.ini` file that admins could configure either manually or through the `MSCONFIG.EXE` utility for previous versions of Windows.

When you are presented with your choices (or in some cases, if your timeout is set to 0, you have no choice because it just boots right to XP), Ntldr uses Ntdetect.com to find out which hardware is installed. Using what's called an ARC path from the `boot.ini` file (in layman's terms the ARC path tells Ntldr where to find the next process in charge, called the Ntoskrnl), the ARC path indicates the hard drive and partition of your system files. Ntldr, before turning over control, reads the Registry, selects a hardware profile and control set, and then loads device drivers. Finally, Ntldr hands the process off to `Ntoskrnl.exe` and `Hal.dll` (the Hal is the Hardware Abstraction Layer, and yes, it is strange that it shares the same name as the *2001 Space Odyssey* computer).

When `Ntoskrnl.exe` is in control, it calls upon several files such as `Winlogon.exe` (which then calls up `Lsass.exe`); eventually you get to your login screen. All that in about a minute.

Although the process typically remains consistent across XP installations, there were times when an XP master had to alter this process. Quite honestly there was only one thing you could change if you started having boot problems—and that was the `boot.ini` file. Sometimes Ntoskrnl couldn't be found, or there were other issues that required you to alter the file to allow debugging. The manual way to alter the file was to edit the `boot.ini` file through Notepad. The MSCONFIG utility made the process much easier with a graphical tool to help you configure your options, and it inserted various switches to alter the boot process.

Now let's consider how this process has changed in Vista

The Vista Boot Process

Having detailed the boot process from previous Windows versions under the NT Kernel, we move forward into the Vista process. A computer, when turned on, goes through the standard POST and the BIOS checks the MBR. The MBR reaches out for the first sector of the hard drive or external media and loads the boot sector, which loads the Windows Boot Manager (`bootmgr.exe`), which controls the boot flow.

The Windows Boot Manager reads the Boot Configuration Data and then displays selections, much like Ntldr did through the `boot.ini` file (selections are offered only if you have a multiboot situation). Some have asked, "Why has there been a change from `boot.ini` to the Boot Configuration Data (BCD)?" Microsoft has explained that there was a need to improve the "mechanism for describing boot configuration data" because of the development of new firmware modes (like the Extensible Firmware Interface [EFI] designed by Intel). The new boot structure

> **NOTE**
> In Windows Vista, the Windows Boot Manager replaces the old Windows NT boot loader. It works in conjunction with a set of system specific boot loaders that allow the Windows Boot Manager to be blissfully unaware of the specific requirements of each OS on multiboot system. Instead, the task of handling each OS falls to the system specific boot loaders that work with the Windows Boot Manager. You can learn more about all this at www.bootdisk.info.

also assists with some of the new diagnostic tools available in Vista, such as the Startup Repair tool and Multi-User Install shortcuts.

The next step in the process is the OS boot loader (`winload.exe`), which essentially calls for the Microsoft Vista kernel (still `ntoskrnl.exe`) to load; it then loads the hardware abstraction layer (still HAL and still fun to say) and device drivers. Finally, you get your logon screen. Once again, all that done in about a minute.

Editing the Boot Process

You recall Boot Configuration Data (BCD) during our discussion regarding the `boot.ini` file that you could edit this file in Windows XP. You could literally open it in Notepad and make edits. You could also use the System Configuration tool (MSCONFIG) or make changes from the command line with the `bootcfg` command in a command window.

> **NOTE:** Systems that use EFI have their own boot managers. The Windows Boot Manager installs as an EFI application and appears as one entry on the EFI menu. When that entry is chosen, the `bootmgr.exe` takes over and displays the Boot Configuration Data.

> **NOTE:** Another new tool in the process is called `winresume.exe`. This resumes Vista from hibernation. Each instance of the OS loaded on a system has its own `winresume.exe` file. What this means is, in the event the system is resuming from hibernation, as opposed to a standard boot process, this tool helps to bring the system back from the hibernated state. In this case the Windows Boot Manager uses the Boot Configuration Data (BCD) to locate the winresume.exe process.

Steven Patrick mentioned these changes on his Microsoft blog at http://blogs.msdn.com/spatdsg/ where he said:

> BCDEdit (`Bcdedit.exe`) is a command-line tool that edits boot options in Windows Vista. It replaces `Bootcfg` (a boot options editing tool that is included in Windows XP and Windows Server 2003) and `NvrBoot` (a boot options editing tool for EFI-based computers).
>
> Use BCDEdit to edit the boot configuration in Windows Vista. You can continue to use Bootcfg and NvrBoot and to edit the `Boot.ini` file in versions of Windows earlier than Windows Vista, even if they are installed on a computer that also has Windows Vista installed.

In Vista you need to know how to edit the Boot Configuration Data (BCD). BCD information is stored in a data file located either on an EFI System Partition (for EFI systems) or, in most cases, in the \Boot\Bcd folder on the system volume.

There are a couple of ways to alter the BCD:

- From the command-line using the `bcdedit.exe` tool. (Keep in mind you need to open the command prompt with elevated privileges.)
- Through the BCD Windows Management Instrumentation (WMI).
- Through the System Configuration Utility (`Msconfig.exe`). It has been overhauled for the new OS but has some great configuration options (such as `/noguiboot` which we used earlier to see the Aurora boot screen) or safemode and debug options that make it easier to receive help from product support services.
- The Advanced tab in the System Properties dialog box.

In-depth Look at BCD

Most likely you aren't interested in knowing the inner architecture behind BCD, although if you were you could download a BCD.doc file from Microsoft's website to learn more about how it functions, see: http://www.microsoft.com/whdc/system/platform/firmware/bcd.mspx. One cool thing within this document is the way it explains how the BCD relates to the `boot.ini` ARC path, which makes the whole process feel closer to home for those of us who are ARC path gurus.

However, there are a few points you should know, especially if you are working with multiple OSes on the same machine:

- If you plan on running previous versions of Windows on the same machine with Vista, be sure you install the previous versions first.
- If you install Vista side-by-side with a previous version of Windows, the Ntldr is still going to take over after you choose that OS from a list of options offered to you. So, the Ntldr and the `boot.ini` file will still be usable for that OS. The changes you make to the `boot.ini` file on a multiboot system don't have any effect on the Vista boot process.
- Editing the BCD requires elevated permissions (keep this in mind if you are using the command-line utility `bcdedit.exe`).

From within the command-line (with elevated privileges), type the following for more information regarding the `bcdedit.exe` command.

    Bdcedit.exe /?

For more information on how to work with the `bcdedit.exe` command-line tool, consider the bcd.doc whitepaper from Microsoft mentioned earlier. It is filled with various examples on how to use the tool to configure debugging, create new boot entries, specify the default operating system, and so forth.

Tony Campbell
http://vista.beyondthemanual.com/

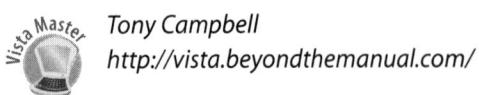

A few tips on using bcdedit:

1. Operating systems are identified using a GUID so you'll need to take note of any GUIDs you want to change before running the commands (try piping the contents of the database into a text file before you start by typing `bcdedit /enum all >bcd.txt`).

2. To change the default operating system (the one that is selected if the countdown expires) you can type `bcdedit /default {GUID}`. Remember, the GUID must be inside a pair of braces!

3. To change the boot loader timeout, use `bcdedit /timeout timeout`, where timeout is the number of seconds the boot loader will wait for decision on which operating system to select. If the timeout expires, the default operating system is selected (see Point 2).

4. To remove an entry no longer required, use `bcdedit /delete {GUID} [/f]`. The `[/f]` switch is necessary in this case to force the deletion of a known operating system, such as Window XP.

EasyBCD—A Free GUI Tool

One thing you might consider, in addition to the choices we've discussed here, are third-party tools that can help you work with your system's BCD. One such tool that we like is EasyBCD (developed by Neosmart Technologies, it can be found at `http://neosmart.net`). The main reason we like it is because it's geared toward users of all knowledge levels and can assist with dual booting with pretty much anything. It also offers a GUI interface to perform your edits (as shown in Figure 1.8). Best of all, it's free!

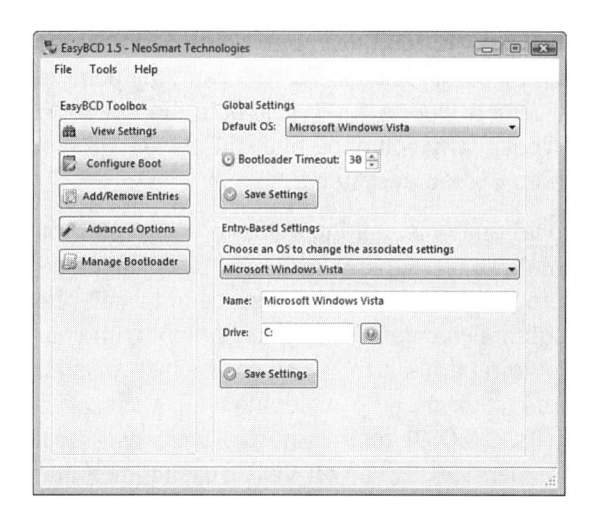

FIGURE 1.8
EasyBCD has a free, GUI interface to configure your BCD.

Dual-Booting XP and Vista

Dual booting is defined by Wikipedia.org as "the act of installing multiple `operating systems` on a `computer`, and being able to choose which one to `boot` when switching on the computer power." You might configure your system to dual boot when you have applications you need to run that don't function on the same operating system. You might want to test new operating systems (for example, during the Vista beta process many installed Vista in a dual boot environment with XP so that they could retain the stability of XP while testing Vista). You can also use dual booting in the development process where you are creating applications to work with different OSes. Keep in mind, that running different operating systems on the same hard disk, even when those operating systems are created by Microsoft, will invite compatibility issues.

Alan Wright
Network administrator and trainer

> I prefer to use completely different hard disks when I set up different OSes. Then I can just change the drive I am using when I want to boot into a different system.

If, however, you did want to boot XP and Vista from the same disk how would you do it?

First, consider what we discussed earlier about the MBR. It points to the Ntldr (in the case of XP) or to the Windows Boot Manager (`bootmgr.exe`) in Vista. It can only point to one or the other, and in a situation where Vista is loaded, it WILL point to the Windows Boot Manager. Vista dominates the MBR. That's why you need to install the XP OS first and then Vista if you want to dual-boot both operating systems.

Hard drive partitions are your first concern when implementing a dual-boot system. You need to put each OS on its own partition. You can use separate drives or the same physical drive with partitions, but just make sure that Vista has enough space to install. The frustrating thing here is that your drive might be completely taken up already with your XP OS. You can purchase a third-party tool to repartition the drive or find free tools (or trial tools) to do it (for example, GParted, the Linux-based partitioning tool). Microsoft is providing Business Desktop Deployment (BDD 2007) tools, and this includes a tool called Windows PE (preinstallation environment) 2.0 based on Vista's capabilities that will allow you to repartition your drives (along with a host of other things).

More information about Windows PE is included in Chapter 8, "System Recovery and Diagnostic Tricks," in the section, "Windows PE 2.0." However, if you boot off your Vista DVD and choose the Recovery Options from the Install screen you will actually be booted into a Windows Recovery Environment (WinRE) from which you can choose the WinPE command prompt.

James Bannan wrote a great article on what to do next at http://www.apcstart.com/4054/how_to_dual_boot_xp_and_vista where he said:

> Boot into PE, and load DISKPART from x:\Windows\System32. This is the Vista version of DISKPART, so the SHRINK option is available. Select the appropriate volume first (usually SELECT VOLUME 0) and type in SHRINK. This isn't a configurable process as it is via Disk Management in the Vista GUI. SHRINK just goes through and recovers what space it can. On a 20GB NTFS partition with a basic XP installation, SHRINK dropped the partition by 10GB, which is enough for Vista (just!). It's likely that defragmenting free space on the partition you're shrinking will help a lot.

Once your system has the space available on another partition, install Vista into that partition. When you finish the install and reboot the new boot manager will display your option to boot into Vista or into "Earlier version of Windows."

Removing Vista from Your Dual-Boot System

Removing Vista from a dual-boot system probably sounds like a strange thing to do. But under some circumstances, it can be necessary. Let's say you have your XP system and you've been running a beta/RC1 version of Vista in a dual-boot configuration. As the date approaches for the OS to be out of date, you might want to just go back to XP.

Long Zheng (www.istartedsomething.com) give us the steps we need to uninstall Vista from our dual boot situation:

After playing around with Vista for a few days, you may want to remove it from your system, and reclaim the hard drive space. Microsoft has made this step very simple as well.

1. Boot your computer in to Windows XP.

2. Ensure you have the Vista DVD image emulated or in the DVD drive.

3. Go to "Start" and "Run". Type in `e:\boot\bootsect.exe /nt52 ALL /force` (replacing e: with the drive letter of your Vista DVD).

4. Restart the computer, and you will notice the boot selection menu is gone.

5. Format the partition/drive where you had Vista installed.

6. Remove two files (`Boot.BAK` & `Bootsect.BAK`) on your XP drive's root folder (C:), these were backup files of your previous bootloader, now no longer useful.

7. Optional: Restart to ensure it still works.

8. Use your partition software to merge your partitions together.

And now you have returned your computer to its previous state, without Vista and without the new bootloader. If anyone has any issues, please post it in comments and I'll try to resolve it.

MSCONFIG: The System Configuration Tool

The System Configuration tool is more of a diagnostics tool, but we want to discuss it in general because it also includes some great settings for configuring the startup of your system.

You start the System Configuration tool by clicking your Start orb, typing `msconfig` in your Search bar, and then pressing Enter. You can also open the Run dialog box and type `msconfig`.

You will see five tabs, and we will give you insight on how to use each one.

General

The General tab has one heading, called Startup Selection, and three options to choose from:

- **Normal**—Boots the system without any diagnostic services. If you are trying to diagnose a problem, you should select one of the other two options. When you are certain the problem is resolved, just click this setting to boot your system normally again.
- **Diagnostic**—This mode starts your system with basic services and drivers. With only the minimal services and drivers running, you can proceed with troubleshooting confident that your system is stable on a basic level, so the problem must be coming from higher up.
- **Selective**—This option allows you to start your system with basic services and drivers (just like diagnostic), but it also allows you to specifically configure the use of additional services and startup applications so you can slowly determine what is causing the problem in your boot process. You can go through and turn on items one at a time from the Service or Startup tabs and see how your system reacts when you reboot.

Boot

The Boot tab lets you configure boot options, including timeout settings and advanced settings, such as these:

- **Safe Boot: Minimal**—Boots to the Windows GUI but only running critical services. Networking functions are also disabled. If you find your system is working at this level then you might want to try turning on services to see if they cause any further issues.
- **Safe Boot: Alternate Shell**—Boots to a command prompt. Critical services are running, but networking and the GUI are disabled. From here you can perform command-line diagnostics.
- **Safe Boot: Active Directory Repair**—Boots to the Windows GUI running critical services and Active Directory.
- **Safe Boot: Network**—Boots to the Windows GUI, running critical services and networking. If you don't think your problem is in the networking services then having the network turned on for your system will allow you to access resources you might need on the network or Internet for diagnosis.
- **No GUI Boot**—Does not display the Windows Vista splash screen when you are booting. Instead, as mentioned earlier, the Aurora screen appears.
- **Boot Log**—Stores information from the boot process in a log located in `%systemroot%` called `ntbtlog.txt`. These logs can be sent to other technicians for their opinion on what might be causing your system to crash.

- **Base Video**—Just like VGA mode in times past, this mode loads the system with standard VGA drivers instead of those that specifically relate to your hardware. This option is good for eliminating problems with video drivers.
- **OS Boot Information**—Shows all the drivers during the boot process as they load up.
- **Make All Boot Settings Permanent**—Usually when you make changes, you can undo them simply by selecting the Normal boot process from the General tab (as mentioned earlier). But if you select this option, those changes can still be undone; however, the caveat is you have to manually go back and uncheck the options you've checked.
- **Timeout Settings**—You can configure different countdowns for your multiboot systems. You can try to type in what you like, but it will ask for a number between 3 seconds and 999 seconds.
- **Advanced Settings**—These advanced options enable you to configure such things as the number of processors, the amount of memory, and Global Debug settings. Keep in mind that these options are last-resort choices to diagnose your systems and are usually used under the direction of Microsoft support services.

Services

The Services tab shows a list of all the services that start with the computer when it boots. You can see the current statuses of these services (running or not) and can enable or disable them from here. You can also deselect the checkbox to prevent that service from starting up the next time you boot the system. In disabling services, however, you are forced to use the Selective Startup in the General tab.

You can also select Hide All Microsoft Services to show only the services from third parties. Be careful when you decide to disable a service because you might cause other problems while attempting to search for the one causing your original dilemma. Some services are required for your system to operate properly. Other services, if disabled, may throw off your diagnostic approach because you may be affecting other aspects of your OS. In other words, know why you are disabling a service before you do it, and understand how that service may impact other services or features of your system.

Startup

Provides a list of applications that start up with the boot. You can see the name of the application, the manufacturer, the location of the executable, and the Registry key for the startup application. You can also see a date when you might have disabled the application.

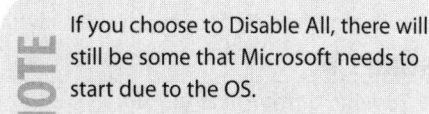

> **NOTE:** If you choose to Disable All, there will still be some that Microsoft needs to start due to the OS.

From here, you can deselect the checkbox to stop the application from running on the next boot. If you feel there is a problem with a specific application, you can also confirm from here the location of the application.

Terri Stratton
Microsoft MVP

Many OEMs include programs that you may not want running at boot. This is the place to disable them. You'll still have access to them when you need them though.

> **NOTE** This is one great little feature. So great in fact that for XP users, Microsoft released a little fix download that enables you to add the Tools tab to your XP System Configuration tool (because it's not there by default). What's great about this is that it's a central location to all sorts of tools and even a few preconfigured command-line options. For example, you can enable/disable the UAC from the Tools tab. We discuss the UAC options a little later, but just the fact that you can, with one click, enable or disable it, makes this a worthy tool to remember.

Another way to disable these options is to locate the path for their startup in the Registry and remove the link for the application. The path is HKLM\Software\Microsoft\Windows\CurrentVersion\Run.

Tools

The Tools tab provides a list of diagnostic and informational tools and shows the location of these tools. From within this tab, you can literally "Launch" any tool, or you can note the location or name of the tool itself, as shown in Figure 1.9.

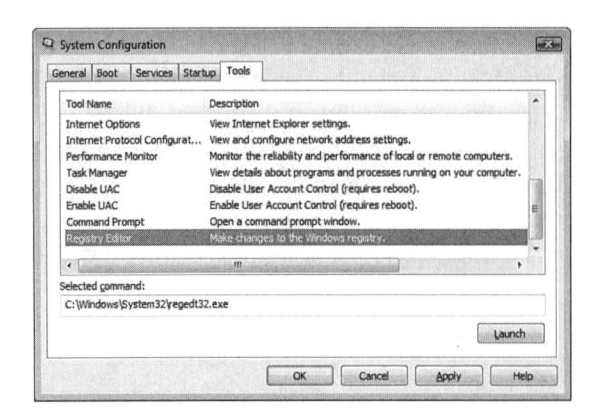

FIGURE 1.9
The Tools tab from msconfig.

Additional Information

A great third-party tool is called the MSCONFIG Cleanup tool. Sometimes you have to disable certain applications in the Startup menu, such as certain spyware and malware applications you find. Disabling these applications from MSCONFIG does prevent them from running, but it doesn't remove them from your system or, more specifically, from your system's Registry. The goal of the cleanup tool is to go into the Registry and remove these items. You can find this tool on www.softpedia.com through the search field. It was developed by Virtuoza.

Shortcut Menu: "Shift" Your Shortcuts

If you have ever sent a document to the Recycle Bin, you have probably wondered why there are two different ways to delete a file. If you right-click a file or folder and select Delete, it goes to the Recycle Bin (see Figure 1.10). However, if you want to permanently delete a file, you hold down Shift and select Delete and you skip the Recycle Bin middle man (see Figure 1.11).

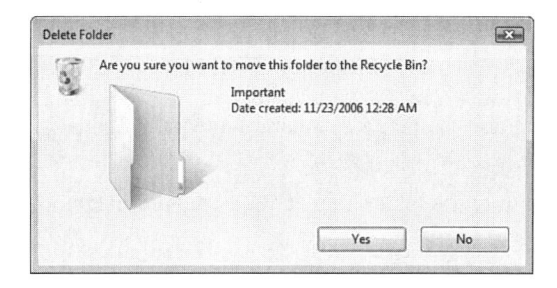

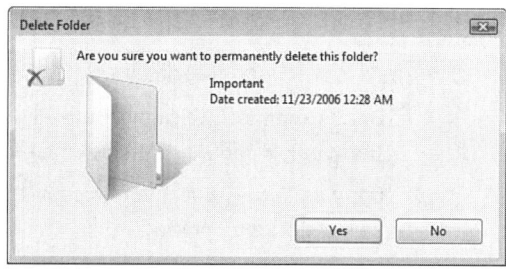

FIGURE 1.10
Sending items to the Recycle Bin with a simple right-click and Delete.

FIGURE 1.11
Deleting items permanently with a Shift button right-click and Delete.

Well, the Shift button isn't only helpful for deletions; it's helpful for a few other things as well. For example, if you right-click a folder, you normally get the view shown in Figure 1.12. But if you right-click it with the Shift button held down, you get something a little different (see Figure 1.13).

FIGURE 1.12
The options when you right-click a folder.

FIGURE 1.13
The options when you right-click a folder holding down the Shift button.

Two new options come into view:

- **Open Command Window Here**—If you choose to open a command window, it opens the window rooted in the selected folder.
- **Copy as Path**—Allows you to copy the path of the folder back to the system or network server's original point.

If you have ever wanted to send someone a link from a network share and had to traverse the path all the way back to its source to give them the full path name, then this tip is for you. By remembering the hidden context menu found by holding Shift when you right-click, you can quickly get the address of any folder or file.

The hidden context menu comes up the same way when right-clicking a file. The new options that appear in this case, however, are

- **Open As Read Only**—Ensures that changes you make to the document are not saved back to the original
- **Pin to Start Menu**—Enables you to add any file to the Start menu
- **Add to Quick Launch**—Enables you to put the file or application directly on your Quick Launch bar

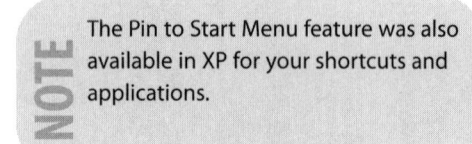

NOTE: The Pin to Start Menu feature was also available in XP for your shortcuts and applications.

- **Copy As Path**—Does the same as above, copying to the clipboard the path of the file all the way back to the system or network share

Windows Explorer

Where are your files? "On my hard drive," you might reply. Okay, silly question, silly answer. More specifically, if you had to locate them—every last one of them—could you do it? Ten years ago that would have been a simpler question, but today, with hard drives in the hundreds of GB, it's not so simple anymore.

We used to think of our data residing on a drive, on a partition, or in a specific folder or subfolder. Trying to continue that line of thought will soon become impossible, so Microsoft has begun the process of moving away from the drive-and-directory storage model. With some systems holding more than 10,000 folders with data strewn throughout, not to mention email into the thousands of messages, address books, contact management information, and so forth, it was time to make a move toward a new storage mechanism. Microsoft has taken a step in the right direction.

Windows Explorer has received a major overhaul. The new interface has been structured to provide you more control in browsing through your files. Consider the interface in Figure 1.14.

In the interface you can see the following options:

- **The Address Bar**—Shows you the path to the folder you are in. It also enables you to navigate backward and sideways within the hierarchy.
- **The Search Box**—Enables you to search for filenames, metadata, and text within the document, in this case within the current folder
- **The Details Pane**—Shows the metadata for any selected file
- **Organize**—Enables you to create new folders; cut, copy, or paste folders; and change the properties of a folder or the layout of the Explorer window
- **Views**—Enables you to adjust the size of folder icons, choosing details or extra large icons

> **TIP**
> New Address Bar Nickname. Because of the way the address bar tracks the way a person arrives at the location by allowing him to navigate backward to any part of the hierarchy, it is sometimes referred to as the *breadcrumb* bar—reminiscent of the story of Hansel and Gretel who left a trail to follow their way back. For example, if you have a specific path in the address bar, you can navigate back to any part of the hierarchy by selecting the folder name in the address bar. You can also navigate in alternate directions to any part of any level by selecting the arrows to the right of the level in which you want to work. This offers more dimensions to your search for your items.

40   Tricks of the Windows Vista Masters

FIGURE 1.14
Windows Explorer: the new interface.

You might also notice that some virtual folders display recently changed documents or saved searches and so forth.

Saved Searches: What Are They, and How Can You Make Your Own?

Originally called Virtual Folders in earlier builds of Vista, these searches are saved in XML virtual folders. They update dynamically as items come under the scope of the search as the XML query continues to update. One of the key ways these searches work is through metadata properties (which we discuss at the end of this chapter).

You will know if folders are virtual saved searches by the color in which they appear in Explorer. Normal folders are yellow; virtual saved searches are blue. To create your own virtual saved searches, all you have to

> **TIP**
> If you like the old style in the address bar, you can still input files in that style and Explorer will understand without a problem. You can even view the folder structure the same as always by either right-clicking into the address bar and selecting the Edit Address option or by pressing the Alt+D shortcut.

do is set up a search and then save that search using the Save Searches option right on the address bar. The great thing about this is that the search continues to update with changes. So, if you plan ahead, you could create a good list of virtual searches you want to save for future use.

Enabling the Preview Pane

The options you have available on the command bar in Windows Explorer are context sensitive in the sense that they change depending on the folder you are in or the file you have selected. For example, if you are in a folder filled with pictures, you will see an option for Slide Show on the command bar.

> **TIP**
> Getting Back Your Classic Menus: If you want to see your old "menu" options when working in Windows Explorer, you just have to press the Alt button once and the menus appear. You'll notice that the menus will not continue in your Explorer each time you open and close Windows Explorer. If you want to make sure Windows Explorer always uses the menu options, alter your Folder Options (which is actually easy from Explorer if you have the menus on). Select Alt to turn on the menus. Then select Tools, Folder Options. Go the General tab and you can tell Vista to use the Classic folders.

Another nice new feature is the Preview Pane. If you are looking at pictures in XP, you could always see thumbnails of your pictures. But with the Preview Pane (enabled by selecting Organize, Layout, Preview Pane), you can see larger representations of those pictures. In addition, Vista has the capability to handle files types like documents and videos, in addition to pictures (see Figure 1.15).

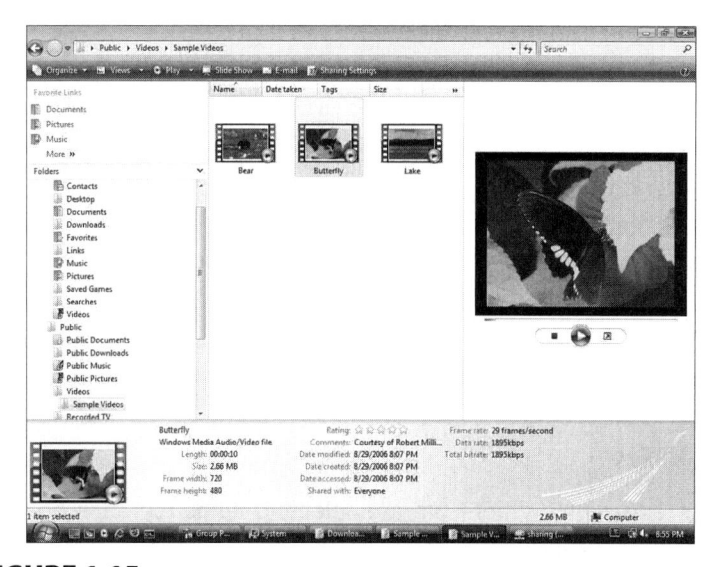

FIGURE 1.15

The Windows Explorer Preview Pane lets you see pictures, files, and videos in a side window.

Improvements to the Explorer UI

New visual effects enable your entire Vista experience to be more visually appealing. For example, files and folders are given expressive icons that allow you to appreciate the contents of those files and folders before even opening them. These are called Live Icons, and they work for many types of files, including Word documents, PowerPoint slideshows, photos, and so on, as shown in Figure 1.16.

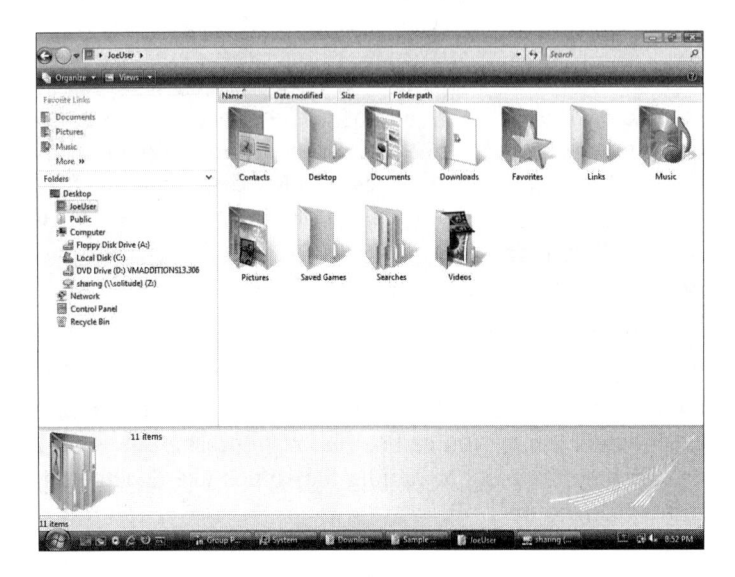

FIGURE 1.16
Live Icons make your files and folders more visually appealing, but also make it easier for users to identify the inner contents of the folder.

As an added bonus, when you grab files to move over to a different folder, you now see the actual quantity of items you're moving directly in the middle of a graphic of one of the files. This lets you know whether you have accidentally grabbed too many or forgotten a file that should have been moved.

Having a restructured Windows Explorer is a great asset visually, but it will mean nothing unless you become proficient in using its new features.

Selecting Files with Check Boxes.

Many of us have had the experience where we are selecting items (perhaps holding down Ctrl and selecting multiple files) and we click one too many. It's not a huge problem, but it's frustrating. On the blog site http://techtalkblogs.com , Chris O'Conner of SDM (http://sdm.com.au/) says:

> You can select multiple files in XP or Vista by holding down the CTRL key and clicking on the files that you need. It works, but it's a little cumbersome—especially if you forget to hold the CTRL key down and you lose all of your previous selections. In Vista you also have the option of using checkboxes to do the selections. To enable the checkbox feature open the Folder Options dialog (by pressing the ALT key from within Windows Explorer and then choosing "Tools", "Folder Options") and then scroll down and check the "Use check boxes to select items" option. Now when you open up Windows Explorer again you will be able to use Checkboxes to select multiple files.

In addition, in the columns you can choose the checkbox next to the Name column to quickly select all the files in a folder. One area where this feature can come in really handy is for you Tablet PC users. It's so hard to select files with the pen, now you can use the checkboxes!

Search: The Next Generation

Here is the truth—you've been searching for things from the minute you started using a computer and by now you believe you know all the options. With Vista, searching becomes a whole new world and you need to know not only how to work with it, but also how to configure your files to help you with searches in the future.

To start with, in Vista you are going to see many ways to search. So what you are looking for in a search is what determines how you will search for your items. For example, if you are simply looking for a file or folder that you know is located in a standard location (such as Documents or Pictures), you can navigate to that folder from an Explorer window and use the Search box from there.

What about a program? What about a website in your browser history? What about a file located somewhere in your personal folder? In Vista you can use your Search box at the bottom of the Start menu to find any of those items. So if a program is buried within a variety of folders and you can't remember where, just start typing the name and the Search box gives you a variety of options based on the name. If you have a website in your favorites or in your recent history, you can just search for it from here.

File List Headings (which are the headings above the file list in a folder, including options like Name, Date Modified, Author, and so forth) enables you to search for files within specific months, or by a specific author, and so on using the drop down arrows that appear when you select the heading. And you can use the Search folder to perform more advanced searches using multiple filters.

Search Box Tips

When you are working with the file/folder search box, you want to find files quickly. The real key to this is making sure you name files logically or include pertinent information as metadata to the file. We will discuss this in-depth momentarily. For example, say you go to a folder and type in the name you are looking for (Expense Report Germany); immediately all the files that don't correspond disappear, making it easier to select the file you need. You could also type partial words like "exp"; the search box brings up all the files with those letters in the title or within the content.

Another cool feature is that you can find a file by type: document, picture, or music. In the search box, just type one of those and it filters out the others. You might want to be more specific about the type of file—for example, is it a .bmp or .jpg? You can do that, too, by typing in the extension of the file. (Using wildcards such as *.jpg generates a clearer search.)

Now let's talk about tags. When you create files, you are asked whether you want to add any tags (see Figure 1.17). This could make finding files, especially pictures, much easier, but only if you take the time to set the tag. You can also search by author, but you could see how that would be helpful only if you have a few items from one author on your system.

Terri Stratton
Microsoft MVP

If you're on a network in a business environment, being able to search by author is a great tool. You can search for documents and spreadsheets created by specific people.

The reason these search filters work is because Windows searches through everything—the name, contents, properties, tags, and so forth. But you might want to search more selectively. That's possible, too. For example, you can search by the property you are looking for by specifying the property and the term separated by a colon. For example, entering "Name:Disney" brings up only the files with "Disney" in the name. "Tag:Wedding" brings up only files with the tags set with the word "Wedding" (great for pictures). "Modified:11/18/2006" gives you the files modified on a certain date. If you enter a specific year, it gives you files modified within that year, although that might be too broad for your search.

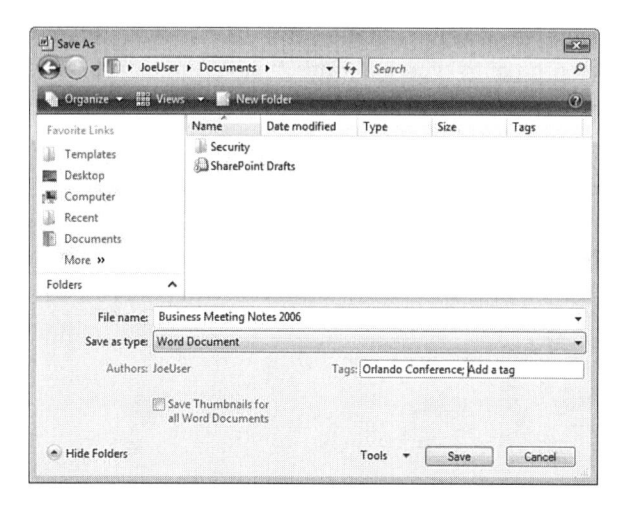

FIGURE 1.17
Tags enable you to specify data to help you find these files again.

Almost any property in the file list headings can be heard. Here is where search becomes very cool. Let's say you have a document and you don't remember the name or where you put it but you have it in your hands and it's six pages long. You can type "Pages:6" in the Search box and it will find all the documents of that size!

You can also use Boolean filters to refine your search a bit more. For example, you recall the standard ones—AND, NOT, OR (make sure you use capital letters when using these because otherwise Search thinks these are real words). Even better, you can combine Boolean filters with the file property searches, for example, "Author: Ed AND David" which finds files authored by both persons. You can find more information on Boolean filters and file properties in the Vista help files.

Natural Language Search

Structure is wonderful and we love to structure our documents and search for those documents based on that structure. But many users might find it difficult to really learn the structure of searches. As an administrator, you might have many issues with helping your users find their files. One cool new feature is the capability to find files with natural language search. That's right, no Boolean, just normal thoughts.

Here is an example. You are looking for music by both Pearl Jam and Soundgarden. Without natural language search, you have to type in "Kind:Music artist (Pearl Jam AND Soundgarden)". With natural language, you just type in "music by Pearl Jam and Soundgarden."

To turn on the natural language feature, go into Control Panel, type **Folder Options** in the search bar, and click the Folder Options link when it appears. Select the Search tab and then enable the checkbox for Use Natural Language Search, as shown in Figure 1.18.

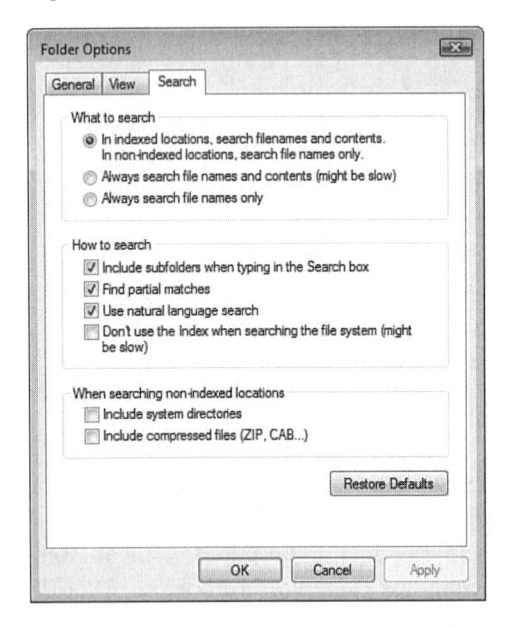

FIGURE 1.18

Alter your Search settings from within your Folder options.

With natural language search turned on, you can still search with Boolean filters but now you can use a more comfortable style, too. For example, you can search for "e-mail from Jaclyn McGovern sent today" or "pictures of family in Florida taken December 2005."

File List Heading Tips

Yet another great timesaver that administrators need to get used to and train their users to get used to is the use of file list headings. The concept is simple: You open a folder and can see your files (all 1,000+ of them), but you also want to filter them based on specific properties in the headings—for example, the name, date, or author headings. Next to each property is a drop-down arrow that enables you to specify what you are really looking for. For example, if you choose Date, you get a drop-down that even includes a calendar (shown in Figure 1.19). This makes it much easier to filter out your files.

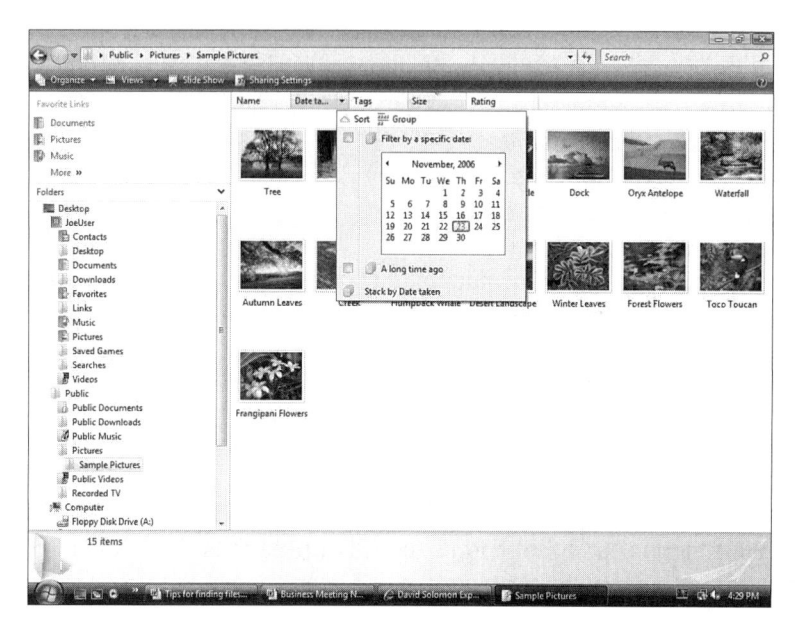

FIGURE 1.19
Filter your files based on heading lists.

You'll notice in Figure 1.19 that you can choose to stack your files. This causes your files to be arranged into piles (stacks) based on the criteria. If you stack based on authors, all the files compile; then, if you want to see all the files from one author, you can just pick the stack.

You might not like that stacking your files hides your choices under stacks by author name. You could choose to group your files instead, which groups files by criteria but allows you to see the grouping.

Beyond the Standard Search: Advanced Search Options

We've mostly been explaining how to use the standard search features. But if you go to the Start orb and select Search, the Search folder appears and you can see you have a lot more from which to choose. Sometimes you don't know the folder your file is in. Or maybe the files are located in several folders at the same time but you want to pull them together. Or maybe you have several criteria to look for and need more depth to the search. That's when you use the Search folder.

You can alter the location of an advanced search. By default, it looks to Indexed Locations (which we discuss in greater detail in the next section). Indexed information

> **NOTE**
> If you are reading all this and yet still using XP, don't feel left out. Microsoft has released the Windows Desktop Search 3.0 so you can download the engine to your XP machine. It doesn't look exactly the same, but the more important thing is that it works. To download and learn more about the Windows Desktop Search 3.0, go to http://support.microsoft.com/kb/917013.

includes personal folder information (Documents, Pictures, Music, the Desktop, and so forth). It also includes email and offline files. You can add more information to the Index if you want. You can also alter the set of locations used and choose dates, file sizes (if you know the file is large or small), and then various properties to narrow the search.

Some Final Search Points: Internet Search, Control Panel Search

In addition to the Start menu search helping us to find applications, files, and so forth, this kind of search can also show us our favorites or history items. But you might also want to search the Internet. The moment you start to type in the Search box, you will see an option for you to search the Internet. This takes you to the Microsoft Live Search site and shows you the results.

If you have a hard time navigating around the new Control Panel, don't worry. When you open Control Panel from off the Start menu, you can use the search features here to help you locate the applets you need, too. For example, if you want to get to Parental Controls, just start typing; within moments you'll be shown the Parental Controls utility before you get past "par" in the search.

As you can see, the Search features are integrated into everything, making this one of the best new tools in Vista. However, without knowing how to take full advantage of it, the users on your network won't appreciate it or benefit from it. Make it a key matter for training.

Metadata: Organizing Your Documents, Music, and Pictures

Metadata is the latest rage in document organization, as well as sharing over the Internet. Even on sites that work with file sharing, tags have been incorporated to make searching for files easier. Metadata has been included in files for quite some time. In previous versions of Office, for example, you can add the author to the metadata of the document, or comments and keywords to the document. For music files, you can establish the artist, album, track, and so forth to round out the underlying information for the file. Pictures can be tagged with information that helps to organize them, and many picture-organizing applications make it easier to add these tags.

With Vista, metadata becomes more an integral part of the OS because you can search for so many parts of that data. Ronald Barrett, the Senior Network Administrator for ERE Accounting in Manhattan says:

> Adding metadata details to your folder display items is not difficult. You can right-click any of the column headings and select More. Then you can choose from any of a long list of details. Normally, certain items are viewable from the Details view; then depending on which type of folder you are viewing (music or photos), these details change. But it's good to know you can add columns that you need.

How Do You Add Metadata?

The first key to adding it is being aware that it needs to be added in the first place. Hopefully programs will become more aware of the needs to make metadata properties more accessible.

Word 2007, for example, has the option to add Document Properties (click the Office button and select Prepare, Properties). In addition, when you attempt to save a document from Office 2007 while on Vista, it asks you whether you want to add tags to your document.

Another way to add metadata is to right-click a file, go to the Details tab, and then add your information directly into the file.

Some photo-editing programs, such as the Vista-incorporated Windows Photo Gallery, enable you to easily add tags to your photos . You can quickly group your pictures by using similar tags this way.

After you have your metadata attached, you can use the search features to search based on that metadata. You can choose within your searches to Organize by Tags or Stack by Tags.

> **NOTE:** There is one very big caveat to the whole metadata approach to data organization—preexisting files. We all have thousands of files by now, and who is going to go back and add that metadata? Now, you might not want or need those files organized that way, but if you do, we feel your pain.

Erasing Metadata Before You Share a Document

There are different ways to get rid of your metadata, aside from going through and trying to manually remove it all, before you share your files with others.

Erasing Metadata from Vista Options

Vista enables you to make a duplicate of a file that eliminates all the metadata (or allows you to choose which metadata to keep in the document).

To do this, you right-click the file, select Properties, and then select the Details tab. Down at the bottom is a hyperlink labeled Remove Properties and Personal Information. If you select this, you are shown the Remove Properties dialog box, which enables you to create the copy or simply remove the properties from the current document.

Erasing from Office 2007

One of the great tools from Office 2007 is the capability to erase hidden metadata from a document before you share it with others.

With the document open in Word, Excel, or PowerPoint 2007, click the Office button and select Prepare, Inspect Document. Click the Inspect button to get the process started, and it should take no time at all for it to return with the results that include additional metadata you might want to eliminate, including track changes and other personal data.

As you consider the results, you can select Remove All for different parts of the document. Or you can select Reinspect for the document itself. After you have removed all the hidden data, the document is ready to be sent out without fear of that information being shared with others.

Chapter 2

MASTERING THE CONTROL PANEL

Configuring the Control Panel

When you open the Control Panel from the Start menu you will notice the Default View is designed to appeal to most users by making the selections more intuitive and less intimidating. You also have the option to switch to the Classic View by selecting the link on the Navigation pane, as shown in Figure 2.1. Because the Classic View displays all the Control Panel applets in one dialog, it's the view I prefer and this chapter is based on using the Control Panel in that view.

IN THIS CHAPTER

- Configuring the Control Panel
- Breaking Down the Control Panel Applets
- Color Management
- Indexing: Find the Needle in the Haystack
- Offline Files: Synchronizing Your World
- Parental Control
- Power Options: Don't Hibernate, Shutdown, Standby—Just Sleep
- Speech Recognition: You Talk, Vista Listens
- Tablet PC: The Flintstones Meet the Jetsons

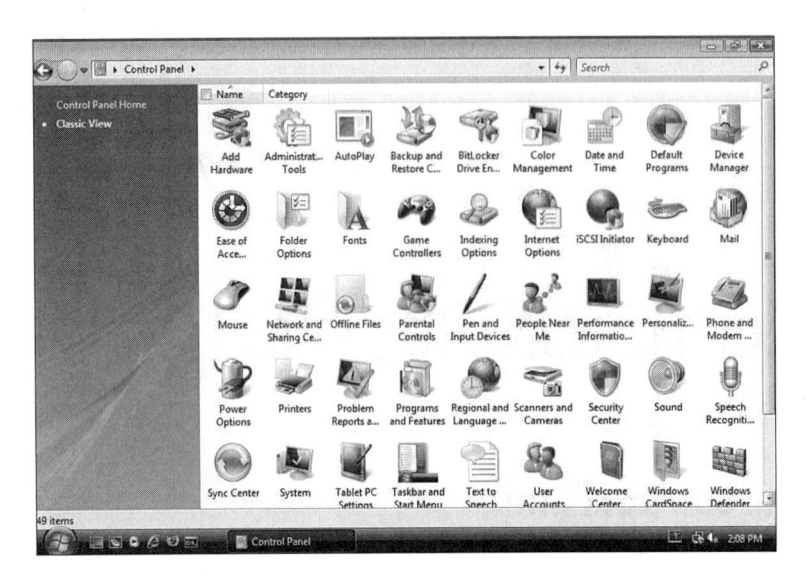

FIGURE 2.1
The Classic View is the way to go if you want to find your utilities quickly.

You'll notice immediately that roughly 50 applets are in your Control Panel (almost twice as many as in Windows XP). *Applet* is another name for the utilities found in the Control Panel. *Applets, utilities, tools*, and so forth all pretty much mean little programs to help adjust your system.

Expanding Control Panel from the Start Menu

You might want to avoid the Control Panel pane altogether. You can have your Control Panel utilities appear from your Start menu by doing the following:

1. Right-click the Start orb and select Properties.
2. You should see the Start Menu tab; select Customize.

> **TIP:** You can group your applets in Control Panel when in Classic View by selecting the Category column and selecting Group. The groupings are somewhat intuitive, placing all the Mobile PC options under one group heading, and all Hardware and Sound options under another, and so forth. Keep in mind that the Search options in Classic View allow you only to search by name. To search using tasks and keywords, you have to be in the default Control Panel Home.

> **NOTE:** There is one good thing we want to mention about the Control Panel Home. If you use the Control Panel Home view, it shows you Recent Tasks so you can see the most recent things you've done in Control Panel.

3. The options for Control Panel should, by default, be labeled Display As Link, which enables the Control Panel to be selected from the Start menu. But you can select the option Display As Menu to make the Control Panel expand off the Start menu so you can quickly select your applets.

If you still want to open your Control Panel from the Start menu, you'll notice that the link doesn't work. But you can still right-click the Control Panel option and select Open for it to open in its own window.

Getting to Applets As Quickly As Possible

Some of the 50 applets you see in the Control Panel you will never, ever use. Some you will use every day. One cool way to make a specific applet handy is to open Control Panel and drag the applet you want to your Quick Launch toolbar. But, what if you have a bunch of applets you want to get at quickly? You probably don't want to clutter up your Quick Launch toolbar.

Another way to quickly get to your applets is to actually make a direct call for it. Control Panel applets are files stored in your System32 folders, and they have a .cpl extension. If you want to look at these, open Windows Explorer and navigate to the Windows\System32 folder. Then right-click in a white area in the folder and select to Arrange Icons by Type. You can now scroll down to see all the standard applets, as shown in Figure 2.2.

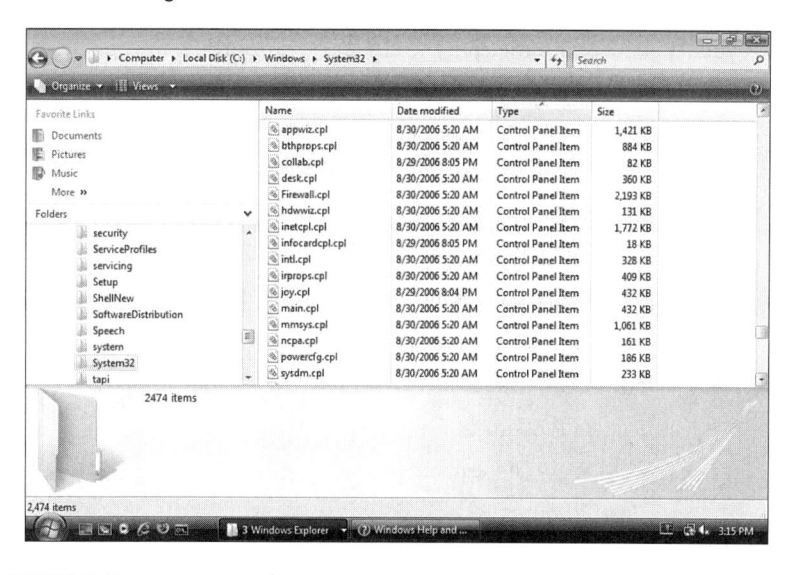

FIGURE 2.2
Know your applets.

Now you can issue a command to open an applet by going to the Start orb and typing it in the Search pane. You can even determine an option parameter to open the applet in the tab you want! How cool is that?

> **NOTE:** These tips work just as well in XP as they do in Vista. They are still not widely known, so it's important to share this information before getting into the depths of Vista Control Panel.

You could also do a search for all *.cpl files, which gives you the full list, including files that are not in the System32 folder. You can run these files by using either the rundll32.exe or the control.exe command and then the filename. At times, you might need to add other parameters to get the functionality you want.

You can find more information on these other parameters at MediaChance (http://www.mediachance.com/faqdll.htm). For example, you can configure an applet with multiple pages to open to a specific page by appending a comma, the @ symbol and a page number (starting at zero). To launch the Display Properties dialog to the Appearance page type:

```
Run("rundll32.exe","shell32.dll,Control_RunDLL desk.cpl,@0,2")
```

To open an applet, type the following from the Start menu, the Search bar, or the Run dialog box:

```
Control <name of applet.cpl>, options
```

So, for example, if you type **control desk.cpl**, the Display Properties open. Table 2.1 includes a list of some standard Control Panel applets.

Table 2.1—Canonical Names for Standard Control Panel Applets

Applet cpl file	Applet Name
Access.cpl	Ease of Access Center
Appwiz.cpl	Programs and Features
Ncpa.cpl	Network Connections
Powercfg.cpl	Power Options
Sysdm.cpl	System Properties
Timedate.cpl	Date and Time Properties
nusrmgr.cpl	User Accounts

Windows Vista has gone a step beyond XP in providing easy-to-remember canonical names. Even if the filename changes, the canonical name remains the same and continues to work. For example, instead of typing `desk.cpl` for the Display Properties, you would type `control.exe /name Microsoft.Personalization`.

You can learn more about this at http://msdn2.microsoft.com/en-us/library/aa905329.aspx.

Table 2.2 lists some of the canonical names of applets that ship with Windows Vista.

Table 2.2—Canonical Names of Vista Applets

Applet Canonical Name	Applet Name
Microsoft.EaseOfAccessCenter	Ease of Access Center
Microsoft.ProgramsAndFeatures	Programs and Features
Microsoft.NetworkAndSharingCenter	Network Connections
Microsoft.PowerOptions	Power Options
Microsoft.System	System Properties
Microsoft.DateAndTime	Date and Time Properties
Microsoft.UserAccounts	User Accounts

For a full list of the new syntax for opening Control Panel applets go to http://msdn2.microsoft.com/en-us/library/aa905328.aspx

Software developers can create additional applets for Control Panel and can add their own canonical names to the list.

Creating an applet is easier than in XP. You can create an executable and register it rather than trying to figure out or go through the difficulty of creating a CPL file. To learn more about how to add and register your own applet in Control Panel, see "Developing for the Control Panel" at http://msdn2.microsoft.com/en-us/library/aa905328.aspx.

Creating a Customized Control Panel Folder

If what you really want is a single location that lists your most frequently used Control Panel applets, without having to clutter up your Quick Launch toolbar, you can create your own Control Panel that shows only the applets you want. Do the following:

1. Right-click the Start orb and select Open.
2. From the Start Menu folder, create a new folder called whatever you like—My Control Panel is a good name.

3. Now open Control Panel in a separate window and go to Classic View.
4. With the two folders side by side, select the applets you like best from Control Panel and copy the link(s) over to your new folder (don't worry, this doesn't actually move the applet; it just creates shortcuts to it in your new folder).
5. Test your new panel by selecting the Start menu, opening your homemade Control Panel, and then clicking one of the applet links. (Or you can put the folder on your Quick Launch bar.)

Breaking Down the Control Panel Applets

There are roughly 50 out-of-the-box applets to look at in Control Panel. Some of them are simple; others more complex. There is no need to cover each and every one of them here. Instead we focus on the ones that have newer functionality over previous versions of the OS and on those newer ones that you should be aware of.

Add Hardware

Add Hardware installs legacy, nonPlug-and-Play hardware or hardware that the OS doesn't recognize. It's recommended that you use the CD that came with the hardware to install the drivers for it. You are also likely to find drivers on the manufacturer's website. But, if you don't have one, by all means keep moving forward through the steps.

After you move through some screens confirming that you have, in fact, installed the hardware and do, in fact, want to install drivers for it, a screen that gives you the following two options displays:

- **Search for And Install the Hardware Automatically (Recommended)**—Vista tries to detect the new nonPlug-and-Play device you are trying to install. Sometimes this works, but sometimes it doesn't. When it works, it installs an alternative driver (usually from the same company), and the device works. But, it's best to find the correct drivers for your devices because it improves performance and prevents a variety of technical issues.
- **Install the Hardware That I Manually Select from a List (Advanced)**—This option enables you to find the driver you need from a group of types and models. Where this might help you is if you research your problem online and someone says, "Oh yeah, I had the same problem and just used such-and-such driver and it worked." If that's the case, you could try this option.

Sometimes with a new operating system and legacy hardware, you have to do the research to see how or if it will work. Workarounds are common, so be flexible with the advice given and try it all until your device is up and running. Or, if it's that old (gasp!), it might be time to upgrade! Microsoft has a tool called the Upgrade Advisor that tells you, in advance, any compatibility issues you face with your hardware or software and it then recommends solutions. It can assist in upgrading from XP to Vista, as well as in upgrading from one flavor of Vista to a higher edition. You can download the tool at http://www.microsoft.com/windows/products/windowsvista/buyorupgrade/upgradeadvisor.mspx

The Loopback Adapter

Network gurus need to have their testing forum. The loopback adapter is a useful tool for testing different network protocols on a system that doesn't have a network adapter already installed. Douglas Comer, author of *Computer Networks and Internets* (fourth edition), says:

> Loopback is used for testing or debugging problems. Loopback simply means that data sent out will be delivered back to the source (usually without actually going across a network). Either protocol software or network hardware can provide loopback, depending on what one needs to test. For example, pinging address 127.0.0.1 causes the IP software to test loopback by handing the datagram back to ICMP on the same machine. One advantage of loopback is that it allows one to configure protocol software and test device drivers even if the computer is not connected to a real network.

To install the loopback adapter: From the Add Hardware applet, go through the steps for adding a hardware device. Select the option we mentioned earlier for adding hardware manually. From within Network Adapters under the manufacturer Microsoft, select the Microsoft Loopback Adapter. The adapter now shows up in your network settings.

While most (if not all) people have network adapters in their machines, there are valid scenarios for using a loopback adapter. Dave Hermans, of Schriek, Antwerp, Belgium, a .NET Consultant and blogger wrote at http://davedotnet.blogspot.com/ after installing Vista:

> The next step that I wanted to do was to install Virtual Server and create a Team foundation server on it. So I did. And of course I need to be able to connect to it over network. But since I'm working disconnected from any company network most of the time and I need two-way communication between host (my visual studio development machine) and client (the virtual Team foundation server), I found out on previous installations (XP + WS2003) that the best way to do this is to add a loopback adapter to the host and make both machines connect to it. So I set off to add a loop back adapter to my Vista host like I did so many times before on my XP installs. And behold, it works! Now all you need to do is assign both the host and the guest a static IP in the same subnet mask and you're in business!

Nima Dilmagani, of Nima Dilmagani's Technology Blog (http://nimad.wordpress.com), had a similar story.

> For my talk at the SF launch I need to do a demo of a client computer calling a SharePoint server. Because I have one computer to do this on, I have to run the server inside a VPC and install the client software on the host computer. Then I need to use the Microsoft Loopback Adapter to connect these two.

AutoPlay

AutoPlay enables you to configure settings for different types of media you might try to play, as shown in Figure 2.3.

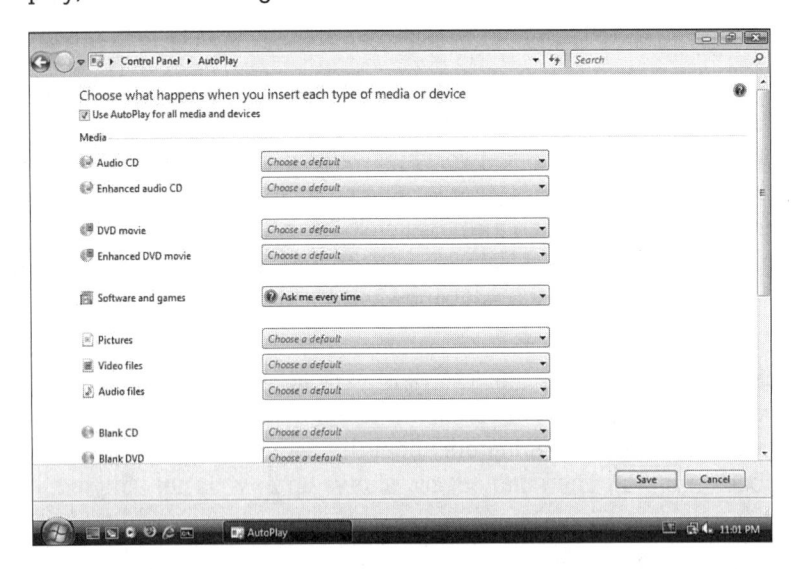

FIGURE 2.3

CDs, DVDs, games, and so forth can be preconfigured to run or not from the AutoPlay settings.

This applet gives you a single location to determine the desired result you want when inserting various types of media. You can configure a DVD to automatically play within Windows Media Center, or some other application if you like. Or you can determine that pictures or audio files use specific options.

> **NOTE**
> The AutoPlay options include settings for enhanced audio CDs or enhanced DVD movies. What are these? Well, sometimes artists include additional items on their CDs, such as music videos and so forth. These are CDs or DVDs that have different format types on them and so require additional settings.

In XP, the AutoPlay options were set by default to automatically run a disc's AutoPlay program. In Vista, the default is for it to ask you every time. But you can change this by going into your AutoPlay settings and changing the setting for Software and Games to Install or Run Program.

Date and Time

People are really liking the new Date and Time applet, mostly because of its ability to add two additional times for other time zones (as mentioned in Chapter 1, "General Tips and Tricks of the Masters").

There are still the following three tabs:

- **Date and Time**—Enables you to change the date, time, or time zone.
- **Additional Clocks**—Enables you to configure two additional clocks with their own time zones. When you hover your mouse over the time, you see the time in these other locations.
- **Internet Time**—Enables you to synchronize with systems on the Internet for the proper time. You can change the time to synchronize or stop this from happening altogether. You can force it to occur immediately or change the servers it checks the time with.

What everyone seems to love is the new clock graphic that displays when you click the time, along with the fact that now you can scroll through the calendar and look at other dates without fear of changing the date. You cannot change the date unless you go into the settings, so you can scroll through the calendar all you want.

Default Programs

Default Programs is a quick place to find your default program associations and file-to-program associations. For example, if you are tired of your MP3 files opening with Media Player and want them to open with WinAmp or some other player, you can make the changes here.

When you open the Default Programs applet, you have four options. (Keep in mind that you can also open the Default Programs applet by selecting the Start orb and then Default Programs.)

- **Set Your Default Programs**—Do you need to select between Firefox and IE 7 as your default browser? Here is where you can tell Vista which one is your go-to application. The same is true for your email, contact management information, media files, and photos. One nice feature is the ability to configure different aspects of the default settings. For example, you can configure certain protocols like FTP to open IE 7, while HTTP opens Firefox.

- **Associate a File Type or Protocol with a Program**—For an expanded view of all file types and protocols and their associated applications, you can select this option to ensure all the file types you have can be opened by the application you prefer.

> **NOTE**
> Changes made under the Set Your Default Programs settings are per user. They won't affect others on your computer. By contrast, the options you select for Set Program Access and Computer Default are for all users on the system.

- **Change AutoPlay Settings**—Opens the AutoPlay applet discussed previously.
- **Set Program Access and Computer Default**—Yet another way to specify which programs access certain information. You can select the following: Computer Manufacturer (if a manufacturer established preconfigured settings), Microsoft Windows (for an all-Microsoft default world), Non-Microsoft (allows you to use only non-Microsoft programs and access to those programs is removed unless you select Custom), and Custom (for a mix and match of applications; this is the most logical choice for most users).

Device Manager

Device Manager first became our trusted friend in Windows 95; it has changed locations through the years and now has its own applet in Control Panel. We are so proud to see this tool grow and make it to a full-fledged applet. Okay, enough nostalgia—this is one of the best tools available when you have a hardware problem. Why? Because it's not afraid to flash big yellow or red icons at you to tell you what's hurting.

With Device Manager, you can see which devices are installed and functioning properly. You can right-click the system and select one of two options:

- **Scan for Hardware Changes**—This checks for the PnP hardware already installed. A good use for this is in troubleshooting devices. Sometimes you might right-click a device and actually delete it from Device Manager. But, because it is still physically connected, the scan finds that device again and asks you to supply drivers for it. Sometimes this can help you to find out the source of a hardware problem.
- **Add Legacy Hardware**—If you select this option, the Hardware applet runs and asks you to select between the option to search for the drivers or to allow you to select your own.

> **TIP**
> To quickly get to the Device Manager settings, you can just right-click Computer from the Start menu and select Manage. Device Manager is integrated within your Computer Management tools from the Administrative Tools options. You can also type **devmgmt.msc** from the Start menu search bar. You can also right-click Computer, go to Properties, and choose Device Manager from the Tasks pane.

You can also update drivers by right-clicking an option and selecting Update Drivers. You can modify settings from within the Properties of the hardware devices you have.

There are a few other things you can do with Device Manager, and it's important to keep these in mind:

> **TIP**: Driver Verifier is a utility included in Vista to troubleshoot and isolate driver problems. You run it from a command prompt under elevated settings. For a quick check of all drivers, just run `verifier /all`. For more information, see the Knowledge Base article http://support.microsoft.com/kb/244617.

- **Driver Rollback**—From the Properties of any given device, you can open the Drivers tab, which has an option to roll back the driver. When you have a problem with a device after you have installed an updated driver, you can select this driver to roll it back to its previous version.

- **Device Conflicts**—Sometimes two hardware devices require the same resources from your system and battle back and forth over these resources, causing a hardware conflict. You can use Device Manager to disable devices you do not need or want, or to resolve the conflict by going into the Properties of a device and opening the Resources tab for a manual resolution to the problem.

- **Signature Verification Tool**—Another great tool in Vista is the Signature Verification Tool (sigverif.exe). Vista, like XP, uses a driver-signing process to ensure that drivers have been certified through Microsoft to work correctly. Sometimes you might purposely select to install devices that have not been verified. Other times, this might happen unwittingly. If you type **sigverif.exe** in the Start menu's search field and select the application that appears in the list, sigverif performs a scan of your system for any unsigned drivers. That's not to say that all these are bad drivers. But, when you are troubleshooting a problem, it helps to have all the facts.

The Alternative to Device Manager: DevCon

DevCon is a tool you run from the command line that allows you to enable, disable, restart, update, remove, and query devices individually or as a group all from the command line. You can download the DevCon toolset from Microsoft by first going to the Knowledge Base article Q311272.

Dave Hermans, mentioned previously (http://davedotnet.blogspot.com/), was having some difficulty installing the loopback adapter (discussed earlier) from the standard Hardware applet. Apparently, the Microsoft manufacturer wasn't showing up in his options (because it was Vista Beta 2 he was working with). So, he installed DevCon and typed **devcon.exe install %windir%\inf\netloop.inf *msloop**. It installed the drivers for the loopback adapter.

Folder Options

We've had to go into Folder Options in the last chapter. But let's quickly review what you can do in the Folder Options settings:

General

Nice features in Vista are the Details pane and the Preview pane. If you prefer to go back to the classic look, you can change this option here. You can change two other settings here: the ability to open a folder in its own window or a new window and the ability to open a folder with a double mouse click or a single mouse click.

View

This folder has a variety of options from which to select. Most of the options are pretty straightforward, but the reasoning behind why you might use some of these options might not be so apparent. Table 2.3 lists the settings.

Table 2.3—Explorer Window View Settings

Setting	Definition
Always Show Icons, Never Thumbnails	Thumbnail previews are beautiful to look at in Vista, but they slow down your system. You can go back to the icon view to free up your system's performance a bit.
Always Show Menus	You can turn on menus by pressing the Alt key, but with this option the menus will always be there.
Display File Icon on Thumbnails	Another graphic element that could be removed if your system seems slow.
Display File Size Information in Folder Tips	When you rest your pointer over a folder, it tells you the size of the folder.
Display Simple Folder View in Navigation Pane	Displays folders with lines that connect folders and subfolders.
Display the Full Path in the Title Bar (Classic Folders Only)	In Vista, by default, you can follow your path back to the beginning and navigate easily. However, if you are using the classic style, you won't see the full path you are in by default—unless you click this option.

Setting	Definition
Hidden Files and Folders. Show or Not to Show	Sometimes files and folders are hidden and you want it kept that way unless you need to work on them.
Hide Extensions for Known File Types	If your system recognizes certain file types and which applications open them, then the extension (.doc, .jpg, and so forth) doesn't show up. You might want to turn this off so you can see the extension of the files you are working with to ensure that files are not maliciously disguised software.
Hide Protected Operating System Files (recommended)	System files are hidden by default, but if you know what you are doing, you are going to need to see these files from time to time. Deselect this option to bring them back into view.
Launch Folder Windows in a Separate Process	Causes Windows to open each folder in a separate part of memory. This is a good idea to troubleshoot problems with your system crashing frequently. But you can take a performance hit with this option selected.
Remember Each Folders View Settings	Sometimes you might want certain folders to open with certain settings. This option does that for you. Other times you might just want Windows to open all your folders with the default settings. In that case, deselect this option.
Restore Previous Folder Windows at Logon	Automatically reopens the folders you were using when you last shut down in order to preserve a work flow.
Show Drive Letters	Most of us like to see the drive we are on. But you can hide the drive letters by deselecting this option.
Show Encrypted or NTFS Files in Color	Deselect this if you want encrypted or NTFS files to appear normally.
Show Pop-up Description for Folder and Desktop Items	ToolTips display when you rest your pointer on folders and desktop items, but you can turn that off.
Show Preview Handlers in Preview Pane	Turning this off improves performance because it won't show things in the preview pane.

Table 2.3—Explorer Window View Settings (Continued)

Setting	Definition
Use Check Boxes to Select Items	This was discussed in Chapter 1. It enables you to select check boxes near folders and files instead of holding down the Ctrl key to select multiple folders and files.
Use Sharing Wizard (recommended)	For sharing folders, the default is for the Sharing Wizard to open and help. The Vista Masters generally hate this wizard and prefer to handle sharing all on their own.
When Typing into List View: "Automatically Type into the Search Box" or "Select the Typed Item in the View"	This one might seem hard to understand at first. If you are in a folder and it is in List view, when you type, it could immediately put that information into the Search box or it could find the typed item in the view itself. If you quickly test each setting and then open a folder, change your view to List and then type in a known filename, you will see that they both do the same thing, just in different ways.

Search

Microsoft wants us to be able to store documents that are similar in folder structures we are familiar with; however, Microsoft now wants to make those similar documents available regardless of where they are stored. Microsoft's solution to this problem is a new concept called the Search Folder. For this reason, we have the Search tab (shown in Figure 2.4) in the Folder Options and we can configure our search settings as follows:

- **What to Search**—Here the default setting is best for performance because, if the location is indexed (which we will be getting into momentarily), it searches through filenames and content. If not, then only filenames are searched. Leaving the default will most likely yield the most useful results quickly if you keep your documents in indexed areas such as your profile folders. However, if you want to search everything with filenames and contents (the slower option), you can select that, too.

- **How to Search**—This offers a variety of logical options, but the Use Natural Language Search selection is one you really might like to set up for users because, as mentioned in Chapter 1, this will certainly help users who never got the whole Boolean thing. You can also tell the system Don't Use the Index if you are trying to troubleshoot a problem with the index.

- **When Searching Nonindexed Locations**—This enables you to decide whether you want to always include system directories and archives as part of the search. With different types of archive files that do not register a search handler (in other words, there is no program to open them registered), they are ignored in the search; however, Zip and CAB archives are handled directly by Vista.

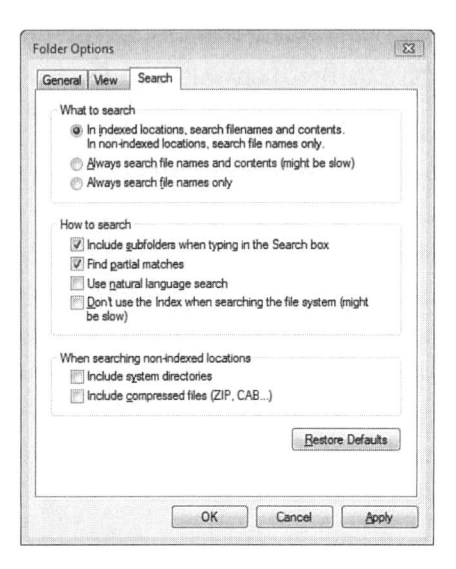

FIGURE 2.4
Folder Options, Search settings.

iSCSI Initiator

If you've lived exclusively in the world of the ATA/IDE interface—the type of interface that connects the vast majority of hard drives and optical drives inside a PC—you probably aren't too sure what an iSCSI initiator is. To understand this applet, you need to understand a little about the evolution of enterprise storage solutions to fully appreciate the iSCSI format.

Any reasonable person can install his own Ethernet network these days. Many use their networks to back up their data to another networked location (be it another computer, a network-enabled storage device, and so forth). It's the cheap approach and works well. But, let's say you want to keep all your storage on its own network. Going one step further, you can create a storage area network (SAN) by installing Ethernet cards and keeping all your storage on one network, while all real traffic is based off another Ethernet card in the system. This is called the *poor-man's SAN*.

Well, what's the rich-man's SAN? That involves Fibre Channel host bus adapters (HBAs) and devices, which are considered very expensive technologies. If you use all Fibre Channel, you pretty much get the SAN of your dreams rather than the poor-man's version, but you could spend your entire budget for the year (or five years, depending on your budget) trying to implement it.

In comes the middle-class-man's SAN. Internet Small Computer System Interface (iSCSI) uses TCP/IP for its data transfer over a common Ethernet network. You get the SAN functionality with pretty decent performance (not quite Fibre Channel yet, but it's improving each day). The catch, of course, is that you need iSCSI devices to make it work—and the OS needs an initiator to communicate with the iSCSI devices. iSCSI devices are disks, tape drives, optical drives, and other storage devices that you can connect to. In the relationship with the other device, your computer is the initiator and the device is the target.

In Vista the initiator is included. However, you can download the initiator from Microsoft for Windows 2000 (sp3), XP, or Server 2003. The Control Panel applet (shown in Figure 2.5) lets you configure and control the interaction between your system and the device.

If you want to work with the iSCSI initiator from a command line, you must use the `iscsicli.exe` command.

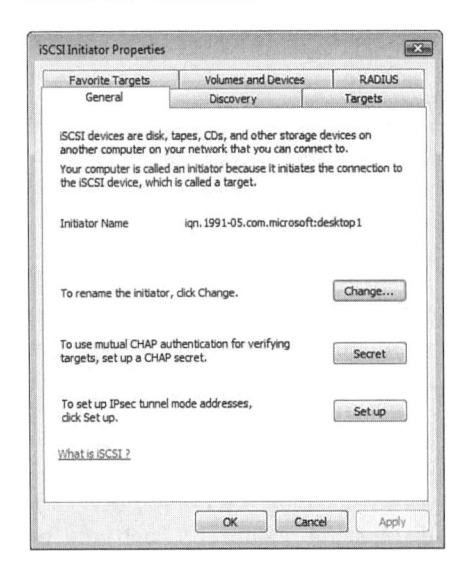

FIGURE 2.5
The iSCSI Initiator applet.

Pen and Input Devices

This enables you to configure your pen and input settings (although there is a Pen applet available with Tablet PCs that allows for a greater level of configuration). Keep in mind that now you don't need a Tablet PC to take advantage of electronic ink.

You can now enter handwriting information directly into ink-capable applications, such as Microsoft Journal or Microsoft OneNote, using tablet devices (such as a WACOM Intuos USB tablet, the ACECAD, or the SolidTek USB tablets). Not only this, but the indexing and searching capabilities of Windows Vista recognize handwriting, allowing you to use the native search to find notes you have typed on your keyboard or written with a pen on a tablet. How incredible is that?

> **NOTE** Truthfully, if storage solutions are not your biggest concern, there is no need to focus too much on the iSCSI initiator. However, if you do want to get more information on it, you should read individual device information from the vendors and how to configure the initiator.

> **TIP** Writing on your Tablet PC's screen may be familiar to you by now. But using these new tablets may not be. One expert recommended aligning the tablet with your monitor (right in front of it, as opposed to the side like a mouse pad) so that you'll get used to the hand-pointer correspondence. You will be a master in no time.

Three simple tabs are presented in this applet: Pen Options, Pointer Options, and Flicks.

The Pen and Pointer options are relatively straightforward. They configure what happens when you tap once or twice or hold down your pen. On the Pointer tab you can configure visual feedback for your clicks, like a single or double circle or larger blue circles depending on what you've done.

But it's the Flicks tab (shown in Figure 2.6) that probably catches our attention the most.

Flicks are defined as gestures that help you use your pen more effectively. You can flick to copy, paste, delete, or undo something. You can flick to scroll up or down or backward or forward in your web browser. Consider flicks like keyboard shortcuts for your pen.

To configure your flicks, do the following:

1. Open Control Panel and click Pen and Input Devices.
2. Click the Flicks tab.
3. Select the radio button by Navigational and Editing Flicks, and then click Customize. The Customize dialog box appears.

4. Select from the list of predefined flick actions, or add any key combination you like.
5. On the same tab, adjust the sensitivity of your flicks to give the best performance without accidentally setting off a flick.

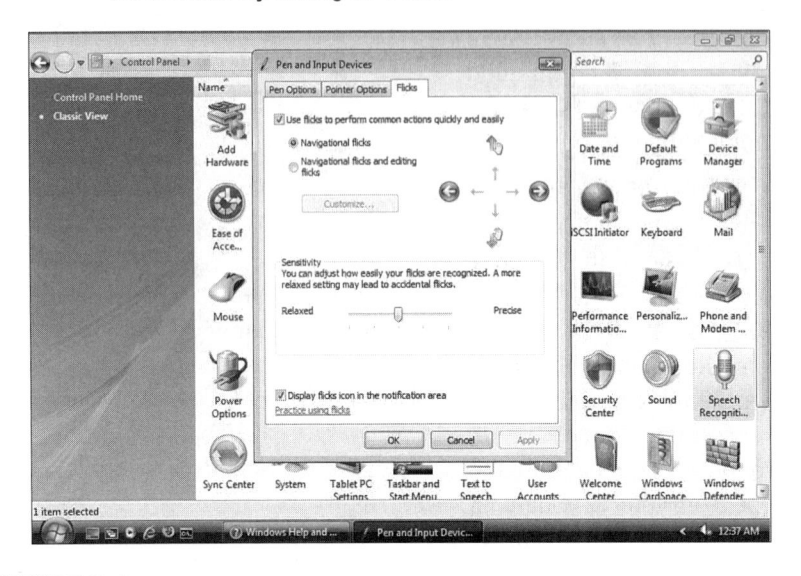

FIGURE 2.6
Learn how to Flick.

Sometimes the system will try to help you incorporate flicks. When you perform an action that might be better using a flick, a notification pops up telling you that there is a wizard to help you learn to use flicks. It appears only three times total and never more than once in a 24-hour period, so you might want to take advantage of it early on.

Printers

The Printers applet shows you printers and fax machines your system is aware of. This applet is similar to its XP cousin, but there are a few changes—for example, a Color Management tab has been added to the properties of your printers to make it easier to configure your device color settings.

When you add a printer, you will notice that now you have the option of adding a network, wireless, or bluetooth printer. This

> **TIP**
> Practice makes perfect. You can open your Pen and Input options and select the Flicks tab; down at the bottom (as you can see in Figure 2.6) is an option to Practice using flicks. Select this to open the Pen Flick Training from Help and Support. Give this a whirl and see if it helps improve your fancy flick-work.

shows that the OS is up-to-speed with possible options. If you right-click the printer you've installed and open the printing preferences, you can change the layout options and the Paper/Quality settings. You can select which printer is your default by right-clicking the printer and selecting Set As Default. You can share it on your network and so forth. If you right-click and open the Properties of your printer, that's where you see the majority of your options, including the choice to print a test page.

Managing Print Jobs

To see the jobs printing off a printer, you can double-click the printer icon from the Printers applet. It opens a dialog box that shows you what's printing. From here you can select certain jobs and select to Pause them or Cancel them, if necessary. The print queue window shows you the print job's document name, status of the printing, owner, number of pages, size of the job, time and date it was submitted, and port.

In some locations, printers are set up with servers and a special team of administrators handles them. In smaller environments, printers might be connected to certain users' machines while others in the office print documents "through" those systems to the printer.

In those cases, if you are the user who has the printer connected, you might want to be aware of how to manage these jobs so you can do things like stop one job to make sure another job prints first, and so forth.

Print Server Properties

You may be thinking, "My Vista system is not a print server." In reality, though, if you have a printer on it that is shared out for others to use, your machine is functioning like a print server for your home/office.

What are some things you might want to do as a Vista Print Server? Well, we discussed the print spooler in the note. You might want to change the location of this file to improve performance. You may also want to configure availability settings or set up a printer pool. Let's look at each tab's capabilities.

> **NOTE** The Print Spooler is a service that runs in the background and controls the flow of your print jobs. When you print a job, it goes into a temporary location on your disk (which explains why you can print a document and then close it but it will still print because that document has already been spooled and doesn't need to be opened any longer). The spooler service unspools jobs when it's their turn to be printed. Sometimes, however, things get a little "stuck." Go into your services, stop the Print Spooler, and then restart it when this happens. When you are having problems with a printer and you've tried several standard troubleshooting approaches, you should just stop/restart the service.

- **General**—You can add/modify the printer location and comment information, change your printing preferences (such as the layout or paper source and quality), and print a test page.
- **Sharing**—You can share or stop sharing the printer. You can also install additional drivers for client systems that may use different operating systems (so that older OSs have the driver available to them automatically when they connect). You can also determine the location of print rendering.
- **Ports**—You can select a port to print to; add, configure, or delete ports; and configure bidirectional printing if your printer supports it (which is a printer feature that allows the printer head to print when it's moving left to right and right to left). You can also configure printer pooling, which is great when you have more than one print device connected to your system and want to make it so that a person can print to one logical printer. If one print device is busy, it automatically sends the print job over to the other printer. Whichever print device is available first is the one that prints.

> **NOTE**
>
> The Sharing tab has a check box that indicates that rendering of the print job will take place on the client (not the server). This aspect of printing has changed back and forth from server to client, from one OS to the next. It all comes down to processing power. Sometimes the server is thought to have more power so it should do the rendering. But servers these days may also serve in multiple roles, which uses more of their processing power; therefore, the client should do the rendering. Well, now it looks like it will continue on the client side unless you deselect this option on your Sharing tab.
>
> The printer driver renders the print job to the Page Description Language (PDL) the printer uses instead of the Enhanced Meta File (EMF) or XML Paper Specification (XPS) format used by the printer driver. The PDL is then sent to the server, which now has less work to do because the client has handled the bulk of it. Along with the processing load being shifted as a benefit, this also corrects problems with drivers being different between client and server and allows users to print jobs while offline (not connected to the printer). When the user does reconnect to the print server, the job then prints.

- **Color Management**—This tab just has a button that takes you to the Color Management applet.
- **Security**—You can configure different groups to have different permissions with the printer. You can Allow or Deny persons or groups to Print, Manage Printers (which involves changing settings on the printers), Manage Documents (which allows you to stop/start/pause print jobs), or set up Special Permissions.
- **Device Settings**—Enables you to configure printer-specific settings that vary with each manufacturer or model printer. You can configure paper tray assignments, font cartridge settings, and so forth.
- **Advanced**—This tab (shown in Figure 2.7) enables you to configure scheduling and spooling settings. Here is where you can really manage your printer:

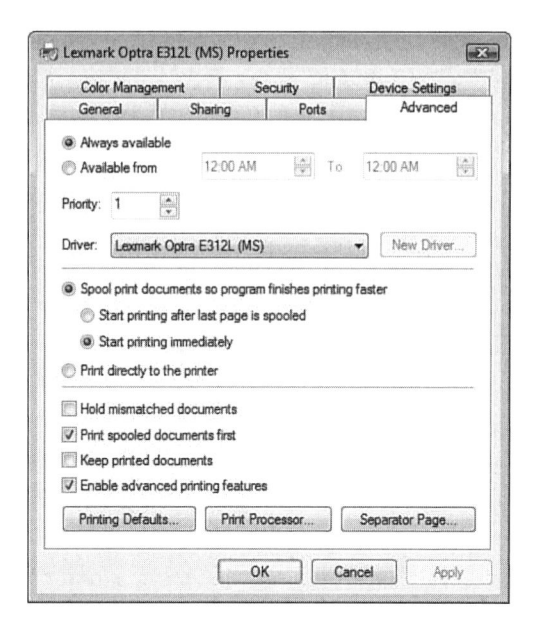

FIGURE 2.7
Advanced Printer setting options.

- **Availability**—You can leave it as always available or lock down the times you want this printer available. Consider this scenario: You have a very expensive color printer that some users want to have access to. You tell them they can print to it from 10am-12am each day. You then configure this setting on their logical printer (which is the one they connect to), and they are locked into that print window.

- **Priority**—The logical printer can have different priorities. For example, say two people print to the same print device but use two different logical printers (one with a setting of 1 and the other with a setting of 99). Let's say one is for managers while the other is for document processors; the priority will determine where in the queue the job will stay. So, a manager's job will be advanced beyond that of others because the logical printer she is using has a higher priority.

- **Print Spooler Settings**—You can start printing immediately or wait until the job has finished spooling. Or you can tell it not to spool at all.

> **TIP**
> If you want to change the location of the spool folder in Vista, open the Printers applet. Right-click in the white space under the printers and select Server Properties. Next, go to the Advanced tab and type in the new path for the new location of the spool folder. Then you can stop and restart the print spooler service or reboot the system.

- **Final Settings**—You can hold mismatched documents, print spooled documents first, retain documents after they have been printed, and so forth.

Regional and Language Options

This applet assists in choosing a keyboard layout and the layout of how your system displays number, currencies and so forth. You have four tabs to work with:

- **Formats**—Allows you to configure the default way your computer renders number, currency, date, and time. You can select a specific format, based on a country in the world, and the options adjust to that country. But you can also select to Customize that format, which gives you several more tabs to configure the display of measurements, long and short dates, and time format. For example, let's say you prefer to use military time (00:00 to 24:00 hours), which is how many countries prefer to look at time. You can also keep all your options based in one format, but customize that one option to read differently.

- **Location**—This is an easy setting to assist with some programs that provide local news and weather.

- **Keyboards and Languages**—You can configure an input language and a display language. An input language involves changing the keyboard layout to support other keyboard layouts. You can read and edit documents in multiple languages by selecting the proper keyboard layout. You can even try different U.S. keyboard layouts, such as the Dvorak keyboard for improved type speed. You can also change the display language from this tab. The display language is the language you see in wizards, dialog boxes, and menus.

- **Administrative**—You can choose the language for non-Unicode programs, and you can copy your regional settings to reserved accounts (which include the default user account and the system accounts).

> **NOTE**
>
> The standard QWERTY keyboard is not the most efficient method of character placement on modern keyboards. It was a good way to keep typewriter keys from hitting each other and sticking, but the modern keyboard was designed to alternate the keys, causing typists to actually underperform. The Dvorak keyboard rearranges the letters to increase speed now that we have modern equipment.
>
> To illustrate the superiority of his keyboard, Dvorak retrained 14 Navy typists during the World War II period. Within a month, they were producing 74% more work and were 68% more accurate. There are varying reports on the speed/accuracy improvements people have if they switch, but it's a guarantee that there will be improvement. Sadly, the Dvorak keyboard may never be widely implemented because Qwerty is already so entrenched.

The two different kinds of language files are as follows:

- **Windows Vista Multilingual User Interface Pack (MUI)**—This provides a translated version of most of the user interface, but it's only available for Windows Vista Ultimate or Enterprise.
- **Windows Vista Language Interface Pack (LIP)**—This provides a translated version of the most widely used areas of the OS interface. You can download these freely from Microsoft, and they can be used on any edition of Vista.

The Language Bar

This appears on your taskbar after you add certain services such as input languages, keyboard layouts, handwriting recognition, speech recognition, and so forth. The Language Bar lets you quickly switch between the different methods from your desktop. The settings you can configure from within the Keyboards installation relate only to how the bar is displayed—whether it is docked or hidden or floating, and so forth.

The Administrative Tab

The final tab in our discussion on regional settings is the Administrative tab. The top options include changing the system locale. Basically this allows you to change settings for applications that do not use Unicode. Sometimes you need to change the system locale when you install other languages on your system.

The other section of options includes copying settings to reserved accounts (shown in Figure 2.8). You can copy the settings you have configured to the default user accounts (for new users who are created on the system, they will now receive the settings you have configured). Note that this doesn't affect preexisting user accounts, only newly created ones.

You can also copy the settings to the default system accounts. By doing this, you can configure the display language and keyboard layout for the Welcome screen. Once you have copied over these settings, users should be able to see the options from their Welcome screens when they log on. If they don't, something isn't configured correctly and you should go back and make sure you copied the settings.

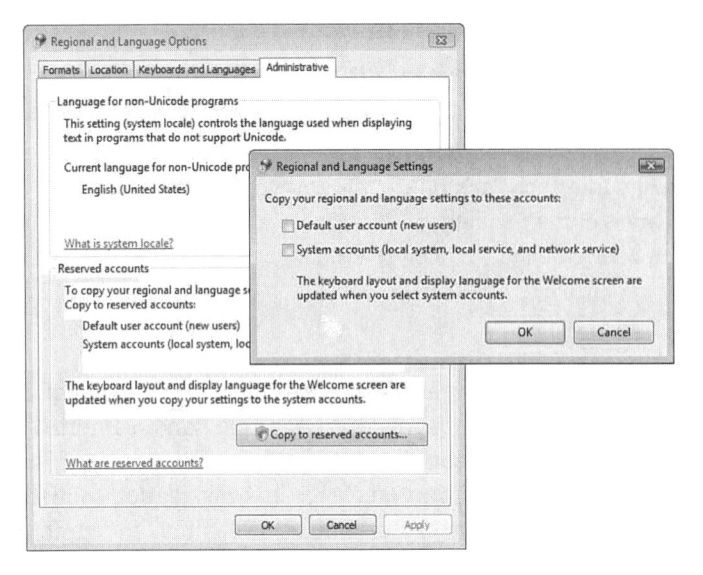

FIGURE 2.8
Copying Regional and Language settings.

Sync Center

We are a synchronizing generation. We sync our desktops to our servers, and we sync our digital cameras, email, cell phones, portable media players, camcorders, PDAs, laptops, and so forth. We sync everything. Now we have a single applet that helps us know how we're doing—how in sync we really are.

Brien M. Posey, in an article for Windows Networking (http://www.windowsnetworking.com/articles_tutorials/Preview-Windows-Vista-Sync-Center.html) wrote about his personal challenge with keeping in sync and the need for the new Sync Center applet.

> The reason why Microsoft created the Sync Center is because users often store data in multiple locations. For example, I already mentioned that I have data stored on a file server and on my laptop. However, I also have data stored on my Pocket PC based cell phone and on my Creative Zen Vision. As you can see, I have data scattered among multiple devices and ,until now, there has not been an easy way of keeping this data synchronized so that there is a consistent experience from device to device. This is where the Sync Center comes in. It allows you to manage the synchronization relationships between a group of PCs, a PC and a server, or even a PC and a mobile device (such as a PDA). The Sync Center allows you to define synchronization relationships, schedule synchronizations, perform manual syncs, abort a sync, or view the current synchronization status.

Later on in the chapter, in the section, "Offline Files: Synchronizing Your World," we discuss Offline Files (which is closely tied in with the Sync Center). First, though, it's important to know that the Sync Center is a different tool altogether. It's not a synchronization application looking to take the place of your device's standard sync application. Essentially, when you install your device's application for synchronization, the Sync Center establishes a behind-the-scenes relationship with your device that enables the center to display information like a progress bar and report any problems or conflicts. Keep in mind that if you are going to sync a laptop and desktop you must have both running Vista. Your other devices (cellphones and so forth) will also have to be Vista-aware to work with the Sync Center.

In terms of Offline Files, you still have to configure your Offline File settings separately, but then you can go to the Sync Center to see how the progress is going with the sync and handle any conflicts (discussed later in this chapter).

Another nice feature of Sync Center is that you can schedule your synchronization. So, for Offline Files, although you normally sync, go on a business trip, and then resync (perhaps manually doing the syncs), you can use Sync Center to work more on a schedule.

When you attempt to sync different devices with the Sync Center, you have to start by setting up a new sync partnership (with the exception of Offline Files, where it's automatic). You might have difficulty establishing a partnership if the device isn't connected properly or if the device isn't configured to work with Sync Center. So, your older devices probably won't work here (unless the software developers provide some new sync software for them).

Text to Speech

Does everyone remember Windows Sam? How many of you couldn't help but type in things like, "Shall we play a game?" (Rent the movie *Wargames* if that line doesn't resonate with you.) Windows Sam is fun to play with, but not smooth enough to want to use often (unless we absolutely have to). But now we have Anna. She is wonderful in comparison. Test this applet and note the difference in the quality of text to speech (TTS) in Vista.

> **TIP** For XP users who want to sync up a little better, too, Microsoft released a tool in 2006 called SyncToy. The number of users who are managing multiple copies of data across a variety of devices, systems, and drives is increasing daily. Keeping track of all that can be a huge burden, so Microsoft offers this free tool to help until you have Vista up and running with Sync Center. Version 1.4 will even run on Vista, so you can continue to use it if you like.

Other TTS applications are available for use that work off the principles Microsoft has implemented within the OS. The Speech Application Programming Interface (SAPI) is an API developed by Microsoft to enable Windows applications to use both speech recognition and synthesis. Developers can utilize this API to create their own types of TTS applications. As a fun example, you can check out http://www.bellcraft.com/deskbot/ and find some cool characters to download and try.

> **TIP**
> In the past, we could download different voices. The same is true today for different voices and different languages too! However, a more recent project is underway for us to record our own voices: http://www.modeltalker.com/mt.php. Model Talker is a development company for the construction of synthetic voices. You record your own voice and the synthetic one can use the recording to even say words you haven't recorded before. It has some real potential, especially for those who have started to lose their voice.

Windows SideShow

Windows SideShow is one technology to watch for. It has real potential. The concept is that laptop manufacturers and others can create a secondary or alternative display to allow users to view critical information without turning on the laptop. It's literally a sideshow, in that things like meeting schedules, contact information, map directions, and email can all be accessed without all the turmoil of turning on the system. The auxiliary displays aren't all created just yet, but the ideas include keyboards, LCD display casings (like mini-picture frame displays), remote controls, cell phones, and so forth that will display information located on your Vista system. Some are even thinking of light gaming capabilities.

When the host machine is on, it checks in with the SideShow devices and you have real-time updates. If the host machine shuts down, the information is then cached in the secondary or alternative system. You can do a quick search online for SideShow products and you'll see some of the innovative thoughts being put together.

Once you have a device that works with SideShow, you can go into this applet and configure your gadgets (calendar, email, and so forth) to work with it.

Windows Update

Windows Update is a way to connect to a Microsoft database that has drivers, patches, security fixes, and so forth to keep your Vista installation up-to-date.

From home, you can configure your Windows Update setting to connect to Microsoft and update your system or do it manually. If you are a network admin, consider the idea of using Group Policies to configure these settings for your workplace. And, if you have a large enough environment and a small enough network connection to the Internet, you might want to consider setting up a Windows Update Server. This downloads updates; then your network systems check in with the server and download from the internal system. It's a great way to ensure that all your systems are protected with the latest security patches and fixes.

> **NOTE** There are some newer features to Windows Update in Vista that should be noted. First, this isn't a web application like earlier versions were. The functionality is part of the Control Panel and checks in with a database at Microsoft. Now your Windows Defender and Windows Mail are updated through the update process so that new anti-spyware lists and junk mail filters are in place.

With Windows Update you configure your system to work on a schedule of your selecting (or none at all if you prefer to handle checking for updates manually, which is not recommended). In the past, many users disliked that updates required reboots often and that these reboots pushed a request box at the user every 10 minutes until the user complied with the request. Now the user can select longer periods of time for that dialog box (up to four hours) and the dialog box is not as intrusive.

You can alter the settings of your updates through the Control Panel settings (shown in Figure 2.9). So, you might decide to change these settings to download the updates but let you decide if you want to install them.

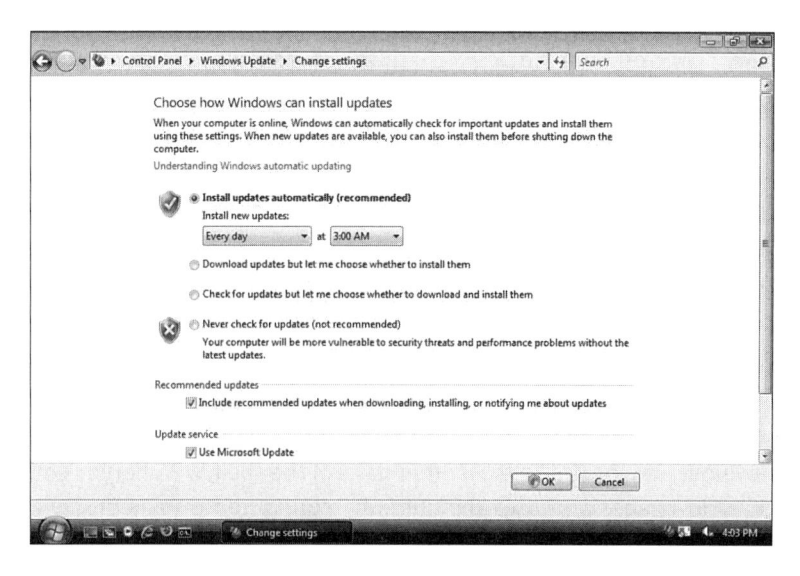

FIGURE 2.9
Select how Windows can install Updates.

Color Management

The Color Management applet enables you to configure a variety of color settings in Vista. This is the result of a team effort between Microsoft and Canon to establish a better screen-to-print match and support for more reliable printing with today's powerful color devices such as digital cameras and modern printers.

This might seem like a brand-new Vista tool, but it is actually available for download from Microsoft for XP systems, too. The XP version is a PowerToy that enables you to view and edit color management settings, configure color profiles for different devices (display, printer, scanner), and even view overly detailed properties for those profiles (including a 3D rendering of the color space gamut).

> **TIP**
> This book is not just one big rah-rah cheerleading session for Microsoft. Sometimes we have to encourage something more than the Redmond giant provides. For example, if you are an intermediate user (or advanced user) with Vista on your home desktop, Windows Updates are a fairly safe option. But other products are available for Enterprise environments. You could go to the next level with a Windows Update Service Server. You could push beyond that with Shavlik Technologies NetChk Protect product, which is the top-rated independent patch-management solution right now. The choices are yours, but whatever you do, you need to keep your OS up-to-date.

Michael Bourgoin
Program Manager at Microsoft for the Desktop & Graphics Technologies Color Team

With Windows Color Management (WCS) in Windows Vista, we have the first stage of a multirelease effort to enable seamless color management in Windows. In Windows Vista we have in place the "engine" for WCS, with support for ICC version 4 profiles as well as WCS XML profiles. We also have the WCS processing pipeline that supports high dynamic range, wide gamut, and high precision (up to 32 bpc floating point) color, but there are still parts of the system and some applications that aren't taking full advantage of it yet.

The first release is mainly targeting IHVs who are in the process of rewriting drivers to use the new XPSDrv driver architecture, PrintTicket/PrintCapabilities mechanism, and WCS. The main place where most end users will notice a difference due to WCS is in the Windows Photo Gallery. Unlike most other parts of the shell, WPG honors embedded color profiles in images and uses the currently configured display profile as its destination profile when displaying images onscreen. If you change the default profile associated with a display, that affects the way WPG displays images (this is not the case with the shell in general). [Note: You must relaunch the WPG after changing the display profile for it to recognize that change because the WPG apparently checks and obtains the current display profile when it starts up.] In WCS, the current profile associated with a display is assumed to match the current state of that display. Unlike ColorSync on the Mac OS, we do not use color profiles to force the display to a different state—we don't modify the video gamma LUTs when a display profile changes.

The Vista Color Management control panel centralizes color management settings and profile/device association activities that had been scattered in multiple locations on Windows XP. You can install/uninstall color profiles (both WCS and ICC profiles), associate profiles with devices, and set defaults for devices and the WCS in general. Also, on Vista you can associate different profiles with each of multiple displays (unlike as is the case on Windows XP). Finally, it supports per-user as well as system-wide color settings.

A number of whitepapers and presentations from WinHEC and DriverDevCon conferences on the Windows Color System are available at http://www.microsoft.com/color. The entire collection of WCS design specifications covering all the algorithms used in the WCS baseline device models and gamut mapping models are available on MSDN at http://msdn2.microsoft.com/en-us/library/ms536900.aspx.

Now, if any of that made sense to you, you are going to love this tool in Vista. If not, don't feel bad—it's a tool that will mostly appeal to digital photographers who are serious hobbyists or experts in the field. So, if you are wondering whether this is an applet you need to work with, the short answer is that it doesn't provide a huge advantage for most users. It just provides convenience, especially because most users who need color management are using a somewhat closed-loop process with Photoshop.

Keep in mind that from the scanner/camera to the computer to the printer, you are dealing with different devices that have different characteristics and capabilities with colors. Beyond the hardware, even programs have different capabilities. For example, the same picture, opened by two different photo-viewing applications, might produce different results to the viewer.

Color management maintains consistency between different devices and applications to produce a more uniform appearance. Is it perfect? Experts in the field say you should have realistic expectations regarding color profiling within Vista. It will get you closer to consistency but not an exact match due to a

> **NOTE** Here are just a few points about color profiles for those who are curious. Normally, a profile is installed automatically with your device, for your device's color settings. If you need to install additional ones, just open the Color Manager, select the Profiles tab, select Add, and then select the location of the new profiles (most likely a CD with your device). Now, why would your devices need different profiles? Take a printer, for example. Different types of paper might require different profiles to ensure that the quality of the print job is consistent.

variety of problems with different light (transmissive versus reflective) and ambient lighting effects—not to mention the differences between color possibilities between your monitors and printers. The final verdict is that you should rely on hardware color calibration if you are doing serious work. And, if digital photography is not something you are serious about, even Microsoft recommends you leave these settings to their defaults.

What's Coming in the Future?

WCS was designed to work in combination with a feature called the Color Policy Database (CPDb). This feature was discussed in 2003 and 2004 WinHEC presentations and you can read more about it here http://www.microsoft.com/whdc/device/display/color/WCS.mspx. The CPDb was a metadata-driven rule base that allowed retrieval of profiles and settings based on metadata presented in a query (things such as paper type, ink set, resolution, camera settings, and so forth). The idea was that device installers could install usage rules along with their profiles, and color professionals could author their own new rules to help with workflow automation. With the CPDb, we really would have had a color solution that "just worked" for the vast majority of users. Due to schedule and resource constraints, it was put aside, but we look forward to seeing more on this in the future.

Another great WCS feature that had to be put aside temporarily is the Display Calibration Wizard. This is a simple visual display calibrator using video clips and onscreen controls (similar to the Display Setup wizard in the Windows Media Center Edition). But stay tuned for this feature in a future Windows release.

Indexing: Find the Needle in the Haystack

In Windows XP, when you did a search, you generally found what you were looking for. But it was rare that you were impressed by the Search engine. To begin with, XP shipped with the Indexing service (a service meant to speed up and simplify your searching) disabled by default. You could turn it on if you knew it needed to be on, and you could even make advanced option configuration changes (if the dialog box didn't scare you to death). Without the Index service turned on, the Search was awful; with it turned on, it was better, but frustratingly slow at times.

Vista is a decent improvement over XP in the area of searching. To begin with, Indexing is on by default, but only on your documents (including your pictures, music, and videos), offline files, and email messages. So, if you are searching one of these types of files, you will be impressed. And, if you want to control what the Windows Search

Engine (WSE) indexes, you can use the Indexing Options in the Control Panel applet to configure things a little better.

When you open the Indexing Options applet, you can quickly see the locations that are included and the number of items indexed. You can also see whether certain locations are excluded. Certain folders do not require searching through normally, and it would be better to keep these excluded from the Index to ensure speed.

> **TIP**
> You might get the idea that you should index all your drives and every folder for the best success. This is a mistake and really bogs down your system. Only select locations that include personal data that you truly need to have indexed.

You can select the Modify or Advanced options.

Modify Index Options

When you click the Modify button on the Indexing Options window, Vista opens the Indexed Locations dialog box. Initially you might not see much, but you can select to see all locations; this expands out the directory tree. Once you can see all locations, you can include or exclude locations by selecting the check box next to each location.

Advanced Index Options

The Advanced indexing options (shown in Figure 2.10) enable you to make a variety of configuration changes to your index.

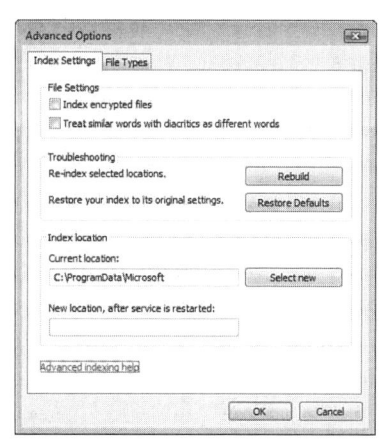

FIGURE 2.10
Advanced Index options.

The Advanced Index options have two tabs. The first is Index Settings, and the second File Types. First, we'll look at the options on the Index Settings tab:

- **Index Encrypted Files**—Enables the indexer to add files that are encrypted with NTFS encryption. Note, this is not the same as .zip or .cab files.
- **Treat Similar Words with Diacritics As Different Words**—Controls how the indexer handles accented words. *Blasé* and *Blase* would generally be the same word to the indexer; but you can change that with this setting so they are indexed separately.
- **Reindex Selected Locations**—This rebuilds the whole index from the ground up, which is necessary at times if you feel the index needs a do-over to speed up your searches.
- **Restore Defaults**—Brings everything here back to factory settings.
- **Index Location**—Enables you to change the location of the index file, which requires a restart. Click the Select New button and determine the new location.

With the File Types tab, the most commonly supported file types are indexed. But if you want to index additional file types, you just have to select the check box next to the file type you want. You can also select to Index Properties Only (which includes meta data for those files, which is possibly all you need or can index), or you can select to Index Properties and File Contents (which indexes content itself, if that's possible).

Offline Files: Synchronizing Your World

The concept of offline files is simple. It's similar to viewing offline web pages when you aren't connected to the Internet. The difference is that you can actually make changes to your offline files. Imagine this scenario: You are working on a set of documents located in a folder on a network server. You are taking a business trip but would like to continue to work on those files while you are away. You could just copy the folder, make changes, and then manually determine and copy back the files you want on the server when the trip is over. This causes multiple versions of the same document to be floating

> **TIP**
> Indexing is a very system-intensive function, especially if you are indexing a large amount of data (for example, if you decide to index an entire drive with many GB of data). The Index engine usually waits until your system is idle before proceeding, and it is best to let the indexer run through the night for larger jobs.

> **NOTE**
> If you install an application that is index-aware, such as Office 2007, all the file types and search handlers are registered automatically. So you don't have to worry about the email index for Outlook 2007 because it should work as soon as you install it. Some have had difficulties with Outlook 2007 being indexed if they upgraded Outlook from 2003. One solution is to uninstall Office and reinstall it again.

around in the event you forget to update the server and someone accesses the older versions of the documents. Or, you could synchronize that data through Offline Files. This feature has actually been around for awhile, but it has been improving over the years and it receives a major overhaul in Vista (and its very own applet, finally).

Configuring a file or folder for offline use is quite simple. You find the folder on the network share, right-click, and then select Always Available Offline. If you want to work with documents offline—even if you have a network connection—from the folder you are working in, you should see an option on the toolbar to Work Offline. When you are ready to resynchronize your documents, you just select Work Online from the toolbar.

To configure your offline files, open the Control Panel applet and you will see four tabs:

- **General**—You can enable or disable offline files. You can open Sync Center (discussed earlier) to check for synchronization conflicts or force the synchronization immediately. If you select View Your Offline Files, the Offline Files Folder opens.

- **Disk Usage**—You can easily see how much space your system is using for offline and temporary offline files. You can also alter the amount allotted. You move sliders to the right and left to configure your offline or temporary offline files. It might seem odd to have two different configurations. Here is how it works: Offline files are local copies of network files that you can use when you are disconnected from the network. Temporary offline files are local copies of recently used network files that are cached for you to use when you are disconnected from the network. Essentially, the temporary offline files are not configured by you, but by Windows when you connect to network files. Windows can also remove them at will, as opposed to your offline files, which you have configured and will not be removed unless you say so.

- **Encryption**—With one click, you can encrypt your offline files. In the event your offline files include sensitive information, you might want to go to the next secure level by encrypting. This encrypts only the files on your system, not on the server itself. You don't need to decrypt a file before using it; this is done automatically based on your user account being verified by your system. This is especially important because most offline file use is done for business purposes, on laptops, for those who travel. In the event of a theft, having these documents encrypted could be essential.

- **Network**—Configures your offline files for slow network connections. In the event you are connected to a slow connection (although in the office and technically online), the work is done offline and the system checks for a slow connection every 5 minutes by default (but you can alter the check time).

> **TIP** You can delete temporary offline files to free up space on your system.

How the Synchronization Works

There are some nice improvements in offline files between XP's implementation and Vista's. First, Vista uses a new and faster algorithm to ascertain which files/directories are different between the server and client. Second, Vista uses a process called Bitmap Differential Transfer to sync changes. To understand this and the benefits, you must first know that in XP the entire file (if changed) was copied back to the server. However, with Bitmap Differential Transfer only the specific blocks that have been modified while offline (disconnected from the server) are sent up to the server. This allows for faster synchronization of only modified data.

Along with performance improvements as a result, Vista can now handle larger files such as .pst and .mdb files (unlike XP, which could not). In Vista, no file types are excluded.

Keep in mind that Bitmap Differential Transfer works only from the Vista client up to the server. In synchronizing the other way, from server to client, the entire file is sent.

Among the other great changes is that Vista synchronizes only the current user logged in (unlike XP, which tried to sync all the users of the machine) and you can also script your synchronization using WMI.

Sync Errors, Warnings, and Resolutions

Connecting your laptop to the network results in one of three things. If you changed your offline files, they sync back to the server. If someone changed the server's files, the files sync back to you. It sounds simple, doesn't it? What is the third option? An error or conflict occurs with which you must deal.

For example, what if the network is unavailable? Or what if you changed the files and somebody else changed the same files? Whose files should continue to exist? And you can't just go by the time stamp because what if you worked on the files all weekend and they are perfect, but someone else opened the files and made a minor correction after you? Should her changes stay and yours be tossed away? These are all problems that must be considered:

- **Sync errors**—Occur when a device isn't plugged in correctly or the server is unavailable. Usually the simple resolution is to check your plugs and see why the server isn't available before you try to sync again.
- **Sync warnings**—Not as serious as the errors. These just try to give you an indication that something isn't going well and that you might need to take action before you get an error. One example is that your laptop's battery is dying, keeping you from being able to finish the sync unless you do something to keep it going.

- **Sync conflicts**—Occur when the system doesn't know what to do with the files. There is a conflict that shows two different files that have been modified and the system cannot make the call as to which one is correct. Another example is when one file is deleted between the two locations. What should be done? Delete the file in the other location, or copy the remaining file back to the deleted location?
- **Resolutions**—Generally, you can see your problems from within the Sync Center. Errors and conflicts (but not warnings) also show up on your taskbar with a little Sync Center icon that has a red circle with an x for an error or a yield sign that indicates a conflict. You can click this to check out the errors.

> **TIP**
> For Sync conflicts, you need to make a decision. Which one should you keep? Many people go with the latest version of the file. But if you aren't sure, you can select to open the files and take a look at them. That might help you to resolve the conflict. If you decide in the end that it might be better to keep them both, you can just opt for that, the Sync Center will make a secondary copy of the file with a different name, and these two files will no longer be in sync with each other.

Parental Control

For years the Internet has been friend and foe in people's homes. The education it can bring a child can be both helpful and harmful, and limited methods of control have been available without having to purchase additional software to control your children's habits when they're surfing the Net or playing certain games, or even the times they are able to access the Internet. Vista now provides all that capability through the Parental Controls applet.

To begin, you should log in to Vista with an account that has the administrative privileges and then create an account for your children. You can create one account for all your children (which makes it easier to manage) or one for each child (which enables you to establish settings based on their ages). Regardless of which route you choose, these newly created accounts must be implemented as standard user accounts for Vista's parental control features to work.

From within Control Panel, under User Accounts and Family Security, you can select the Setup Parental Controls for any user option and it takes you to the Parental Controls options.

After you access the main control panel (shown in Figure 2.11), you can then determine whether you want to turn Parental Controls on or off. You can also turn Activity Reporting on or off. This option gives you information about the sites your children visit, the amount of time spent online, the number of email messages they receive, who they exchange email with, and so forth. You can also select View Activity Reports to see the account's history pattern.

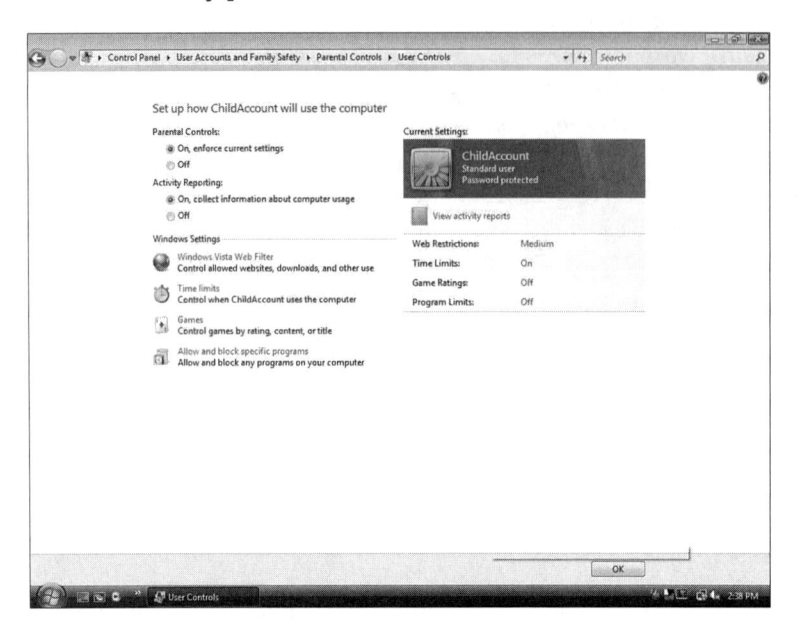

FIGURE 2.11
Control your child's web use and see activity reports to keep you informed.

In addition to this, you can also determine the following:

- **Web Restrictions**—These determine which sites your child can visit and what they are allowed to download.
- **Time Limits**—Determine the time your child can use the computer with the account you provide. This is an excellent tool to help children who are sharing one computer, if you've given them different times to be on it. It's also a perfect way to prevent a child or teenager from getting up in the middle of the night and using the computer without your knowledge.

> **NOTE**
> With Activity Reporting, you can look at the sites your children have been viewing, or trying to view, and can provide access to those sites with one click. You can also save the report to a file you can hold onto for later. The maximum amount of time reported is one week, depending on the space allowed for the log. You can also view activity from the Event Viewer logs under Applications and Service/Microsoft/Windows/Parental Control (although it's much easier to read the report within Parental Controls).

- **Games**—Determine which games your children can play by choosing from a variety of settings.

One of the Microsoft blogs had many questions regarding the way this works. This is a reprint of one of the postings from the Program Manager of Parental Controls, Brian Trenbeath. It is in response to a user's question regarding how game ratings work.

The rating information is included in a file called the GDF (game definition file) that is part of the game. However, just because a game supports our GDF format, it doesn't mean it has been rated by the different ratings boards throughout the world. This is up to the publisher/developer to do and include in the GDF. It is a very common scenario for a game to be rated by the ESRB (U.S. rating system) but not some of the others. This means the game will show up as unrated if such a rating system is selected.

For games that don't include a GDF (anything done before now) there are 2 possibilities: 1) We have a list of over 2,000 tier 1 games that Windows Vista recognizes and pulls down the data much like Media Player grabs artist and album information, or 2) The game shows as unrated. Parental Controls allows you to bulk block games that are unrated as well as selectively allow those you are comfortable with on a per-game basis.

- **Allow and Block Specific Programs**—You can control which programs your children can access even after they are installed on the computer. So, if you have your tax or business software on your computer but want your children to be able to use the same one, not to worry. You can prevent them from even opening your applications.

Manually Configuring the Allow-Block Websites List

We previously mentioned that the recommendation is that you worry only about "allowing" sites because trying to handle the thousands of blocked sites will exhaust you. And being that Parental Controls is a home

> **NOTE**
>
> Question: Does it matter if I am using Firefox or IE 7 to surf the Web? Or can my children download a separate browser and surf in that way?
>
> It doesn't matter which browser they use; the settings are established at the operating system level and connected to their account so that, regardless of the browser they are using, you are still in control.
>
> However, kids are pretty smart these days. They might try to download an executable browser like Browzar (www.browzar.com) but you can prevent this by not allowing installs. They might also try going through portal sites that have a safe web address but allow them to surf through the site. Or they might try a simple tool called Bart PE, which allows them to reboot the machine and run an OS off memory so that they can surf the web and then reboot back into Vista. The point? Parental Control does not remove all online fears.

feature—not a network-oriented feature—admins do not have to worry about figuring out how to block sites for their entire organizations with Parental Controls.

However, many users still want to know how to do this even if it's not going to be used at work. The concept starts simply: Go to your Allow or Block Specific Websites section. You can quickly type an address in the Website Address pane and then click Allow or Block. After that is done, to work manually for faster progress, click the Export button and save the file.

When you attempt to open the file, you will notice it has an odd file type association. It's called a WebAllowBlockList file. Aside from the Parental Control being able to open the file, you won't see another option associated with it. Right-click the file and select Open with (and then select Notepad or some other text editor).

Now, you'll notice that the file isn't all that complicated to work with.

```
<WebAddresses><URL AllowBlock="1">http://microsoft.com/</URL><URL
AllowBlock="2">http://badstuff.com/</URL></WebAddresses>
```

You can see that a code of 1 is for Allow and a code of 2 is for Block. From here, you can add as many sites as you would like. When you are done, you can go back and import the file back into your Parental Controls.

Obviously, there are a billion sites you can add to the blocked sites. You can do this manually or pick up a filter off the Net and then configure the entries to work with your Parental Control entries. That might be more work than you wanted, though. Which is again why we recommend you either allow sites only or use standard filtering techniques (not based on sites specifically).

Keep in mind, if you let your kids know that you can see every site they go to regardless of filtering, then that should solve a good deal of your troubles. Prove it to them one day over dinner by saying "so, how is your research going... I saw you were looking up information on such-and-such today."

> **NOTE**
>
> If you do want to use a blocked list that has already been created, you have to do some configuration maneuvers to get them to work with the simple file for Parental Controls. To find a good list, from your search engine look for URL deny lists or URL block lists. You could even try lists for ISA servers and so forth, or you could just export the list of your current home protection software.
>
> You might also check out Rich Krol's block lists, which work with ISA Server. These are two XML files: blocklist.xml and BNSD.xml (one for porn content and the other for spyware):
>
> http://www.tacteam.net/isaserverorg/download/blocklists.zip

Power Options: Don't Hibernate, Shutdown, Standby—Just Sleep

In XP, when you decide to turn off your computer you get three options: Stand By, Turn Off, and Restart. If you know how—and most likely if you've been working with XP for more than a day, you do—you can hold down Shift and get the Hibernate option. You probably understand that Stand By is the fastest to recover from but still requires power from your battery (if you are using a laptop) or power supply. If you Hibernate, you freeze your system and you can leave all your applications up, but it takes longer to come back to life from hibernation than Stand By. The benefit, however, is that you don't use battery life.

Vista's Sleep Mode gives you the best of both worlds. It is actually the default way to shut down your system, both desktops and laptops. When you select the Start orb (the fancy name for the Start button), a power button (shown in Figure 2.12) appears that enables you to put the system in Sleep Mode. For desktops, this means your system state is written from RAM to a file called `Hiberil.sys` and then your system goes into Stand By. This provides a quick return from sleep when you sit back down at your computer, but it also ensures recovery in cases of emergency (in the event the power goes off). The system is actually still drawing power for things such as the CPU, the RAM, and a few chipset features.

On laptops it works slightly different. Initially when the system is put in Sleep Mode (by closing the lid, leaving the system idle for any extended period of time, or telling it to sleep), your system state is only put in Stand By without writing to the hard disk and Vista uses a low power mode (better than in XP) to keep the state alive. Power is being drawn from the battery as it is in Stand By mode, but not as much power is used. Still, though, given enough time, you will run low on power. Before that happens—thanks to monitoring by the system—your system wakes up, does a hibernate, and then shuts off.

When you turn on a system from Sleep Mode (either a laptop or a desktop), if it hasn't "hibernated," it should return quickly and restore your system and applications instantaneously, just as Stand By does. If it has hibernated, it comes back to life the same way a hibernated system does with XP.

> **NOTE** Desktops, by default, also go into hybrid Sleep Mode if you leave them for an extended period of time. Microsoft says this saves huge amounts of energy, thus assisting the environment with global warming issues.

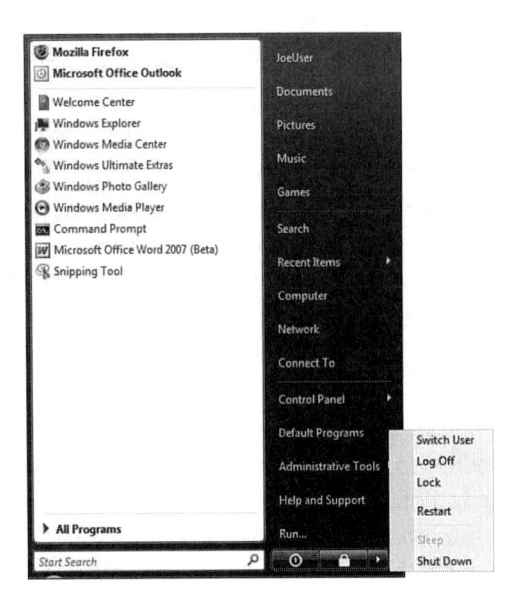

FIGURE 2.12
Sleep Mode offers the best of both worlds between Stand By and Hibernation.

Disable Hibernation

When a system goes into hibernation, Windows places a file on your hard drive that it uses to store data about your current computing session. If you do not use Hibernation Mode, or your computer does not properly support it, you may want to disable hibernation and clear the file off your hard drive to free up some space (the file will use as much space as you have in physical memory, so if you have 1GB of RAM, it's going to use 1GB of your hard drive space).

There are two ways of disabling this: through the command prompt and through the Windows user interface.

To disable Hibernation using Disk Cleanup, do the following:

1. Click Start, All Programs, Accessories, System Tools, Disk Cleanup.
2. In the Disk Cleanup Options window, click Files from All Users on This Computer.
3. If User Account Control prompts you to allow the action, click Continue.
4. If prompted to select a drive, select the drive in which Windows Vista is installed and click OK.
5. Disk Cleanup scans the hard drive and presents you with a list of options.

6. Check Hibernation File Cleaner, and then click OK.
7. When asked Are you sure you want to permanently delete these files?, click the Delete Files button.

Your power options don't give you the option to disable Hibernation, but you can do it from the command prompt. To disable hibernation using the Command Prompt, do the following:

1. Click Start, All Programs, and then right-click Command Prompt.
2. From the context menu, click Run As Administrator.
3. If User Account Control prompts you to allow the action, click Continue.
4. In the command prompt window, type `powercfg -h off`.
5. Close the Command Prompt window.

Shortcut Keys to Sleep

What some experts have found frustrating about the new Sleep Mode is the lack of quick keystroke support to enter it. In XP, you could press the Windows key+U+H and you were hibernated. Not anymore. Now you press the Windows key and the Search box opens. As mentioned in the Shortcuts in Chapter 1, you can use key successions. For example, first press the Windows key, then press the right arrow, and then Enter (to go into Sleep Mode). Or you can press the Windows key, then press the right arrow three times, and then press the up and down arrows (or use letters) to access the various shutdown or switch user options.

Configuring Power Options

When you open Control Panel in Vista under Power Options, you are now presented with power plans from which to select. These power plans are designed to configure hardware and system settings to maximize energy (called Power Saver), maximize performance (called High Performance), or a balance of both (called Balanced). If you are used to earlier power options, these power plans aren't new—they used to be called *schemes*. The difference is that now you can easily select one of three default options, unless you want to get more involved.

You can configure the options in any one of those default plans or configure your own personal plan that suits you. Options you can configure include the brightness of your display, how long your display stays on during periods of inactivity, requesting a password when it comes back from sleep, and a variety of other settings.

The real key to changing your settings is in Advanced Power Management settings. Configuring Advanced Power Management settings (shown in Figure 2.13) is not as easy as it was under XP. Now you have to go through Control Panel and into your System and Maintenance settings to find Power Options (or just switch to Classic view and click Power Options). From here, you can edit your plan settings and look for the option to Change Advanced Power Settings. This enables you to have a greater level of control over your settings.

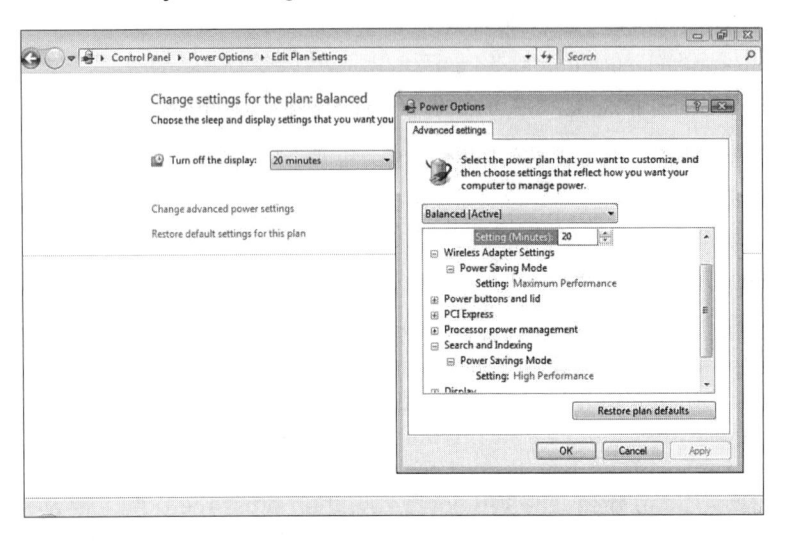

FIGURE 2.13
Advanced Power Management settings are harder to find.

Group Policy Settings

It has been a long-time complaint that Power Settings could not be configured through Group Policy. You could do one of two things. First, you could use an Administrative template (for XP users trying to make these changes, look for EZ GPO Power Management for preconfigured templates you can import). Or you could give users administrative rights and have them log in, change the settings, and log out (which is not even close to being a real-world fix to this problem).

In Windows Vista all your power management options can be configured through Group Policy. Most users are balking online about how easy it is to turn off Sleep Mode, but on a corporate level if you are an administrator who wants to control power usage, Group Policy can save your company a significant amount of money. The settings are located under Computer Configuration\Administrative Templates\System\Power Management. Use your Group Policy Object Editor to make these changes on an individual system or to establish a policy for your entire organization (if you are using Active Directory–enabled Windows Servers).

The numbers change depending on who you are talking to, but some are saying you can save $50 and more per user on energy savings. That may not sound like a lot, but when you add up millions of users who will be running Vista, it can truly have an impact.

Speech Recognition: You Talk, Vista Listens

Section by Joli Ballew
Technology trainer and writer with over two dozen books to her credit
www.joliballew.com

Windows Vista offers speech recognition tools for those who would rather speak than type when communicating with their computers. After it has been set up, Vista's speech recognition offers you yet another input method, one that is ultimately better than other methods if you have difficulty typing or mousing due to an injury or disability or if you simply lack the typing skills necessary to input data quickly. You can find the Speech Recognition options in Control Panel, but better than that, you can find it by typing Speech in the Start Search window. When you open Speech Recognition, you'll see the options show in Figure 2.14.

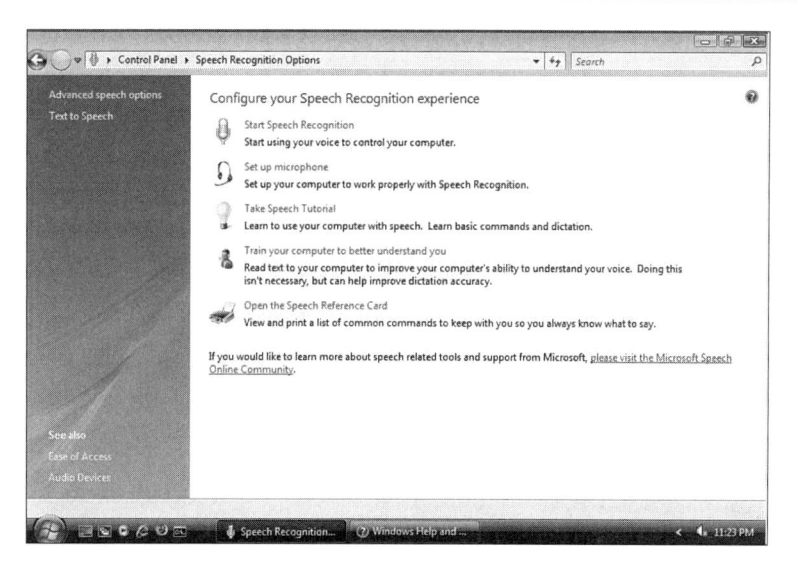

FIGURE 2.14
Configuring your Speech Recognition experience.

The order in which the items are listed isn't necessarily the order you should take when you first start using speech recognition. However, to start, you should click Start Speech Recognition. Vista will walk you through the setup process.

Starting Speech Recognition

When you click Start Speech Recognition, a wizard starts to help you through the process. You'll need to have your microphone or headset installed prior to starting for the easiest setup. As you're working through the wizard, you'll be prompted to select your input method (microphone, headset, other), properly position the microphone, and speak a few words in your natural speaking voice. With that done, you'll see the option to enable document review. By enabling document review, you can improve the computer's capability to understand what you say, by allowing the computer to learn words and phrases you use when you speak.

Start Listening

After setting up Speech Recognition, you'll see the listening window shown in Figure 2.15. It continues to say Sleeping until you tell it to Start Listening. After you say the words *Start Listening*, the speech recognition interface changes to denote what you're doing. That can be talking, clicking the taskbar (as shown in Figure 2.15), or performing some other task. The Listening option shows what you'll see if the Speech Recognition tool is waiting for you to say something. Figure 2.15 shows what you'll see after you say "Start listening."

FIGURE 2.15

Sleeping, Switched to taskbar, Listening.

Opening the Speech Reference Card

Obviously, "Start listening" is a command Speech Recognition knows. But what else does it understand? To find out, open the Speech Reference Card (refer to Figure 2.14). A Help and Support page opens with all kinds of information regarding speech tools. Click Common Speech Recognition Commands (see Figure 2.16).

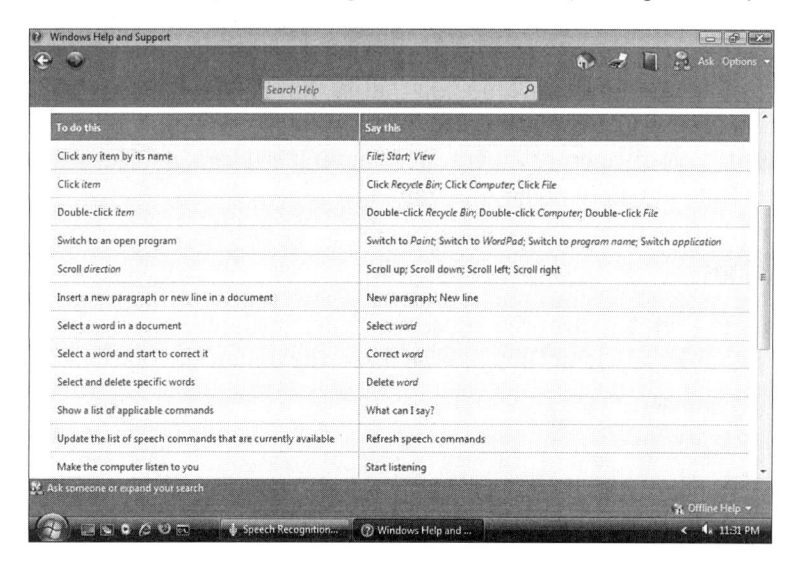

FIGURE 2.16
Frequently used Speech Recognition commands.

Here's how this works: First, with the Speech Recognition tool running, say, "Start listening." Follow that with "Move speech recognition." Now, open Internet Explorer or any other window that can be scrolled up or down. Say, "Scroll down;" then say, "Scroll up." You'll get the idea how these commands work after playing with them a bit.

Taking the Speech Tutorial

Although you'll be able to start communicating with Speech Recognition immediately, it's best to take the Speech Tutorial as soon as you can. You can access the Speech Tutorial by selecting Control Panel, Speech Recognition Options (refer to Figure 2.14). The speech tutorial will help you understand how speech recognition works and how to customize it to suit your needs and preferences.

> **TIP:** It's recommended you print and keep a copy of these commands handy so you know what to say.

In this particular page of the tutorial, you're asked to say, "Show speech options." If your computer understands the command then you are doing fine. If it does not, you'll see "What was that?" in the Speech Recognition window.

Training Your Computer to Better Understand You

Finally, you can continue to train your PC to better understand you by completing the Voice Recognition Training, available by selecting Control Panel, Speech Recognition Options, Train Your Computer to Understand You Better. During this training, you'll be prompted to read the text on the screen and Vista will learn how you speak, what nuances are included in your voice or accent, and more. It's recommended you work through the Speech Tutorial before doing this training.

Advanced Speech Options

You'll probably want to visit the advanced speech options, available from the left pane of Control Panel, Speech Recognition Options. You'll see the options in Figure 2.17.

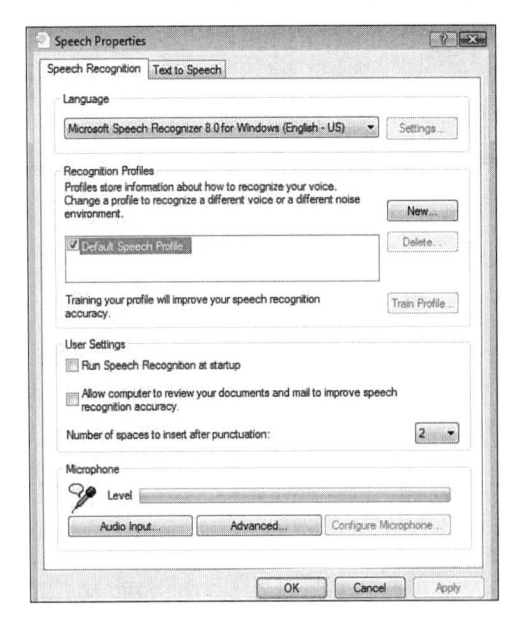

FIGURE 2.17
Configuring advanced Speech Properties.

As you can see here, you can create additional speech profiles, which is useful if more than one person uses the Speech Recognition program on this PC. In that case, you can select to run Speech Recognition at startup and configure microphones and audio input levels. If you're interested in Text to Speech capabilities, notice there's a tab for that, too.

> **TIP** If you are thinking that you are just going to stick with your Office 2003 speech engine, well, it has been removed in Office 2007. Now that the speech engine is integrated directly into the OS, you no longer have it as part of the Office applications. The good news with this is that you configure the speech properties one time for both your OS and your Office.

For some excellent information on the Microsoft development of speech technology over the past decade, check out this link: http://msdn.microsoft.com/msdnmag/issues/06/01/speechinWindowsVista/.

Tablet PC: The Flintstones Meet the Jetsons

Whenever you see a Tablet PC, doesn't it look like one of Fred Flintstone's writing tablets? Same shape, different material. Some might have thought Tablet PCs were a fad that would disappear. But they are actually beginning to find their own niche in the market. In fact, one prominent blogger, Chris Pirillo and his new bride Ponzi used Tablet PC's (TabletKiosk's. UMPC v7110 256/40 (white, of course) to be exact) to read their vows to one another. Chris says "They're sexy, compact, and perfect for this kind of event."

Terri Stratton
Microsoft MVP
Publisher and News Editor of "The Tablet PC" web site at http://thetabletpc.net/

Most Tablet PCs are convertible models and look just like a regular notebook. Slate models, and now ultra-mobile PCs have no keyboard or one that detaches. They have had a niche since they were first introduced, especially in the medical field, but are now becoming more mainstream. Windows Vista has a lot to do with this as there will no longer be a need for a separate image created specifically for Tablet PCs.

So, with the leaning toward a more T-PC world, Vista now sports a few applets to improve our Tablet PC population, including the Pen and Inputs applet and the Pen Tablet applet. And a Tablet PC Settings applet is available as well, shown in Figure 2.18.

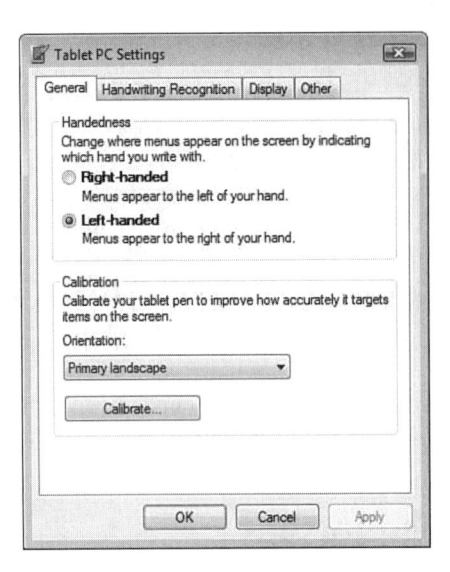

FIGURE 2.18
The Tablet PC Settings applet enables you to configure your tablet.

Let's discuss each tab and see which new features you can work with:

- **General**—You can configure the tablet for a person who is right- or left-handed. You can also calibrate the Tablet PC.
- **Handwriting Recognition**—Has a personalized recognizer, which uses your own data from the handwriting recognition personalized recognizer tool combined with the information it gathers from the automatic learning tool. It also improves its capability to recognize your handwriting.
- **Display**—Allows you the ability to adjust screen orientation.
- **Other**—The Other tab has a link to the Pen and Input Devices applet, discussed earlier.

Tablet PCs have many tools to help you work more smoothly with your pens. Keep in mind what we discussed earlier in the section "Folder Options" about being able to select multiple files and folders more easily with selection boxes next to the items. You can even click one box in the upper-left of Explorer that selects all the items within for you. Turning on this feature with your Tablet PC can really make your life easier when working in Windows Explorer. Terri Stratton says:

> **NOTE**
> These are just the Control Panel applets in Vista, but on Tablet PCs you also have the Tablet Input Panel (TIP). This panel hides by default when you don't need it, but the features of the panel help you (like the Control Panel applets) to configure your system for pen usage and Tablet settings.

Vista Master This is the tool that I've found to be one of the most useful for Tablet PCs. In previous versions of Windows, when in slate mode, it was necessary to bring up the onscreen keyboard or map a button to access the Control key.

Chapter 3

MASTERING ADMINISTRATION

The Desktop Tech: A Modern-Day Hermes

If you research the Greek god Hermes, you come to appreciate the similarities to your desktop administrators. He was the chief messenger between humans (computer users) and gods (network administrators). He was the swiftest—nobody could get there faster than Hermes—and was later called Mercury in Roman mythology. He was also called the "most shrewd and resourceful" of the gods. Yes, all these descriptions aptly fit our desktop admins.

Although the Control Panel tools (discussed in Chapter 2, "Mastering the Control Panel") are a necessity to an admin. It's the Administrative Tools specifically and the System tools that are your greatest allies. We are going to discuss the tools and then some of the important considerations within Vista for desktop admins to keep in mind.

IN THIS CHAPTER

- The Desktop Tech: A Modern-Day Hermes
- User Accounts
- Computer Management
- Sharing System Resources
- The System Window
- More Useful Tools

Depending on the situation, the desktop admin (also called the desktop tech, hardware tech, and so forth) can be the put in the role of network admin for a small network that uses all Vista machines instead of servers (or a mixed Vista-XP-Other) environment. The admin can be responsible for a department of systems that are connected to a larger network, in which case the responsibility would most likely include troubleshooting desktop issues, printer connectivity issues, hardware problems, and so forth.

The website www.infotech.com gives some clear job descriptions for the technology world.

> **Vista Master**
> The desktop technician's role is to provide a single point of contact for end users to receive support and maintenance within the organization's desktop computing environment. This includes installing, diagnosing, repairing, maintaining, and upgrading all PC hardware and equipment to ensure optimal workstation performance. This person will also troubleshoot problem areas (in person, by telephone, or via email) in a timely and accurate fashion and provide end user assistance where required.

Regardless of the role you play, be it a professional administrator or an at-home PC guru, you should be prepared to use the tools at your disposal. It's true that being part of a larger network can tie your hands on some of the resolution options. You might just have to call in the network systems admins. But the focus here is purely on what Vista has to offer. What can you, the Vista Master, do to administer the system? Well, you start by adding other user accounts to the network (small office or home).

User Accounts

You can create new users in a couple of different ways. You can use the Computer Management MMC Console, or you can use the User Accounts applet from the Control Panel. The User Accounts applet found in the Windows Control Panel gives you most of what you need for adding users to a simple system. For a network situation, you should use Administrative Tools that can configure the Active Directory (the identity management database for Windows Servers).

Literally Creating the Accounts

This part is simple. You can open the Control Panel, select the User Accounts and Family Safety option, and then select User Accounts. Or if you are working in Classic mode, you can just go directly to User Accounts from the panel, select Manage Another Account, and then select Create a New Account. You will have to choose a type of account: Standard User or Administrator. Standard User accounts are recommended if you are going to have others using the machine who you do not want to provide permissions to because they might pose a security risk (inexperienced users or children). After the account is created, you can change the password for it, change the picture, and establish Parental Controls (which you learned about in the last chapter).

Terri Stratton
Microsoft MVP

One of first things I do (as I use classic mode and 'display as menu' on Computer, Control Panel, etc.) is to right-click the Start orb, select Properties, then Customize, and add Administrator Tools to both All Programs and the Start Menu.

A more advanced way to create an account is through your Administrative Tools, Computer Management (which opens the Computer Management MMC) console. You can also right-click Computer and select Manage to open this console. Using this method can give you a greater level of control over your accounts in that you can configure Group memberships, password settings, and profile/home directories all from a centralized location.

From here, you can expand Local Users and Groups, right-click the Users folder, and select New User (or select the Users folder and select New User from the Actions pane under More Actions).

Type in a username and full name—the description is optional (see Figure 3.1). Then enter a password and one of the following options to go with the account:

- **User Must Change Logon at Next Logon**—The first time the user logs on to the system, she is asked to provide her own personal password, as opposed to the one you've assigned.
- **User Cannot Change Password**—Forces the user to use the password you created.
- **Password Never Expires**—With this option, the user never has to worry about changing her password.
- **Account Is Disabled**—Makes it so that the account is temporarily inaccessible. This is a good option if a user account is going to go unused for an undetermined amount of time but you think the user might be coming back. You can disable

> **TIP**
> If you want to delete a user account, you can do that from within the same User Accounts applet. When you attempt to delete the account, it asks you if you want to delete everything or if you want to have a copy of the user's Documents, Favorites, Music, Pictures, and Videos folders on your desktop. It will not copy email messages or other settings, but this is a great way to preserve the user's personal items or more easily move them over to another machine.

her account as a preventative security measure but not delete it until you know the account will never be used again. This frequently comes into play in corporate environments as employees come and go (and frequently come back again).

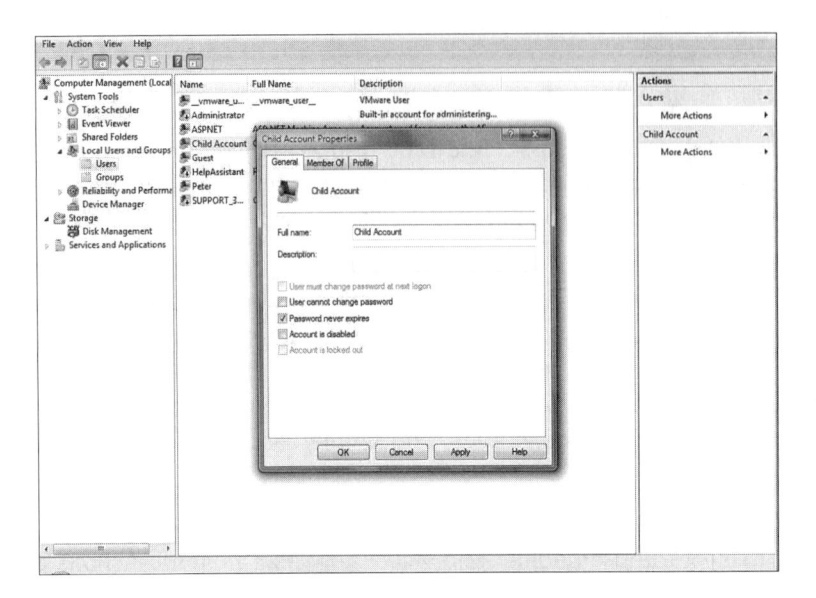

FIGURE 3.1

Creating a new user account through the Computer Management Console.

Using Net User to Create Accounts

When I was in fourth grade, they taught us the programming language BASIC in an after-school program. We used simple command statements like these:

```
10 Print Hello
20 Goto 10
```

There's something oddly fun about seeing "Hello" scroll up and down the screen. Some of us just love the command prompt way of doing things. For many Windows gurus, they can just get things done more quickly via a command prompt, but I also have no doubt that for many vets it also goes back to those early days of BASIC and Commodore 64 programming. So, if you want to create a new user in Vista from the command prompt, you can use the `net user` command.

Start by opening a command prompt in elevated mode, as was discussed in Chapter 1, "General Tips and Tricks of the Masters." Then type **net user /?** to see your options. The /? tells Vista to list all the options you can associate with the `net user` command.

To try one example, type the following:

```
net user tim 0u812! /ADD
```

This creates a user named Tim with the password of 0u812!. To confirm this, open your User Accounts applet and see that this new account exists.

For more information on how to use the `net user` command see the Microsoft Knowledge Base article: http://support.microsoft.com/kb/251394. And there are other uses for the "net" command, you can find here: http://www.chicagotech.net/netcommand.htm

Modifying Your User Accounts

Without going into a discussion of Active Directory and Vista, you have to know that modifying user accounts in this discussion involves the Vista-only angle. Obviously, Active Directory modification allows for more options, but the focus here is Vista.

From within the User Accounts applet, in addition to changing a user's password or picture, a sidebar is available from which you can choose one of the following:

- **Create a Password Reset Disk**—You'll need a floppy drive or a USB drive to start the process. The concept is simple: You are asked for your password and then that is stored on your disk as a `.psw` file. In the event you forget your password, you can log on with your disk. Keep in mind that anyone can use the disk to log on so this is something you don't want to leave around for others to get a hold of. This password is only for your local system logon. If you log on through a domain controller into an Active Directory domain at work and you forget your password, you will need your network admin to give you a new one.

- **Manage Your Network Passwords**—You can store passwords for networks or websites you visit through this option so Windows will log you on automatically when you visit those servers or sites. Just type in the computer name on the network or the URL and then enter your username and password. (Again, this is not for an AD domain, but it can be very helpful if you have a small peer-to-peer network with a member server and so forth.) The Vista Security Team (http://blogs.msdn.com/windowsvistasecurity/) also said:

> **CAUTION** It's very important to remember that a person might forget his password and that you as an admin can then reset it. However, if you do this, the user actually loses access to encrypted files, email messages that are encrypted, and stored passwords for servers or websites. This is another reason it's a good idea for users to use their password reset disks. When they use the password reset disks, they are changing their passwords and this doesn't harm their access to encrypted resources.

Vista Master: Stored User Names and Passwords in Windows Vista includes a Backup and Restore Wizard, which allows users to back up user names and passwords they have requested Windows to remember for them. This new functionality allows users to restore the user names and passwords on any Windows Vista system. Restoring user names and passwords from a backup file will replace any existing saved user names and passwords the user has on the system.

- **Manage Your File Encryption Certificates**—We will discuss encryption in Chapter 5, "Disk Configuration and Volume Tricks," but this option helps you manage smart card certificates or even personally created certificates for encryption. You can back them up in the event the certificate is lost as well.

- **Configure Advanced User Profile Properties**—Profiles are basically your likes and dislikes for the system to store and remember when you log on. So when you sit down and log on, you see the mountain background but when another person logs on, he sees something else. If you don't use a network and just work off your own system, you have all your profile information stored on the local system. But if you move around from machine to machine, rather than reconfiguring a local profile on each system, you can configure a roaming profile. This means the profile is stored on an accessible server and when you log on, your settings are brought down to your system from that server. So, you can move around all you want and you still see the mountain background. But, if you log on and the profile you have isn't available (say, the server is down for maintenance), you will still be able to log on with a locally cached profile.

- **Change My Environment Variables**—The most technical option of all in User Accounts is this one (shown in Figure 3.2). Environment variables tell your computer where to find certain types of information. You'll notice that there are user variables (for settings specific to users and their profiles) and system variables (which indicate locations of critical system resources). These variables can be edited or added to.

    One reason for doing this can come into play when creating a boot CD (as we

> **NOTE:** There have been some changes in the way profiles work under Vista. Although roaming profiles solve one problem (that of users moving from one workstation to another), they cause others. For example, those profiles can become quite large and cause excessive logon times. Folder Redirection solves some of these problems because the profile data is separated from the user data. Another change is the location of the profiles. Previously stored under Documents and Settings, they are now stored under Users. They aren't nested so deeply as they were before and are structured more intuitively. For more information on the changes, do a search for the "Managing Roaming User Data Deployment Guide" from Microsoft. Type this into Google and you will be directed to a document for download.

discuss in Chapter 8, "System Recovery and Diagnostic Tricks"). Boot CD's generally use a variety of command line tools that are not located in the standard set of environment variable folders, so it's beneficial to edit the environment variables for the system so that when you want a tool, you do not need to navigate to the specific folder that holds that tool. You can type it from any folder location and the system knows where to look to find it.

These options have changed somewhat from the past and so it's good to note the changes listed in Table 3.1, which was posted on Jason Conger's blog at http://blogs.msterminalservices.org/conger/2006/09/12/profile-and-environment-variable-changes-in-vistalonghorn/. However, as Jason notes on his blog, it's important to bear in mind that these changes can cause problems with login scripts. Particularly scripts that have hard-coded paths.

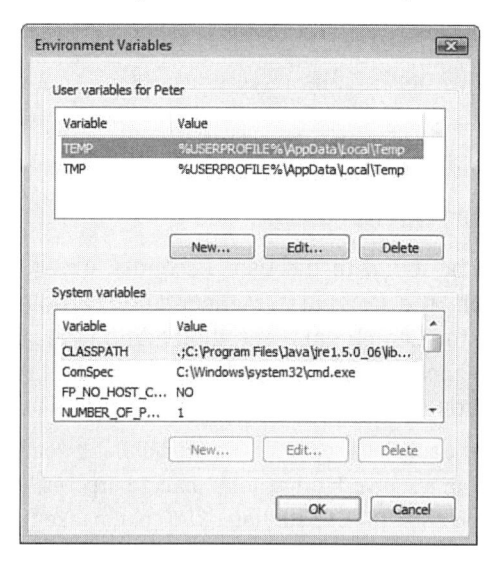

FIGURE 3.2
Environment variable changes.

To quickly access specific locations that have parameters set in the environment variables, you can go to the Start orb and type the variable into the search or Run command dialog box. For example, although Vista allows you to go directly to the user folder when you select the Start orb and see the username on the upper-right side, you could simply type %userprofile% in the Search pane and the folder structure for the user logged in displays. The same goes for any of the other variables.

To configure environment variables from a command prompt, you can use the **setx** command. Type **setx /?** to see a full list of parameters for its use.

Table 3.1—Changes in Environment Variables from Windows XP to Vista

Before Vista	In Vista
ALLUSERSPROFILE=C:\Documents and Settings\All Users	ALLUSERSPROFILE=C:\ProgramData
APPDATA=C:\Documents and Settings\<username>\Application Data	APPDATA=C:\Users\<username>\AppData\Roaming
HOMEPATH=\Documents and Settings\<username>	HOMEPATH=\Users\<username>
TEMP=C:\DOCUME~1\<username>\LOCALS~1\Temp	TEMP=C:\Users\<username>\AppData\Local\Temp
TMP=C:\DOCUME~1\<username>\LOCALS~1\Temp	TMP=C:\Users\<username>\AppData\Local\Temp
USERPROFILE=C:\Documents and Settings\<username>	USERPROFILE=C:\Users\<username>

Additional Options from the Computer Management Console

Although the majority of your settings can be found in the User Accounts applet, you can configure more advanced settings from the Computer Management console (or create your own console by typing `mmc` from the Search pane and then adding the snap-in Local Users and Groups). You can double-click any user and add the user to different groups or go to the Profile tab. From here, you can configure the following for a user:

- **Profile Path**—Your local computer already has a local path for the profile. But if you want the profile to be stored elsewhere on a network drive, for roaming purposes, you can configure the Universal Naming Convention (UNC) path here. (UNC paths take the following form: \\servername\sharename\folder.)

- **Logon Script**—Enables you to type the location of the logon script. These scripts can be helpful in performing all sorts of tasks, such as mapping your network drives. You might not be a scripting guru and that's okay—you don't have to be. You can find plenty of configurable free scripts on the Internet. For example, check out Don Jones' site http://www.scriptinganswers.com to learn more about logon scripts and other forms of scripting as well.

- **Home Folder Local Path**—Even though users have a Documents folder, you might want to configure the location for another home folder for a user. This can be local or remote.

Chapter 3 Mastering Administration

- **Home Folder Connect**—If the home folder is remote, you can configure a drive letter for the connection so the user sees the folder as a personal drive letter in which she can store documents. That folder, if located on a server that is backed up daily, lets your users feel safe about their data.

Vista Master: We found this great little tip about accessing a hidden user panel from Serdar Yegulalp on the SearchWinComputing.com site (you can read more from Serdar at www.thegline.com). He mentioned typing the following command from either an elevated command prompt or the Search pane:

```
control userpasswords2
```

This opens a User Account's dialog box from which you can manage group memberships and passwords. You can even click a button on the Advanced tab under Advanced User Management that opens another MMC console but one that includes only Local Users and Groups.

Computer Management

Administrative Tools comes with a list of mini-apps to work with, but the Computer Management option provides a grouping of tools in one console. It may not be the super console you would like to have (which you can create if you like), but it is a decent toolset collection.

The Computer Management tool, shown in Figure 3.3, allows you to manage local or remote systems through one console. You can monitor system events, work with hard disks, manage performance, schedule tasks, and so on.

Under System Tools, the following are available:

- **Task Scheduler**—Create and manage common tasks that your computer will carry out either automatically, or at the times you specify.
- **Event Viewer**—Used to view logs about events associated with file and directory replication, DNS, security, and more.
- **Shared Folder**—Categories include: Shares—Used to create shares and list all system shares. Sessions—Any open session from the local computer or a remote computer is listed. Open Files—Files being used by users or other computers are listed.

> **TIP:** To create a super MMC console go to the Start orb and type **mmc** from the Search pane. Then select File, Add/Remove Snap-In and select all the Snap-Ins you like. When you're done, select File, Save As and select the location for your .msc file.

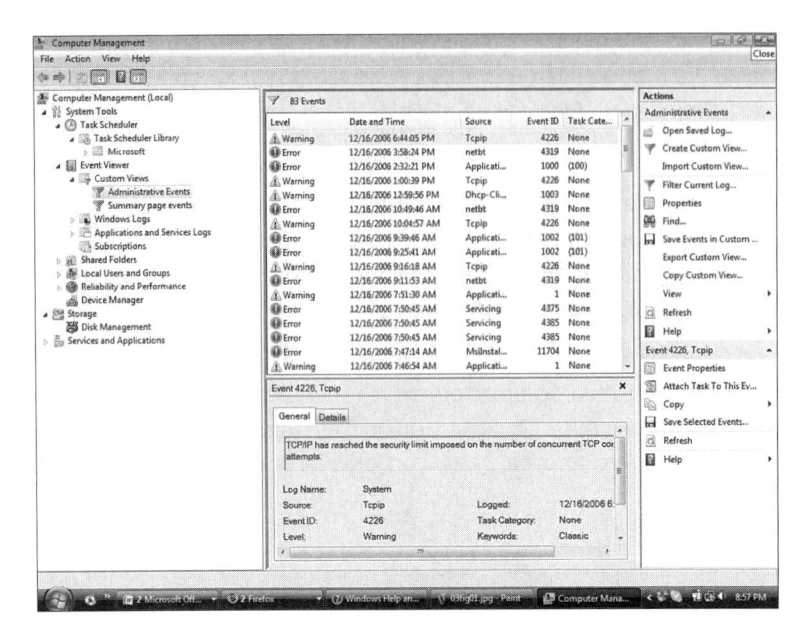

FIGURE 3.3
The Computer Management console includes a bevy of tools.

- **Local Users and Groups**—Used to make user and group accounts on the local computer.
- **Reliability and Performance**—Provides preconfigured diagnostics of your systems reliability and performance. You can also define your own counters to watch in real time or over a predefined period.
- **Device Manager**—Used to view all system resources.

Under Storage you'll find this option:

- **Disk Management**—Used to create, format, or delete simple, spanned, mirrored, striped, or RAID-5 volumes. Also provides information about the disk regarding the status and health.

Under Service and Applications are the following:

- **Services**—Lists all services (started or not) and the Startup Type (Automatic, Manual, or Disabled).
- **WMI Control**—Windows Management Instrumentation control allows monitoring and controlling system resources.

We've already discussed Local Users and Groups. Reliability and performance (in Chapter 8, "System Recovery and Diagnostic Tricks"), as well as disk management (in Chapter 5), are discussed later, while Device Manager was discussed in Chapter 2. This section discusses Task Scheduler, Event Viewer, and Services.

Task Scheduler

Vista really gives the Task Scheduler a much-needed overhaul. Now you can configure the Scheduler to perform tasks on a timed basis and to respond to situations that occur on a variety of levels. The response system can even restart a service that has failed or send an email to the admin when a certain event has occurred.

The Task Scheduler is integrated with Event Viewer now so that it can react to situations based on trackable events that occur. There is also a way to view the task history. You can see which tasks are running, have run, or are scheduled to run.

In addition, an entire Task Scheduler Library has preconfigured tasks with which you can work (see Figure 3.4).

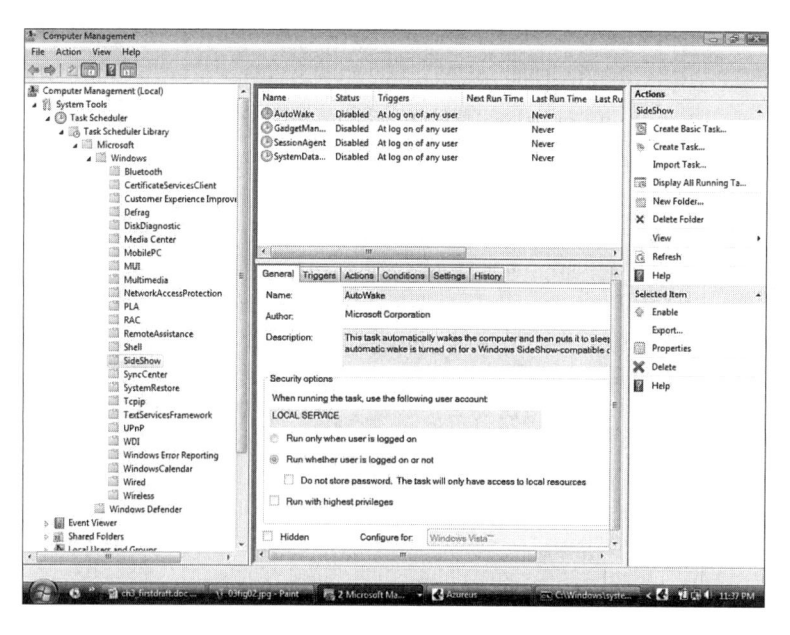

FIGURE 3.4
The Task Scheduler has an entire library of options, or you can create your own using the basic options or the more advanced tabular dialog box.

Triggers and Actions

A *trigger* is what causes the task to run, and an *action* is what you have configured to occur in the event the trigger goes off. Some triggers are schedules you put into effect. For example, if you specify that every day at 1:00 p.m. a certain action should occur, the trigger is the scheduled time. But a trigger can also be when a user logs on, when the system starts up, when a specific event occurs, and so forth. An action is whatever task the system executes in response to the trigger. Actions can include running a program, sending an email, or even displaying a preconfigured message. There is a list of possible actions to take, including running scripts with the `cscript.exe` application, copying a file with Robocopy, starting and stopping services, shutting down the system, and a host of others.

> ### Copying Files with Robocopy
>
> Some (well, Tim Sneath in particular, but we agree with him) have called Robocopy (Robust Copy Utility) the coolest command-line tool in Vista. Many of us have used Robocopy for years because it was the only way we could copy large file structures. In the past we always had to get it from the Windows Resource Kit, but it's now in Vista for everyone to use.
>
> Here are a couple of cool points about Robocopy: It has a whole bunch of switches (the original documentation was more than 30 pages long). Type in **robocopy /?** and watch the magic. There are really too many switches to get into here, so you'll have to research it a bit to see what it can do. I'm sure you'll find that it's quite flexible. For example, if a network link goes down during the copy, it doesn't shut down, it just waits. You can configure the wait time parameters. It's great for mirroring large file shares because it only copies files that have changed and you can throttle the traffic so you don't use up your entire connection when you are going over a slow link.
>
> One thing to keep in mind, if you are backing up user folders, use the /XJ switch to exclude copying junctions.

Scheduling a Task

You can do this in several ways. First, from the console, you can open the Actions pane and select Create Basic Task. This walks you through the following options:

- **Create a Basic Task**—Start with a name and description.

- **Trigger**—You can work from a schedule (daily, weekly, monthly, one time) where you set time parameters for the triggered event. You can also select When the Computer

Starts, When I Log On, or When a Specific Event Is Logged. In the case of the latter, you can select the Log, the Source, and even the Event ID that triggers the next step.

- **Action**—You can start a program (and choose which program that is), send an email (with the information for the email), or display a message (and write the message you want displayed).

> **TIP**
> The time settings relate to the time zone that the system is currently in. However, if you check the Universal box, the time zone connects to Coordinated Universal Time (UTC); this is a good way to have multiple computers across multiple time zones perform a task on the same time schedule.

- **Finish**—You can review your new task and tell it to open the properties of the task. When this happens, you can see a much more complicated tabbed view of a task. These options help you go beyond the basic task. You can create and manage your tasks in this way, or you can create a task from the more complicated tabs to start with.

To create a task that goes beyond what you can do when creating a Basic Task, select the Create Task option from the Action pane. This offers a dialog box with five tabs to configure your tasks. The tabs include the following:

- **General**—Enables you to configure the name and description of the task, under which user account it should run, and whether it should run only when that user is logged on or not.
- **Triggers**—Here you can schedule an extensive list of triggers, starting with the time triggers you can set up. If you change the Begin the Task options, the settings will. The most complex of the triggers involves Events.
- **Actions**—The actions you can perform are no different here from what they were from the basic settings. You can configure a program to run, send an email, or display a message: Or you can do all three if you like. That is the benefit to using the advanced tabbed task creator. You can configure different actions to occur from here.
- **Conditions**—This tab enables you to specify conditions to your task. For example, you may want certain tasks to run only if the system is idle. Other conditions might depend on whether the computer is running on AC power or battery power, or if it is or isn't connected to a specific network.
- **Settings**—Allows you to determine whether you can start the task manually, what to do if your task couldn't run on schedule, what to do in the event a task is running too long, and so on.

Importing and Exporting Tasks

All of a task's properties (triggers, actions, conditions, settings) are held in XML files. You can export these XML files and import them on other systems.

Importing is quite simple; you can see the import option on the Action pane while working with the task manager. To see the export option, you must open the Task Scheduler Library folder. You can export the tasks you have created or export the preconfigured tasks within the library (although this would make sense only if you have configured them differently in some way). To export a task you select the task, right-click and choose to export. Choose the location for the .xml file that will be created. To import you can right-click any of the task folders and choose import task and then select the .xml file you want to import.

The AT Scheduler, Command Prompt Options, and Scripting

The AT command is the tool that was historically used to schedule tasks through the command-line in previous versions of Windows. Call it nostalgia, but for some reason Microsoft hasn't removed the at.exe command from Vista even though it has replaced it with the schtasks.exe command. What does this mean? Well, if you have worked with the AT command for many years and are comfortable using it, you can still use it in Task Scheduler. All tasks created with the at.exe command must run on the same account, which you can configure through the AT Service Account Configuration option from the Actions pane.

But, if you want to work with the latest tool, the schtasks.exe command enables you to do many of the same operations on local or remote systems. You can create, delete, query, change, run, and end scheduled tasks. Type one of the following commands for help on using schtasks.exe:

```
schtasks /Create /?
schtasks /Run /?
schtasks /End /?
schtasks /Delete /?
schtasks /Change /?
```

Scripting the Task Scheduler has been made more fun now that you can go beyond at.exe and even schtasks.exe. With Vista, you can access the Task Scheduler API through scripts. Microsoft provides a nice article on this at http://www.microsoft.com/technet/scriptcenter/topics/vista/tasks1.mspx.

This article walks you through the beginning stages of scripting the task scheduler, and whoever wrote it is more than intelligent, but knows how to take dry-programming-speak and turn it into a fun article.

Chapter 3 **Mastering Administration** **115**

Having Some Fun with the Task Scheduler

Fun? Are Vista Masters allowed to have fun? Well, in addition to saving the universe, we need to enjoy our work. Here are some fun things to try with your Task Scheduler:

- Need your religious or comedic fix in the morning? You can also set the task scheduler to start up an installed Daily Scripture program, or a set Bible reader, or if comedy is more your needed wake-me-up go to the Calvin and Hobbes site (or whatever comics make you happy).

- Need an expensive alarm clock? Set Task Scheduler to start up one of your music applications to open and play your favorite songs (or if you are a heavy sleeper, you can have a Godzilla MP3 set to go off, too). Want to live the movie *Groundhog Day*? Set the Sonny and Cher song "I've Got You Babe" to go off the same time every day?

- Make coffee and pick up your dry cleaning? Sorry, perhaps in the next version of Windows.

Adam Pash
In, "Hack Attack: Using Windows Schedule Tasks," at Lifehacker.com

Okay, so it's the middle of the night and you've defragged your hard drive and scanned for viruses. Before you get up and start working, though, you'd like that oh-so-fresh feeling that only a newly-rebooted Windows PC can offer. Try this bit of code for your Run line: `C:\WINDOWS\\system32\\shutdown.exe -r -t 01`

Note that because this command closes all applications and then reboots the system you might want to have a task run that restarts certain applications—perhaps your email client or an Office application you use every day.

Adam Pash
"Hack Attack: Firefox extension packs," at Lifehacker.com

No matter who you are, if you spend a lot of time on the Internet, chances are you have a set of pages that you visit to start the morning just like your morning paper. You're computer has been freshly restarted and is just sitting there, waiting for you to wake up—why not let it fetch your favorite pages so that your morning reading is ready and waiting for you. Set up a task to open Firefox just as you did above, then add all of the websites you'd like to visit following your run line separated by a space. The resulting line should look something like this: `C:\Program Files\\Mozilla Firefox\\firefox.exe" lifehacker.com del.icio.us/username nytimes.com wikipedia.org gmail.com`

The Vista Event Viewer

We've been using Event Viewer for years, but most people check it only when there is a major problem. They see if they can quickly discover which service stopped or what caused the glitch; then they forget about it again until the next big problem. This is not truly taking advantage of the powerful technology at our fingertips. Although upon first look, Vista's Event Viewer can appear overwhelming, let's see if we can tame it a bit.

> **NOTE**
> For more tips on using the Task Scheduler or other tips, check out www.lifehacker.com. This site has one tip for running a vbs script that allows you to keep track of your weight each day in an Excel spreadsheet. The script is free to download along with a bunch of other free scripts you can use to clean up your hard drive and so forth. You can spend hours on this site looking at all the cool tools and articles.

The Event Viewer (shown in Figure 3.5) enables you to see more than the standard Windows logs (Application, System, and Security logs). Now there are Applications and Services logs, which include diagnostic logs, logs for specific applications within Vista, like your IE logs. In the past, you had to hunt to find logs for certain applications, but Microsoft has tried to bring them all together here.

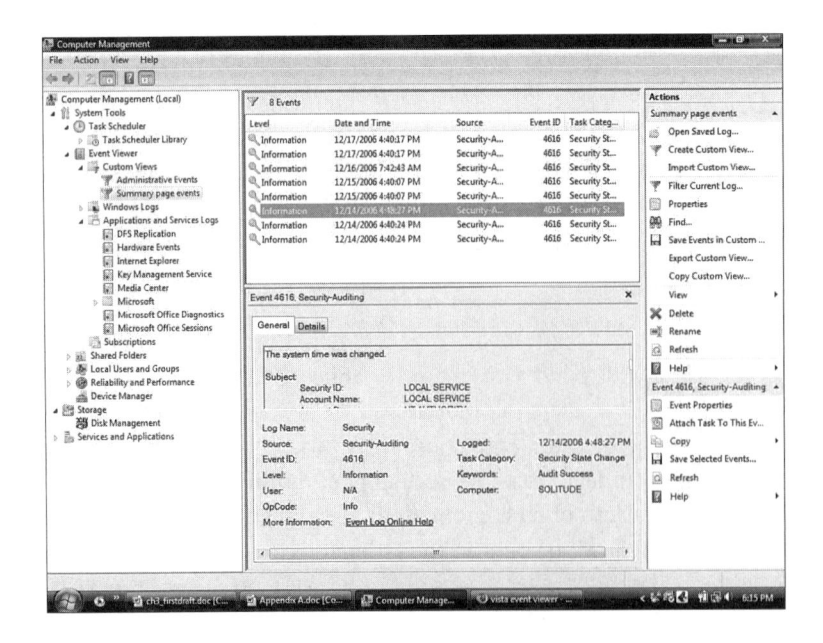

FIGURE 3.5
The Vista Event Viewer is more robust, offering an Enterprise monitoring functionality.

Custom Views: More Than Filters

So many events come into the Event Viewer that it's almost impossible to track down the problem you are investigating without some form of filter. Views allow you to create filters that not only filter the events of one log, but also enable you to select multiple logs to view. To create a custom view, you select a log, open the Action pane, and select Create a Custom View, shown in Figure 3.6.

> **TIP**
> We just discussed the Task Scheduler and how great it is with assigning events as triggers that require actions. Well, instead of memorizing the events you want so you can put them in Task Scheduler, you can find the event you want in the Event Viewer, right-click it, and select Attach Task to This Event (or you can find this option in the Action panel). This enables you to create a basic task that you can configure further from the Task Scheduler.

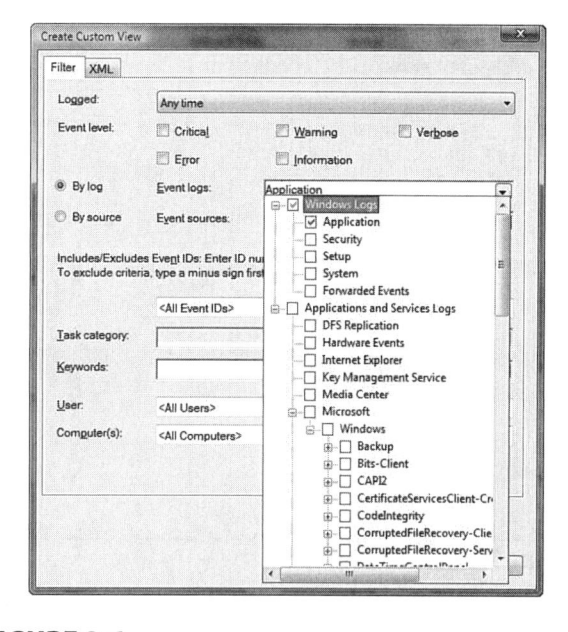

FIGURE 3.6
Creating a custom view and choosing the logs included.

From the Custom View dialog box, you can configure the following options:

- **Logged**—Enables you to provide a time frame for the events.
- **Event Level**—Critical, Warning, Error, Information, and Verbose.
- **By Log**—Select the Event log or logs from a checkbox hierarchy.
- **By Source**—Select from a source hierarchy, including applications and services.

- **Event IDs**—If you know the specific ID you are looking for, you can put it here or enter several IDs separated by commas.
- **Task Category and Keywords**—Select from the checkboxes that drop down. Filtering by keywords is a new feature we can all appreciate.
- **Users and Computers**—You can have the view look for specific users and can even filter through multiple computers.

XML Event Viewer Details

XML is everywhere in Vista. Event Viewer is no exception. If you look at the properties of an event, you will be met with a scary-looking XML structure (shown in Figure 3.7). You can switch over to the Friendly View if that makes you feel better.

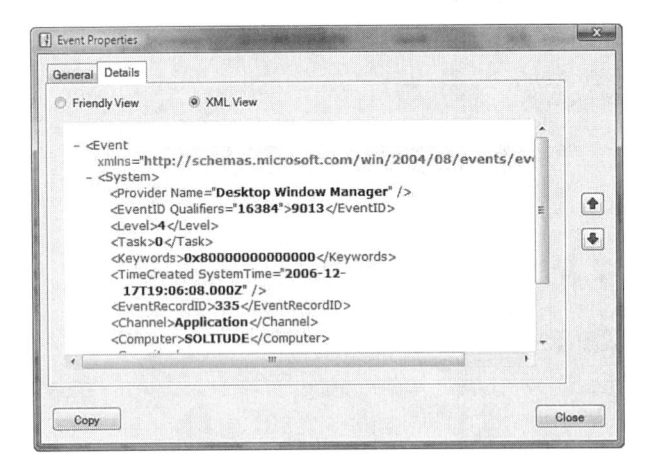

FIGURE 3.7
XML is everywhere in Vista, including Event Viewer details.

Why is the information stored as XML? It makes it easier for applications to take advantage of it for centralization and consolidation of the data. Other applications such as Microsoft Operations Manager (MOM) and Systems Management Server (SMS) (and others that are in the works) can take advantage of the XML open-sourced format of the data.

You can right-click any event and choose "Event Properties" to obtain more information. From the Properties, the General details provide the information you most need to troubleshoot that particular event, if the event indicates a problem with your system. You'll notice that you still have the ability to request help from Microsoft through the Event

Log Online Help option, which usually says something like, "Sorry, even though we created the program we have no how idea to help you…we're really, really sorry." Okay, so it doesn't say that, but it is frustrating much of the time.

> **TIP** Do you really want to know what the Event IDs are telling you in Event Viewer? Check out EventID.net. This is an online community of tips and tricks from other admins who are all seeking event enlightenment. At the time of this writing, close to 9,000 events existed in the Event ID database with about 500 event sources and about 15,000 comments provided by almost 3,000 contributors. It's worth checking out if you have difficulty understanding an event.

Subscriptions

You can collect logs from remote systems and save them onto your local system through subscriptions. For this to work, you have to configure the collector (the system that collects the events) and the remote source systems.

To configure the source systems, type the following command from an elevated command prompt

```
winrm quickconfig
```

To configure the collector computer, type the following command from an elevated command prompt

```
wecutil qc
```

On the source computers you will need to add the computer account of the collector to the local Administrators group on each computer.

After the systems are configured to forward and collect events, you can create new subscriptions through the Event Viewer. There are more details you might need to consider depending on your environment, such as opening ports for your firewall to allow the event management exception and so forth. Going through the Help information from the Event Viewer offers a great deal of information on how-to advice and troubleshooting problems.

Services and the SC.exe Command

Services are the underlying core OS features that handle any number of things on your system, from web services, to print services, and so forth. You've no doubt seen the services console before in XP or Windows 2000 because it has been around a long time.

The services structure hasn't changed much in Vista. You might notice a few more services in Vista. You now have the option to turn off some services to reserve system resources. But from within Service, you can do the following:

- Stop, start, pause, resume, or disable a service. You can also see the description of what each service does and which other services rely on it to work.
- Configure recovery actions in the event of a service failure (like restarting the service).
- Configure a service to run under the security context of a user account that is different from the logged-on user or the computer account.
- Configure hardware profiles that use different services enabled or disabled.
- Export your services information to a .txt or .csv file.
- Monitor the status of each service.

> **NOTE:** If you enable or disable a service and your computer cannot start up, try starting the system in Safe Mode. Safe Mode is preconfigured with core services to start regardless of whatever settings you might have configured. Once in Safe Mode, you can make the changes to put the service back on that you accidentally shut off.

You can use the sc.exe command to communicate and configure the Service Control Manager and services. You can also use the net start or net stop command to stop and start services, but SC is much more powerful.

An example of the **sc.exe** command is the following:

    sc config <service name> start=<mode>

You can start with the following modes:

- auto—A service automatically started at boot, regardless of a user logging on or not
- boot—A device driver loaded by the boot loader
- demand—The default, a service that is manually started
- disabled—A service that is prevented from starting
- system—Started during kernel initialization

For more information on SC, type **sc.exe /?** from a command prompt.

Sharing System Resources

We discuss networking in Chapter 7, "Master Vista Networking," and NTFS permissions in Chapter 5, "Disk Configuration and Volume Tricks," but here we want to talk about the simple concept of sharing. You have files, other networked users want access to those files, and sharing is the key. How is it done, how can you monitor what is being shared, and who is accessing it on your system?

Sharing Files Through the Public Folder

The Public Folder (in XP called the Shared Documents folders) is the convenient and easy way to share files. Putting things in the public folder allows anyone who can access your computer to see and use the files as well as anyone who has been granted access to the files remotely via the network. There is only one set of public folders per computer, so all users on the computer add things to the same location.

To see the public folder, select the Start orb and then click Documents. You'll see a folder called Public in the Favorite Links pane. When you open it, you can see that other folders have already been created to make this easier: Public Documents, Public Music, Public Pictures, and so forth. All you have to do is copy or move the files over that you want to share to these locations.

> **NOTE** It's good to note, for novice sharers out there, that you cannot share individual files, only folders and all the files those folders contain. Sharing a folder means allowing access to that folder by users across the network. You can configure the level of access users can have through that network share, too. But keep in mind that you don't want to share everything you have, especially if you are working off a wireless network with no security settings (as many people are these days) because you are just inviting strangers into your computer.
>
> Be careful about your sharing. Oh…and lock down your wireless network, too. We will talk more about this in Chapter 7, "Master Vista Networking."

Anyone with a username and password on your computer can sit down and access these folders, but you can determine how people across a network connection can (or cannot) access them.

If you want to make sure a person has a username and password on your system to access those folders, open the Network and Sharing Center (click Start, Network and click the Network and Sharing Center button on the Command bar). Look for the arrow next to Password-protected Sharing and then turn it on or off. Make sure, too, that the Public folder sharing is on. You can alter the permissions people have in accessing the Public folder by selecting the Public Folder Sharing option and then selecting one of the following options:

- Turn On Sharing so Anyone with Network Access Can Open Files
- Turn On Sharing so Anyone with Network Access Can Open, Change, and Create Files
- Turn Off Sharing (people logged on to this computer can still access this folder)

One thing to take note of is that this method of sharing doesn't allow you to structure permissions on a per-user basis. If individuals can access the Public folder, then they all have the same set of permissions that you apply. If you want to give different users different permissions, or if you don't want two copies of files on your system one in your real folder and one in the Public folder), you might want to share out a different folder altogether on your system.

Sharing Any Folder

You can right-click a folder and select Share. By default, this turns off the File Sharing Wizard. You can choose to share with users who are configured on the system with user accounts, or you can just allow everyone to access the folder through the share. This means users on other systems will be able to access the share even if they don't have an account on your machine.

If you don't like the wizard and prefer to share folders manually, you can turn off the wizard. Open the Control Panel and select Folder Options. Select the View tab and scroll down to the Use Sharing Wizard (Recommended) checkbox and deselect the box. Now, when you right-click a folder and select Share, you will be taken to the Sharing tab under the folder's properties. You will also see that the Share option is grayed out for the basic sharing. Instead you have to use the Advanced Sharing options (see Figure 3.8).

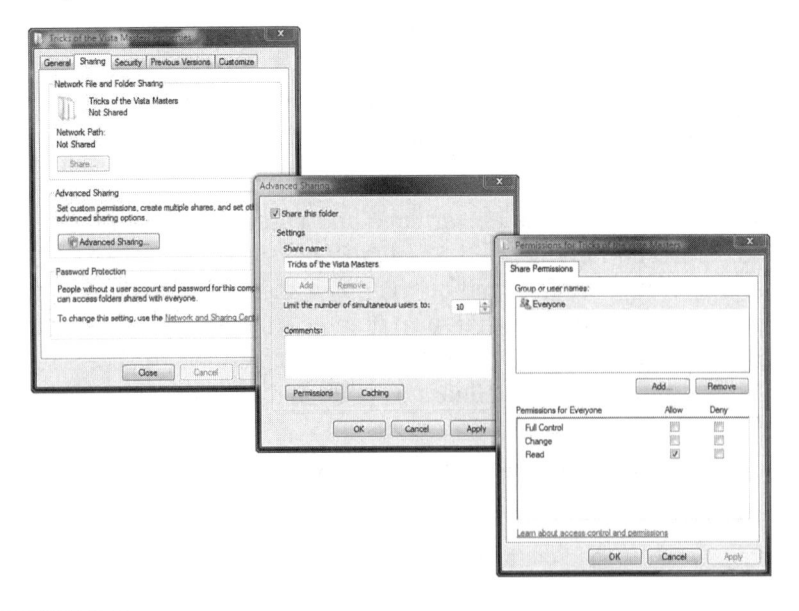

FIGURE 3.8
Configuring the Advanced Share Permission settings.

You might notice that you can also determine the number of users who can access the shared folder at any given time. The default setting is 10. You can control this further. If you know for a certainty that you only have 1 other person, for example, that will access the share, you can lower this to 1, and this will prevent others from accessing (or trying to access the share).

> **TIP** After you configure a shared folder, you can go back and click the Add button to share it again! Why would you want to do that? Well, you can configure a share with different names AND different permission sets.

The permissions you see aren't all that complicated to understand. You have Full Control (Allow or Deny), Change (Allow or Deny), and Read (Allow or Deny).

If we broke these down into smaller explanations, you would have the following:

- **Read**—Allows you to read a file (meaning read, listen to, view, watch, and so on with that file) and execute the file (if it is a program)
- **Change**—Allows you to read and execute the file, but it also allows you to write to the file (that is, open a Word document and make changes) or delete the file
- **Full Control**—Allows you to read, write, execute, and delete the file; plus you can take ownership of the file if you want and change the permissions of the file

Allow/Deny is an interesting dilemma. If you, as a user or a group you belong in, is assigned Deny in any way, shape, or form, on the object (printer, folder, drive share, and so forth), the Deny permissions are stronger than any of your Allow permissions.

To illustrate, let's look at an example of a shared folder. By default, everyone (which includes you) is given Full Control to access that folder through the share. However, you are part of a specific group that has been denied the ability to Read the folder. So this means that through the share, you won't even be able to open the folder to look inside. However, you could change these permissions for the group you're in because you have that ability through the Full Control set of permissions. After changing the permissions, you could then enter the folder.

If you think this is complicated, wait until we throw NTFS permissions into the mix.

Other ways you can share a folder are covered in the following sections.

Shared Folders in Computer Management

From within Computer Management, you have the Shared Folders options. You can right-click the Shares folder and select New Share. Regardless of your folder options, this turns off the Create a Shared Folder Wizard.

From within Computer Management, you can do a couple of great things with Sharing. If you select the Shares folder, you can see all the folders and drive letters (even hidden ones) that are shared out on the system (see Figure 3.9). From here, you can right-click any share and choose not to continue sharing that folder. You can also go into the Properties of the share and alter the configuration, including the Share and NTFS permission settings.

FIGURE 3.9
We are back in Computer Management, this time looking at the Shared Folders options.

If you select Sessions, you can see the users connected to your shares, which computers they are on, how long they have been connected, and so on. From here, you can right-click any user connected in a session and close the session.

You can also select the Open Files folder to see which files are being viewed, and you can right-click any file and close it. You should notify a user before you do this because otherwise the work they are performing on the file might be lost.

Creating a Hidden Folder Share Is $

Why would you want to hide a share? Dorin Dehelean explains the reason to http://www.windowsitpro.com by saying:

> To improve security on a Windows-based network, append a dollar sign ($) to your share names to hide shares from users. When you use this step in conjunction with tight NTFS and share permissions, you reduce incidental attempts by unauthorized users to click folders they shouldn't open. If users can't see the folders, they won't try to see what the folders contain. For authorized users, you can use a logon script to map the hidden share to a drive letter. Thus, only users who are authorized to access the folders will know the folders exist. Only technically savvy unauthorized users who know the exact path to the share can reach the restricted folders—and NTFS or share permissions will still deny these users access.

For someone to connect to those hidden shares, he must know they exist and then type in the share name correctly when he maps to that share.

Connecting to Shares

You can view shares over the network by opening the Network window and viewing which systems exist that have shared folders to which you can connect. This is certainly the easiest way. Or, you can connect to a system using a mapped network drive.

A mapped network drive is basically a configuration in which you select a drive letter and type in a universal naming convention (UNC) path to the resource with which you are looking to connect. It sounds complicated—and it can be.

Right-click Computer or Network and select Map Network Drive to see the options. Or, from within Computer, you can select the option to Map Network Drive. When you select the option, you see the dialog box in Figure 3.10.

To map the drive, you select an available drive letter and then select the path. The path is `\\servername\sharename\<path>`. So, if you wanted to connect to a computer named Solitude to a share named Sharing, you would type `\\solitude\sharing`. You could also click the Browse button to see which shares are available, but you won't see hidden shares. To connect to those, you have to enter the share name with a $ at the end.

You can also choose to reconnect at logon so that you will reconnect each time to that share and will not have map the drive each time.

Keep in mind that you can also connect to the server by using an IP address. So, you can also type `\\serveripaddress\sharename`.

> **NOTE** Keep in mind that Network Discovery must be enabled in your "Network and Sharing Center" in order to use network mapping. If you aren't able to map to a shared out folder on another system, and you know the permissions are set properly, check to make sure that system has Network Discovery turned on.

126 Tricks of the Windows Vista Masters

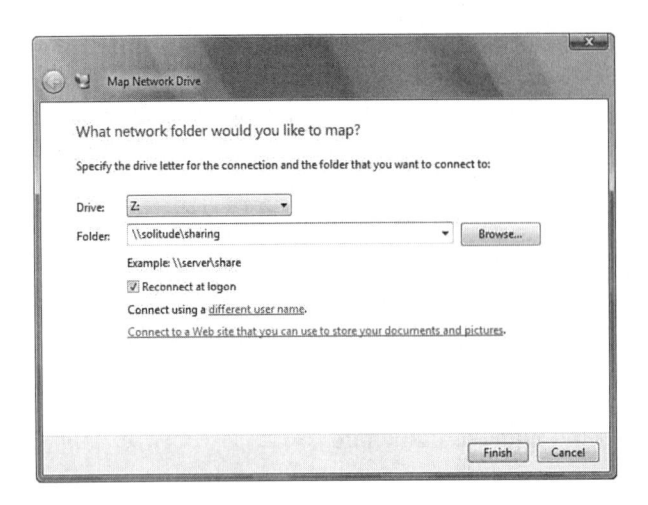

FIGURE 3.10
Mapping a network drive.

To map a drive from a command prompt, you use the NET USE command by typing the following:

```
NET USE <drive>: \\<server>\<share>\<path>
```

The System Window

Want to configure your workgroup or network? Or configure Remote Assistance or Remote Desktop? Need protection? If so, you need to go see the Godfather, also called System.

You can find System in the Control Panel. Or you can right-click Computer from the Start menu and select Properties. You'll start off with a new graphical screen that gives you some basic information: the version of Windows, your Windows Experience Index (which we discuss later), your computer name workgroup/domain name, and the Activation options (see Figure 3.11).

> **NOTE:** There are a couple of cool things to keep in mind with net use. You can also use the IP address of the machine for the server. Or you can use a fully qualified DNS name (such as webserver.company.com). Instead of choosing a drive letter, if you just type an asterisk (*), net use just picks one for you from the available options. Finally, you can include more than the share name. You can include the folder itself so that in your scripts, if you use net use, you don't have to just connect people to a share—you can put them into a specific folder if you want.

Chapter 3 Mastering Administration 127

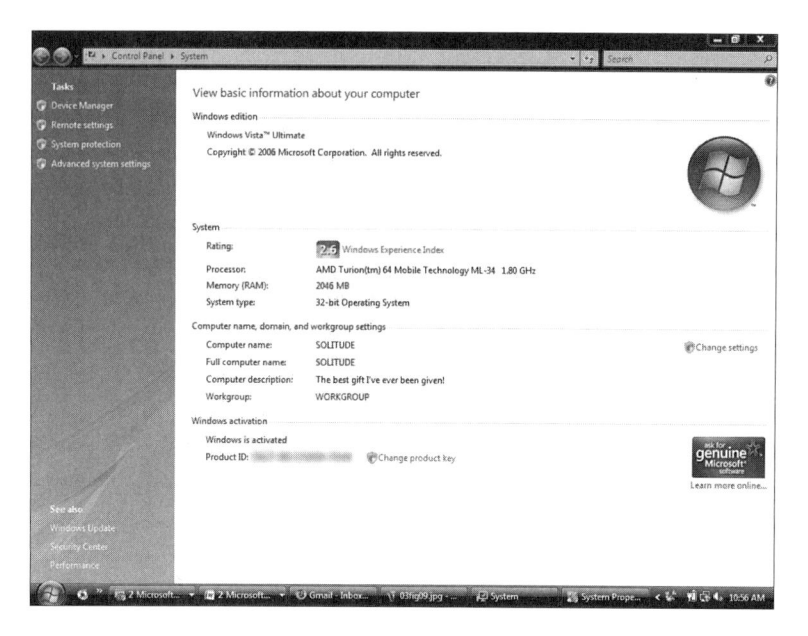

FIGURE 3.11
Your initial System screen, before you get to any of the good stuff.

On the left is a list of tasks. Click the Advanced System Settings link to see the System Properties, which includes five tabs. Let's discuss each one.

Computer Name

On the Computer Name tab, you can change the description for your computer. If you want to join a domain (or workgroup), you can select the Network ID button, which starts an easy-to-use wizard that guides you through the process. If you don't need or want help, you can select the Change button and answer the questions for switching between a domain and a workgroup.

To join a domain, you must have a domain controller available (logically) and have a user account on the domain with the capability to join systems to that domain. Interestingly, if you are connected to a domain, you must still have those credentials to un-join and go back to a workgroup. This prevents users from removing themselves from the domain without permission.

> **TIP:** The fastest way to open System is to hold down your Windows Key and then hold down the Pause key (or on some systems the Pause/Break key).

From the Change options, you can also change your computer name. Or you can configure a DNS suffix for the system (which you don't have to worry about unless you are part of a domain, and even then it's rare) or change the NetBIOS name for the computer.

Hardware

The Hardware tab contains two options. The first is Device Manager, which we talked about in Chapter 2. The second is Windows Update Driver Settings.

If you select the Windows Update Driver Settings button, you will see the Windows Update Driver Settings dialog box and be presented with three options:

- Check for Drivers Automatically (Recommended)
- Ask Me Each Time I Connect a New Device before Checking for Drivers
- Never Check for Drivers when I Connect a Device

Advanced

The Advanced tab gives you options to enhance your system's performance. For an admin, this is like a candy store of options. There are three sections to focus on in this window: Performance, User Profiles, and Startup and Recovery. Each has a Settings button you can click to modify your system's advanced system properties.

Performance

When you click the Settings button for Performance, you'll find that there are three tabs with which you can work:

- **Visual Effects**—Choose to configure Vista for best appearance (which turns on all options) or performance (which turns off all options). Or you can go through all the options and manually make adjustments that will give you what you need. If your system is acting sluggish, your best option is to turn off some of these and see whether performance improves, without losing all your favorite effects.

- **Advanced**—You can change the Processor Scheduling to either Programs or Background Services. And you can configure your Virtual Memory.

  The options under Processor Scheduling relate to how your processor (which can only handle so much work at a time) divides its attention among multiple applications. If you leave the setting to Programs, the processor devotes the majority of its time to the program running in the foreground (that's whatever program you are currently working in). If you select Background Services, the processor devotes time equally to all applications.

- **Data Execution Prevention (DEP)**—This is the final tab under Performance. DEP monitors your system to ensure that programs use system memory properly. Although DEP is a software-based protection feature, some processors are also DEP enabled for hardware protection. The two options you can configure are Turn On DEP for Essential Windows Programs and Services Only and Turn On DEP for All Programs and Services Except Those I Select. Then you can configure which programs you don't need monitored.

> **TIP** If you or your users complain that programs are running too slowly, you should ensure that this is on Programs so that the active program gets the majority of the processor's attention. However, if you or your users frequently run background processes, such as macros, you should give all applications equal time slices (which are called *quanta*) by enabling the Background Services option.

> **NOTE** DEP has been known to cause problems with some older applications. If you run into a conflict and trust the application that causes it, you should turn on DEP for all programs and configure it so that it doesn't check the applications you want to be able to run.

Understanding Virtual Memory

Virtual memory is something you generally don't have to worry about. If you open this setting, you can see that the option at the top makes you feel good inside—it tells Vista to handle it without your help. However, any true Vista Master knows what it is and how to configure it if needed. Ronald Barrett, the Senior Network Administrator for ERE Accounting in Manhattan, says:

> Imagine your computer is like an office. Your hard disk is your file cabinet and your desktop is your, well…desktop. Every time you want a file or folder, you have to get up and go to the file cabinet. That slows down your workday. But, say you have a set of folders on your desktop that can hold the latest work—that is your RAM. In addition, you have a little spot right in front of you for the stuff you need immediately—that's your cache. You can start to see how it all comes together for your workflow. Your virtual memory involves a situation in which your computer is working hard, moving files back and forth between the RAM, but finds that it needs more space. There is no more RAM and it doesn't want to put it back in the large file cabinet of a hard disk; what can it do? Instead, a pagefile is created (also called a *swap file*). This is on the hard disk (back in the file cabinet), but it's really an extension of the RAM itself so that RAM can quickly access what it needs. So, even though it's on the hard drive, it's called virtual memory. Got all that?

Now, even though we said you can let Microsoft handle it, the fact is that there are some best practices Vista knows but ignores.

If you have multiple drives, you can divide the pagefile between all the drives you have (drives, not partitions). The more drives, the better. You should also try to get the pagefile off your system file drive (c: drive). If you have any drives that are fault tolerant (discussed later), you should keep the pagefile off these drives.

Microsoft generally sets the minimum size of the pagefile to the amount of RAM you have plus 300MB. The recommended size is 1.5 times the amount of RAM. You can increase beyond that if you want. Generally, though, it's best to go with the recommended and just split it up amongst your drives and get it off that system drive (but not on fault-tolerant drives).

User Profiles

Explained earlier as your likes and dislikes for your desktop, you can use the user Profiles tab to delete profiles on the system from here. You can also copy profiles to give to other user accounts and configure roaming or local user profiles if you have a profile configured as roaming.

Startup and Recovery

The Startup and Recovery options, shown in Figure 3.12, haven't changed from Windows XP.

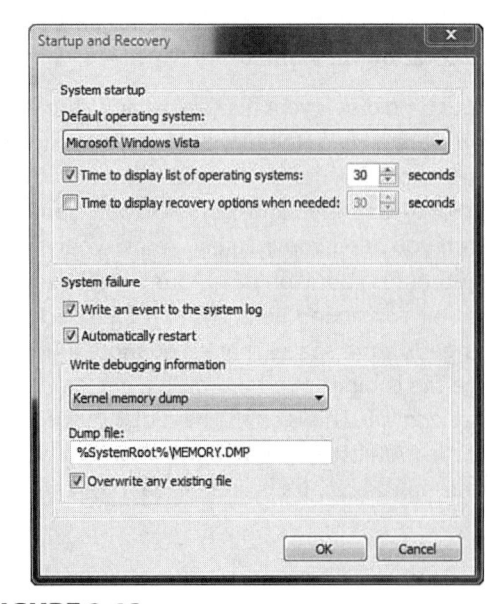

FIGURE 3.12
Startup and Recovery options.

The System Startup section lets you select the OS to which to boot up (only important if you have multiple OSes on the same machine) along with a boot time. You can also configure startup to automatically show the recovery options for a period of time (instead of pressing F8) during bootup.

The recovery options are for those special "blue screen of death" moments that occur in all our lives. (Although, hopefully, their frequency will be much less in Vista.) Sometimes you want the system to reboot and get it over with; other times you want to see the blue screen before the system reboots so you can see what's happening.

Terri Stratton
Microsoft MVP

One of the first things most techs and support personnel that I deal with advise is that users turn off the 'automatic reboot' feature so that they can see the problem without having to use the Event Viewer, which may or may not give the same information. This is especially true now that so many errors can recover without a reboot (although not a blue screen).

In addition, you can configure the extent of the memory dump that occurs, the location of the dump file, and so on. Here are the types of memory dumps you can configure, besides none, which is self-explanatory:

- **Complete Memory Dump**—Records the entire contents of memory. Basically, during the crash, your RAM is copied over to the pagefile, which is then saved as the memory.dmp file during the reboot process.
- **Kernal Memory Dump**—Records only kernel memory, driver memory, and HAL memory (which should suffice to know what crashed the system).
- **Small Memory Dump (64KB)**—Lists the stop message and parameters, loaded drivers, processor context, and running thread information.

To understand what has actually occurred, you need to analyze the dump file. You can download the latest Windows debugging tools from http://www.microsoft.com/whdc/devtools/debugging/default.mspx. In addition to the tools, plenty of documentation is provided.

System Protection

The System Protection feature lets you create restore points so you can quickly jump back to a point in time when your system was working perfectly. This feature affects only the system; it does not undo files, photos, or other items you have created on your system.

So, for example, if you've installed a program or new driver and the system cannot handle it, you can try to uninstall the problem. If that doesn't work, you can use a restore point to jump back.

System Restore is an option from All Programs, Accessories, System Tools. You can run this wizard when you want to restore a previously created restore point. But, you create the points from your System Properties. Restore points are automatically created every day and when you install new applications and drivers. You can also go into your System Properties, open the System Protection tab, and select the Create button to take a snapshot of the system as it is at that moment.

> **TIP**: You can configure the times for System Restore points by going into the Task Scheduler, looking through the Task Scheduler Library, under Microsoft, Windows, SystemRestore. Under the SR task, you can see that the task provides two triggers, one for a time schedule (default is 12:00 a.m.) and one for system startup.

Restore points require at least 300MB of space on any given hard disk where they are turned on.

Remote

Remote is where the settings for Remote Assistance and Remote Desktop reside. The Remote Assistance feature is more helpful than most people give it credit for. I cannot count how many times family members have called asking for assistance and I just had them send me an invitation so I could see what they are doing and either take over or walk them through the changes.

The settings are simple. You can set Remote Assistance to make connections that allow desktop control. You can also determine the length of time for the invitations to be valid. To invite others to use your system or accept invitations, go to the Windows Help and Support dialog box and look for the Windows Remote Assistance options.

Remote Desktop enables you to connect to another computer as if you were sitting at it. So, for example, you can access your work computer from home (if your work computer is on, configured to use Remote Desktop, and the Firewall allows the connections).

To connect to a system, you use the Remote Desktop Connection tool under Programs, Accessories. You can configure quite a bit, including the display settings and the use of resources.

> **TIP**: In Vista, the Remote Desktop can span multiple monitors. You must type `mstsc /span` at a command prompt to accomplish this. To toggle in and out of full-screen spanned mode, you press Ctrl+Alt+Break.

More Useful Tools

We cannot pick apart every last little feature. It's just not practical or necessary when you have an Internet filled with article after article that will round out your knowledge on any one of these tools. The key is to know they exist and to know what they do—a true master takes what she's been given and adds to it. Here are some of the other tools you can use to help you administrate:

- **Data Sources (ODBC)**—Uses Open Database Connectivity to move your data from one type of database to another. So, for example, you can move data that was created on FileMaker Pro into an Excel format.
- **Defragmenter**—Found under the Accessories, System Tools, the defragmenter is no longer a graphical tool that you can watch move your data blocks around. But you can and should still schedule it, using either the tool or the Task Scheduler. It is set up by Task Scheduler to automatically defragment the drive once a week at 1:00 am, but if you know the system isn't on at that time then you will want to change the time.
- **Disk Cleanup**—Lets you free up disk space by searching through your folders for unnecessary or unused files. One great example of an unused file is the hibernation file. You can delete it from here (usually the size of your installed RAM).
- **Print Management**—Manages printers and print servers on a network.

Other tools such as the Memory Diagnostics Tool and the Reliability and Performance Monitor are addressed in chapters to come.

The following are some other resources an admin should know about and have in her utility belt:

- **Windows Vista Resource Kit**—Resource Kits are must-haves for any serious admin. These are sets of command-line tools that simplify the managing of Windows through a command prompt. The Windows 2003 Resource Kit is a free download that works on a variety of Windows systems and contains close to 200 tools. The Vista Kit can be purchased and includes a book and CD. Microsoft has a site dedicated to Resource Kit information: http://www.microsoft.com/windows/reskits/default.asp.
- **Sysinternals**—Mark Russinovich's incredible site of free tools has not been phased out now that he has moved into the Microsoft world; they have just been moved to this new location: http://www.microsoft.com/technet/sysinternals/default.mspx. Some tools to look out for are PageDefrag, Process Explorer, AutoRuns, BGInfo, and a bevy of others.
- **Adminpak (Windows Server 2003 Service Pack 1 Administration Tools Pack or Windows Server 2003 R2 Administration Tools Pack)**—These are free tools you can install on your Vista desktop if you plan on administering servers on your network. You

might have some difficulty running these to start with, but you just need to register the DLLs for the tools. An article at http://4sysops.com explains how to install the pack on Vista.

- **4SysOps.com**—It's not a collection of tools, but a website that is great for system admins to keep up-to-date on the latest and greatest tools and how to use them.
- **Microsoft BDD 2007 (Business Desktop Deployment)**—BDD 2007 contains important deployment tools for Vista, such as ImageX, WSIM (Windows System Image Manager), and WDS (Windows Deployment Services). You can download it at Microsoft Connect.

Chapter 4

SECURITY ENHANCEMENTS

Security Overview

To say that Microsoft puts out operating systems that are inherently insecure is untrue and, quite frankly, unfair. It's also easy to forget just how big a target Windows represents. When you have an OS that hundreds of millions of people use, it creates an irresistible target for people who like to crash through for money, fame, or fun—it's impossible to win. Not to mention the fact that the biggest security hole in any OS is the user! The majority of compromised systems occur when the end user practically opens the door for those of malicious intent.

I know what you might be thinking. What about flaws like easily exploitable ActiveX controls and so forth? Fair enough. There's no question that Microsoft has not always shown foresight when it comes to PC security. But it's a mistake to think that Microsoft isn't taking PC security seriously, especially when it comes to Windows Vista. IE 7 has made some incredible improvements to prevent breeches. Improvements to the Security Center have been introduced with Windows XP Service Pack 2, a two-way firewall, the Windows Defender antispyware tool, and a host of other features under the hood to keep you more secure. Does all that make Vista impregnable? No. Operating system security will never be perfect. But Vista is still a big step in the right direction.

IN THIS CHAPTER

- Security Overview
- Understanding Vista's "Hidden" Security Features
- User Access Control
- Internet Explorer Security
- CardSpace/InfoCard— Don't Leave Home Without It
- Windows Defender
- The Malicious Software Removal Tool— Postinfection Removal
- Windows Firewall

Evolution of the Vista Security Process

The technology within Vista is a fun new world to explore, and we are going to get there shortly. But to really be a master Vista user, you have to read a little on the story of security development. We promise to keep this brief.

Since the evolution of the Internet, Microsoft has been getting hammered from all sides about how awful its security was and how it needed to do something about it. In 2002, Microsoft formed the Trustworthy Computing Initiative (TWC) to address the flaws in security and privacy. This initiative, which you can read about at http://www.microsoft.com/mscorp/twc/default.mspx, is built on four principles:

- Security
- Privacy
- Reliability in our software, services, and products
- Integrity in business practices

One of the products of the Trustworthy Computing focus is the Security Development Lifecycle (SDL). This is a process for software development that has two main goals: One is to reduce the number of bugs in the code, especially in relation to security; the second is to accept that there will obviously be bugs remaining and to make it as difficult to exploit those bugs as possible. One aspect of the SDL is that engineers are required to attend security training. This helps developers and designers eliminate errors being made during the development process from design to release. However, when errors *are* made, every effort is used during the peer review process to catch and fix them. To that end, specific tools are run that look for missing Sourcecode Annotation Language (SAL) annotations, buffer overruns, array bounds issues, integer overflows, banned-APIs, banned cryptographic functions, and so forth on all the developer's code.

To learn more about how all this is being done, you can check out MSDN blogs, (specifically some of the blogs posted by Michael Howard at `http://blogs.msdn.com/michael_howard/default.aspx`). You should also check out Michael's book *The Security Development Lifecycle*: `http://www.microsoft.com/MSPress/books/8753.asp`. Michael Howard is a Security Developer for Microsoft and he was kind enough, in harmony with the spirit of this book, to cooperate on the early part of this chapter by editing and contributing material towards it.

Finally, because security is an ever-changing game, you can keep up-to-date on the latest Microsoft methods and information at http://www.microsoft.com/security/windowsvista/default.mspx.

Understanding Vista's "Hidden" Security Features

In the sections to follow we will be discussing tangible tools that are provided that you can configure and work with, such as Parental Controls. But you still should have a grasp of the underlying technology (and terminology) for Vista security.

Address Space Layout Randomization

One type of security attack is called *return-to-libc*, which tries to run a system function based on a standard location for that function in memory. These attackers need to locate the code to be executed while other attackers try to execute shellcode within a stack; however, they need to find that stack first.

The purpose of ASLR is to move the system functions around in memory so that they aren't always located in the same spot and thus cannot be predicted. So, attackers can only guess at the location. There are 256 possible locations from which to choose, giving an attacker a 1/256 chance of finding his mark, which is unlikely. In the event of a false guess, the application usually crashes without hindering security.

Randomization like this makes the attacker's life harder.

This brings us to rootkits, which have become a popular system attack in recent years. Rootkits are processes that spoof their way into protected memory and then run in stealth with full privileges, communicating with a host system out on the Internet through unprotected ports. For a rootkit to work properly, it has to locate itself in system memory. With ASLR, there is no longer a haphazard way of processes locating themselves in memory. A table of registers keeps track of where things are located. A rootkit couldn't place itself in memory without registering on that list. After the rootkit registers, it's no longer a stealth process. You can see again, that even though ASLR is a behind-the-scenes feature, it's one we should appreciate.

Windows Service Hardening

The goal of Windows Service Hardening is to ensure that as many background processes as possible are prevented from having direct access to system resources. In addition, WSH ensures that processes are now run with the lowest possible privileges. They are also isolated from one another.

The benefit is that attacks to the file system, Registry, network, and other resources are hindered because malware cannot use system services to attack. In previous versions a service would run with the Local System account (high privileges), but now many run with the Local Service or Network Service, which reduces the overall authority of the service itself. In other words, when a process is run with a higher set of privileges the system trusts any actions that process is programmed to initiate. This is where the danger comes in. But running under reduced privileges prevents these attacks from going forward.

Windows Service Hardening cannot prevent the attack if your system is vulnerable. There are other services, such as Windows Firewall, whose job it is to take care of that. But Windows Service Hardening can limit the damage done if the attacker is seeking to exploit services because it won't allow it.

How does WSH work? Now there is a per-service security ID that means each service has its own ID with permissions that can be specific between the service and the resources being accessed. In addition, services are given a network firewall policy that prevents that service from being accessed from outside the standard boundaries of the service.

Windows Integrity Control

Another invisible feature of Vista that you should understand is the Windows Integrity Control (WIC). Previously, a system used Access Control Lists (ACLs) to determine whether an individual could modify an object. For example, if you attempt to access a file, and that file has a permission setting that denies you access, you are done, you have no access. Files, folders, processes, threads, Registry keys, and so forth all have ACLs.

Now, however objects also have an Integrity rating. There are four levels: low, medium, high, and system. Standard users receive medium, and elevated users receive high. Processes that you (as a user) start receive the integrity you are running (medium or high). But this isn't the case if the file already has a setting of low on it. System services receive the highest-level system rating.

How does this work? Well, let's say you are running IE 7 in protected mode (so it's running with a level of low integrity) and something from the Internet wants to write a virus to the operating system. The attack fails because, if it tries to access an object with a higher integrity level, it is stopped.

Objects that don't have an integrity code assigned are treated as medium so that lower-level integrity processes cannot harm them.

As for changing integrity levels, only users with the Change Label privilege can change integrity levels to a higher level. The primary point in WIC is that an object cannot be modified if it has a higher integrity level than that which is trying to modify it.

Windows Resource Protection

The initial plan in Windows Vista was going to be that the Windows Integrity Control would secure the system files in Vista. Over the course of the beta process, however, things changed. Instead Microsoft came up with a new set of permissions and modified the file protection structure into Windows Resource Protection. This is an update to the Windows File Protection features found in Windows 2000 and XP. WFP protected system files by running in the background and detecting attempts to replace protected system files. When a protected file is under threat of replacement, it notifies the WFP, which looks up the file signature in a file catalog to see whether the new version adheres to Microsoft standards. If it does not, it replaces the new file with the correct one from the dllcache folder (located under the system32 folder), which contains a backup of *all* .dll, .exe, .fon, .ocx, .sys and .tff files. Additional file types are backed up there, too.

Windows Resource Protection works in pretty much the same way; however, it also includes some advancements. For starters, when a program tries to install a protected file that the Windows Installer knows is not allowed, it won't install the file—rather it just logs an error. WFP used to be allowed to install the file by the installer and then it would undo the change. Another enhancement includes the capability to protect Registry keys. The Vista installer simply will not alter Registry keys that are marked as protected.

WRP protects critical files that are installed by Windows Vista with the following extensions: .acm, .ade, .adp, .app, .asa, .asp, .aspx, .ax, .bas, .bat, .bin, .cer, .chm, .clb, .cmd, .cnt, .cnv, .com, .cpl, .cpx, .crt, .csh, .dll, .drv, .dtd, .exe, .fxp, .grp, .h1s, .hlp, .hta, .ime, .inf, .ins, .isp, .its, .js, .jse, .ksh, .lnk, .mad, .maf, .mag, .mam, .man, .maq, .mar, .mas, .mat, .mau, .mav, .maw, .mda, .mdb, .mde, .mdt, .mdw, .mdz, .msc, .msi,

> **NOTE**
> The original plan was to use WIC to control Windows Resource Protection (WRP). This was changed such that all operating system files are unlabeled (which as we mentioned earlier, defaults them to medium integrity). The default ACLs for these files are set up so that only the Trusted Installer has write access—everyone else, admins included, has read and execute.

> **TIP**
> If you want to work with and alter integrity levels, you need to use the new command `icacls`. To run this, you must give your account the new Vista privilege modify object labels. You can find that in the User Rights part of Group Policy on a Vista machine.
>
> Another developer Microsoft acquired, along with all his great free tools, is Mark Russinovich. You can use two of his SysInternals tools—AccessChk and Process Explorer—to display a process's integrity levels (although you cannot change the levels with these tools). Visit http://www.microsoft.com/technet/sysinternals/default.mspx to learn more about them.

```
.msp, .mst, .mui, .nls, .ocx, .ops, .pal, .pcd,
.pif, .prf, .prg, .pst, .reg, .scf, .scr, .sct,
.shb, .shs, .sys, .tlb, .tsp, .url, .vb, .vbe,
.vbs, .vsmacros, .vss, .vst, .vsw, .ws, .wsc,
.wsf, .wsh, .xsd, and .xsl.
```

WRP makes it harder to delete a system file because all files are owned by the Trusted Installer service by default. You could, as an admin, take ownership of the file and then modify, rename, or delete protected resources.

> **NOTE:** The WRP concept is the same as the WFP, but the backup files are located in a different place. Now you check \Windows\Winsxs\backup. Only critical files are included in this directory, and Microsoft claims the size of the cache directory and the list of files copied to the cache cannot be modified. Vista gurus on the Internet claim otherwise as they try to reduce the overall installation size of Vista in order to shrink it down.

How to Modify HOSTS on a Vista System

Section by Mark Minasi
http://www.minasi.com/newsletters/nws0611.htm
Newsletter #58

The HOSTS file is in the same place that it's always been in Windows: \windows\system32\drivers\etc. But that directory has a different set of NTFS permissions than Windows has ever seen, as by default administrators can't delete files, nor do they own those files. You can give yourself enough control of HOSTS to modify it by first taking ownership of it, then granting yourself full control to HOSTS. That's most easily done from an elevated command prompt.

From the elevated command prompt, type these two lines:

```
takeown /f c:\windows\system32\drivers\etc\hosts
icacls c:\windows\system32\drivers\etc\hosts /grant yourusername:f
```

Those are two new Vista command-line tools. The first lets you take ownership of a file or folder, as its name suggests. That line that you typed is the simplest form of takeown: just add a "/f" and the name of the file or folder to take ownership of. (Takeown even lets you take ownership of things on remote systems, which can be convenient.) The second command lets you adjust NTFS permissions and file/folder integrity levels — it's intended to be the replacement for cacls, which has been around since NT 3.1, and its syntax closely mirrors cacls's. In that command, I'm using the /grant option to allow me to give the account "yourusername" full control; that's what the "F" stands for.

> **TIP:** An "elevated command prompt" means that you right-click the Command Prompt icon and choose "Run as administrator," and then click "Confirm" when you get the User Account Control prompt.

ACLs Versus Integrity: Who Wins?

Paper covers rock, rock crushes scissors, scissors cut paper, WIC eliminates ACL. And that's a good thing.

If you are a Windows 2000/XP guru, you know how ACLs work. If you are new to this discussion, then we will give you a quick overview. Everything and everyone is on a list; a Discretionary Access Control List, or simply put, ACL. These lists are maintained on the objects themselves so that when a person/device/process attempts to access an object (file, printer, and so forth), the subject presents a token that includes groups the subject is a member of. The object compares that to the list. If any group has a Deny setting attached, the object is denied. Denied settings are at the top of the list so that denial is quickly determined. If access is granted, it's with a list of permissions as to which type of access. It all sounds so great and protected. Unfortunately, there is a catch.

Any subject that is not on the ACL of an object is put in a different category. Think of it like an average person who goes to the Oscars without a ticket. They get to the door, but they're not on the list, so it's all over for them. But let's say a special section is reserved for those people without tickets. It seems odd, but let's just imagine the Academy doesn't know what to do with them and so puts them in a category. Once in that "Everyone Else" category, there is always a way to sneak in. How? Do they go to the door and pretend to be a star? It wouldn't work. The same is true of malicious code trying to spoof being a real user on your network; it's very hard to do. But from the vantage point of the "Everyone Else" category, it's possible to find a way in because you are one step closer.

With Integrity Control, the normal users in the network all have medium permissions. Medium doesn't give them enough to damage anything. In our Oscars illustration, it would be as if everybody on the "Everyone Else" list were allowed into the building but were completely isolated from the all the stars, onsite staff, and so on. So you can never have an effect on services or other higher integrity–oriented situations.

Additional Features to Vista Security

The rest of this chapter delves into the configurable Security features, such as User Access Control, Defender, Parental Controls, Firewall, and so forth. But some other security features that you can find in other chapters include

- **Authentication**—This is found in Chapter 3, "Mastering Administration," which covers the process of user account creation, the Vista login process, new smart card devices, and so forth.

- **Network Access Protection**—Found in Chapter 7, "Master Vista Networking." This discusses the new agent that prevents your system from communicating on the network unless it is completely up-to-date with security patches. In that chapter, we also discuss IPv6 and some other changes with networking that are important to keeping your network running smoothly and securely.
- **Data Protection**—Found in Chapter 5, "Disk Configuration and Volume Tricks," this discusses the new BitLocker Drive Encryption feature.

> **NOTE** The security features in this chapter are by no means exhaustive. Hackers are lunging and camineering every day, and Microsoft is trying to parry and perform what they would call in fencing *prise de fer*—that is "taking the blade" from their opponents by controlling their opponents' weapons. Entire books, seminars, webinars, blogs, and so forth are dedicated to Vista security; we recommend you continue your studies, not only on the practical implementation, but also on the underlying philosophy. Only then will you become a Vista "Maestro di Arma."

User Access Control

Use Vista for 10 minutes and you'll probably encounter Vista's User Account Control. Use Vista for an hour and you may even find it the most irritating new Windows feature you've come across in a long time. Use it for a week and you might be ready to take an axe to your system. Admittedly, that could be an expensive resolution.

During Vista's beta process and early shelf life, UAC has often dubbed the most hated new feature of Window Vista and yet that's usually because people are not really sure what its purpose is. To truly appreciate it, you have to think about pre-Vista Windows operating systems. Usually people were either provided with Administrative privileges to make certain system changes or they were locked down so they couldn't even change the time without an admin's intervention. There needed to be a balance. UAC strives to achieve that balance by giving standard users more capabilities with their own systems (such as changing the time, adding fonts or printers, and so forth), while not giving too much so as to cause security risks.

Here are a few of the new capabilities that standard users now have:
- View system clock and calendar
- Change time zone
- Install Wired Equivalent Privacy (WEP) to connect to secure wireless networks
- Change power management settings

Chapter 4 Security Enhancements

- Add printers and other devices that have the required drivers installed on the computer
- Install ActiveX Controls from sites approved by an administrator
- Create and configure a virtual private network (VPN) connection
- Install critical Windows Updates
- Change the desktop background and modify display settings
- Use Remote Desktop to connect to another computer

Deb Schinder, in an article entitled "Working with (and around) Windows Vista User Account Control" for TechRepublic.com said this about UAC:

> **Vista Master** Once upon a time, we had the Power Users group to allow more experienced users to do things like install printers and programs. With UAC, there's no need for the Power User mode, but it's still available for backward compatibility with previous versions of Windows. If you want to use the Power Users group on Vista, you need to apply a security template that changes the default permissions on the registry and system folders so that they'll be the same as with Windows XP.

In Windows Vista, all users (including admins) run in a standard mode. This causes frustration to admins working with Vista but we will get to that soon enough. Let's first consider how this benefits admins and users alike. Standard users now have more control over their systems, allowing them to do their work without having admin privileges and without bothering the administrator. Conversely, standard users do not have the ability to do things that will hinder their machines or the network, so admins will have less to worry about. This not only prevents users from accidentally messing around with their system or the network, but it also prevents malware from installing sneakily in the background. When such an attempt does occur, a prompt comes up and the user is unable to proceed without providing admin credentials.

The process we are talking about is called Administrative Approval Mode, and it treats everyone like they are standard users. When actions are taken that require administrator-level access, it requires administrative credentials to proceed (see Figure 4.1). Even if you are an administrator who is already logged in, you are still required to confirm an action, although you won't have to enter a password to do so.

> **CAUTION:** Although it should go without saying, I must also emphasize that you should never provide administrator password credentials to a standard user. It defeats the entire purpose of separating standard users from those with administrator credentials.

FIGURE 4.1

For a standard user, an action requiring Administrative privileges calls for credentials.

This sounds like a good thing—and it is. But at the same time, when an administrator is logged in to Vista and tries to access a resource that requires administrative credentials, the system still sends a little pop-up that requires you to agree before moving forward. In a normal day when you are just working, you could go the entire day without seeing one of these. But administrators will have to go through this process constantly.

Here are some of the reasons you will see a prompt for elevated confirmation:

- Install and uninstall applications
- Work with Windows Firewall
- Install drivers or configure Windows Updates
- Add, remove, or modify user accounts
- Configure Parental Controls, run elevated command prompts, and so forth

One danger in getting too used to seeing these prompts is that we may just agree without reading what we are giving permission to. So, we should take a moment to make sure we requested the application that's asking for permission. In addition, we should ensure that our antispyware and antivirus applications are up-to-date so that nothing accidentally gets through.

How UAC Keeps Track of Privileges

When you logged on to a Windows NT/2000/XP system, it took your username and password and then, based on those credentials, it prepared a token for you. That token included your group memberships and user rights. When you attempted to access a resource, the resource would compare its ACL against the group memberships found in your token and allow/deny access based on this.

With UAC, administrators receive two tokens from the local security authority (see Figure 4.2). One of these tokens is for their administrative account, and one is a standard user token that offers a filtered set of access. When you log on, the desktop is launched (explorer.exe) using the standard user's token. This is considered the parent process, and all other processes are based on this parent and therefore also run with the standard user token. So, even if you logged on as an administrator, the system is running you with the Standard User access. When you try to access something that requires higher privileges, it uses the Admin token, but not before requesting your permission through the dialog box. For this to work, a new system service was created called Application Information Service (AIS) and it launches the applications with the elevated Admin token.

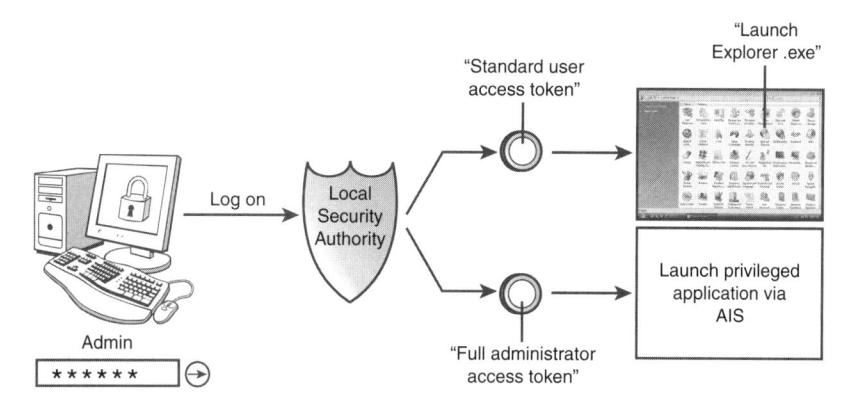

FIGURE 4.2
Token creation in Vista.

The Standard User Access Token

Your Administrative token includes your SID, your group memberships and user rights, and an Integrity level of high (which we discussed a little earlier). But what about that standard user access token?

> **TIP** In the event that you have difficulty running processes with elevated credentials, your AIS service might not be working. Check your services first to make sure this isn't the problem. To do this go to Administrative Tools, Services.

Tricks of the Windows Vista Masters

Mark Minasi
"Getting to Know User Account Control"
http://www.microsoft.com/technet/community/columns/secmvp/sv1006.mspx

In designing UAC, Microsoft reckoned that of the 34 possible privileges and many group memberships that a Windows Vista user account can have, nine privileges and four groups confer the ability to do some damage to a system. The "Notorious Nine" privileges (as I call them) are:

- SeCreateTokenPrivilege, create new Windows tokens
- SeTcbPrivilege, "act as a part of the OS"—essential for a RunAs-like operation
- SeTakeOwnershipPrivilege
- SeLoadDriverPrivilege
- SeBackupPrivilege
- SeRestorePrivilege
- SeImpersonatePrivilege
- SeRelabelPrivilege, the privilege to change a Windows integrity label (new to Windows Vista)
- SeDebugPrivilege, the privilege to look into other people's processes

The "Fearsome Four" groups are all local built-in groups:

- Administrators
- Backup Operators
- Network Configuration Operators
- Power Users

The first three groups clearly confer some of the Notorious Nine privileges, hence their inclusion; we'll see why Power Users is in there in a moment. If UAC sees that your account has either one of the Notorious Nine privileges or the Fearsome Four group memberships, upon logon your account will get two tokens.

Your standard token contains your Security ID (SID), an integrity level of medium, and all privileges and group memberships that are not part of the dangerous ones mentioned here (in Mark Minasi's tip). You will be given Deny-only memberships in the four groups that are considered dangerous above. This means that any resource that allows access based solely on one of those groups causes you to be denied with this token. And any resource that denies access based on those groups will also deny you. What does all of this mean? Basically, it means the standard access token (while better for users because it includes more capabilities than before) is locked down for security for administrators.

The Administrator Access Token

So, you're logged in as an admin but holding back the admin token, using only your standard token. Now what? When you open a program like Solitaire, the standard user token is used. That's fine. But now you open a command prompt to perform some advanced configuration changes and find that you cannot do it. That's because you need to be running in elevated mode. Elevated mode means you need to provide the credentials to the system to use the administrative token. If you started the program already, it's too late. You cannot change modes after you've started the program, so now you have to restart your command prompt with elevated credentials.

There are a few ways you can elevate a program. You can right-click the program and select Run As Administrator (and you will see one of those little shields next to this option). You can change the properties of the program permanently to require elevation by going into the Properties, selecting the Compatibility tab, and selecting the check box Run This Program As an Administrator under the Privilege heading.

There are also situations in which the application automatically knows, or is told, that it requires elevation—for example, if a manifest file tells it to run elevated. These files are XML text files that are in the `.exe` or within the same directory and would give the direction to run elevated to Vista.

Windows Vista heuristically detects installation programs (usually running with the word *setup*, *install*, or *update* somewhere in the name). Windows Vista also heuristically detects updater and uninstallation programs. The UAC takes an educated guess (based on certain rules and background knowledge regarding various file types) on whether the application is an installer, updater, or uninstallation program.

Additional reasons elevation may be called on involves the Program Compatibility Assistant (PCA), which monitors the installation of a program. The PCA tries to automatically determine the compatibility mode settings the program needs; if it fails, the PCA asks whether it can run again with

> **NOTE** If the Run This Program As an Administrator isn't available, that could be because it's blocked from being elevated, the program doesn't require elevation to run, the application is part of the current version of Vista, or you just might not be logged in as an administrator.

different settings, causing it to change the settings on the Compatibility tab to request admin approval.

Finally, the Application Compatibility Toolkit knows some of the applications you use absolutely need to run with elevated rights. The ACT is a set of tools that create shims that mark an application with the correct run level for the parent process that launches the application. A shim is a dynamic link library (DLL) used to fix a single compatibility issue. Microsoft has gone through thousands of applications to prepare which shims each legacy application needs. That information is contained on every Vista machine in a file called `sysmain.sdb` located in the %windir%\apppatch directory. Normally you can open sdb files using the command-line tool sdbinst.exe included with Vista, however in this case, because it is a system file, Vista will not let you crack it open.

> **TIP:** Before deploying Vista, developers and IT admins should ensure that the applications are going to be stable. Testing is a must, and the Application Compatibility Toolkit v.5.0 is one tool we recommend you work with. The other is the Standard User Analyzer, which diagnoses problems with applications running under a standard user. Both tools provide logs that show where standard user mode could cause a problem for applications. You can also look for applications running with elevated privilege through Event ID 592, the Process Tracking Audit.

Audit Process Tracking and Audit Privilege Use

Section courtesy of TechNet
http://technet.microsoft.com/en-us/windowsvista/aa905117.aspx

The audit process tracking setting enables real-time monitoring of process elevations. For example, the IT department can enable audit process tracking with Group Policy and track each time an administrator in Admin Approval Mode or a standard user elevates a process to a full administrator process.

To audit process tracking:

1. Click Start, click Run, type `secpol.msc`, and then click OK.
2. In the Console pane, expand Local Policies, and then select Audit Policy.
3. In the Details pane, right-click Audit process tracking and select Properties.
4. In Audit process tracking Properties, select Success.

The audit privilege use setting enables real-time monitoring of elevated process creations.

To audit privilege use:

1. Click Start, click Run, type `secpol.msc`, and then click OK.
2. In the Console pane, expand Local Policies, and then select Audit Policy.
3. In the Details pane, right-click Audit privilege use and select Properties.
4. In Audit privilege use Properties, select Success, and then click OK.

UAC and File and Registry Virtualization

Legacy applications are always a problem with newer operating systems. It would seem that this would never be truer than with Vista because many legacy applications weren't designed to understand and work with standard user accounts. Often legacy applications attempt to write to protected file system areas (like Program Files) or to the Registry, and this just won't work under Vista with a Standard User setting.

However, Microsoft has created an intermediary plan to help legacy applications function even better than they did with XP: file and Registry virtualization. The concept is simple. Instead of these applications writing to the real protected file system areas or Registry, they are redirected to a special location within the user's profile.

Blogger (and Microsoft Certified Solution Developer for Microsoft .NET) Wenfeng Gao wrote at http://wgao.blogspot.com/:

> Windows Vista includes file and registry virtualization technology for applications that are not UAC compliant and that have historically required an administrator's access token to run correctly. Virtualization ensures that even applications that are not UAC compliant will be compatible with Windows Vista. When a non-UAC-compliant administrative application attempts to write to a protected directory, such as Program Files, UAC gives the application its own virtualized view of the resource it is attempting to change, using a copy-on-write strategy. The virtualized copy is maintained under the user's profile. As a result, a separate copy of the virtualized file is created for each user that runs the non-compliant application.
>
> For example, if an application attempts to write to "C:\program files\appname\settings.ini" and the user doesn't have permissions to write to that directory, the write will get redirected to C:\Users\username\AppData\Local\VirtualStore\Program Files\appname\. A write to HKLM\Software\AppName will get redirected to HKCU\Software\Classes\VirtualStore\Machine\Software\AppName.
>
> Virtualization is enabled by default in Windows Vista. Virtualization does not apply to applications that are elevated and run with a full administrative access token. Virtualization is disabled for an application if a program includes an application manifest with a requested execution level attribute.

Microsoft is threatening to remove this feature in future versions, so hopefully software developers are trying to get their programs to work with the new security features in mind through the UAC.

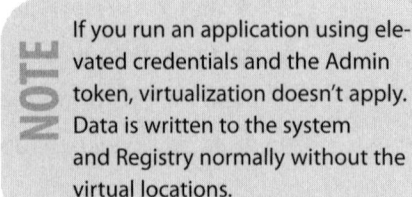

> **NOTE**
> If you run an application using elevated credentials and the Admin token, virtualization doesn't apply. Data is written to the system and Registry normally without the virtual locations.

Wengfeng Gao
Blogger and Microsoft Certified Solution Developer for Microsoft .NET

Although virtualization allows the overwhelming majority of pre-Windows Vista applications to run, it is a short-term fix and not a long-term solution. Application developers should modify their applications to be compliant with the Windows Vista Logo program as soon as possible, rather than relying on file, folder, and registry virtualization.

Configuring UAC Settings

While much of what we've discussed about UAC up to this point has been prelude, it's important to understand all that information before you go about changing settings that involve UAC. Now that you know what UAC does, what should you do if you want to turn it off or part of it off?

Here are several ways to turn it off:

- **MSCONFIG**—Go to the Tools tab and scroll down. Select the Disable UAP line and select Launch. Reboot to make the change apply.
- **Registry**—From your Registry editor, go to: HKEY_LOCAL_MACHINE\Software\Microsoft\Windows\CurrentVersion\Policies\System. Locate the EnableLUA DWORD and set this to 0.
- Open Control Panel and go into the User Accounts applet. Disable it from here.
- **From Group Policy**—You can use `gpedit.msc` if you are working with the local policy, or you can also use `secpol.msc`. For AD policies, you need to type `gpmc.msc`.

The next few sections look at the specific steps required to configure UAC through Group Policy.

Disabling Admin Approval Mode

As mentioned above you can disable or alter the functionality of UAC through Group Policy (local or domain). Here are the steps for changing the local security policy to disable "Admin Approval Mode."

1. Log on with an administrative account.
2. Enter `secpol.msc` into the Start menu's search box to open the Local Security Policy window.
3. From the Local Security Settings, select Local Policies, Security Options.
4. Find User Account Control: Run All Administrators in Admin Approval Mode. You'll need to scroll down the list to the group of settings related to user account control.
5. Disable this setting and then reboot your system.

Disabling Prompt for Credentials

To change the setting on your system with regard to the Installer knowing and acting on the program you are trying to install you can alter this setting.

1. Use the steps in the previous section to navigate to the User Account Control: Detect Application Installations and Prompt for Elevation policy setting.
2. Change the setting to Disabled.

On home systems the default is for this to be enabled and to determine whether the elevated mode is necessary for the install. On Enterprise systems this is disabled by default.

Changing Elevation Prompt Behavior for Standard Users

You can also configure how the elevation prompt reacts for a standard user. You may want to disable the request for a prompt so that users do not even know they can ask for your credentials to install something.

1. Again, in the Local Security Policy window, navigate to the User Account Control: Behavior of the Elevation Prompt for Standard Users policy setting.
2. Choose one of the following: No Prompt, Prompt for Credentials (requires a username and password of an admin account for it to run in elevated mode and is the default option) or Prompt for Consent (the default option for admins, requests only consent but does not request a password).

For the Home user, the default is for the user to be prompted. For Enterprise users, the default is for the user to be denied the choice.

The Best Prompt Choice: Maybe

The best option for admins who are sick of the elevation prompt is the User Account Control. Behavior of the elevation prompt for administrators in Admin Approval Mode changes from Prompt for Consent to Elevate Without Prompting.

This keeps the UAC running in the background but when you do request a process run in elevated mode, it won't ask you for approval. To try it, right-click the command prompt option and select Run As Administrator; that opens in elevated mode without first prompting you.

Additional Options

- **Admin Approval Mode for the Built-in Administrator Account**—Normally you wouldn't use the Built-in Administrator account (in fact, it's disabled by default). If you enable it and decide to use it, the account is not running in Admin Approval Mode by default, but you can change this so it works just like all the other admin accounts. This mode protects the administrators by having them work as standard users for normal day-to-day tasks and then prompting for elevation mode.

- **Detect Application Installations and Prompt for Elevation**—Enabled by default in the home version and disabled in the Enterprise version, any time an application installation starts, the user is prompted whether to allow it or not.

- **Only Elevate Executables That Are Signed and Validated**—Disabled by default, this policy enforces PKI signature checks on any interactive application that requests elevation of privilege. Enterprise administrators can control the admin application allowed list through the population of certificates in the local computer's Trusted Publisher Store.

- **Only Elevate UIAccess Applications That Are Installed in Secure Locations**—Enabled by default, only applications launched from the `%Programfiles%` (including subdirectories) or `%windir%` location are given privileges to run because the permissions in this location prevent the executables from being user-modifiable, and therefore more safe.

- **Switch to the Secure Desktop When Prompting for Elevation**—By default when User Account Control prompts appear, the screen darkens. With Secure Desktop enabled, other software running on the machine is blocked from interacting with the user's interface. This feature makes it more difficult for malware to trick the user because everything stops and you have to consent, or not.

- **Virtualize File and Registry Write Failures to Per-User Locations**—Enabled by default, this policy allows non-Vista–compliant applications to run properly by redirecting Registry and file system writes that require administrative access.

> **NOTE:** The Virtualize File and Registry Write Failures to Per-User Locations setting is enabled by default. However, if you are confident that all your applications for your situation are UAC compliant (which might be the case if you are just getting started and have carefully selected approved applications), then you can turn off this option.

Internet Explorer Security

Internet Explorer has been around for a little over a decade and has been riddled with security holes to such a degree that over the past few years, it has been losing ground to other browsers on the market, such as Mozilla's Firefox browser. With the release of IE 7, Microsoft attempts to recapture the market by matching the feature set of newer browsers and also plugging up the holes. We discuss the features (including tabbed browsing) and more in Chapter 10, "Group Policy Power," but for now let's talk security.

> **NOTE:** Internet Explorer 7 can be downloaded for XP, but keep in mind that many of the advanced security features work only in Vista because of the new security architecture.

One point to mention with IE 7 is that IE is no longer integrated with Windows Explorer. Now, when you perform an operation such as opening a file or trying to view a web page, each process takes over and performs its own task; they are not joined and this is a major security enhancement.

Protected Mode

We are going to discuss Windows Defender momentarily, but on the antispyware/malware front, IE 7 helps to protect us by having a new Protected Mode. This works off the UAC features we discussed earlier, which has IE working under a low Integrity setting so that—aside from searching the Web—a standard user cannot do much more than that. No software installation (or worse, malware sneakily installing itself), no file changes without you being aware, no changing your home page or search engine settings…in short, none of the things that make you want to scream. This is because IE 7 is only allowed to play in its own sandbox, isolated from all the other applications or processes. Data can only be written to the Temporary Internet Files folder, and this folder is also given a low integrity, so a fence is put around it as well.

Now, what happens when a program wants to get out from under this protection? Let's say you download something and you really do want it to run. A broker process asks for your permission so you definitely know what is going on and have to approve it before it can write anywhere other than the Temporary Internet Files. That's right—no malware sneaking in without your permission (so be sure you read the boxes that display and ask you for permission; don't just arbitrarily say yes).

> **NOTE:** As great as Protected Mode is, you can turn it off (not that this is recommended). Go to your IE settings by selecting Tools, Internet Options, the Security tab. You can disable a check box labeled Enable Protected Mode (Requires Restarting Internet Explorer).

What happens when Protected Mode is disabled? Internet Explorer has the same capability as your user account, which is a much more dangerous scenario.

What if you absolutely need to access certain things through IE and you are having way too much trouble going through the UAC/Protected Mode road blocks? For example, certain banking websites have been giving users trouble through IE7 with Vista. You can disable the UAC or the Protected Mode, or you can right-click IE and choose to run it as an Administrator, which starts the application with a higher integrity level. This might or might not resolve these issues with your bank. Another idea is to try a different browser and see if this fixes the problem.

To consider some other ways for your XP systems to run browsers in a more protected environment, try the tool Drop My Rights created by Michael Howard of Microsoft. Here is a site that explains a little more about this tool and others for browser (IE, Firefox, and so on) safety: http://cybercoyote.org/security/drop.shtml.

The Phishing Filter

Protecting users from phishing is part education of your users, part technology. The scenario is simple: A user gets an email from a bank (possibly even what appears to be his own bank) or another merchant that is familiar to him (such as Amazon, eBay, or PayPal), asking for some information. If the user thinks the site is valid and doesn't know how to determine otherwise, he is at risk of providing information that may be sensitive to his financial or personal identity. The user might enter his information. Typically, the site then redirects the user to the real company site so the user doesn't even know he has been tricked.

These sites look so real sometimes that it can be very difficult for people to know otherwise. The Phishing Filter helps by notifying users if a site is suspicious. It can do this by comparing the site you type in to a list of known phishing sites already on your computer. If you type in a site that isn't on that list but seems suspicious, the computer checks that site automatically, too. Sites are sent to a Microsoft server for confirmation. This provides up-to-the-minute security for users because these servers are updated constantly with new phishing sites. This global database is maintained by a list of providers, as well as user reports that come in from users who stumble on sites that appear "phishy."

Because the phishing filter is not a Vista-specific feature, it works in XP or any other OS on which you can install IE7.

What Happens When You Go to a Suspicious or Bad Site?

When you come upon a site that the phishing filter knows is a scam, the Address Bar turns red and a Phishing Website message displays in the Security Report area, as shown in Figure 4.3. You'll notice that it recommends you don't proceed but still gives you the option to go forward if you choose to.

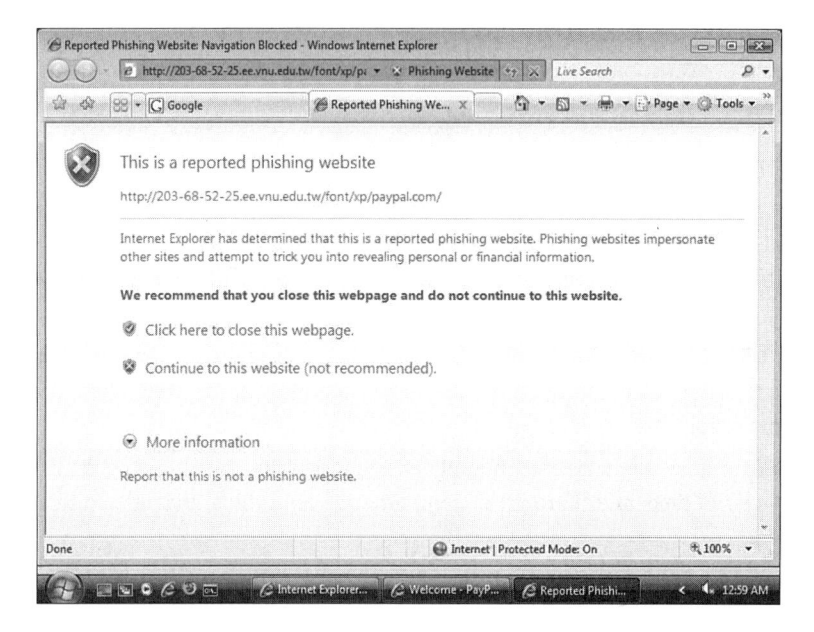

FIGURE 4.3
Hook, line, and sinker. We say no thanks.

Note that if you decide to turn off the automatic filter, you can still check the validity of a site by selecting Tools, Phishing Filter, Check This Website. Just keep in mind that sometimes sites might not be registered with the Microsoft servers. It's not a perfect science, and if you are looking at a new site, it might not have it in the database. That's why the following tips about what else to look for in a phishing site are also important. If you do come upon a site you think is a scam, you can use the Report link to have Microsoft check it out officially for future visitors.

> **NOTE**
> If you happen to come upon a site that isn't clearly a phishing site but IE is suspicious for some reason, the Address Bar background turns yellow and a Suspicious Website message appears in the Security Report section.

156 Tricks of the Windows Vista Masters

Terri Stratton
Microsoft MVP

You can also report sites that are legitimate but may show as phishing or suspicious. One scenario where this might happen is when a site hasn't registered all domains and sub-domains with both the www and without, for example, http://www.domainname?.com will resolve correctly, but http://domainname?.com could prompt the warning.

What to Watch For

There are a few things users can do beyond trusting the technology to protect them from phishing sites. If a site makes them nervous, they can also use the phishing tool to check on that site manually. Anyone who browses the Web should always be aware of the following:

- **Address Bar URL**—If a user sees the IP address rather than a real name or sees sites that look partly correct using part of the name of the company or incorrect wording, she should become suspicious.

- **Page links**—Some links might be real, but others might be fake. If a user moves her cursor over a variety of links and there is no continuity between them, that should raise red flags, too.

- **View the source of the form submittal**—Usually you have to type information into a form and send it off. Teach users how to view the source of a form and match the button's address action to the site it supposedly is sending information to. So, if you think it's going to citibank.com and it's really going to imgoingtostealyourmoney.com, that's a big tip off.

- **Obvious text or graphical anomalies**—The truth is that these guys are good. You usually won't find too many mistakes on a site that has been created by professionals. But, for the amateurs, you might catch mistakes in spelling (or a site such as bankland.com could be represented as bank1and.com using the 1 instead of an *l*). With graphics, you might even see free web hosting advertisements and so forth, which is not normal for a respected banking institution or merchant to use.

> **NOTE**
> Another common trick these days is to mix character sets within a URL. This allows a spoofer to present users with websites that can look exactly like the real thing but use a foreign language character set to fool the user. Even though it's not viewable to your eye the computer will actually be sending you to the false site. IE7 now notifies a user when this happens. This feature is enabled by default and functions with or without the phishing filter being turned on.

- **SSL icon**—Sensitive data is encrypted and sent through a secure socket layer. Users don't need to understand the hows and whys of it all, but they should be trained to look for the lock icon in the status bar that tells them everything is secure for sending sensitive data. This isn't the most important thing, though, because scammers know how to set up their own SSL servers with IIS, so even a bad site can appear correct. Again, the professionals will have this covered, and the amateurs won't.

> **NOTE**
>
> One trick scammers use involves covering over the IE address bar with a minimized version of another IE window that displays the address of the real site. If it is overlaying the fake address just right, your users see only the real address. For this reason, you need to prevent pop-ups, too.
>
> Another new feature in IE7 is that the address bar is never hidden, even in pop-ups. This is because the address is the easiest way to see whether a site is bogus, so if a window displays with no window, you won't know whether the address is real. Now, IE7 takes that capability away from scammers.

Some Additional IE Security Features

There are a few more security features that every user of Vista should know about. The next three sections detail the most crucial of these.

Use of Add-Ons

Add-ons include the likes of ActiveX controls, browser extensions, browser helper objects or toolbars, and so forth. Sometimes we love certain add-ons, such as Flash players, because it expands the standard capability of IE to give us more animated or interesting content. However, some add-ons can cause problems, cause pop-ups, or even contain spyware.

Sandi Hardmeier
http://www.ie-vista.com/
Content courtesy of
http://msmvps.com/blogs/spywaresucks/archive/2006/04/02/88876.aspx

One of the lesser known features of Internet Explorer 7 is the "No Add Ons" mode. A shortcut is automatically added to the All Programs Menu in the System Tools folder (All Programs, Accessories, System Tools) when Internet Explorer 7 is installed. Alternatively, you can create a shortcut on your desktop or Quick Launch bar with the following target path:

"C:\Program Files\Internet Explorer\iexplore.exe" -extoff

Primarily a troubleshooting tool, No Add Ons mode allows you to start IE with all add-ons such as toolbars and activex controls disabled. If you are seeing problems when using IE in normal mode, and those problems go away when using No Add Ons mode, then obviously a third party product is at issue.

In addition, you can control the add-ons allowed within IE7 by selecting the Tools option and selecting Manage Add-Ons, Enable or Disable Add-Ons.

ActiveX Opt-In

The number-one security concern for most people is basically that ActiveX controls can be very unsafe. They can install quietly and be a real nightmare to get rid of. With the ActiveX Opt-in feature, you can approve which ones will run.

The way it works is when you go to a website, ActiveX controls are disabled by default (unless they meet the requirements in the following list). You are presented with a warning screen that asks whether you want to run the control or gather some more information regarding it.

ActiveX controls that are not disabled are as follows:

- Common controls that are on a preapproved list because they have been tested and are considered safe.
- Those controls that are downloaded from IE7 are considered secure.

Enabling or disabling the ActiveX Opt-in is done on a zone-by-zone basis through the IE security settings. The option Allow Previously Unused ActiveX Controls to Run Without Prompt lets you enable or disable.

URL Handling Protections

This is not a configurable feature but one you should be aware of. There is a new URL parser. Attackers used to take advantage of a technique that allowed executions of code within a URL. A standard method was to have a long URL that would cause a buffer overflow and then, at the right moment, position a command to execute. It can sound

> **TIP**
> You can go to a website, have a problem, and spend forever trying to figure out why it's not working. For instance, maybe it worked before but doesn't work now. You start blaming Microsoft, IE7, Vista, Bill Gates, and so forth, but try running your IE with No Add-ons first. If this resolves your problem with the site—even though it's not the way you want to run IE all the time—you know you have a problem with a third-party product, not IE. You can then use the Manage Add-Ons tool to disable all your add-ons and then go back and enable them one at a time until you determine what is causing your problem.

crazy, but it worked. Fixes were made and other exploits found, but IE7 now checks the URL's reliability before letting it execute within your browser.

CardSpace/InfoCard—Don't Leave Home Without It

Discussing the concept of digital identities can be difficult with the average computer user. One writer mentioned that we have different forms of personal identity—for example, a passport, a driver's license, a credit card, a Social Security card, a birth certificate, and so forth. Each one of these is used in different situations, and some can be used in multiple situations—for instance, when buying items, you can use that credit card more than once.

Some of our identities are made up, whereas others are given by a valid authority. For example, you might tell someone your nickname and that's how you will be remembered—that's your created identity. Whereas if you are given a credit card, that's a form of identity provided by an outside agency.

Your online identities are important to maintain as well. And we have no shortage of these. So, the problem occurs when a variety of digital identities are provided by a variety of sources, and there will never be a way to control all of that. So, instead of trying to control it, Microsoft has decided that what's really needed is an identity metasystem. Microsoft and others have been working together to create this metasystem to define the standards necessary to make this work. The end result in Vista (and there will be an add-on for XP and Server 2003) is CardSpace (code-named InfoCard). Microsoft says its goal in promoting this system and encouraging vendors and others to use it is to "let people on any machine, running any operating system, use digital identities as easily, as effectively, and as securely as they today use their identities in the physical world."

To read a bit more about the development process and the underlying architecture for CardSpace, check out this article from the MSDN site: http://msdn2.microsoft.com/en-us/library/aa480189.aspx

You might still be wondering, "But what IS CardSpaces?"

Imagine it's like a wallet. Your wallet contains a variety of identities you use in the real world. The wallet isn't a new form of identity; it holds the identities. CardSpaces allows you to choose from a portfolio of digital identities. Some you perhaps created yourself, and others you can obtain from merchants, banks, and so forth. This is a new technology, so it might take a while for it to catch on. Figure 4.4 shows the card management console.

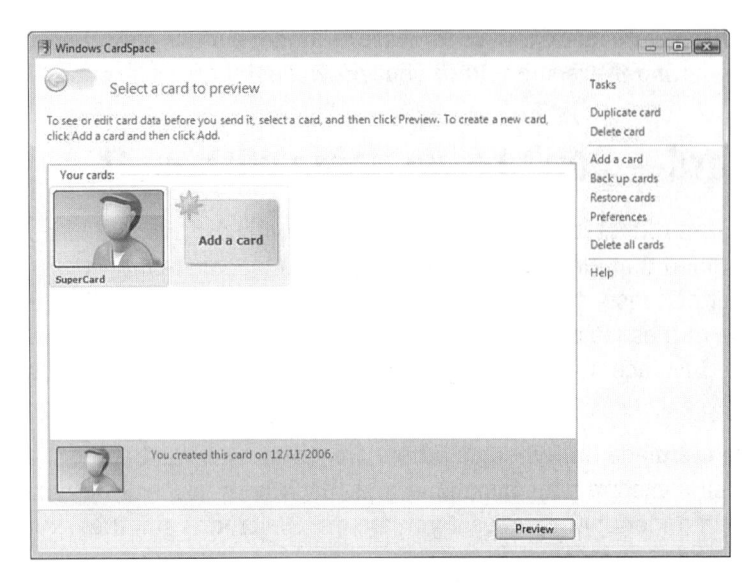

FIGURE 4.4
Create, delete, duplicate, back up, and restore your digital identities.

These four aspects are considered the most important:

- **Support for any digital identity system**—Basically, different systems have different requirements and provide different tokens to the user for access. There is no way to guarantee that Amazon is going to use the same structure as another merchant, and that's okay. The key is that both merchants understand and implement the same support for the identifiers so you can go to each site and present the identity for that site without a problem.

- **User control of digital identity**—In some cases you create your own identities (such as with your email sites and with a variety of merchants). You can also receive identities from other institutions. You maintain these yourself on your system and then can choose which identity to send the merchant you are accessing. When you access the merchant, you are presented with a screen that asks you to choose a particular InfoCard. Microsoft wants to make this whole process easy enough so that even new and inexperienced users can do it. After a card is chosen, CardSpace makes a request to the identity provider for a security token.

- **No more password-based login for websites**—The idea behind this is that users access sites with their self-made usernames and passwords. Although this is encrypted for many sites, phishing is still a very popular way to steal the identities of others. With CardSpace, you can create your own identity with specific information that you include and the website agrees upon, but with no password. This is still not a perfect solution because phishing sites can still accept your identity token and learn important information.

- **Increased confidence in the website**—People have been tricked, so now they are afraid. In the past, SSLs have worked to help alleviate some of that fear so users now check their browsers for the little lock that shows them that they are in a secure session. But this doesn't mean the site isn't a bogus one with SSL implemented. What's really needed is a new way for sites to identify who they are—a new form of certificate validation so the user can be confident she isn't dealing with a scam site.

> **Identity Management Pitfalls**
>
> Identity management, identity theft…who doesn't have concerns? Movies portray it as so easy for a person to steal your "identity" and have you in huge amounts of debt or make you take the fall for crimes committed in your name that many people are scared to death. For this new concept to work, vendors and such need to support it and users need to be able to easily understand it. No, not you, the person reading this book, but if your grandma uses a computer and goes to websites, she is the target audience for this kind of technology. It has to be simple and functional without requiring you to be an identity management expert. Unfortunately, until it's out for a while, we won't be able to see if that's going to happen.
>
> One thing CardSpace does to ensure that your privacy is intact when using CardSpace is run in its own desktop. This means that, when you are running CardSpace, everything else stops and no other applications can function or interact with it.

Windows Defender

First, what is Windows Defender? It's Microsoft's answer to spyware (keyloggers, bots, rootkits, and so on). It's a relatively simple tool (with an easy-to-use dashboard) that can be used to perform an immediate scan of your system to look for the latest spyware and eliminate it from your system. Or, you can have it working in the background to stop spyware from infiltrating your system ahead of time.

> **TIP** Some of us leave our systems on 24/7. If you don't, you should know that Defender is set up by default to scan your system at 2 a.m. each day. You might want to adjust this to work with your schedule. To change that, go to the Tools menu and select Options. Then change the Automatic scanning Approximate Time.

Spyware can do any number of things to annoy you and slow down your system, such as displaying pop-up ads, altering your

Internet settings, and even using private information without permission. Beneath the simple dashboard of Defender, the underlying engine is constantly working in the background to protect you, even looking into Zip files (or other archive file formats) to see whether you have harmful software within, even before you open the files (which is a huge benefit because many spyware/malware creators use archive installers).

SpyNet

One of the benefits to Microsoft being so large, with such a huge install base, is that a group of people from all over the world called SpyNet are assisting in finding new spyware and other harmful programs and reporting them to Microsoft. SpyNet essentially allows for a voting option on software that hasn't been categorized as harmful or safe. You will be able to see how other users have rated the application and what percentage installed it or declined to install it. This gives users a greater opportunity to be in control of what is installed on their systems at a much earlier stage than before. If Microsoft sees that people are uninstalling a particular type of software, it can check it out itself and add that to its definitions of software that Defender automatically detects.

> **NOTE**
> Initial versions of Windows Defender included the capability to browse downloaded ActiveX controls and a Tracks Eraser (which could erase application tracks for Microsoft or other third-party applications), but these have been removed. IE 7 allows you to view and lock down ActiveX controls as we discussed earlier.
>
> It's also good to remember that Defender is not an antivirus protection software. However, you will still need to get yourself some good antivirus protection, even with Defender.

Vista Masters run in packs sometimes. SpyNet is an optional club (or gang, whichever makes you feel cooler about participating). You can choose not to be a part of it at all, or you can choose Basic or Advanced membership by selecting Tools and then SpyNet.

With Basic, Defender sends Microsoft some information regarding software it encounters on your system that isn't classified. You aren't alerted if Defender detects software or changes made by software that have not been analyzed for risks.

With Advanced, Defender does notify you if it detects software or changes made by software that have not been analyzed for risks. Windows Defender sends more information to SpyNet about spyware discoveries made on your computer, including filenames and directories, how the software works, and changes that it makes to your computer—information that is used to help warn and protect other Windows Defender users.

Advanced Defender Information

The truth is that Defender was designed for simplicity, so you might be fooled into thinking it only scans and that's it. But additional tools are included and there are a few tricks you need to know to allow your applications to work with Defender at times.

Advanced Options

From within the Defender dashboard, you can select the Tools button and it will take you to the Tools and Settings area. From here, you can select Options, which allows you to configure how you want Defender to run. We mentioned previously that you can change the time setting for when it runs.

You can turn real-time protection on or off. You can also determine the security agents you want to run (that is, Auto Start, IE Settings, Services and Drivers, and so forth) and notification settings, along with files/folders you want skipped over.

Application Exclusion

Sometimes you might have a conflict between an application you personally choose to run and Windows Defender. I recently came across a poster who asked the following question on one of the techs sites that I frequent:

> "I have an application I've permitted to work with my firewall exceptions called Comcast Rhapsody, and Windows Defender continues to ask me about it. How do I let Defender know to permit this application?"

The answer to that question is that you need to exclude the application from the scan. To do this, select Tools, open the Options dialog box, scroll down to Advanced Options, and click the Add button to find the application you want to exclude from the scan. It's important to know what you are excluding. If you exclude a folder, that folder and all subfolders are excluded from scans (both manual and automatic) as well as real-time protection and even the software explorer. So, if you want to leave yourself that open, you may, but we recommend you specifically choose the application you need Windows Defender to ignore.

Command-line Defender

In the event you need to, you can also run Windows Defender from command-line parameters. For example, you can type `%ProgramFiles%\Windows Defender\MSASCui.exe -Hide -CheckForUpdates` to hide the Windows Defender window and also check for updates. You can use a variety of commands, including `-QuickScan`, `-FullScan`, and so forth.

Group Policy and Defender

Another cool thing in Vista is the capability to now use Group Policies to control things we couldn't before. Windows Defender Settings are now built in to the policies for Vista.

From the Group Policy Object Editor (from the Start Orb, type `gpedit.msc`), browse to the following path: `<Policy>\Computer Configuration\Administrative Templates\Windows Components\Windows Defender`.

Here are the policies available:

- Turn on definition updates through both WSUS and Windows Update.
- Check for New Signatures Before Scheduled Scans.
- Turn off Windows Defender.
- Turn off Real-Time Protection Prompts for Unknown Detections.
- Enable Logging Known Good Detections.
- Enable Logging Unknown Detection.
- Download Entire Signature Set.
- Configure Microsoft SpyNet Reporting.

Software Explorer

The most interesting feature in Defender is a tool called Software Explorer. Software Explorer shows you the programs you have set to start up on Vista or those that are currently running. You can view network-connected programs and Winsock service providers as well.

How does this benefit you? When you run Task Manager, you usually see processes you recognize pretty quickly; others you might have to research to know why they are running but there will be some that will come up as `svchost.exe` applications. This doesn't help you to know what these really are because they are shells that surround executable DLLs. Task Manager doesn't tell you what's inside those `svchost.exe` shells, but as you can see from Figure 4.5, the Software Explorer does.

Software Explorer gives you basic details and allows you (when possible) to end a process or go to Task Manager with the click of a button.

Here are some of the types of information provided through Software Explorer:

- **Auto Start**—This lets you know whether the program will start with Vista automatically.
- **Startup Type**—This provides the location where the program is registered to start, for

example, the All Users Startup Folder or the Registry and so forth.

- **Ships with Operating System**—This is a nice touch because if it ships as part of the Vista installation, that should make you feel better about it because you know it's not harmful (hopefully).
- **Classification**—Lets you know whether the application has been reviewed for potential risks to your privacy and security.
- **Digitally Signed By**—Lets you know whether the application has been signed and by whom. Microsoft recommends you trust only software that has been signed or vouched for by a third party.

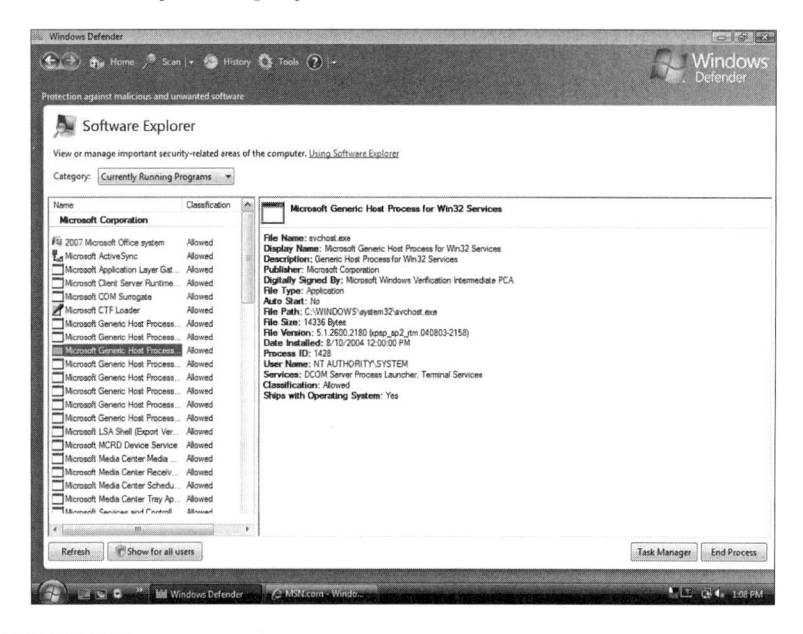

FIGURE 4.5
Software Explorer gives you more control over processes running.

You can alter the way information is presented to you. You can choose different categories and also determine whether you want applications shown to you based on the publisher or the startup type (which lets you know whether it's started by the computer or the user).

> **NOTE:** You can learn more about using Windows Defender from http://www.microsoft.com/athome/security/spyware/software/support/howto/softwareexplorer.mspx.

Beyond Windows Defender

There are other tools on the market for spyware/malware protection and for viewing processes running on your system. There is no way to list them all and give opinions on each—plenty of magazines do updates on the latest software and their feature sets. However, one tool has caught our eye. The legendary Mark Russinovich has created a tool called AutoRuns. A graphical version and a command-line version of the tool are available. The first time you run it and see what it does, you are bound to gasp (see Figure 4.6). The detail it offers is really incredible. For another tool that shows processes and threads (if you care to go that deep with your system), check out the new tool Process Monitor v1.0.

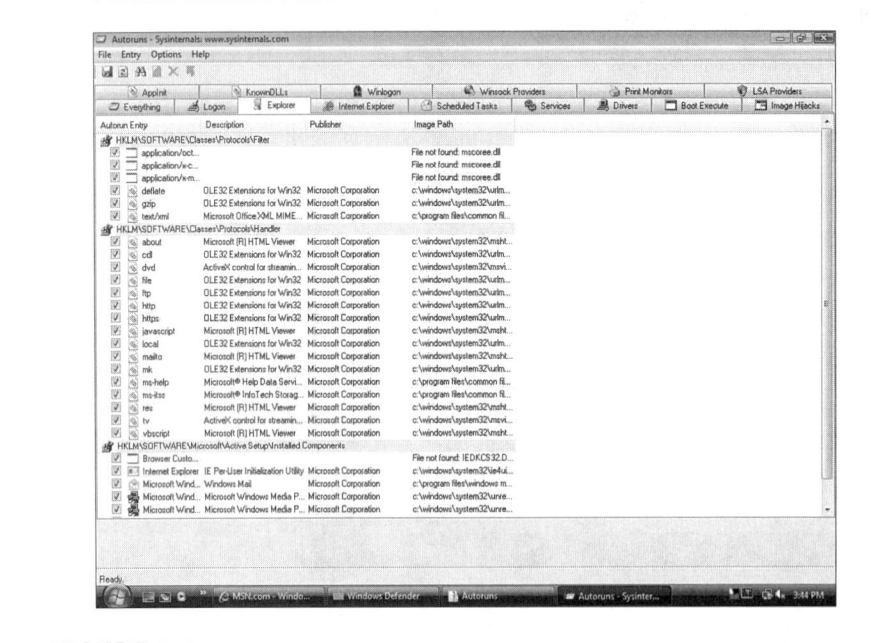

FIGURE 4.6
AutoRuns will blow you away with the amount of detail about your system.

AutoRuns shows you the auto-starting locations for all the programs that are configured to start during the boot process or during your login. AutoRuns shows you much more than the MSConfig utility (which some believed was removed from Vista, but it still exists and is an excellent tool). After you run AutoRuns, it shows you startup applications and a list of Registry and file system locations for your applications. These include logon entries; Explorer add-ons; IE add-ons, including Browser Helper Objects (BH's); and a host of other things, including Windows Services and Winsock Layered Service

Providers. You can see everything all at once or switch to the tab that contains the section you need most. If you want to disable any of the items, you just uncheck the box next to it. You can delete the entry as well. There is a lot you can do with this tool, so enjoy!!!

> **NOTE** There are plenty of other tools to work with from Sysinternals that allow you to see system resource usage and configuration, as well as troubleshoot Windows. Sysinternals was purchased by Microsoft, but the tools are still available through the Microsoft site at http://www.microsoft.com/technet/sysinternals/default.mspx.

The Malicious Software Removal Tool— Postinfection Removal

The Malicious Software Removal Tool (MSRT) Postinfection Removal most likely sounds both gross and cool at the same time. The fact is people either don't have antivirus stuff installed or don't update their signatures. Either way, bad things happen to good computer users, and Microsoft, although not an antivirus maker, doesn't want MyDoom running on its OS. It's bad for business. So, it gave us the MSRT, not as a preventative tool, not to scan our files and protect us 24/7, but to scan system memory to see whether anything is currently running that is on its list. If it finds something bad, it crushes the process that caused it and deletes files or Registry keys associated with it, but it does not go searching for other instances of it like an antivirus software should do.

Here is what Microsoft has to say about its tool:

> The Microsoft Windows Malicious Software Removal Tool checks computers running Windows XP, Windows 2000, and Windows Server 2003 for infections by specific, prevalent malicious software—including Blaster, Sasser, and Mydoom—and helps remove any infection found. When the detection and removal process is complete, the tool displays a report describing the outcome, including which, if any, malicious software was detected and removed.
>
> Microsoft releases an updated version of this tool on the second Tuesday of each month, and as needed to respond to security incidents. The tool is available from Microsoft Update, Windows Update, and the Microsoft Download Center.

To see a list of malicious software families that Microsoft has already focused on with the MSRT, check out this site: http://www.microsoft.com/security/malwareremove/families.mspx

Microsoft provides you with different ways of running MSRT on your system: using Windows Update, the Microsoft Download Center, or an online version of the tool. It's your choice.

When the tool runs in the background (as it usually does without you even being aware of it; it's called quiet mode), it keeps a log for itself located in the `%windir%\debug\mrt.log`.

The log looks something like this:

```
Microsoft Windows Malicious Software Removal Tool v1.20, September 2006
Started On Wed Sep 13 16:02:55 2006
Results Summary:
————————
No infection found.
Return code: 0
Microsoft Windows Malicious Software Removal Tool Finished On Wed Sep 13
16:03:06 2006
———————————————————————————————————
———————.
Microsoft Windows Malicious Software Removal Tool v1.21, October 2006
Started On Sat Oct 14 03:00:21 2006
Results Summary:
————————
No infection found.
Return code: 0
Microsoft Windows Malicious Software Removal Tool Finished On Sat Oct 14
03:00:33 2006
```

After the tool runs, it disappears until the next version is released. Or you could just run the tool manually or online and you'll see results immediately.

In addition to the log file, you can also check the Registry to see whether the tool has run:

```
Subkey: HKEY_LOCAL_MACHINE\SOFTWARE\Microsoft\RemovalTools\MRT
Entry name: Version <GUID> (1d21fa19-c296-4020-a7c2-c5a9ba4f2356) - Note,
this is for the November 2006 version of the MSRT)
```

You can find the list of version GUIDs on http://support.microsoft.com/?kbid=891716&SD=tech#E2ACAAA in the FAQ section.

In addition, at that link, you can find information regarding Deployment of the Microsoft Windows Malicious Software Removal Tool in an enterprise environment. Some options provided include scripting it to run on your systems (a sample login or startup script is provided). You can also use SMS to deploy the tool. If you have Active Directory running your enterprise, you can also use Group Policies to deploy the tool.

Some might not like the infection report being sent back to Microsoft, although this helps Microsoft to see what malicious software is being detected and to what degree it is spreading. But you can turn this off in the Registry.

Add the following Registry value to the system:

```
Subkey: HKEY_LOCAL_MACHINE\SOFTWARE\Policies\Microsoft\MRT
Entry name: \DontReportInfectionInformation
Type: REG_DWORD
Value data: 1
```

If the computer is connected to an SUS server, this functionality is already disabled because of the following Registry key value:

```
HKEY_LOCAL_MACHINE\SOFTWARE\Policies\Microsoft\Windows\WindowsUpdate\WUServer
```

Windows Firewall

Windows Firewall in Vista goes well beyond the XP version because in XP only inbound traffic is blocked, allowing outbound traffic to go unmonitored. That was a big complaint for the XP firewall because various forms of malware and such make outbound connections without users' knowledge. That left many security-conscious XP users with no choice but to use a third-party solution such as ZoneAlarm, which is capable of blocking both inbound and outbound traffic. With Windows Vista's improved firewall, you can block outgoing traffic, too.

When you first open Windows Firewall, though, you might feel betrayed because it looks almost the same as the XP version. Where are the Outbound settings? Apparently, during beta, complaints were made that the two-way firewall was complicated, so Microsoft hid the settings and turned it off by default.

To work with these Advanced settings, you can start your own customized MMC console and add the snap-in for it—but it's much easier to go through your Administrative Tools and select the Windows Firewall with Advanced Security option. You can also

> **TIP** If you are working with the MSRT tool and using a Windows Server Update Service (WSUS), you might not get the tool. You need to make sure you selected the Update Rollups to synchronize with MU. This is not done by default, so you have to be sure you select Update Rollups under Update Classifications.

> **TIP** To configure outbound connections and customize the Windows Firewall in various ways, type **wf.msc** from the Start orb, under Search.

configure through a command line from an elevated prompt using the `netsh avfirewall` command. But before we go into great detail on the latest and greatest Firewall options, let's quickly review the options for monitoring incoming traffic.

Windows Firewall (Simple Settings)

So, if you just open the Windows Firewall Control Panel applet, you are going to be met with a simple screen that you could have just as easily found (with a whole lot more information about other security features) from your Security Center. Your information screen tells you whether your firewall is on, whether it's working, how alerts are set, and which network location the firewall covers.

Selecting the Change Settings option displays a three-tabbed dialog box. The tabs are General, Exceptions, and Advanced. Let's go through these and see how they have changed or stayed the same with their XP SP2 counterparts. Seeing the two side-by-side is what is going to really help you ease into the new Firewall tool. It's not so scary.

> **NOTE**
> Having Firewall with Advanced Security work through an MMC console allows for some possibilities that were previously unavailable. This is because now you can configure your own personal settings or establish settings on a remote system or through Group Policy to affect a larger number of systems at once.

> **NOTE**
> You hear the term *stateful* or *stateful inspection* quite often with firewalls. Most people who don't know what that means will mumble something like, "hmmm...stateful...yes, right." Vista Masters know what it means—not intuitively but because they looked it up on Google and Wikipedia. It's a technology and concept that ensures that all inbound packets are the result of an outbound request. For example, if you click a web page link, you are making an HTTP request and can therefore receive information back. Another example is your email application, which makes a query to a mail server. The goal is to avoid having packets coming in without you making a request. There are exceptions you can configure, as we discuss shortly, but now you have a handle on the terminology.

General Tab

From the General tab, you can turn your firewall on or off and select the Block All Incoming Connections options (see Figure 4.7). This last one is a good option if you are traveling and connecting to less-secure, public networks and need the added protection of not having exceptions. Exceptions are explained in greater detail in the next section.

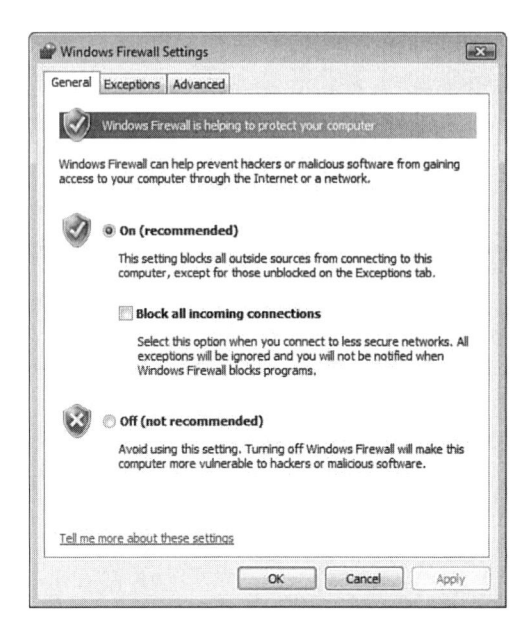

FIGURE 4.7
Use the General tab of the Windows Firewall Settings dialog box to enable and disable the firewall.

Exceptions Tab

You will want to allow certain programs through the firewall. The Exceptions tab lets you quickly select which programs those might be (see Figure 4.8). If you are unsure as to what a certain program does, you can select it and select Properties. For example, if you select Bits Peercaching and click the Properties button, a box appears that tells you about the program or port.

If you don't see the program you need, you can try to add it by clicking the Add Program button. Or, if you need to open a specific port, you can do that too by clicking the Add Ports button. For both programs and ports, you can configure the firewall to allow any computer (within your network or on the Internet) access through the firewall via a particular program. Or you can configure it to allow only your subnet (network) or even specific IP addresses (or a set of subnets).

> **NOTE:** All applications that communicate from your computer over the network or the Internet do not need to be in the exceptions list. If your computer initiates the communication, Windows Firewall creates what is called a *stateful* exception for that connection. This allows your device to communicate with the other device on required ports. So, you need to establish exceptions only when an external system initiates the communication to your computer.

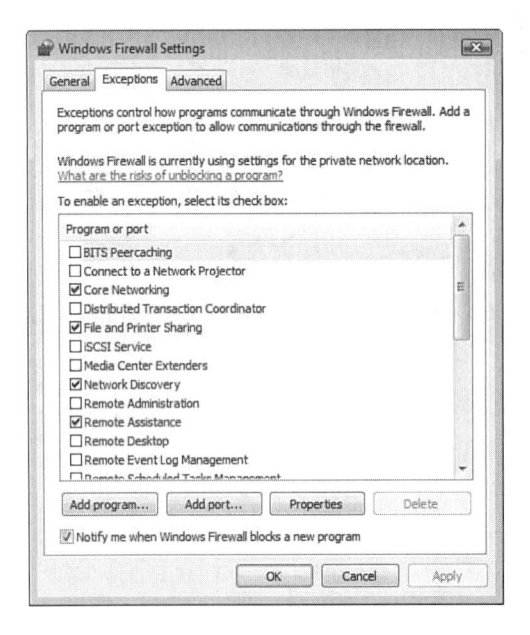

FIGURE 4.8
Use the Exceptions tab to permit specific programs or ports through the firewall.

Advanced Tab

This tab has seen something of an overhaul since Windows XP. The main reason is that in XP SP2 all the Advanced features left for Firewall had to be placed on that one tab. In Vista, you can choose the network connections you want protected and choose to restore defaults (see Figure 4.9).

Windows Firewall with Advanced Security

Advanced Firewall concepts could be an entire book in themselves (and they are). At the least, Microsoft and others have written some pretty long manuals to help users learn the ins-and-outs of firewall configuration.

Here is a good manual to start with (WF_AdvSec.doc): http://www.microsoft.com/downloads/details.aspx?FamilyId=DF192E1B-A92A-4075-9F69-C12B7C54B52B&displaylang=en.

But to get you moving in the right direction, let's discuss some of the more advanced aspects of Vista's new firewall.

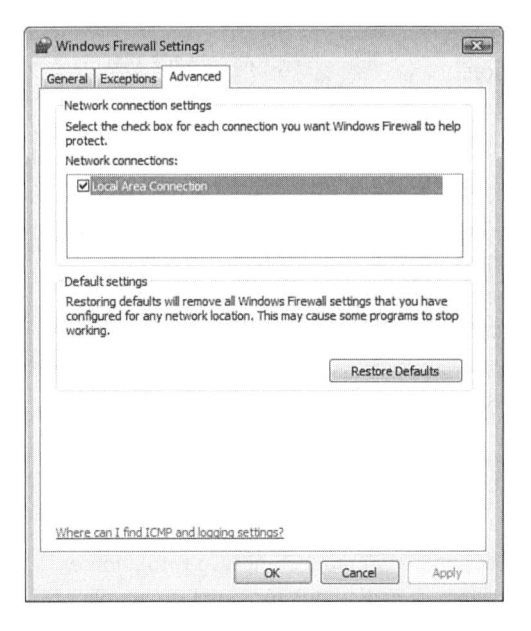

FIGURE 4.9
The Advanced tab enables you to choose which available networks you want the Windows Firewall to protect.

New Features of Vista's Firewall

Desktops sit still, but laptops are consistently moving. Obvious? Sure, but it still needs to be said because it's this mobility that makes portable systems vulnerable to new environments like an airport or Starbucks Wi-Fi connection. With the Windows Firewall, you can configure rules based on profiles that relate to three category settings:

- **Domain**—For when your computer is connected to an Active Directory domain.
- **Private**—For when a computer is connected to a network that has a private gateway or router.
- **Public**—For when a computer is connected directly to the Internet or to a network that isn't considered a private network or a domain.

The Vista Firewall is network-aware in the sense that it can determine based on the network (domain, private, public) the settings necessary to help protect the user for any given situation. Although that takes the lion's share of the workload off your shoulders, you are the one who needs to configure the policy that will be applied after the category network you are on is determined. Obviously, the more vulnerable the situation (such as a public Internet connection), the more strict the policy should be.

Another feature of the Vista Firewall is Authenticated Bypass. This enables you to use IPSec authentication to configure some systems to bypass rules you have in place. This gives you granular control over your rules. You can also create rules that are based on Active Directory (users, computers, or groups) using IPSec.

> **NOTE** IPSec is a protocol suite that secures IP packets by encryption and/or authentication methods. IPSec also includes protocols that allow for cryptographic key establishment. In Windows XP and Server 2003, the IPSec settings and Firewall settings are configured separately. In Vista, though, they fall under the same GUI and command-line options. Even the Group Policy settings are located in the same place in Vista, as you'll see in the next section.

There are also some more new features of the Windows Firewall that should be discussed here:

- **ICMP Blocking**—The Ping tool is used to send echo request messages to another network location to see whether the system or device being pinged is capable of responding and whether the connections to that device are configured properly. Although this makes it a useful troubleshooting tool, at the same time hackers can use these same requests to find likely targets for their attacks. You can block these messages going in to or out of your network.

- **Server and Domain Isolation**—This enables you to isolate servers using IPSec policies so that only permitted servers can communicate with your system. Domains can also be isolated using IPSec policies between clients and servers. To learn more about isolation concepts, see http://www.microsoft.com/sdisolation.

- **Network Access Protection**—Allows you to create health policies so a computer that doesn't pass its health standard is not capable of communicating with others. For example, if a system is not up-to-date with all its security patches, you can stop it from communicating on the network. To learn more about NAP see, http://www.microsoft.com/nap.

Working with the Advanced Firewall Settings

To work with the advanced settings found in the Windows Firewall, begin by opening your Administrative Tools and selecting Windows Firewall with Advanced Security. The MMC console that appears will look like the one in Figure 4.10.

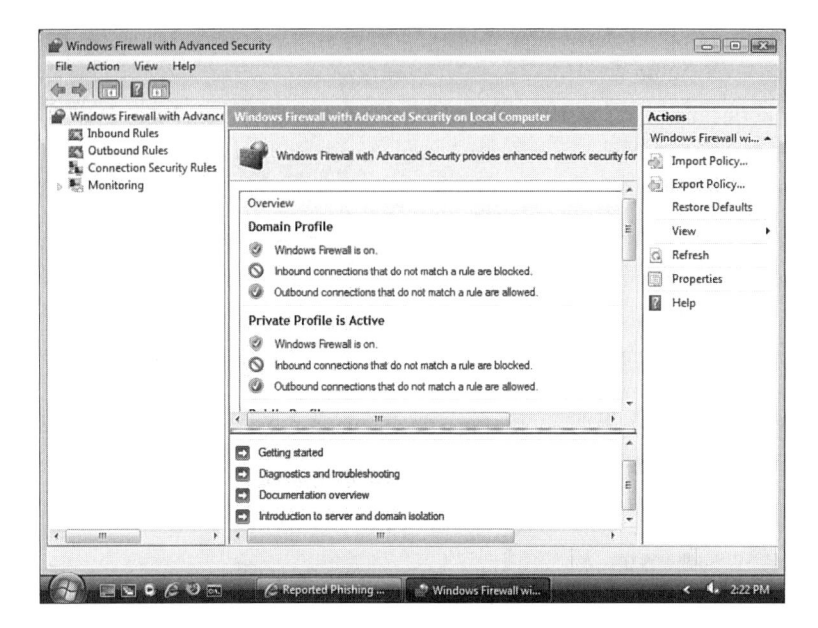

FIGURE 4.10
Windows Firewall with Advanced Security MMC console.

In the Overview pane you can see each profile category and how the settings look. The left pane enables you to view and create connection security rules. The Actions pane on the right gives you context-sensitive options. If you scroll down the Overview pane, you will see a link labeled Windows Firewall Properties. Selecting this link opens the Windows Firewall with Advanced Security on Local Computer dialog box (see Figure 4.11). This dialog box has four tabs, one for each profile (Domain, Private, and Public) and one for IPSec configurations.

Each of the profiles has the same types of settings, which makes learning what they do much easier for you. Here are the settings you can configure:

- **Firewall State**—Turns the firewall on or off for the profile tab you are configuring.
- **Inbound Connections**—Establishes one of three rules for your inbound connections. The Block (default) rule blocks connections that do not match any active rules. The Block All Connections rule ignores the rules and blocks everything. The Allow rule allows connections regardless of the firewall rules.
- **Outbound Connections**—You can choose to Allow or Block connections that do not match the firewall rules.

- **Settings**—Selecting the Customize button brings you to another dialog box with the following options (see Figure 4.12):
    - Display notifications to the user when a program is blocked from receiving inbound communications
    - Allow unicast response to multicast or broadcast network traffic
    - Apply local firewall rules (applies only when working with Group Policy)
    - Apply local connection security rules (applies only when working with Group Policy)
- **Logging**—Selecting the Customize button allows you to determine the location (the default is %windir%/pfirewall.log), the size of the log (the default is 4096KB), whether dropped packets should be logged (the default is no), or whether successful connections should be logged (the default is no).

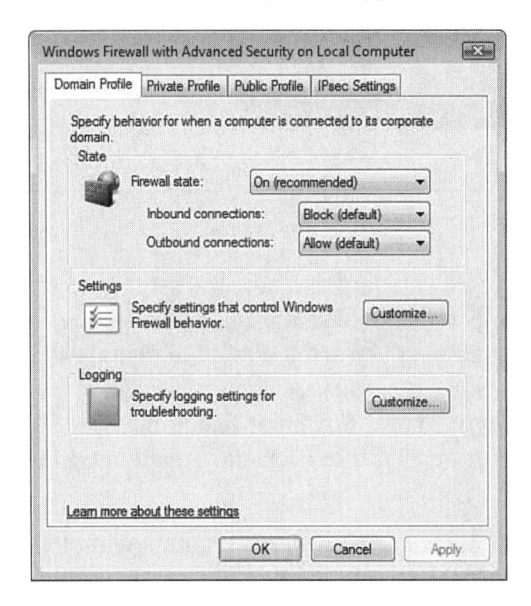

FIGURE 4.11
Windows Firewall Properties.

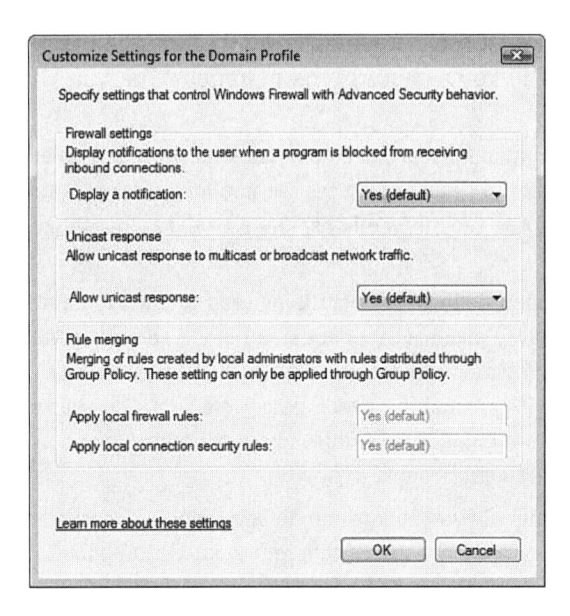

FIGURE 4.12
Customizing Firewall Profile settings.

The next set of options involves IPSec Settings, shown in Figure 4.13.

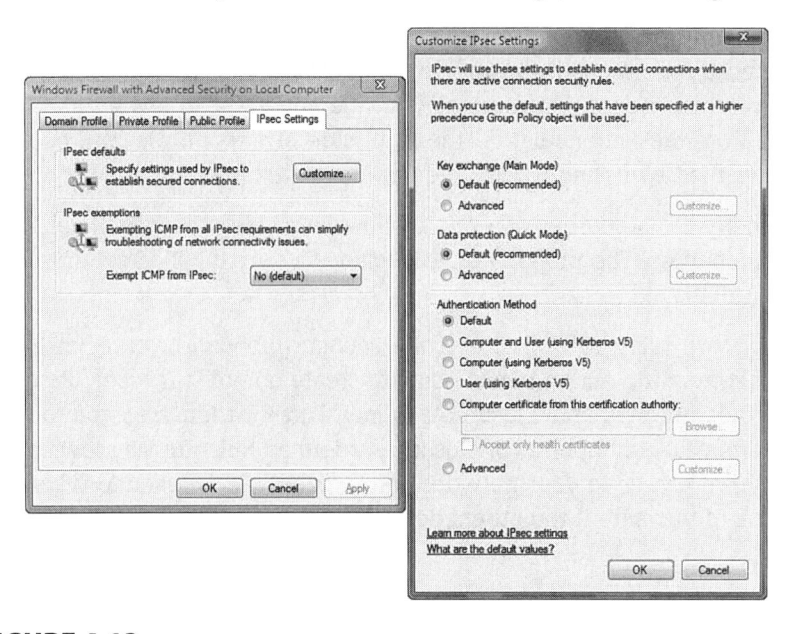

FIGURE 4.13
IPSec settings in Firewall.

Microsoft help documentation (noted previously) provides fairly thorough understanding of the features to IPSec settings. The key aspects of the help docs that you should remember:

- **Key Exchange**—To enable secure communication, two computers must be able to access the same shared key without transferring that key across the network. Clicking the Settings button allows you to configure security methods, key exchange algorithms, and key lifetimes.
- **Data Protection**—IPSec data protection defines the algorithms used to provide data integrity and encryption. Data integrity ensures that data is not modified during transit. Windows Firewall with Advanced Security uses the Authentication Header (AH) or Encapsulating Security Payload (ESP) protocol to provide data protection. Data encryption protects data by concealing the information. Windows Firewall with Advanced Security uses the ESP protocol for data encryption.
- **Authentication Method**—This setting lets you choose the default authentication method for IPSec connections on the local computer, unless a different method is applied by a specific rule or by Group Policy settings. The out-of-box authentication method is Kerberos v5. You can also restrict connections to domain-joined computers or users, or to computers that have a certificate from a specified Certificate Authority (CA).

Inbound and Outbound Rules

If you select the Inbound or Outbound rules options on the left side of the Windows Firewall with Advanced Security console, you are presented with a list of preconfigured rules from which you can choose. You can select a rule you want to enable and then select Enable Rule from the Actions list on the right side of the console. You can see whether a rule is enabled by noting if it is green or somewhat grayed out.

You can view or modify the properties of a rule by double-clicking the rule or selecting the rule and then Properties. The property sheet includes a very detailed set of tabs to configure the rule further.

You can create your own rules as well. Select the section (inbound or outbound) and then select New Rule from the Action menu. You can create one of four types: Program Rule (you pick the program path and executable name), Port Rule (enables you to fine-tune TCP or UDP ports you want opened or closed), Predefined Rule (for Windows functions you want to have access to your network), or Custom Rule (applies to whatever else you might think of to create if the others don't cover your needs).

Tips for Using the Vista Two-Way Firewall

Tip courtesy of VistaHunt.com

http://www.vistahunt.com/windows-vista-two-way-firewall.html

For the most part, incoming traffic can be configured from the standard Windows Firewall console from Control Panel. However, you can configure outbound rules only from within the Advanced Settings console.

Connection Security Rules

The Connection Security Rules section of the Windows Firewall with Advanced Security console lists any rules implemented to enforce a predetermined form of authentication between two computers before establishing a true connection. By default, IPSec is used between two systems to ensure security of the information transmitted.

When you select Connection Security Rules, there are no rules to start with. You have to add your own. So, you must select the New Rule option from the Actions pane. You are then presented with a list of options from which to choose, including

- **Isolation**—This restricts connections based on such criteria as domain membership or health status. You can choose different authentication methods, such as Kerberos or computer certificate. You can ensure that if those certificates aren't healthy (with NAP health policies), they won't be accepted.

- **Authentication Exemption**—This specifies computers that are exempt from connection authentication. You can do this through the IP address or an address range, a subnet, and so forth.

- **Server to Server**—This rule authenticates connections between computers you specify. You specify the endpoints, which can be one computer on each side or groups of computers that are trusted on each side.

- **Tunnel**—This rule is used to authenticate connections between gateway systems. Specified endpoints are handled through IP addresses. Authentication methods include certificates, preshared keys, or more advanced methods.

- **Custom**—If none of the other rule types is appropriate, you can create a custom rule.

> **TIP**
> When you are confident that your system is locked down, the best advice is to perform a security audit. Several good companies will do this for free. One company called Security Space gives you one free audit—and you will be amazed at how detailed the information they provide is. Check out http://www.securityspace.com to learn more.
>
> Another great firewall tester can be found at http://www.atelierweb.com/.

Vista Firewall Versus Third-Party Solutions

We mentioned earlier that both XP and Vista protect you with an incoming firewall. And with Vista, you can configure the outbound settings to protect you as well. True, the average user will not be able to truly understand the advanced settings; so, although it's a great feature, it's not a user friendly one. Some experts would recommend looking elsewhere then for a firewall solution, and we have to be honest in saying that this might not be a bad idea.

One important thing to remember with Vista is this: Just because the firewall provides a similar level of protection as XP SP2 at the beginning (before configuring outbound security), this does not mean the threat level is the same. Vista has so many other security features such as UAC control, Windows Defender, IE7 Protected Mode, and so forth (discussed earlier in the chapter), that even without outbound filtering, you get a tremendous improvement to your security.

That being said, our primary focus here is whether a third-party solution is necessary for outbound filtering and the types of filtering that are available.

The best third-party solution recommended is ZoneAlarm Pro (www.zonelabs.com). This software is not only useful for its firewall, but also includeidentity theft protection, spy site blocking, privacy protection, and a new feature called Game mode (for when you are playing and do not want to be disturbed during the game). For years, ZoneAlarm has gotten good ratings from *Personal Computer World* and CNet.com, amongst many others. One of the key compliments, besides its feature set, is that the interface is easy to use (unlike the Vista interface for advanced settings). The main complaint is that ZoneAlarm usually has conflicts with other software on a system and workarounds are necessary to ensure everyone plays nice together.

Some other good possibilities for third-party firewalls include:

- Outpost Firewall Pro from Agnitum (generally ranked number 2)
- Kerio Personal Firewall from Sunbelt (considered the best budget solution)
- Norton Personal Firewall
- McAfee Personal Firewall Pro

In addition to these products, there are quite a few free firewalls you might consider.

ZoneAlarm offers a free firewall that reviewers like, but for the best free firewall (according to *PC Magazine*), you need to check out the Comodo Personal Firewall (www.comodogroup.com). Reviewers liked the interface, it passed a number of leak tests, and it resists being terminated (an important firewall feature).

You might also check out Jetico Personal Firewall (www.jetico.com), which outperformed even commercial products in leak tests—although some felt that it was too complicated, which is the same problem with the Vista Firewall.

Chapter 5

DISK CONFIGURATION AND VOLUME TRICKS

Vista File System Review

In the years between the launch of Windows Vista and the release of Windows XP, one of the more anticipated features of Vista was a new file system called WinFS. About two years before Vista's release, however, Microsoft announced that WinFS was being pulled from Vista's feature list. There is an entire MSDN blog discussion dedicated to the subject of the Windows Vista file system development and WinFS, covering such topics as is WinFS a file system, what happened to it, and so forth. Let's review the story from the beginning.

In the beginning Bill Gates created Windows...well, actually before that was MS-DOS, which was really QDOS, which was based on CP/M-80... but I digress. Windows was eventually created, borrowed, bought, whatever. Operating systems need to be installed on hard drives, and those drives need to have file systems. Why? Because there has to be a way to store and locate information on those rapidly spinning platters. The question is how? That's where the file system comes into play.

IN THIS CHAPTER

Vista File System Review

Disk Management

Understanding NTFS Permissions

EFS and BitLocker

ReadyDrive

Previous Versions

A hard disk is one form of data storage device, and generally your data is written to sectors (also called *blocks*) in 512-byte sections. A file system keeps track of which sectors are used and which sectors aren't. It also holds a table that indicates which files are in which sectors. Operating systems come with built-in file systems to organize data. Windows specifically supports the latest flavors of these two file systems:

- **File Allocation Table (FAT)**—FAT was named after its design. A table keeps track of which area of your storage media is available for use, and which portions have data already written to them. This table makes it easier to find where portions of your data that make up a file are located. FAT has developed over the years to allow for longer filenames and larger hard disks. FAT32 is the latest version of this disk file system.

- **New Technology File System (NTFS)**—It was first introduced in Windows NT and has also undergone advances over the years. NTFS allows for permissions to be placed on specific folders or files, quotas, compression, mount points, and metadata. We discuss NTFS a little later, but this has been and continues to be in Vista the disk file system of choice.

The Rise and Fall of WinFS

Now that we've established the two primary Windows file system formats, what then is WinFS? Well, it was not meant to be the next DISK file system. WinFS actually stands for Windows Future Storage (and, yes, it was strange and misleading to use the *FS* part of the acronym but have it mean something else). Although disk file systems generally organize data in a hierarchical fashion (fancy words meaning you have folders inside folders in a hierarchy of data that the file system keeps track of), WinFS was meant to be more of a database file system. It would keep track of files based on their metadata (underlying information or data about the files, such as the author, the type of file, and so forth).

> **NOTE** What is said in the previous paragraph is factually correct. However, here is a comment from Quentin Clark, Director of Program Management for the WinFS team, that gives us some cool insight on how it was perceived during development: "There is one factual bit—internally to the team WinFS was "File System" not "Future Storage"—while it's absolutely true as you say it's not really a disk file system, but rather layered on NTFS, our purpose of it was as a file system as most users understand them—the place their files are stored."

In the past you would search for a file by its name, maybe with an idea of which folder the file might be in, but under this new structure you could search for a file based on metadata (that you have to provide for the file for it to be indexed). The WinFS premise, which had been in development for many years, was to have data and metadata viewed in a relational database format. In other words, NTFS would still be the disk file system and the files would still be in physical locations on your hard disk, in physical sectors; however, WinFS would be capable of transcending the common view of that data and seeing how one piece related to another. This would allow some incredible possibilities with advanced searching, even beyond what Vista can do now.

For example, let's say you wanted to search for the phone numbers of all the people you emailed on Friday who also took pictures with you at the last office party. Sounds like a crazy example, but the point is that you are talking about your address book, your pictures, and your email being searched and having that data cross-checked with each other application for you to see the results. With FAT and NTFS, that was impossible to do, but WinFS was going to change that.

To make the relational concept real, you have to be able to see the connection. Think of photos of people I am meeting with today or this week, mail from customers who are currently high opportunities in my Customer Relationship Management (CRM) application, restaurants I have been to near this address (such as a friend's house), or pictures of my wife and I on a particular vacation that I also posted to a photo site. The data itself doesn't matter, but if I can think of a reason to connect it, WinFS should be able to query and return my search.

So, what happened to WinFS?

It's difficult to say for sure. Initially, although touted as one of the three main pillars of Vista, it was dropped from the Vista release because it wasn't ready to be included (although many beta testers said it was working pretty well). It was going to be released as a separate add-on, but then even that dream ended on June 23, 2006, when the WinFS Team announced that WinFS wouldn't be released as a separate feature and would instead have the technology used in other technologies like ADO.NET and future versions of SQL Server.

You can read the blog about WinFS's demise as a Vista feature at http://blogs.msdn.com/winfs/.

If you want to read more about WinFS, the Wikipedia site has a great deal more detail on the architecture and so forth at http://en.wikipedia.org/wiki/WinFS.

So, why are we discussing a feature that *isn't* in Vista? Mainly because of the hype that surrounded it. It's important to note that although Vista didn't ship with WinFS, the concept of being able to search metadata has definitely been enhanced in Vista, as we discussed in Chapter 1, "General Tips and Tricks of the Masters." Quentin Clark, on the WinFS blog site said the following "There are many great technical innovations the WinFS project has created–innovations that go beyond just the WinFS vision but are part of a broader Data Platform Vision the company is pursuing."

That Data Platform Vision was explained in greater detail by Paul Flessner, Senior Vice President of Microsoft, when he said "We have a vision to meet the needs of the coming data explosion and the next generation of data-driven applications. We see you, our customers, requiring a data platform that can store and manage all of the different varieties of data, XML, email, time/calendar, file, document, spatial, etc. You will be able to do this with security enhanced rich services such as: search, query, analysis, sharing, and synchronization. You will be able to access this data from birth to archive and on any device. So your smart-phone will be able to work with a mega-service in the cloud. This is the core of our vision, which we think of as *Your Data, Any Place, Any Time.*"

WinFS and SQL are the future of that primary vision, but Vista is a launching point for many of those goals.

Transactional NTFS and Transactional Registry

Before we get into the technical side of this let's put your mind at ease: You already know what a transaction is. You know when you go to buy something online and something goes wrong, that initial feeling that your order didn't go through but maybe that the site took your money anyway. But then you realize that the "transaction" failed and you feel better. This means that even though you selected the item, entered all your credit card information, and so forth, something went wrong. So, instead of the process partially completing, the entire transaction failed.

In contrast, you know when you try to upgrade your OS and something goes wrong, and your whole system is now unbootable, and you scream for a long time? That's a failure, too, but it's not a failed transaction. Part of the process failed causing the whole thing to be a failure, but it didn't undo the transaction, didn't go back in time to the point before the transaction took place. This is not a good thing for you or your system.

Hence, the need for transactional improvements. In truth, Microsoft cannot guarantee that things aren't going to fail from time to time for any number of reasons. But it can at least guarantee a consistent way for your system to handle the failure. That's where transactional NTFS and Registry comes into play.

A new piece of Vista is the Kernel Transaction Manager (KTM), which enables Vista to use transactions. Keep in mind that this entire feature is a developer feature. Yes, it protects the end user from pain, but the KTM allows developers to create installation code that requires the completion of the entire transaction because otherwise a rollback process will be kicked off and the entire process will be reversed (called an *atomicity* or *atomic transaction*). The KTM does this for both NTFS and the Registry. It can retrace the steps that have been completed and undo them on both ends to reverse portions that have completed.

Chapter 5 **Disk Configuration and Volume Tricks** 185

The Common Log File System (CLFS) API is used to log the process of the transactions for data and event management. In the past, logging was a performance-sapping process, but CLFS (released with the SDK for Server 2003) simplifies the process and reduces the impact on performance.

Disk Management

If you open Computer Management and select the Storage options, Disk Management setting, your disk drives and CD/DVD drives become a simple, block-like blueprint before you, as shown in Figure 5.1.

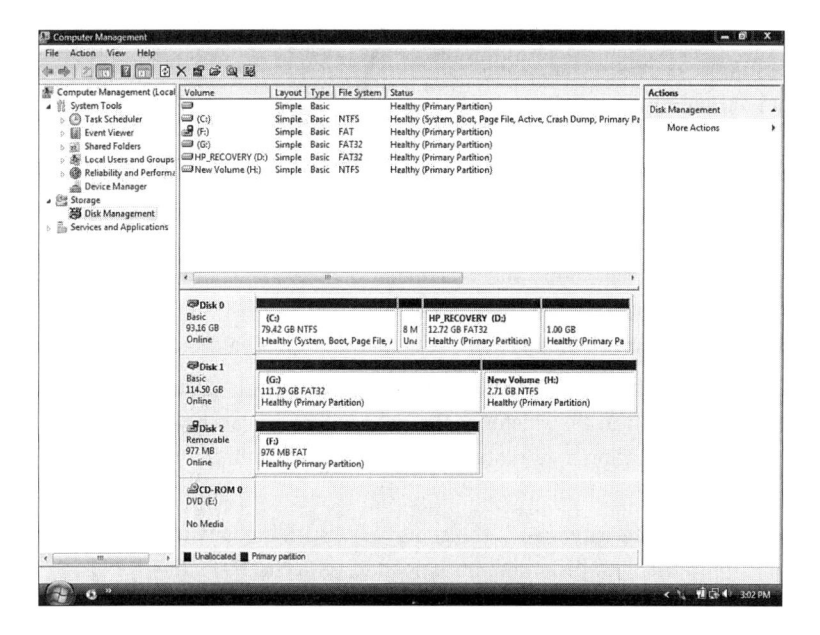

FIGURE 5.1
The Disk Management options.

The Disk Management tool helps you manage your disks. You can create partitions (volumes), format those volumes with a file system (FAT, FAT32, NTFS), see a readout on the status of those disks, expand or shrink partitions, and more.

Disk Terminology Review

Logically, you cannot work with a tool if you don't understand all the options available. Here is a list of terms you need to know and understand:

- **Basic disks**—These have been around forever. We didn't quite know how basic they were until we had something to compare them to. Here are some basic disk trivia points:
    - They use primary partitions (up to three) with one extended partition that can hold multiple logical drives. A primary partition can contain one file system for that partition. The partition that the OS boots from is generally a primary partition. An extended partition is a container partition that can be subdivided into logical drives that can be formatted and given a drive letter.
    - Basic disks store their configuration information in the master boot record (MBR). The MBR (located on the first sector of the hard disk) and can hold the disk's partition table information and allow the system to locate the boot files to start the OS.
    - Basic partitions can be extended if the same disk has the space to allow for the extension. To do this, the disk must be formatted with the NTFS file system.
- **Dynamic disks**—These first showed up in Windows 2000, and they do not use partitions or logical drives. The entire physical disk becomes one big partition that can then be divided into separate volumes (not partitions, although the concept is similar to logical partitions). The last 1MB region of a dynamic disk keeps the configuration information for the disk group. A disk group is all dynamic disks in the computer:
    - Dynamic disks can contain an unlimited number of volumes (unlike the restrictions of basic disks).
    - Dynamic volumes support the more advanced disk configuration features we will discuss shortly, such as spanned volumes, striped volumes, and RAID volumes.
    - Dynamic volumes cannot be set up on a laptop. The reasons are somewhat logical. Laptops typically have only one drive and you need at least one drive in your OS because that drive has the boot information, as we mentioned earlier.

> **TIP**
> Fred Langa wrote an interesting article in *Information Week* regarding a challenge that a reader sent his way. Fred said he could make a 1-terabyte system (1000GB) for under $500. The reader disagreed, but Fred knew what he was talking about. He proved it was true, and what was the tool he said helped him to do it? Partition Magic? Acronis Disk Director? Nope, he did everything he needed with Disk Manager. There are definitely times when paying the extra money is worth it for the NAS box, or when you can spend a little extra and just use USB drives (which are a little more expensive but easier to work with because no screwdrivers are required). But for the price, nothing beats good old-fashioned internal drives. You can learn a lot of cool stuff from Fred by subscribing to his newsletter (www.langa.com).

Chapter 5 Disk Configuration and Volume Tricks

- **Volumes**—With dynamic disks comes the use of the volume words (*mirrored volume, striped volume, RAID-5 volume*, and so forth). Keep in mind that before dynamic disks, these still existed and were called *mirror sets, stripe sets*, and so forth. There are different types of volume structures that can be used with dynamic disks including the following:
  - **Simple volume**—When you convert a basic disk to dynamic, it creates one single volume that can stay as one volume or can be broken into multiple (unlimited) areas. These are not fault tolerant. Although systems can remotely access these volumes regardless of the type of system (Windows 98/Me and so on), only systems running 2000, XP, or Vista can have a dynamic volume installed into the computer and continue to use it.
  - **Spanned volumes**—This enables you to extend the size of your volume to include other physical disk space. You need at least 2 disks to create one, but you can extend the volume with as many as 32 disks. These are not fault tolerant and cannot be mirrored or striped.
  - **Striped volume**—Increases performance by spanning data across disks. You need at least 2 disks to do this and can use as many as 32. The concept is simple: Instead of writing data consecutively on a single disk (1,2,3…), data is written and retrieved across the striped volume. So data is written between the disks, for example Disk 1 (1,3,5,7) and Disk 2 (2,4,6,8). This increases both the read/write speed for your data. There is no fault tolerance here either, though.
- **Fault tolerance**—We've used that word quite a bit. The basic definition is the capability of your system (or in this case, your data) to recover from some form of hardware failure. If a disk goes down, can your system recover without data loss, or should you start looking for your backup tapes?

Here are the features included in Windows 2000/2003 servers but not included within the software for Vista (note, there are hardware implementations of the same terms; in this case we are just referring to the software options in Vista for disk configurations):

> **NOTE**
> It's important to note again that you cannot create software-based fault tolerance on Vista systems. You can, however, use the Disk Management snap-in on a Vista machine to connect to a Windows 2000/2003 server and administrate the disks remotely. If you want to learn more about disks and volumes, the following Microsoft Knowledge base article will prove helpful: http://support.microsoft.com/kb/222189

- **Mirrored volume (Raid 1)**—Makes a copy of all the data on one drive over to another drive. In this case, you lose half your drive space. In other words, if you have two hard disks with 500GB each (equaling 1000GB), you are essentially going to have only 500GB of data because the other disk is used as a copy.

- **Raid 5 volume**—It's similar to a striped volume, but in this case at least three disks are required, where one is used as a parity for the others. Striping can occur in many ways, but the concept is that if one disk fails, the system can continue running until you replace the disk with no data loss.

Alan Wright
Network administrator

If RAID is an absolute must for your data and you don't want to go out and spend a fortune on a NAS box, check your motherboard settings. Some motherboards offer onboard RAID 1 ability and a few even offer RAID 5. You might have the solution right in front of you and not even know it."

Now that you have the terminology down, you need to know what Disk Manager can do for you. The next several sections explain many of the ways you can manage your system's disk drives in Windows Vista.

Converting a Disk to Dynamic and Back to Basic

Just in case you still aren't clear on why you would convert to dynamic, Diane Huggins (respected author and contributor to *Lockergnome*) mentioned a few good points, which can be found at http://www.lockergnome.com/nexus/windows/2005/08/08/why-convert-to-a-dynamic-disk/. She mentions the fact that dynamic disks can be managed without rebooting most of the time. The number of volumes supported can be as high as 2,000—a much greater number than extended partitions with logical drives can achieve. And, as already mentioned, you cannot access the spanned or striped volume options unless you are using dynamic disks.

To convert a disk from basic to dynamic, follow these steps:

1. Open the Computer Management Console and select Disk Management.
2. Right-click the basic disk (you right-click the disk part of the display, not the part in the middle with the partition information), and select Convert to Dynamic Disk. (Keep in mind before proceeding that you need to have at least 1MB of space for the configuration information that is going to be stored.)

> **TIP**
> To work with your disks from a command line, you use the Diskpart utility. For example, to convert your disk from basic to dynamic, you would type the following:
>
> ```
> Diskpart
> select disk 0
> convert dynamic
> Exit
> ```
>
> When entering the `select disk` command, `disk 0` refers to the first drive on your system, `disk 1` refers to the second drive, and so on. After typing `Exit` into the command line, you should then restart your system.

Here are a few caveats to consider in making this conversion:

- If you think you are going to upgrade a basic partition and then span it so that you increase the space you have on that one partition, that's a great idea. But it won't work if you have a volume that was originally a partition on a basic disk. The upgrade did indeed upgrade the disk to dynamic, but an upgraded disk's functionality is still limited. You would do better to save the information off the disk and restructure the whole thing. In that case you want to remove all partitions and create one partition that spans the disk.
- Multiple operating systems are not recommended with dynamic disks. If you have an OS older than Windows 2000, it won't be able to see the dynamic disks. And if you convert the boot and system partition, the other OS won't even boot.
- You cannot convert laptop disks or USB removable storage into dynamic disks. A dynamic disk can span multiple drives. If you spanned a drive to a USB storage device and that device was unplugged one day, this would essentially break the volume and ruin data. With laptops, usually they only include a single basic disk. Usually if a laptop does have a secondary disk its part of a docking station, which would be considered removable media and would not function if the laptop is removed from the station.

As for converting back from basic to dynamic? Well, that has always been a bit of a problem. You cannot just revert to basic like you could going forward. You need to back up your data, remove all the volumes, and then convert the disk back to basic using the Disk Management tool. That's the standard routine.

Moving Disks Between Systems

When you add a new disk into a system, the first thing you need to do is initialize it. It's not hard to do. From Disk Management you select the disk and choose to initialize it. Then you select whether you want the MBR (which uses the standard BIOS partition table) or GUID partition table (GPT) style (which uses the extensible firmware interface [EFI] and is a newer format for disks). These are initialized as basic disks to start with. You can also decide later to convert from MBR to GPT, but the disk cannot have partitions or volumes on it.

> **TIP** Newsflash: You can convert from basic to dynamic without having to remove all your data and volumes first. No, it's not supported or even recommended, but if you want to try it, be sure to back up first and then give it a whirl. Don't try this on spanned volumes, though because you will lose your data.
>
> To proceed, check out http://thelazyadmin.com and search for an August 15, 2005 article titled "Converting Dynamic Disks Back to Basic Disks." Before you begin, you need a tool from the Windows 2003 Support Tools called DskProbe 2. DskProbe is a sector editor tool that allows you to edit, save, and copy data on a physical hard disk. The tests worked in Windows 2000 and XP (most of the time).

But another thing you can do is take a hard disk and move it from one computer into another computer. Just remove the disk and plug it in somewhere else. Before doing so, though, you should make sure the disk is healthy. You can easily see whether the disk is reported as healthy from either the Status column on the volumes or within the graphical display of your disks.

To uninstall a disk, open Device Manager, right-click the disks you want to uninstall, select Uninstall, and then confirm the device removal. If the disks are also dynamic, you need to open Device Management, select the disk, and select Remove Disk.

After you physically plug the disks into the new computer, you can select Rescan Disks from the Disk Management action options. If any disks come up as foreign, you can right-click, select Import Foreign Disk, and then follow the prompts.

If you are moving spanned, striped, mirrored, or RAID-5 volumes, you should move the entire set of disks. If you don't, you will still be able to access the drive but all the data will be inaccessible. You will therefore be forced to reformat the drive.

Basic Disks/Dynamic Disks—Creating Partitions and Volumes

For basic disks, you can create a new partition by using Disk Management. Just right-click an unallocated region of a basic disk and select New Partition. You can make it a primary, extended partition or a logical drive within an extended partition. You can also select the partition and choose to delete it, but you will lose all the data on those partitions.

With dynamic disks, you right-click the space on a dynamic disk and can then choose to create a simple, spanned, or striped volume. Then just follow the prompts for the information required. You can also extend or shrink a volume or a spanned volume.

Disk Repair and Preventative Management

If you don't change the oil in your car, it might last a while but then one day your engine might stop working. Preventing these catastrophes requires a little thing we like to call preventative maintenance. A several-thousand-dollar repair, in this case, is prevented with routine $30 oil changes. The same philosophy is true of your disks. You want to be able to open Disk Manager and see the little "Healthy" message—that's what it's all about.

Given that, let's consider some of the other things Vista allows you to do to keep that "healthy" reading.

Cleanup

If you right-click any of your disk volumes, the drive letter is displayed enabling you to do a cleanup, as shown in Figure 5.2. You could also begin this from the System Tools options: Click Start, All Programs, Accessories, System Tools, Disk Cleanup.

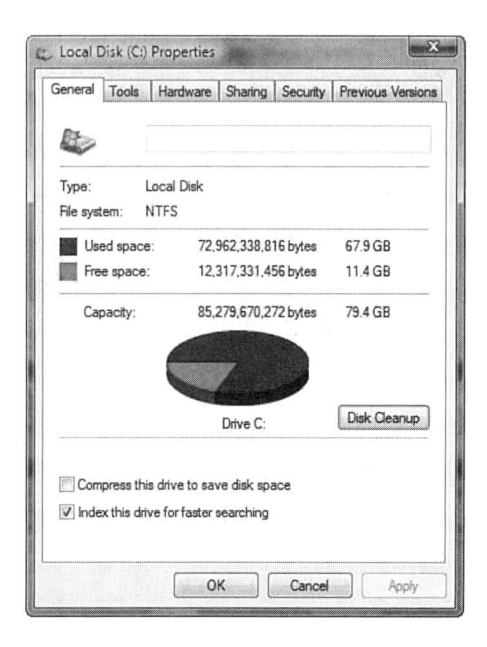

FIGURE 5.2
Cleaning up your volumes.

The fact is you need a little breathing room on your hard drive. You can get this manually by deleting your temporary files, deleting your temporary Internet files, and moving files off drives to those with more space. But an easy method is to use the Cleanup tool and see what it comes up with.

Whereas your temporary files can be deleted manually or through the Cleanup tool, you can also configure temporary files to be deleted on a daily or weekly basis through the Task Scheduler to ensure that your system is clean.

Alan Wright, from Detroit, recommends setting up a schedule that runs twice a week and has you run the Task Scheduler to run a program at that time: `cleanmgr.exe`. In addition, if you want to focus only on the temporary folders and not the entire set of cleanup options, you can run the `cleanmgr` command with switches to modify its behavior. The Knowledge Base article that helps you do this can be found at http://support.microsoft.com/kb/315246/en-us.

You could also set up the following logoff script to run each time you log off that deletes temporary files:

```
RD /s /q "C:\WINDOWS\Temp
```

(Note: RD stands for remove directory. The /s removes all the directories and files in that directory, including the directory itself, the entire directory tree. The /q runs the command in quiet mode so that permissions are not asked of the user when run with the /s switch.)

Disk Compression (To Compress or Not to Compress)

Vista includes compression (as did XP and 2000 before), and compression, as a concept, is easy to understand and easy to implement. You want to reduce the amount of space on a disk or bandwidth if you're sending over a network for specific files/folder. The space is saved through compression, but accessing the data requires decompression (which affects the performance of your system).

There are different types of compression. For example, Zip files are one type of compression. WinRAR, another type, has received excellent ratings for its compression capability. Yet another type, NTFS, allows for another style altogether.

> **TIP**
> For example, Mitch Tulloch, the author of several Windows 2000/2003 books, recommends running `cleanmgr /sageset:1`, which enables you to determine what you want deleted from your system. After you choose your settings, those settings are stored in the Registry so that when you run the `cleanmgr` tool with the `/sageset:1` setting it uses your settings. If you want even more granular control, you can run `cleanmgr /sageset:2` and use that setting to run another task scheduled cleanup. Mitch says you might set the task to run once a day to clean up temporary files and then once a week or month to empty the Recycle Bin.

> **TIP**
> Why are my files blue? This is a common question amongst novice XP/Vista users who might have followed the prompts for cleaning out disk space and had folders compressed in the process. When you compress your files they now appear blue in Explorer so that you know they've been compressed. You can always open the Properties of the file or folder; then under Advanced settings, you can deselect the compression to turn this off.

So, there you have it. Compression can save you some disk space, but use it sparingly because it also causes a performance hit. With disk space costing pennies per megabyte these days, you are better off not compressing your disk, folders, or files if you can help it.

Error Checking Your Disks

Error-checking will check the surface of your hard disk and locate (and if requested, fix) damaged files or bad sectors. This is a simple tool you should run every once in a while on your disk. You open Disk Management, select any partition (not disk, but partition), and then open the Properties for that partition. On the Tools tab is an Error-Checking option. You can run this for the tool to scan for and fix possible errors. If the disk you select is in use, it runs the scan the next time you reboot your system.

It's important to note that systems running NTFS perform this check automatically on startup so you only have to run it if you suspect there might be a problem, or as a routine form of tune-up. However, if you are running a FAT32 system then you might want to run the tool once a month for routine maintenance.

> **TIP** You'll get the best results when checking your disk for errors, if you run it from Windows Safe Mode.

> **NOTE** Defragmentation is another tool we recommend, but as we mentioned earlier, the defragment tool is set to run automatically through Task Scheduler. However, you can always set it to run at any time you like through the System Tools folder in your Accessories folder. Remember, though, that it's no longer graphical.

Chkdsk is the command-line interface for this program. You can learn more about it's abilities at http://support.microsoft.com/?kbid=314835.

Understanding NTFS Permissions

In Chapter 4, "Security Enhancements," we discussed User Access Control and the new method of giving standard user access tokens to users and giving two tokens to admins (a standard token for common use on the system and an admin token for whenever necessary). It's important to remember that tokens are passes into the system but not into the resources.

As a child in Brooklyn, I would go to a place called Astroland (it used to be the old Coney Island amusement park with the Cyclone rollercoaster). I would pay to enter the park (a small fee), but I couldn't get on any of the rides without a ticket (I had to buy those individually). Even worse, I couldn't get on some of those rides, even with a ticket, if I was too short. By the time I got tall enough, I wanted to go to Disney World instead—but that's a different story.

The point is that there were multiple points of access and permission settings involved. The same is true with your OS. You get logged onto the system by providing a username and password. At that moment, the system provides you with an access token. But, your rights on the system or permissions established on the system are what determine what access to resources you have. We discussed sharing in Chapter 3, "Mastering

Administration," and here you will see how accessing folders through the share combines with NTFS for even greater lockdown.

NTFS Permission Settings

Permissions are set on the objects, the resources, not on the users or on the groups to which they belong. So, if you have a printer, a folder, or a disk drive that you want to stop access to, you need to right-click that object, open the Properties of the object, and then open the Security tab. You'll be able to see the permissions set on the object, as shown in Figure 5.3.

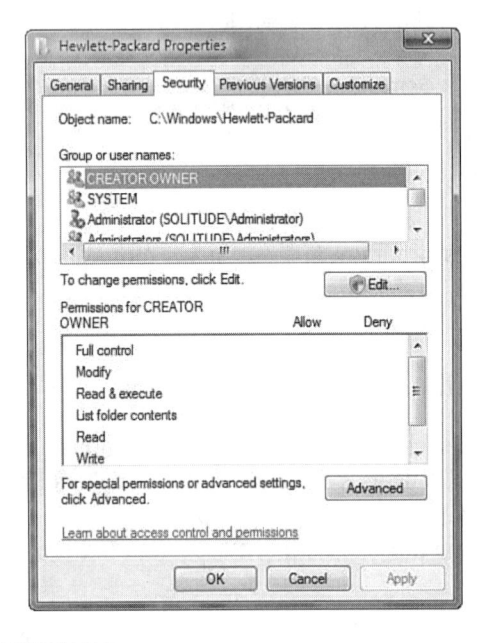

FIGURE 5.3
NTFS Permissions on a folder.

Keep in mind that different resources require different permissions—for example, a printer doesn't need to have the permissions to read or write, but it does need them to print or manage the printer. In this section, we are going to focus primarily on files and folder permissions under NTFS.

Table 5.1 details the six permission categories. The standard ones are Read, Read and Execute, Write, Modify, and Full Control. These can be established quickly; however, if you want more granular control, you can change the settings even further using special permissions.

Table 5.1—Permission Settings

Special Permissions	List Folder Contents (Folders Only)	Read	Read and Execute	Write	Modify	Full Control
Traverse Folder/ Execute File	x		x		x	x
List Folder/Read Data	x	x	x		x	x
Read Attributes	x	x	x		x	x
Read Extended Attributes	x	x	x		x	x
Create Files/ Write Data				x	x	x
Create Folders/ Append Data				x	x	x
Write Attributes				x	x	x
Write Extended Attributes				x	x	x
Delete Subfolders and Files						x
Delete					x	x
Read Permissions	x	x	x	x	x	x
Change Permissions						x
Take Ownership						x
Synchronize	x	x	x	x	x	x

One thing to note is that a file and a folder's permissions are pretty much the same, with the exception of the List Folder Contents settings. By using this setting, you can limit a user's ability to look through a folder even if he has permission to use a file within that folder.

What if a user has access to a file but not to the folder? Will Willis and David Watts (two fine Vista masters in the writing world) wondered the same thing. They say:

> NTFS file permissions override or take priority over NTFS folder permissions. A user account having access to a file can access that file even though it does not have access to the parent folder of that file. However, a user would not be able to do so via the folder, because that requires this List Folders Contents permission. When the user

makes the attempt to access the file, he or she must supply the full path to it. The full path can either be the logical file path (`F:\MyFolder\MyFile.txt`) or use the Universal Naming Convention (UNC). To access the file via UNC, the user must supply the server name, share, directory, and file."

Here's an example

`\\MYSERVER\Win2003Share\MyFolder\MyFile.txt`.

Permissions Are Cumulative, Deny Is Unforgiving

When you get your access token, you have an identifier that includes your security ID (SID) and the IDs for any groups to which you belong. When you attempt to access the resource, your token is checked against the Access Control List (ACL). The ACL contains Access Control Entries (ACEs) for different types of permissions. So, for example, if you try to read a file, the ACL checks to see whether you can even access the file and the ACE determines whether you can read it.

Cumulative permissions are *usually* a good thing. In other words, say you are part of a group called Managers and you attempt to open a folder. The folder has NTFS permissions established that say your account can read the contents of the folder. However, the Managers group to which you belong has permissions saying you can modify the contents. Thanks to your group membership, you can do more than if you were alone. In the event the situation were reversed—you had modify and the group had read—it would still allow you to modify the contents.

Here is the caveat: Deny. If the ACE has you or any group you belong to as being denied permission to access, that setting is the one that will stand. In fact, deny entries are listed at the top of the ACE so that it can quickly be determined what you *can't* do before determining what you *can* do.

Because of the power the Deny option has, by explicitly denying access to a resource regardless of whether the user has other permissions, most network admins will tell you not to use it. Ron Barrett, the lead network admin for ERE, an accounting firm in Manhattan, says:

"Troubleshooting a permissions problem like this on a large network could take forever; it's better to develop a plan for using NTFS permissions in such a way that the user only has the access he/she needs. It's better to assign the permissions to groups of users on larger networks to avoid permission clashes."

This is where it becomes important to understand the difference between implicit and explicit. After you deny someone access, he is explicitly denied. But if you structure your permissions properly, he is implicitly denied by his lack of explicit approval. In other words, he won't be allowed to do what you don't grant him access to do.

Permissions are also inherited from the top down. So, permissions you establish on folders are inherited by default in subfolders and then into files. You can change this behavior by opening the Advanced properties of your Security permissions and deselecting the check box Include Inheritable Permissions form This Objects Parent.

> **TIP** To see what the effective permissions are for a user or group, you can use the Effective Permissions tool. The way the tool works is that it runs through each membership of a group or user, through each share permission, and then through NTFS permission. Next, it takes the overall set of permissions as a result. Effective permissions can be the quick and easy way to determine why a user is having difficulty accessing a resource.

It's time for a quick review. We have discussed the NTFS permission sets, how permissions are cumulative, and how if deny is set on any one of the groups to which a person belongs, or on any one of the permissions, this leads to that part of the access being denied. We've discussed folder permissions dripping down over subfolders and files (meaning you need to be careful about the permissions you give out). Finally, we've discussed a quick tool to determine the permissions set on an NTFS resource using the Effective Permissions tool.

You might have noticed that the Advanced settings has additional tabs for auditing the resource and taking ownership of the resource.

Now let's combine what we learned in Chapter 3 about share permissions with what we have discussed on the NTFS side.

Share Permissions Mixing with NTFS

Say you go to a consulate anywhere in the world and you have many things in your bag or purse, such as a cell phone, a bottle of water, some papers, and so forth. You enter the special security section that determines whether you can enter consulate property. They say, "Yes, you can enter, but you must leave the cell phone and water." Upon entering the building, you see a sign that says "cell phones and water are allowed here." What can you do? Nothing because you left your cell phone and water when you entered the premises.

Sharing and NTFS work the same way. When you go through the share, you have specific permissions that have been given to you. Now, if you've been given full control permissions, you only have to worry about the NTFS side. In fact, this is the highly recommended best practice to share permissions.

Brian Posey, in an article on Windows Security tips, says, "I personally tend to advise people to grant everyone full access at the share level and to assign more restrictive permissions only at the file level. In doing so, the file level permissions will be effective because they are more restrictive than the wide open permissions you assign at the share level."

However, in the event this wasn't done and someone grants read-only through the share, the person who accesses a folder on the NTFS side is given full control, but it no longer matters because the share has already ruled them out.

The way to work out shares is the down-down-across method.

Add up all the share permissions cumulatively, then the NTFS, and then go across, as shown in Table 5.2.

Table 5.2— The Down-Down-Across Method

Objects	Share Permissions	NTFS Permissions	Effective Permissions
UserJoe	Full Control	Modify	Modify
Managers	Change	Deny: Read	Write, Delete

So if we just look at UserJoe, we see how his permissions move across and allow the modify capabilities. But if we put UserJoe into the Managers group, how would we figure out the permissions? If we just went across for both UserJoe and Managers, it might appear that UserJoe's permissions would still be modify. But by using the down-down-across method, we would see full control through the share, deny: read (but allow write and delete)—essentially UserJoe would have write and delete permissions.

We could do a million more examples like this. For example, what if you have a folder called Files in another folder called Folders on your C drive: `C:\Folders\Files`. If you share it out to UserJoe as full control and you share Files out to UserJoe as read, you have an interesting dilemma. If UserJoe tries to access the share through the Files share, his permission is read. But if you go through the Folders share, UserJoe gets Full Control and then can access the Files folder, which still would be Full Control because you are already through the share. Then permissions on the NTFS side would have to be added into the mix.

You can always open Computer Management and expand out the shares to then see the permissions set on each one of the shares by viewing the properties. From the same place, you can see the NTFS permissions set, too.

A command-line tool that admins can play with comes from the Windows 2003 Resource Kit, it's called SRVCHECK.EXE. This tool enumerates the shares on the local or a remote machine.

> **TIP** Richard Wu mentions that you can easily create a batch file that will list all the shares on all the file servers on the network. He tells you exactly how to do this at http://msmvps.com/blogs/richardwu/archive/2006/09/04/Enumerating-Shares-and-their-ACL_2700_s.aspx.

FIGURE 5.4
The SRVCHECK.EXE utility works from the command line.

EFS and BitLocker

We've had Encrypting File System (EFS) for a while now. It's a simple procedure, right next to the compression option on your files or folders if they are stored on an NTFS drive. EFS uses public key cryptography that, in the case of EFS, encrypts the file using a symmetric key (known as a *file encryption key* [FEK]). Then the symmetric key is encrypted with a private key that is connected to the user account. To decrypt the file, the private key of the user is used to decrypt the symmetric key that is then used to decrypt the file itself. (Note, from the Details options, you can add users to be allowed to open your encrypted information.)

This offers you some protection in the event your laptop gets stolen or the hard drive goes missing because the thief won't be able to access those files without your encryption keys. That's why it is very important to back up encryption keys (and your data) so that you don't get stuck in a situation where you cannot access your own files.

Keep in mind that EFS was available only in XP Pro and is now available only in Vista Business, Enterprise, and Ultimate. EFS in Vista supports storing private keys on smart cards and allows admins to store their recovery keys on smart cards.

The best practice with EFS is to back up your recovery keys because if something happens to the key, the data could be lost. So be sure you make a backup, it's a critical step to avoiding data loss with EFS. The key is connected to an encryption certificate. To back up the key, you need to back up the certificate. For this, you need to open the Certification Manager. From the Start orb, type `certmgr.msc` (shown in Figure 5.5).

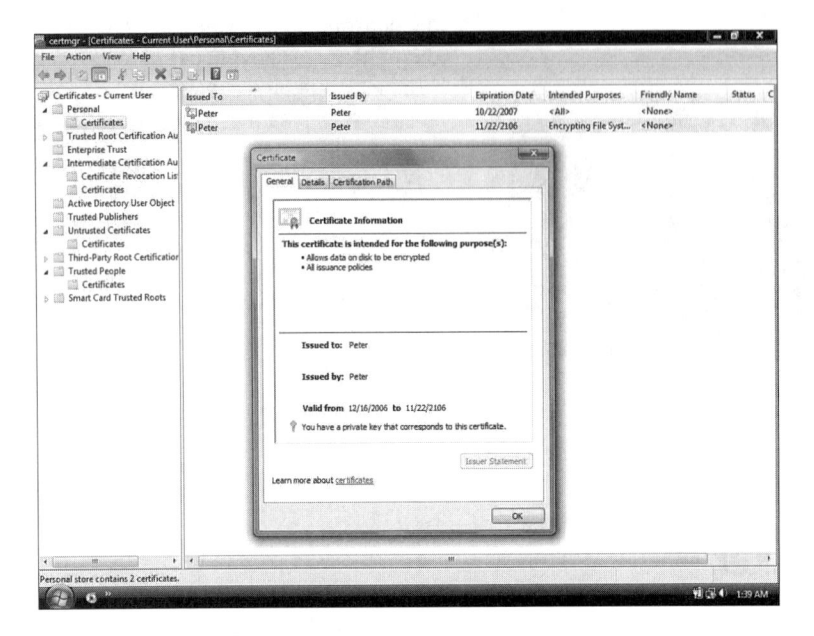

FIGURE 5.5
Use the Certification Manager to back up your EFS certificates (keys).

Expand the Personal folder. You can see your certificates, which you can double-click to see their properties. You need to back up the one labeled Encryption File System or Allows Data on Disk to Be Encrypted under the Intended Purposes heading. The recommendation is that you back up all the certificates if you see more than one (just be sure).

On the Action menu, select All Tasks, Export. Agree to export the private key. On the Export File Format tab of the Export Wizard, select the Personal Information Exchange options and finish the wizard with a password and then a location for your files. Again, you should store these someplace safe off the drive—perhaps a USB drive.

Tim Duggan, co-founder of cliptraining.com, says it's important to encrypt folders like Documents and Temp folders. He also encourages exporting your keys to a private place. You can encrypt your spool folder for when you print. Finally, he mentions that your encryption is only as good as your password. If an attacker can get through your password, she can access your encrypted files, too.

Bill Boswell, a well-respected guru in just about every Microsoft technology, listed a few best practices regarding EFS in an article "EFS: Handle with Care" for Redmond magazine. He said to be sure you join both desktops and laptops to your domain if you have one. "A laptop with the data recovery agent private key on the hard drive is not secure." If you don't have a domain, your next best option is to "immediately export and remove the admin file recovery key from each machine, burn the certificates to CDs, and keep those under lock and key."

Looking Deeper into EFS

What if you are looking at a file and you know it's encrypted but you don't know who encrypted it or the identity of the data recovery agent? One great tool in the Resource Kits is EFSInfo. This shows you which main folders are encrypted and who encrypted the file. It also tells you who the recovery agent is. This could be a real life-saver. In the event you have files on a system and aren't sure who encrypted them, this tool tells you who it was (the one who encrypted) and who the recovery agent might be. That recovery agent, if there is one, can retrieve those files in the event the other person cannot.

Another tool from Sysinternals (now owned by Microsoft) is called EFSDump (http://www.microsoft.com/technet/sysinternals/FileAndDisk/efsdump.mspx). This tool gives you similar information to EFSInfo but in a different format.

Paul Deltree says, "In the event you really get stuck and let's say you had to reinstall Vista due to a major problem and now you cannot access your encrypted files and didn't back up your keys you might try one more thing. http://www.crackpassword.com/ has an EFS password recovery tool. It's worth a try when you have nothing more to lose.

BitLocker Overview

EFS obviously isn't perfect for a number of reasons (most of which include the inability to recover, which has led many admins to never use the technology). In addition, you cannot encrypt an entire volume and there are certain files you cannot encrypt in Windows 2000/XP, such as the paging and hibernation files.

BitLocker offers some newer possibilities that can be especially appealing to traveling businesspeople. If your laptop is lost or stolen, the data you're carrying will be fair game. With BitLocker, the entire drive is encrypted and a thief won't have the option of switching out the drive and attempting to crack through the encryption. BitLocker uses Advanced Encryption Standard (AES) as its encryption algorithm with configurable key lengths of 128 or 256 bits. These options are configurable using Group Policy.

For BitLocker to work, though, you will need one of two things:

- A laptop that has the Trusted Platform Module (TPM) chip version 1.2. The TPM chip is like a smart card that is embedded into the motherboard. It has a predefined number of unsuccessful attempts configured so that a thief cannot force her way in.
- A USB storage device, but your systems BIOS has to be capable of accessing USB devices prior to the bootup of the OS.

Keep in mind that BitLocker doesn't mean you don't need EFS now. BitLocker is designed to encrypt your system partition, but any other data on other partitions or other drives would still be encrypted using EFS. In addition, after your system is running, BitLocker doesn't protect your files whereas EFS does. So, BitLocker is more for peace of mind if your laptop is lost or stolen. The data remains secure. EFS is for the day-to-day encryption of your files.

BitLocker Planning and Recovery

Before implementing BitLocker, you should know a bit about it's requirements and how to prepare your system. For starters, you need a 1.5GB partition on your drive for BitLocker to use. This is not the partition with your OS, but a separate partition.

Mark Minasi wrote about this in his newsletter (http://www.minasi.com/newsletters/nws0611.htm), and he has allowed us to reprint his remarks here:

> I really like Vista Ultimate's BitLocker feature. BitLocker's a pretty neat way to set up a laptop with a C: drive that's entirely encrypted and, even better, in my experience the cryptographic overhead isn't all that bad performance-wise.
>
> The thing that drives people crazy about BitLocker, however, is the odd setup that it requires to work. Despite being called BitLocker *Drive* Encryption, BitLocker actually encrypts just the C: volume and can't work unless your system's first hard disk is divided into two partitions. One partition must be 1.5GB in size, and it contains some basic boot code. You can use the rest of the drive for C:. To make BitLocker work, then, your system's first hard disk must be arranged so that one partition is 1.5GB in size and is marked active, one other partition is at least 16GB in size, and Vista is installed to that partition.
>
> This requirement presents two problems. First, no one seems to know about it, and so people just set up their laptop's entire disk as C: and install Vista. Then, after Vista's installed, they want to turn on BitLocker, only to find that it refuses to install because of the lack of the 1.5GB partition. Second, even if you *do* know beforehand about the 1.5GB partition requirement, there isn't any way in Vista's Setup GUI that would let you create a 1.5GB partition and mark it active.

As is so often the case, however, there's an answer—the command line.

Installing BitLocker on clean system requires the following steps:

1. Boot the Vista install disk.

2. When you see the screen that says Windows Vista / Install Now, click Repair Your Computer.

3. In the subsequent dialog box, select Command Prompt.

4. From the command prompt, type this:

   ```
   diskpart
   select disk 0
   clean
   create partition primary
   assign letter=c
   shrink minimum=1500
   create partition primary
   active
   assign letter=p
   exit
   format c: /y /q /fs:NTFS
   format p: /y /q fs:NTFS
   exit
   ```

5. When you're out of the command prompt, press Esc to return to the Install Now screen.

6. Install Vista as usual. When Vista asks which partition to install Windows to, direct it to C:.

At that point, you'll have a copy of Vista that works fine either with or without BitLocker and that lets you add BitLocker whenever you'd like. In addition, notice the `shrink minimum=1500` command. This is a neat diskpart command that actually lets you *shrink* an existing partition. The documentation says it works only on basic disks, and I've not tried it on a dynamic disk, so I can't comment. In any case, though, it's a pretty neat feature, given that I used to have to buy a moderately expensive third-party utility to resize a partition without losing data.

Having dealt with *that* BitLocker annoyance, though, I should explain a BitLocker annoyance that I can't fix (or understand): You need either Vista Ultimate *or* Enterprise to use BitLocker. It's kind of sad to consider that as far as Vista's concerned, security is clearly a *profit* center.

Joern Wettern (Ph.D., MCSE, MCT, Security+) is the owner of Wettern Network Solutions, a consulting and training firm. He has said, "Once the encryption process starts, plan on going out for dinner or watching a movie. It can take more than an hour."

Again, with encryption there is always the problem with recovery solutions in the event of a problem. If someone loses his key or has a problem with his system and the motherboard is replaced, this could cause a major issue so you need to be prepared.

> **TIP**
> If you are using a USB storage device to hold your key, do not—no, let's make this clearer—DO NOT, DO NOT, DO NOT, keep the key with the laptop. We all know it's so easy to toss the key in with the bag, but if the thief has the key, the thief has your data. End of story. Period.

Put together by Joern Wettern for an article in *Redmond* magazine, here is a large list of articles from Microsoft to help you get started in figuring out all the little idiosyncrasies of BitLocker:

- Windows Vista BitLocker Drive Encryption: Executive Overview
  (http://www.microsoft.com/technet/windowsvista/security/bitexec.mspx)
- Windows Vista Beta 2 BitLocker Drive Encryption Step-by-Step Guide
  (http://www.microsoft.com/technet/windowsvista/library/c61f2a12-8ae6-4957-b031-97b4d762cf31.mspx)
- Windows Vista BitLocker Drive Encryption: Technical Overview
  (http://www.microsoft.com/technet/windowsvista/security/bittech.mspx)
- BitLocker Drive Encryption Frequently Asked Questions: 1
  (http://www.microsoft.com/whdc/system/platform/hwsecurity/BitLockerFAQ.mspx)
- BitLocker Drive Encryption Frequently Asked Questions: 2
  (http://www.microsoft.com/technet/windowsvista/security/bitfaq.mspx)
- BitLocker Drive Encryption
  (http://www.microsoft.com/technet/windowsvista/security/bitlockr.mspx)
- BitLocker Drive Encryption: Technical Overview
  (http://www.microsoft.com/whdc/system/platform/hwsecurity/BitLockerTechOver.mspx)
- BitLocker Drive Encryption Executive Overview
  (http://www.microsoft.com/whdc/system/platform/hwsecurity/BitLocker_Over.mspx)
- Windows Vista BitLocker Client Platform Requirements
  (http://www.microsoft.com/whdc/system/platform/hwsecurity/BitLockerReq.mspx)

The big drawback to BitLocker is the human factor—people forgetting or losing their keys or admins not educating their users properly or configuring BitLocker correctly. These are causes for concern. Paul Thurrott, in an article titled "Vista BitLocker: Boon or Bust?" for Windows IT Pro wrote, "I'm a bit nervous that BitLocker might ultimately do more harm than good. Will the number of people burned by BitLocker's unbreakable encryption exceed those who are saved by this feature? Only time will tell."

ReadyDrive

ReadyDrive (along with SuperFetch and ReadyBoost, which are discussed in Chapter 8, "System Recovery and Diagnostic Tricks") are part of the new technologies Microsoft is using to increase performance and improve storage reliability. It sounds like something out of *Star Trek*, but it's not quite that far into the future. It's not going to give your system warp speed, but it will enhance speed a bit.

If a system has a hybrid drive, this technology enables the system to boot more quickly, come back from hibernation more quickly, and use less battery power. The trick to a hybrid drive is that it uses both traditional hard drive technologies with nonvolatile Flash memory. This means your disk platters, instead of spinning all the time, can rest because the Flash memory is holding a large storage buffer to assist. Theoretically, this could enable the laptop battery life to extend, the drive life to extend, less heat to be produced from the laptop, and possibly faster drive speeds.

How is it that the platters are at rest most of the time? The disk starts to function for only two reasons. The first is if the Flash memory reaches its limit, in which case the drive spins up, moves all the data from Flash over to the disk, and then spins down. The other reason is when data is required (such as a file) that isn't in the Flash memory already.

One great benefit is that the Flash memory doesn't lose data in the event of a sudden power failure. It will retain what was on it. One downside to Flash memory is that it has a shorter read/write lifespan than a hard disk, so this could be a problem with disks lasting less time depending on how the technology is developed over time. It's all in the infancy stages at the time of this writing.

Previous Versions

This Vista feature might be considered a form of backup in some ways. But we want to discuss it here because it's part of the properties you see when you look into folder properties.

Server 2003 has a feature known as Volume Shadow Copy that takes snapshots of your files as part of a restore point. These restore points are used on your system files to jump back to a point in time when your system was in good running order. The same is true with your files. In the event you changed a file or deleted it (whether on your personal system with Vista or on the network with Server 2003), you can jump back to a point in time, open the file, restore it to a different location, or simply have it replace the existing file.

When you perform a backup of your files, it creates a shadow copy of those files. However, when you restore a file by using the previous versions tab off the properties of the file, you will note that previous versions and backup versions of the file exist.

On the Previous Version tab, shown in Figure 5.6, you can see three options for restoring a file: Open, Copy, and Restore.

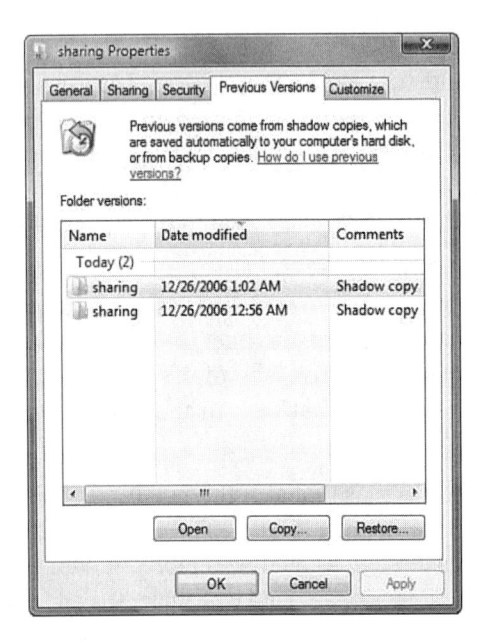

FIGURE 5.6
The Previous Versions tab of the properties of a folder.

To get to the Previous Versions tab for any folder or file you need to restore, simply right-click the folder and select Restore Previous Versions. Or you can go to the Properties of the folder and then to the Previous Versions tab. (This is true whether you are using Vista and restoring files off your own system or are using a network connection to a Server 2003 file server.)

David Brunelle, a network admin for a Seattle advertising agency called Radarworks, wrote the following commentary about the Previous Versions tab on the www.lifehacker.com website:

Vista Master: I wouldn't call it "file versioning." It will use a percentage of your hard drive to record these snapshots. When that percentage is used up, it will overwrite the oldest backup. The more often your data changes—the more often your previous versions will be overwritten. In other words, it's not bulletproof. We have this feature in place on our primary file server that's running Windows Server 2003. It's been a life-saver. In the past, with Windows 2000, if an employee deleted a file, I'd have to hope the file was on the previous night's backup tape and then spend an hour or so restoring the file. No fun. With volume shadow copy, all it takes is going into the properties menu and selecting a previous version of a file (as demonstrated). Also fantastic if you accidentally overwrite a file.

You might wonder what happens if you deleted a file or folder, or renamed it. How can you recover the previous version of that file without going to backup tapes?

First, you need to know where your previous version snapshots are stored. To start with, find the folder where the file was originally located, right-click the folder, and select Restore Previous Versions. From here, you can see a previous version folder that you can double-click; then you will see the deleted file you thought was gone forever. From here, you can drag that file or folder to your desktop.

Advanced Configuration Options for Previous Versions

The default setting for disk space reserved for shadow copies is 15% of the volume size, but you can change this size by using the `vssadmin.exe` command-line tool, which is already present in the OS (so you don't need to find and install new tools). You can use it to create shadows or list shadows.

For example, just type **`vssadmin list shadows`** to see the shadows on the system. But another good use for the `vssadmin` tool, according to Alan Wright, is to change the maximum size using the `/maxsizespec` switch. He says, "It's frustrating not having GUI control over the shadow copies but through `vssadmin` you can alter the amount of space you use. For example, if you want to create a shadow copy and set the size you type: **`vssadmin.exe add shadowstorage /for=C: /on=D: /maxsizespec=1GB`**. You can also use KB, MB, GB, TB, PB and EB for the size settings. And you can resize existing instances." To find out more about this tool type **`vssadmin.exe /?`**.

Another concern you might have is to delete restore points to free up space. Traces of previous versions can continue for a long time, or you might just run low on disk space. In that case, you might want to remove all but the latest restore point. To do this, open Disk Cleanup and click the More Options tab; then, in the System Restore and Shadow Copies area, click Clean Up.

Keep in mind that we don't recommend you remove all but the latest restore point. In the event you come across a virus or malware, you will need that restore point from before the infection in order to bring your system back quickly. Otherwise you will spend a good deal of time trying to clean out the infection, or possibly even reinstalling.

Chapter 6

OFFICE 2007 TRICKS FOR VISTA MASTERS

The New Interface

What a cool sight to see Office 2007 running on Vista. In the bottom-left corner is the Vista Start orb. In the upper-left corner is the Office orb. Together, they are the launching pad for all things Vista and Office. Welcome to the future.

One of the big changes is learning how to work with the new Office layout. The streamlined approach was a necessary change because of the way Office has changed over the years. The first version of Word, for example, had about 100 commands. Now there are more than 1,500 commands, so changes were obviously needed. The new interface (with ribbons) exists in Word 2007, Excel 2007, PowerPoint 2007, Access 2007, and parts of Outlook 2007. You can see an example of the new user interface (UI) in Figure 6.1, which points out several specific new additions to the UI.

IN THIS CHAPTER

- The New Interface
- Word 2007
- Excel 2007
- PowerPoint 2007
- Outlook 2007

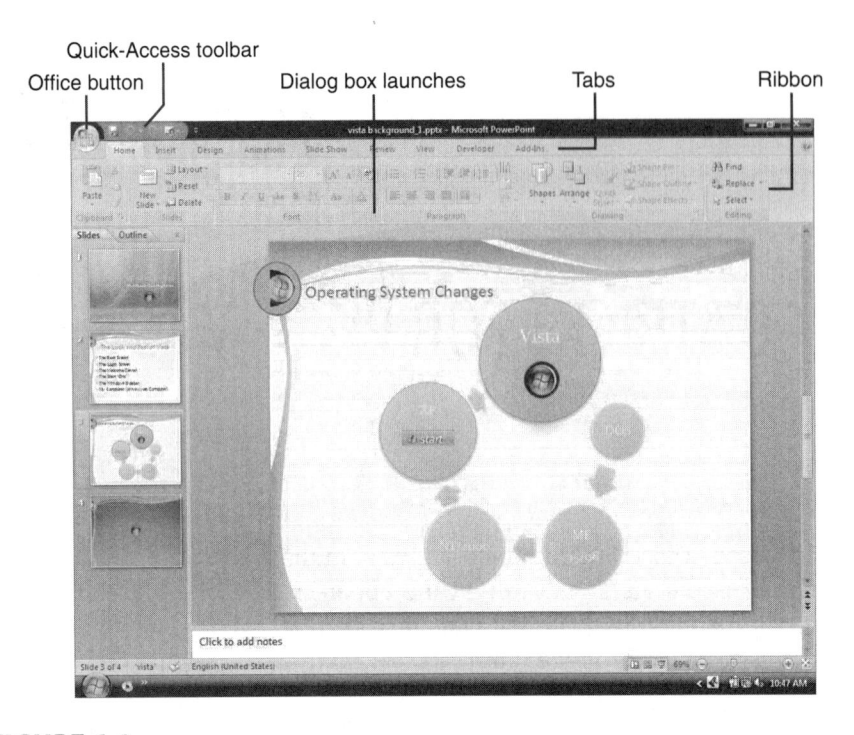

FIGURE 6.1
The PowerPoint 2007 user interface with the new ribbon format.

Terminology for Working with the New UI

It's important to learn the terminology because in this chapter you will see words like *ribbons*, *galleries*, and *tabs* all over the place:

- **The Office button**—The sleek circular launching pad for document options. You can click the Office button to open and create new documents, save documents, prepare your documents for deployment, and access special application options.

- **The Ribbon**—Previous Office versions used menus and toolbars. The Ribbon is the successor to these. Each ribbon has a set of tools specific to the functionality, which cannot be changed unless you're a developer with XML coding experience (you can find articles on the MSDN site that explain how to customize the ribbon at the Office Developer Center http://msdn.microsoft.com/office/). Ribbons organize the various command options in such a way that people can more easily find them than in past versions, and that ensures users have easy access to all the commands that relate to specific options.

- **Tabs**—All ribbons have a tab associated with them so that every tool has a named location to which books like this one can refer. The tab itself is just the little part of the ribbon where the name is located. For example, you might be directed to go to the Home tab in Word 2007. This is the same as being directed to use a tool on the Home ribbon.

- **Galleries**—The galleries give you different choices for formatting your documents and show you live previews of what your paragraphs or tables will look like if you choose a specific option. You can take a gander at what this looks like later in this chapter, in Figure 6.8.

> **NOTE:** In the bottom-right corner of some of the tool groups on the ribbons is a little arrow-pointing icons, called *dialog box launchers*. Clicking one of these icons opens a dialog box or window pane that offers more options related to the tool group associated with that launcher.

> **NOTE:** If at first you think you're missing commands in Office 2007 that you had access to in previous versions, don't assume they're gone. With so many commands, it's impossible to put them all on just a handful of ribbons. So, Microsoft instead decided to make certain ribbons contextual. This means you won't see some ribbons until you take an action that requires them to appear. For example, you can insert a table but you cannot format it unless you have the Design and Layout tabs. These tabs do not show up unless you are working inside the table.

Customizing Your Interface

As we stated in the previous section, you cannot alter the appearance of your ribbons. However, there are plenty of ways to customize your Office applications. For example, you can customize the buttons that appear on the Quick Access toolbar (refer to Figure 6.1). From here, you can add and remove buttons for all the commands you like. To do this, select the down arrow next to the toolbar that allows you to choose from the following options:

- **Minimize the Ribbon**—This enables you to keep your ribbon tabs visible, while allowing you a little more room at the top of your screen. The ribbons reappear if you select the ribbon tab.

- **Show below the Ribbon**—The Quick Access toolbar grows as you add buttons to it, but you might not want it all the way at the top of your document. You can give it a bit more space to expand if you put it below the ribbon.

- **More Commands**—Takes you directly to the Customize Settings window, which enables you to add more commands to your toolbar (see Figure 6.2).

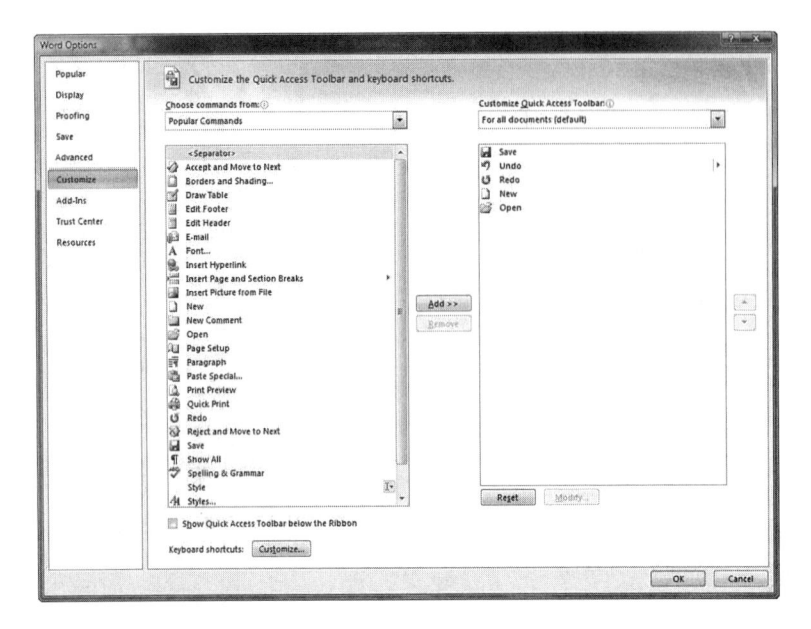

FIGURE 6.2
The Customize Quick Access Toolbar options.

The Mini Toolbar

A little toolbar called the Mini Toolbar shows up when you select text and then move your cursor over the selection. Designed to give you quick access to common formatting options (like bold, underline, and italic, for example), this new feature is on by default. Unfortunately, not all users particularly like the Mini Toolbar, but if you want to turn it off, you can. Select Office, Options, Popular, and click the checkbox to enable or disable the Mini Toolbar.

Tim Duggan
Network Administrator for ERE

> I recommend you disable it. If you are usually selecting text or right-clicking and copying or cutting text, the problem with this toolbar is that it gets in your way and hinders your normal method of work." It's for you to decide if you like it or not. However, if you turn it off, when you right-click text (selected or not) the Mini Toolbar appears with your other options.

Word 2007

Along with a fancy new interface are a ton of great new features we think you will truly appreciate. It's impossible to cover them all, but here are some highlights; we'd like to thank Ed Bott, author of the book *Special Edition Using Microsoft Office 2007* (ISBN-10: 0789735172) for these tips.

Saving Files As PDF (or XPS)

If you have ever needed to convert a file from a Word document to the portable document format (PDF), you know that it can't be done without a conversion tool. With Word 2007, the tools are included. Well, you have to download them first from Microsoft, but they are free. Just go to microsoft.com and search for "2007 Microsoft Office Add-in: Microsoft Save as PDF or XPS." It's a small file (less than 1MB), and after you install it you will see the option to save your documents as PDF or XPS.

What Are PDF and XPS?

Because of the globalization of our modern world, we often share information with people who use different technology than we do. Different applications, different operating systems…how do we share documentation in this world? You cannot force everyone to use a method that YOU like. This is where the PDF and XPS file formats come into play.

PDF is a file format that is very common because it takes your document and preserves it for sharing. So, you don't have to worry that someone will work on it or make changes because it's already set, with all the formatting included, for others to read. To read PDF files, you need a reader program—the most popular of which is the free Acrobat Reader. Adobe gives you the reader for free, but you have to buy the conversion tool.

XPS stands for XML Paper Specification, which is also a format for sharing documents that Microsoft is positioning to compete with PDF. Although PDF is a common standard that you can use to share documents with others, you might not want to use the proprietary method. XPS, which is an open format, allows for the following features:

- A document converted to XPS maintains its look. None of the quality is lost (as is the case with PDF) and your fonts, formatting, and high-quality images continue to look the same.

- You can share the XPS document with everyone because it is based on an open standard. XPS viewers will be free for the world to download and use.
- XPS supports digital signatures to allow you to apply rights to the document.

You can also convert to XPS through Office 2007. However, it's worth noting that Windows Vista also includes an XPS printer driver that enables you to save to XPS directly from Vista by choosing to print-to-file (instead of saving the document to a file). So, in the event you don't have Office 2007, you can still save a document in the XPS format.

Preparing Your Documents for Distribution

Before sending your documents off for others to see and work on, there are a few things you might want to do. To see the tools available for preparation, click the Office button and select Prepare. You will see the following options:

- **Properties**—Document properties (part of the metadata for your document) can be added from here. This hidden information includes author, title, page count, and so on.
- **Inspect Document**—First, it examines the document and determines whether you have hidden data you might want removed; then it presents you with the option of removing that data.
- **Encrypt Document**—This option ensures you remember the password you chose if you encrypt the document.
- **Restrict Permission**—This preparation option is connected to the Information Rights Management (IRM) tools available for Office 2007. The basic concept is that IRM gives you greater control over who can access what, allows you to configure the extent of the access people can have (for example, having a user read the document but not allowing him to print it), and even lets you establish document expiration so that contents within a given document cannot be viewed past a certain date. To understand these tools to a greater extent, search on Microsoft.com for Information Rights Management (IRM) or Rights Management Services (RMS).
- **Add a Digital Signature**—This option enables you to add a digital method of authentication to your documents. The signature (much like a digital certificate) can be added with the backing of a third party that validates the signed document. You could also add a signature that cannot be validated by others.

- **Mark As Final**—With this option, you can make your document read-only and prevent changes. When you select this option, the document has typing, editing, and proofing marks disabled. This is not a security feature—just a deterrent. People can turn it off to do what they want, but it does stop someone from making thoughtless edits to your work.
- **Run Compatibility Checker**—This goes through your document and lets you know which items that you have included will not carry over (or will be altered) if you convert the document to 97-03 compatibility.

The Document Inspector

To start the Document Inspector, a tool that provides access to a wealth of summary and hidden information about your Word documents, you go to the Office button, select Prepare, and then "Inspect Document". When you start the Inspector, you might see a message that tells you to save your document first. Select Yes if this message appears; then you will see your options, shown in Figure 6.3.

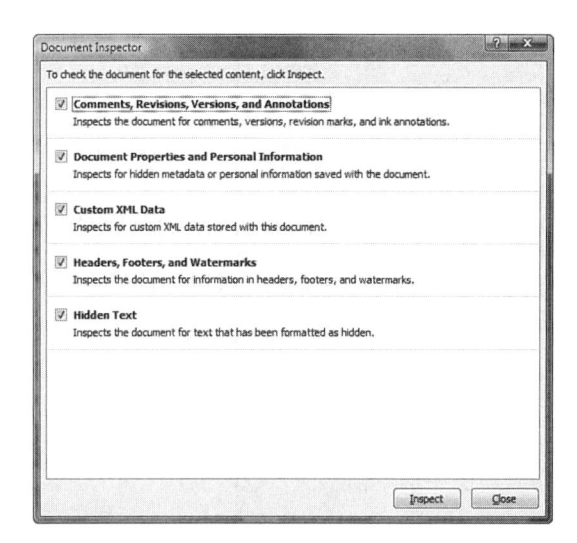

FIGURE 6.3
Document Inspector checks through your document for metadata.

Click the Inspect button to get the process started; it shouldn't take much time for it to return with the results. As you consider the results, you can select Remove All for various parts of the document. Or you can select Reinspect for the document itself. After you have removed all the hidden data, the document is ready to be sent without fear of that information being shared with others.

Full Screen Reading

If you go to the View ribbon and select the Full Screen Reading view, you see the updated version of the view known in Word 2003 as Reading Layout. You can also select it from the Status Bar at the bottom of your screen.

> **NOTE**
> The purpose of the Full Screen Reading layout is to make documents more legible onscreen, first, by hiding most of the user interface. The presentation is further enhanced by using ClearType technology to make the text easier on the eyes. ClearType provides a crisper display on modern monitors. In addition, new fonts are being used by Microsoft to take advantage of the ClearType technology, including Calibri, Cambria, Consolas, Candara, Corbel, and Constantia.

You'll notice in Full Screen Reading (shown in Figure 6.4) that the ribbons are hidden to maximize the reading area. The list of options to choose from includes Increase/Decrease Text Size, Show One/Two Pages, and Allow Typing. These are all available to enhance your ability to read and work at the same time.

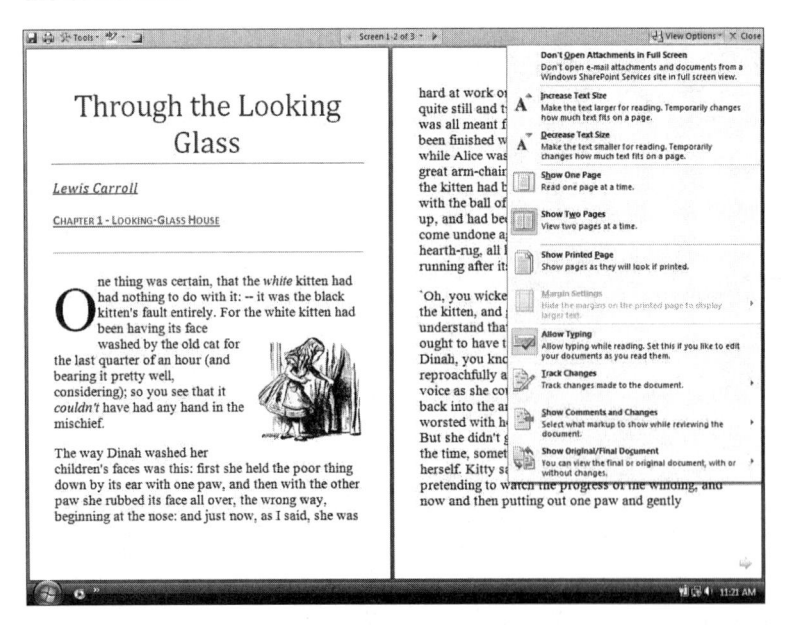

FIGURE 6.4
Customizing the Full Screen Reading view.

Moving from page to page is simple using the up/down arrow keys or the right/left arrow keys to navigate through your documents. In addition, as you move your cursor toward one side or another, it turns into a hand that enables you to turn the pages with a click of your mouse. Finally, at the bottom of the pages are arrows you can select to move from page to page. To exit Full Screen Reading view, click the Close button on the upper-right side of the document.

The Building Block Organizer

One new feature in Word 2007 is the use of Building Blocks. These are basically saved "blocks" of preconfigured items. In the past you could create a document that included a header/footer and a variety of formatting and either save the document and then use it when you needed it, or save it as a template so you could call it up when necessary. You might have even created macros that inserted all the items you needed, including the formatting. Now, however, you can create blocks that can be included separately, at your discretion. For example, you can create a header block and a footer block that are inserted separately. This gives you more control over what you include in your documents.

To create the building block you want, first create the text or formatted section. For example, if you want to create a footer building block, you can make the footer according to your specifications. When it's exactly what you want do the following:

1. To save the footer, select the footer and go to the Insert ribbon.
2. Under Quick Parts in the Text grouping, select Save Selection to Quick Parts Gallery.
3. When you select this, the Create New Building Block dialog box opens; from here, you can determine the name of your building block and the gallery you want it to be a part of (as a footer you can save it to the footer gallery).

To see some or all of your building blocks, you can go to the Insert ribbon, select the Quick Parts options from the Text grouping, and select Building Blocks Organizer (see Figure 6.5). Here you can see a grouping of various types of blocks, including Cover Pages (which is another new feature that enables you to quickly add a cover page to your documents, also located on the Insert ribbon).

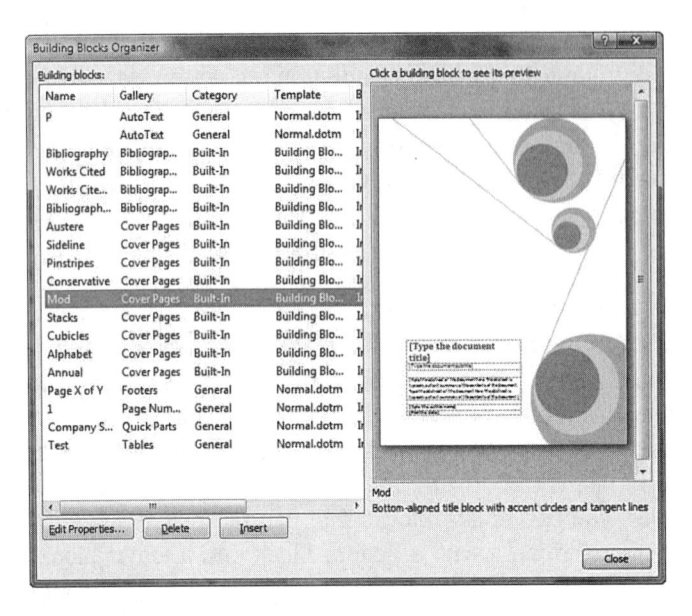

FIGURE 6.5
The Building Blocks Organizer.

Translation Tools

One of the coolest features in Word 2007 for those of us who sometimes work with documents in other languages is the built-in translator tool and the translator tips tool. In addition, in Vista you can add keyboard layouts that allow Word to recognize documents written in different languages. (That feature makes it so you don't see squiggly lines under every word of a document in a foreign language.)

To work with the Translate tool, type the text you want translated and select it. Then, in the Proofing tool group on the Review ribbon, select the Translate button. You can also right-click a selection and select Translate.

The Research pane appears and you can choose to translate from one language to another (see Figure 6.6). The company that assists with the translation is WorldLingo.com. If you find that all the text you selected wasn't translated, it's possible you sent too much. Do the translation in smaller sections of a few sentences at a time. Or you can choose to have an entire document translated by selecting the green arrow. The tool lists 15 languages that can be translated to 14 languages, including English. The only exception is that the document cannot be translated to Arabic.

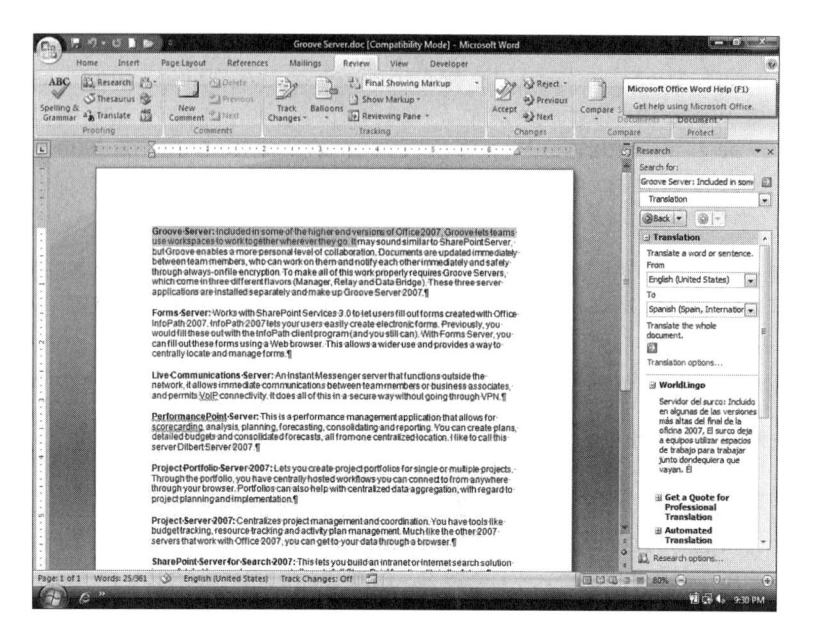

FIGURE 6.6
Word's Translation tool can help pave the way for translating documents from one language to another.

If one of your documents is in a foreign language, you can turn on Translation Screen Tips from the Proofing tool group on the Review ribbon. You can pick from one of several languages, including Arabic, English, French, and Spanish.

Using Word 2007 As a Blog Editor

As you probably already know, the word *blog* is short for weblog, which is a journal (or newsletter, public diary, set of organized rambling, and so on) that is frequently updated and read by anyone in the world who wants to. What you might not know is that Word 2007 makes it easy to write and publish blog posts directly from Word.

First, you need a blog account, which you can get anywhere that publishes blogs (you could also register your own domain and use special blogging software to publish blog

> **TIP** For other languages, you might try searching for other document processors that can work separate from Word (although still cut/paste into Word). The most incredible software available for working with Chinese (and it also has Korean and Japanese) documents is NJ Star (www.njstar.com). It's not a translator, but if you have a document with Chinese characters, it can convert that document into Pinyin for you (the phonetic version of Chinese) and can translate the characters or groupings of characters. It's also excellent for students learning Chinese.

posts to it). Among the popular free blogging services worth trying are Blogger, MSN Spaces and LiveJournal. After you have the account, select the Office orb and select New, New Blog Post. When the Register Blog Account dialog box opens, click Register Now to register your account with Word 2007. If you have more than one blog account, you can register as many of them as you have and then can select whichever account you want to use for your posting.

If you created your document first and now want to post it to your blog site, select your Office orb and then select Publish, Blog. If the site is registered, you can post it up to the mothership. If not, you can register at this time.

Why use Word 2007 to blog?

That's a good question. And the answer is mainly because it is easier for some to use Word to do things. It's a program they are comfortable with and if they can blog from it, maybe they will blog more. Also Word 2007 has some powerful features you can take advantage of, such as the spell-checking and the translation tools we discussed earlier. So, give this feature a try; we think you'll like it...and maybe even mention our book on your blog site!

Excel 2007

Excel is fast approaching the number-crunching prowess of Deep Thought, the fictional computer of *The Hitchhiker's Guide to the Galaxy*. Some would say Excel is "a mere abacus, mention it not," and we would know they've read the book...and are pretty nerdy like us.

John Walkenbach has been writing about Excel for many years now. Here is what John had to say about the new Excel in his book *John Walkenbach's Favorite Excel 2007 Tips & Tricks* (ISBN: 978-0-470-13766-6):

> I've been using Excel for more than 15 years, and Excel 2007 is by far the most significant upgrade ever. For starters, it has a new user interface, new open file formats, a larger worksheet grid, better use of memory and CPUs, new functions, and more templates. Dig a bit deeper and you'll find worksheet tables, 100 levels of undo, easier formula construction, better-looking charts, unlimited color choices, SmartArt, a handy page layout view, new conditional formatting options, new collaboration features, a very useful compatibility checker, workbook themes—and even skins so you can change the look of the entire program.

One of the great changes in Excel 2007 is the increase in worksheet size. David Gainer, the group program manager for the Microsoft Excel team, provided a list of increased worksheet capacity in Excel 2007 on the team's blog site: http://blogs.msdn.com/excel/default.aspx. Table 6.1 lists some of the highlights.

Table 6.1—New Limits in Excel 2007

Change	Old Limit	New Limit
The total number of available columns in Excel	256 (2^8)	16,000 (2^14)
The total number of available rows in Excel	64,000 (2^16)	1.1 million (2^20)
Total amount of PC memory that Excel can use	1GB	Maximum allowed by Windows
Number of unique colors allowed in a single workbook	56 (indexed color)	4.3 billion (32-bit color)
Number of conditional format conditions on a cell	3 conditions	Limited by available memory
Number of levels of sorting on a range or table	3	64
Maximum formula length	1000	8000
Maximum formula nesting levels	7	64

Here are a couple of excellent tips from our good friend and Excel guru Bill Jelen (www.mrexcel.com):

Sometimes people mark cells that they need to investigate later. Some people apply a red font or a red background to these cells. Say that you now want all the red cells to come to the top. Right-click a red cell and select Sort, Put Selected Cell Color on Top. Yes, you can now sort by color!

The good news is that the capability you already have with Excel for creating workbooks, working with formulas, analyzing data, and constructing a variety of charts is essentially unchanged—with the exception of the new ribbon. Over the next few sections, we'll take a closer look at some of the cool highlights for Excel.

TIP: There are now 1.1 million rows and 16,000 columns. That is 17 billion cells, up from 16 million cells in Excel 2003. However, when you open an Excel 2003 spreadsheet in Excel 2007, you have only the 16 million cells. You specifically have to go to the Office orb menu and select Convert to update the workbook file to Excel 2007 and unlock the additional rows.

Naming Ranges

Section courtesy of The New Paperclip
www.thenewpaperclip.com

For the uninitiated, naming a range is a great tool you can use in Excel. It enables you to give a descriptive name to a range (such as Expenses) instead of using the normal notation such as (A10:A25). This is very handy if you work with quite a few formulas in a sheet.

First, you might wonder why you would name a range in Excel. The answer is to make it easier to work with formulas. So, I went looking for the Formulas tab in the Ribbon. And there it was, a whole section on Named cells, which includes the Name Manager (which enables you to control all the name references you have added to your workbook), Name a Range, and a few other Name functions.

Adding in the Analysis ToolPak Add-in

Excel is filled with a tremendous amount of built-in functions, but you can add more functions. One useful add-in is the Analysis ToolPak (ATP) that includes additional functions related to dates, statistics, finance, and engineering.

It's included for free, and all you have to do is open your Control Panel, select Programs and Features, select your Office 2007 installation, and select Change. You'll be allowed to make the change to your Excel by choosing to have the add-in Run from My Computer, as shown in Figure 6.7.

To see a list of all the add-ins, click the Office button and then click the Excel Options button. Click to display the Add-Ins group and you'll see a button toward the bottom of the window called Go. Select Excel Add-Ins from the Manage drop-down list and click Go. Excel opens the Add-Ins dialog box, showing your currently installed add-in routines.

One example of the usefulness of the ATP add-in is the special-purpose date and time formats, such as EOMONTH(TODAY(),0), which gives you the last day of the current month (a great tool for when you're trying to calculate payments that are due on the last day of the month). You can change the value from 0 to 1 to return to the last day of the next month or change it to -1 to return the last day of the previous month (0, of course, returns to the last day of the current month). Other useful functions include WORKDAYS and NETWORKDAYS, which help in calculating project timelines.

Chapter 6 Office Tricks for Vista Masters   **223**

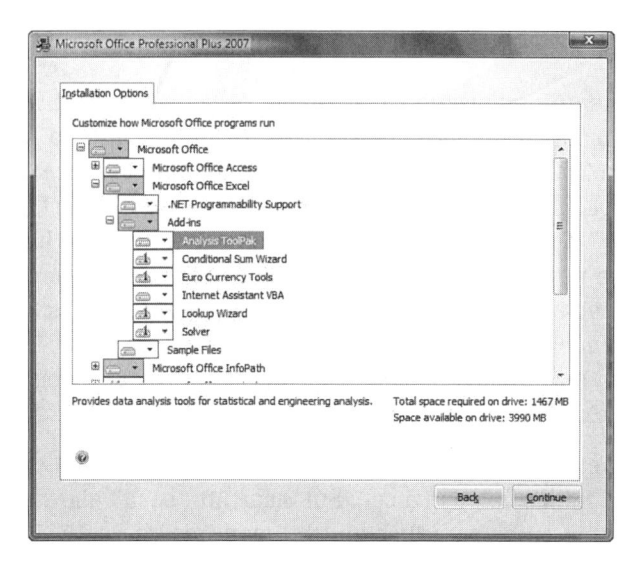

FIGURE 6.7
The Analysis Tool Pack add-in.

Here are a few other add-ins to install directly from within Excel (they are already installed on your computer, you just have to activate them):

- **Analysis ToolPak VBA**—Enables developers to publish financial, statistical, and engineering analysis tools and functions using Analysis ToolPak syntax
- **Conditional Sum Wizard**—Creates a formula that sums data in a range if the data matches criteria you specify
- **Euro Currency Tools**—Formats values as euros, and provides the EUROCONVERT worksheet function to convert currencies
- **Internet Assistant VBA**—Enables developers to publish Excel data to the Web by using Internet Assistant syntax
- **Lookup Wizard**—Creates a formula to look up data in a range by using another known value in the range
- **Solver Add-In**—Calculates solutions to what-if scenarios based on adjustable cells and constraint cells

SmartArt for Excel 2007

As opposed to using Visio to create organizational diagrams of your team structure, business processes, marketing diagram, project management timelines, and so forth SmartArt was introduced in Word 2003 as a way to include basic charting in Office documents. However, the 2003 implementation of SmartArt was a bit bland. In fact, you can see these tools in Office 2007 if you save a document in compatibility mode (using the 97-2003 format) because the new version of SmartArt requires the new document format. Office 2007 includes a much fancier-looking set of lists, process graphics, pyramids, and other business diagramming tools. SmartArt is included in Word 2007, Excel 2007, and PowerPoint 2007. The PowerPoint version is a little better because you can select any existing text, right-click it, and select Convert to SmartArt.

There is one flaw to the Excel version: In the older version of AutoShapes, you could have text in the AutoShape come from a value in a cell. But SmartArt doesn't allow this. Fortunately, you can overcome this problem. Bill Jelen, the man known as Mr. Excel (www.mrexcel.com) has written a way to overcome this problem.

1. First, create the static SmartArt.
2. Use the `Design` and `Format` ribbons to get the graphic as close to finished as possible.
3. Click inside the SmartArt border, but not on any shape in the SmartArt.
4. Press Ctrl+A to select all the shapes.
5. Then press Ctrl+V to paste. You will now have an identical copy of the SmartArt, but this version is made up of AutoShapes. (That's where the trick comes in.)
6. Now select the text in one of the shapes.
7. Click the Formula bar.
8. Type =`<CellNumber>` (to indicate the location of the value), and you are all set.

Sharing Your Excel Data

There are many ways to share your Excel data with others. Here are a few you might have thought about, and one that you probably haven't.

For starters, if you have a SharePoint Server 2007 running Excel Services, you can save your workbook to that server and then others can access your workbook through a browser via Excel Web Access. In addition, you can use dashboard reports to display critical data in your workbook. One good thing to note is that other users do not need to have Excel 2007 installed to use Excel Web Access.

You can also share your Excel workbooks by using a document management server that others can access. If that server is running SharePoint Services 3.0, other collaboration features are available that users can take advantage of, such as automated workflow, document libraries, checking in/out versioning, reporting, and so on. To place your workbook on a document management server, click the Office orb and select Publish, Document Management Server; then indicate the server location and the name of the workbook.

> **NOTE**: If you are sharing workbooks with people who are not using Excel 2007, keep in mind that Office 2007 documents use a new file format based on XML. Documents saved in the new format cannot, by default, be opened using Office 97-2003. The way to get around this is to save your document using the Start orb, Save As, 97-2003 Document. This ensures backward compatibility. Some features, however, will not be available under this "compatibility mode."
>
> If that's not acceptable, you can always visit office.microsoft.com and download the, "Microsoft Office Compatibility Pack for Word, Excel, and PowerPoint 2007 File Formats." This makes it possible to open 2007 Office documents in Office 2000, Office XP, or Office 2003.

Of course, you could also click the Start orb, select Send, and then select Email or Fax. You could also print the spreadsheet and hand it out. You can even save the workbook as a PDF or XPS document and share it with others in a completely different format.

Using Google to Share Data

Section courtesy of Bill "Mr. Excel" Jelen
www.mrexcel.com

Google has a spreadsheet sharing feature that enables two people to collaborate on the same spreadsheet at the same time.

To get started, go to http://www.spreadsheets.google.com. You will need a Gmail account to get a Google Spreadsheet account.

After you sign up, you will have a simple online spreadsheet. It can accommodate up to 10,000 cells but does not support charting, pivot tables, or VBA. The real power, though, is the capability to share the spreadsheet in real time with another person. To begin sharing, click the Share This Spreadsheet link in the upper-right part of the screen. You can then invite others to view the spreadsheet. You can choose to invite people to Edit or to simply View.

When you are done, you can then download the spreadsheet to your desktop in .xls or .csv format. You can work on it and upload it to for the next round of edits.

Dragging Tip to Fill Cells Quickly

One of the cool things about Excel cells is that you can put a couple of numbers in one or two cells, select those cells, and drag. You will notice that the numbers are filled in automatically based on the pattern previously set. For example, type Monday in Cell A1, Tuesday in A2. Select both and then grab the little fill handle (the square dot in the bottom-right corner of the cell). As you drag, the other days of the week will be filled in. After seven cells it starts the week over again on Monday.

Excel can do this with any number of series, from straight numeric patterns to sequences such as the following:

- Monday—Tuesday, Wednesday, Thursday, Friday, and so on
- Jan—Feb, Mar, Apr, and so on
- January—February, March, and so on
- Q1—Q2, Q3, Q4, and so on
- Qtr 1—Qtr 2, Qtr 3, Qtr 4, Qtr 1, and so on
- 1st period—2nd period, 3rd period, 4th period, and so on
- Oct 23 2006—Oct 24 2006, Oct 25 2006, and so on

However, there is a trick to alter the way this works. For example, normally if you just enter a 1 in a cell, or Monday alone, and try the same drag method to fill cells, the default routine is for the 1 to just be repeated (same with Monday). However, if you hold down the Ctrl button as you drag, it augments the default behavior and gives you increments more along the lines of what you normally look for.

Conditional Formatting

Conditional formatting is a feature that enables users to automatically apply formatting to cells depending on the value of the cell or the value of a formula. Examples of how this can be used are provided by David Gainer on the Excel team's web blog (http://blogs.msdn.com/excel/default.aspx). He mentions having all test scores below 50% turn red, or all tasks assigned to a specific person turn green.

Conditional formatting isn't new, but you are going to love some new features in Excel 2007. Directly on the Home ribbon, under the Styles grouping, is the Conditional Formatting selection. Here you can choose to use data bars, color scales, or icon sets to enhance the presentation of your data.

Another cool trick from Bill Jelen, Mr. Excel, is that you can set up a table with 20 customers in column A and 20 numbers in column B. Then you can select the numbers in column B (but not any total cell!). From the menu, select Home, Conditional Format, Data Bars and then select Blue. Excel adds a great visualization—you can now see the relative size of each number on a bar inside the cell!

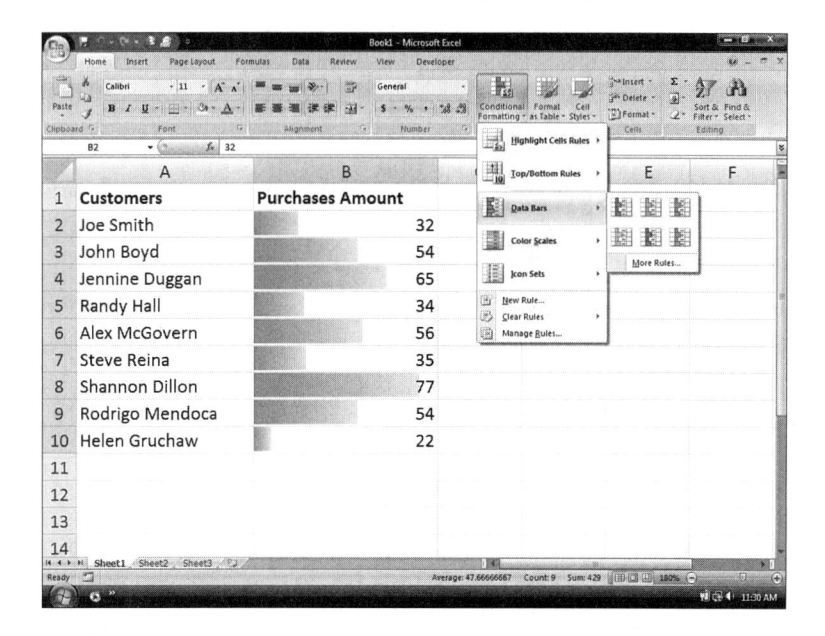

FIGURE 6.8
Conditional formatting.

Going Beyond the Highlights

There is obviously a lot more to learn about Excel 2007. These are a few highlights we thought you would like. For more information on using Excel, we recommend the following:

> Ed Bott, author of the book *Office 2007 Unleashed* (www.edbott.com).

> Bill Jelen, Mr. Excel (www.mrexcel.com), for books and podcasts that will enhance your Excel abilities; he's informational and entertaining.

> David Gainer—Search for his commentary in Excel blogs on the development blog site: http://blogs.msdn.com/excel/default.aspx.

> John Walkenbach is another highly respected Excel guru who has written many fine books on the subject (http://j-walk.com/ss/).

PowerPoint 2007

Some of the best new features of PowerPoint have already been mentioned with Word or Excel. For example, preparing documents before sharing is the same in Excel and PowerPoint as it is in Word. SmartArt is included in Word and Excel, as well as in PowerPoint (although, as already mentioned, it's a bit easier to work with in PowerPoint because you can select text and have it switch into SmartArt easily). You can also save PowerPoint presentations into PDF or XPS format. So, the big question here is, "What is new with PowerPoint 2007 that hasn't already been touched on?"

The answer to this question comes courtesy of PowerPoint expert Echo of Echo's Voice (www.echosvoice.com/2007.htm). Among many others, she included the following key points in her list of great new features in PowerPoint 2007:

- **Text and Shape Effects**—Shadows, reflections, glows, bevels, 3D rotation, and transforms (like the old WordArt shapes).

- **Selection Pane**—Woohoo! A taskpane lists all objects on the slide. We can rename objects (and that name shows up in the custom animation taskpane, YEAH!), change the stacking order, and make the object visible or invisible in the pane.

- **Grouping and Pasting**—To group items quickly in PPT, just select them and press Ctrl+G. To ungroup, press Ctrl+Shift+G. In addition, although you might know that Ctrl+V is a shortcut for Paste. Now, in PowerPoint 2007 you can press Ctrl+Alt+V as a shortcut to the Paste Special dialog box (works in Word and Excel, too.)

- **Charts Are Done in Excel**—No more MS Graph. Charts are now done in Excel. But don't panic! It's not scary, I promise. When we insert a chart in PPT, we still get a dummy chart to begin with, just like always. I think in the long run the change to charting in Excel will make charting much better.

- **The New Presenter View**—If you are an avid PowerPoint presenter, you will love this feature, which enables you to display your PowerPoint presentation on one monitor (or through a projector) but see the Presenter View on your screen. This enables you to customize your slideshow for your audience on-the-fly and preview what your next slide will be so you don't have to memorize the presentation or work with awkward notes.

- **Placeholders**—In 2007, you can now add placeholders to your slide masters. From the View ribbon, select Slide Master to open the Master view. Select a slide layout on the left and then click the Insert Placeholder button and select the type of placeholder you would like.

Working with Themes

Here is an Office-wide feature that unifies the overall look of your presentations. On the Design ribbon, under the Themes grouping, is the capability for you to choose from amongst 20 different preconfigured themes, as shown in Figure 6.9. These themes include color schemes and font options that carry from one Office application to another, allowing you to create presentations that are more pleasing and that work together aesthetically.

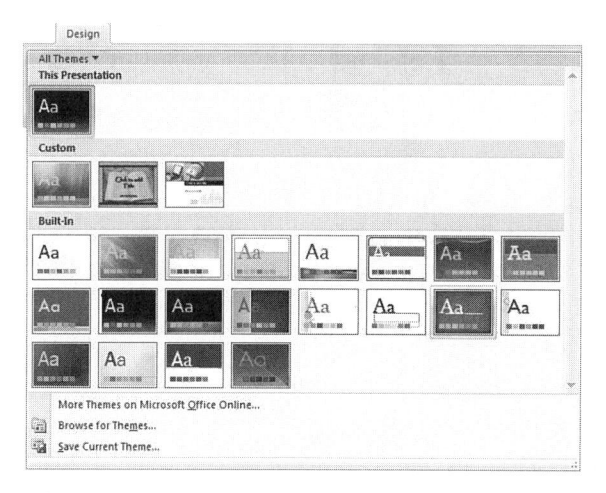

FIGURE 6.9
Themes work from one application to another.

In addition, you can create your own themes by changing the color and font features. You cannot change the effect, but you can select which one you want for your custom theme.

Going Beyond the Highlights

With PowerPoint, there is a lot you can do to impress your audience. The tips discussed here are just a few useful nuggets for those who are already proficient in PowerPoint from previous versions. To start from the beginning and work your way up, check out the useful content these PowerPoint Masters offer:

- **Echo Swinford (http://www.echosvoice.com/)**—A Microsoft PowerPoint MVP (Most Valuable Professional). When she's not working on new media, she is answering almost all the questions on the PowerPoint newsgroup. Echo is also the author of *Fixing PowerPoint Annoyances*, published by O'Reilly.

- **Ellen Finkelstein (http://www.ellen-finkelstein.com/)**—Also has some great articles on her site and has written the book *How to Do Everything with PowerPoint*.
- **Bill Dilworth (http://billdilworth.mvps.org/)**—Another MVP who has some online tips and some online add-ons to enhance your PowerPoint presentations.

> **TIP**
> If you really, really want to master PowerPoint, you first have to see beyond the program itself. Cliff Atkinson has done just that with his book *Beyond Bullet Points* http://www.sociablemedia.com. The true heart of this book is that it is really about people communicating with other people. Cliff says, "By using a commonly available software tool to help you do that, you can find focus, clarity, and engagement."

Outlook 2007

When you open the other applications (Word, Excel, PowerPoint), you cannot help but be wowed or intimidated by the new interface. But then when you see Outlook, you might be slightly disappointed that not much seems to have changed from its predecessors. The interface does have slight differences, and when you compose a new message, you will see the ribbon display the other applications have, but the rest of the changes are under the surface.

Here is a list of some of the newer features:

- **The New To-Do Bar**—In previous versions of Office to see things like your calendar, you had to switch views. In this version all the way to the right is a cool To-Do bar that enables you to see your calendar and a task list that shows you immediate items as well as emails you have flagged. If you flag it, it's now right before you so you won't forget. It also includes tasks from the Microsoft Office OneNote 2007 note-taking program, Microsoft Office Project 2007, and Windows SharePoint Services 3.0 Web Sites.
- **RSS**—You can now subscribe to RSS feeds and download the articles into folders like email messages. This makes them searchable.
- **Outlook Editor Is Out**—Word Editor is in. The Word Editor is the only editor now and you don't need Word to use it; it comes as a special DLL file included with Outlook.
- **Search**—Indexing is working constantly in the background making, your search ability much faster and more powerful than before. Similar to the Vista search capability, you can begin typing letters and the search already begins to search ahead for what it thinks you are looking for.
- **Calendar**—Now you can share your calendar quickly with a feature called Calendar Snapshots, which essentially creates an HTML form of your calendar to share. You can also publish your calendar to the Web so others can see your schedule.

- **Security features**—Junk mail filtering and anti-phishing filtering are included. These two features keep your Inbox from filling up with trash and also keep you away from the ever-growing false set of websites out there.

Just to be fair that not everyone is as excited about the enhancements, you can check out http://chris.pirillo.com/2006/05/26/65-reasons-why-outlook-2007-will-suck/, where you'll find 65 personal rambling points from Chris Pirillo titled "Why Outlook 2007 Will Suck!" He is not just a "Microsoft-Hater;" he has some legitimate concerns and has sent them to the development team for response.

Integrating Outlook 2007 with the Vista Sidebar

Ryan Gregg, program manager for Microsoft Outlook, has announced on his blog two new Outlook gadgets for your Vista sidebar (http://gallery.microsoft.com/).

Outlook Upcoming Appointments—The Outlook Upcoming Appointments gadget shows you your next three to five upcoming appointments from your Microsoft Office Outlook 2007 calendar in the Vista sidebar, just as they appear in the Outlook 2007 To-Do bar. You can double-click appointments to open them in Outlook. The theme of the gadget matches the theme of Office. If you are receiving security prompts, you can turn off the option to see the appointment organizer. This gadget works only with Outlook 2007.

Outlook Tasks—The Outlook Tasks gadget shows you your tasks, flagged email, and flagged contacts from Microsoft Office Outlook 2007 together in the Vista sidebar, just as they appear in the Outlook 2007 To-Do bar. You can sort the tasks by date, category, or priority, and you can include or exclude groups you don't want see. The gadget has two sizes so you can see more or fewer tasks. You can double-click tasks to open them in Outlook and enter new tasks into Outlook through the new item row at the top of the gadget. You can mark tasks complete by clicking the checkbox on the left side of the gadget. The theme of the gadget matches the theme of Office. This gadget works only with Outlook 2007.

Color-Coding Your Outlook Items

Section Courtesy of Annik Stahl, The Crabby Office Lady at
Author of The Microsoft Crabby Office Lady Tells It Like It Is:
Secrets to Surviving Office Life (ISBN-10: 0-7356-2272-8)

I've often been asked whether you can color-code your email messages so you can see, at a glance, which email pertains to which category (such as who it's from, whether it relates to a certain project, and so on). So far, that hasn't been possible. But now, color categories can be assigned to messages, contacts, appointments, tasks, and so on. I love this because I might have a message, a task, and a calendar item all relating to the same project, and when I see that they've all been flagged with the same color, I know that they're all part of one big happy family.

For an existing message in your Inbox, you just right-click it, point to Categorize, and then click a color category. If it's an open message, on the Message tab in the Options group, you can click Categorize and then click a color category. You can change the color associated with a category at any time and create a new color category. And, to make things even easier, a Categorized Mail search folder has been added to Search Folders in the Navigation pane and provides a view of all your categorized mail items.

Getting More from the Outlook Calendar

Section courtesy of Adriana Morriale, Edison, New Jersey
Owner of the training company Custom Computer Training and an M.O.S. Certified Instructor for NJ County Colleges

When creating a new Appointment or new Meeting Request, you can type directly in the Start Time or End Time date box—text such as "next week," "in two weeks," or "tomorrow." Outlook recognizes the text and automatically calculates the date for you! In addition, if you type "noon" in the Time box, 12:00 p.m. is automatically entered."

Chapter 7

MASTER VISTA NETWORKING

The Network and Sharing Center

Windows Vista is a desktop operating system that is designed to be user-friendly. Networking is meant to be as easy as possible for users in Vista, but that doesn't mean we can't squeeze every last little bit out of it, right? Starting with the Network and Sharing Center—found through Control Panel tools—you will notice a beautiful new look to your networked machine, as shown in Figure 7.1.

IN THIS CHAPTER

- The Network and Sharing Center
- Wireless Networking
- Function Discovery
- Media Sharing with Windows Media Connect
- Network Diagnostics
- Windows Meeting Space: Virtual Meetings, Real-time Collaboration

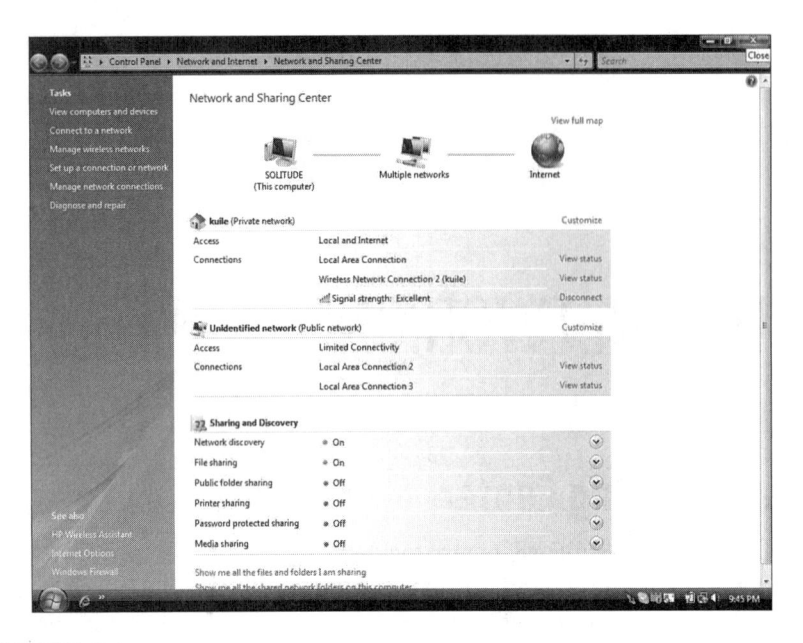

FIGURE 7.1
The Network and Sharing Center: Connecting to a network or making your own home network has never been easier.

The main panel displays a compressed view of the network map, information about existing network connections, and any resources the user can locate on the network (or is sharing on the network—a Links section at the bottom shows all files and folder currently being shared by the user). The task pane gives you access to common network tasks, including Diagnose and Repair, Manage Network Connections, and more.

The Network Connectivity Status Indicator

The NCSI is the networking icon that sits in your taskbar notification area commonly called the systray. It has four states, and you can use these to quickly see whether a problem exists. It either tells you No Connectivity (which has a little red X), Connectivity Problem (which has a warning sign over it), Local Connectivity (which has only the computers), or Internet Connectivity (which has the globe icon on top of it indicating that you have access to the Internet). Another enhancement to this icon is the fact that if you have a notebook computer with a built-in network card and a wireless network card, in the past you would have two network status icons. One of these might appear broken all the time because you don't usually have both plugged in and available. With Windows Vista, one of the benefits with the new NCSI icon is the fact that it consolidates all your network connections to the one icon. Thus, if there seems to be a problem with one of your connections and you hover your mouse over the NCSI icon, you'll see the two distinct network connections listed there individually."

Bob Kelly
Founder of AppDeploy.com—a resource focused on desktop management products and practices.
Homepage: http://www.bkelly.com/
Podcast: http://www.realtime-vista.com/podcast/

NCSI can detect the status of your network pretty well on its own but, like in IE 7 you have to tell it about your web proxy. If you're behind a proxy, NCSI doesn't require that you tell it, but it will react a lot quicker if it knows about it. So, to let NCSI know about it you can use the `netsh` command to set proxy.

Note that the `netsh` command is used for wireless local area network (WLAN) and provides methods to configure connectivity and security settings. You can learn more about `netsh` through an Internet search or by typing `netsh /?` from the command line.

Greg Shields, a senior consultant for 3t Systems (http://www.3tsystems.com) in Denver, Colorado and contributing editor for *Redmond* magazine, gave an interesting war story about tuning Vista networking with the `netsh` command. A network admin named Scott Brondel had emailed a problem he was having trying to join an upgraded Vista laptop to his domain. The system took forever to connect, Group Policies were having difficulty applying, and so forth. He says, "trying to RDP to servers outside of my local subnet would either time-out or just give me the gray background screen. Just about anything not on my local subnet was hit-or-miss." Apparently the problem is connected to Vista's automatic network tuning. Greg says, "Turns out that you may need to tune Vista's automatic network tuning—by turning it off." It worked for Scott.

The Network Map

You might have noticed at the top of the Network and Sharing Center a mini-map of your connection to the Internet with a connecting router between (refer to Figure 7.1). If you select the option View Full Map, you see an expanded view of your computer and everything to which your computer is connected, including network connections (wired and wireless), computer-to-computer connections (called *ad hoc*), and connections to the Internet. The map shows you problems between connections as well, so you can begin diagnosing connectivity issues visually before you make corrections physically.

Preston Gralla, the editor of WindowsDevCenter.com, wrote the following about the network map:

> To see my favorite new networking feature, click View Full Map, and Vista shows you a complete map of all of the PCs and devices on your network, including switches and gateways. Click a device or hover over it, and you'll see more details. So click a PC, and you'll see shared network files and folders. Hover your mouse over a device and details about it will be displayed—for example, its IP address and MAC address.
>
> Does that mean the Network and Sharing Center is perfect? Far from it. The Network Map tends to be flaky in its support of non-Vista PCs, for example. Still, this is a big step forward for networking with Windows.

To note what he is talking about, check out Figure 7.2. You'll see that a computer named Lapcycle couldn't be placed on the map. And yet this system is plugged into the network the same as the others and is accessible. But it is an XP machine, so the word *flaky* seems to apply.

FIGURE 7.2

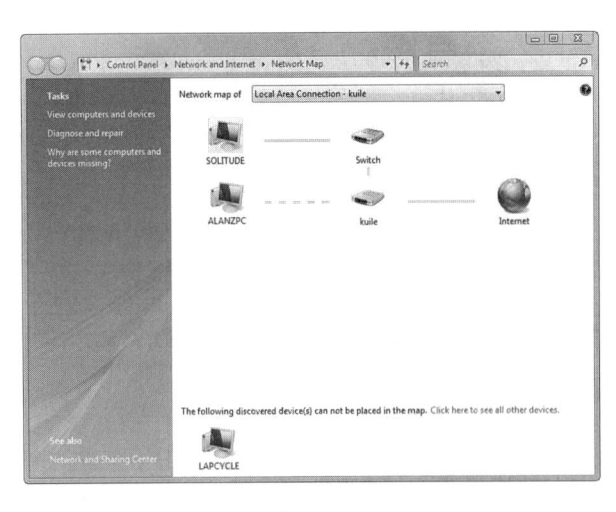

The Network Map is one of the coolest features, but it's still a little flaky.

This could be frustrating in a mixed XP/Vista environment, which many people are going to be dealing with for the next couple of years. You might see your XP systems; you might not. They might appear and disappear at will. At least in Figure 7.2, you can "see" that the machine exists, but it just isn't part of the topology.

Patrick Squire, of MSBlog.org, explains the reason for the problem on his blog at http://www.msblog.org/2006/11/23/link-layer-topology-discovery-lltd-responder/. He says, "The simple reason is that Windows XP couldn't or wouldn't respond to the LLTD Call made by Windows Vista over your network. (LLTD enables device discovery via the data-link layer and determines the topology of a network (802.3 Ethernet & 802.11))."

Link Layer Topology Discovery (LLTD) allows Vista devices to obtain information about other devices on the network and even diagnose problems with them. To fix your XP machines, you can install the LLTD Responder Microsoft released. Find it on the Microsoft download site or through Knowledge base article KB922120.

Gabe Frost
Windows Core Networking blog site
http://blogs.msdn.com/wndp/

> In its basic form, LLTD allows a Windows Vista PC to accurately map the topology of your home network. In short, this map is a rich diagnostic tool designed to be a visual replacement for command-line `ping` (and I suppose `arp`). LLTD Mapper (component which initiates probes and draws the map) heuristics are able to ascertain what types of network elements (which may or may not implement the LLTD Responder) are interconnecting PC/devices that implement the LLTD Responder (component which responds to probe requests). If a PC/device implements the Responder, rich information such as: custom icon, IPv4/IPv6 address, MAC address, configuration URL, etc. is visible within the map.

So, what sorts of devices can have LLTD included besides Vista (and now XP)? Did you know that the Xbox 360 has LLTD included? So, if you connect your Xbox 360 to your network, you should see it in your network map!

In addition, a Windows Rally Development Kit (located at http://www.microsoft.com/whdc/rally/rallykit.mspx) is royalty free and provides all the source code developers need to implement LLTD support. Linux was used as the main reference, but the Windows Core Networking team says the code can easily be ported to other platforms including network routers, access points, NAS, PVRs, media players, and so forth. The blog site notes that in addition to showing up in the Windows Vista network map, devices—which have their own custom icon and attributes—that include a qWAVE-enabled application "can do real-time bandwidth estimation, congestion detection, etc. for adaptive network streaming/transfers."

Customizing Network Settings

For each of your connections, you can provide a name of your choosing and select whether you want that connection to be part of a public or private setting. You also have to determine a location you want to use. This is all done the first time you connect to a network, but you can go back and customize your connections and make changes.

The three network locations are Home, Work, and Public. These settings automatically configure your firewall settings to adjust to the type of network you have chosen. For example, if you select Public (considered untrusted), the firewall settings are more strict because you will be accessing things such as airport networks or the network at the local Wi-Fi coffee spot.

Mitch Tulloch
President of MTIT Enterprises
http://www.mtit.com

> In Windows Vista, there are now three different firewall profiles: Domain, Private, and Public. These three profiles match up with the different network categories available in Vista. A network category (or network location type) is the type of network that a Vista computer is currently connected to. There are basically three network categories, though the UI suggests that there are four. When you log on to a Vista computer for the first time, you're presented with a dialog asking you whether your computer will be used at Home, at Work, or at a Public Location. Choosing either Home or Work basically gives the same result—your network category is set to Private. If you choose Public Location, your network category becomes Public. You can manually switch between categories using Network And Sharing Center, or Vista can detect when the network connectivity of your machine changes and switch categories for you. And if you join your computer to a domain, your network category becomes Domain. That means there are three underlying network categories (Domain, Private, and Public) and these correspond one-to-one with the three firewall profiles available and having the same names.

Each location option causes different settings to be established, for example

- **Domain Location**—The firewall is automatically turned on and is configured through Group Policy settings provided by Active Directory. In addition, all the settings for network discovery and file and printer sharing are configured through the Group Policy.
- **Public Location**—The assumption with this option is that you are physically exposed on an insecure network. The result is that the firewall is turned on and network discovery is turned off, along with all forms of sharing (file, folder, printer, media are all off by default).

- **Private Location**—This assumes you are safe and trust the environment (home or work) to which you are connected, perhaps even knowing that there are other safeguards in place to protect you like a good router with a firewall and security settings. Even still, the firewall is on, but network discovery is also on. All sharing options are still turned off by default, but you can easily enable them.

Wireless Networking

Windows Vista makes managing your wireless connections much easier than in XP. We now have improved management tools and configuration screens to work with to make wireless networking something for the masses.

When you make a connection, you can name it and then save that connection and have Vista connect to the network when you are in the proper range. So, if you take your laptop from work to the coffee house, to work, or to your friend's house, you can configure each connection and then tell Vista to automatically connect to it when you are in range. How important is this? Preston Gralla says, "In a world that's increasingly wireless, and in which many people connect to multiple wireless networks—at home, at the office, and in public hot spots—this is a very big deal."

Alex McGovern
Head of Sales, ClipTraining.com

> Another great Vista wireless feature is the ability to configure wireless connections to accept one connection over another. In my building we have 10 people with wireless access points. With XP if I start off my laptop a little to the left, or a little to the right, I get a different network and I almost NEVER get my own.

You can set precedence of one network over another, but you can also ensure that you don't connect to the wrong network.

Preston Gralla
Editor of WindowsDevCenter.com

> Windows XP automatically connects to the strongest nearby network, which causes problems if the strongest network isn't necessarily the one to which you wanted to connect. With Vista, you first have to accept a wireless connection as one of your permanent ones before it will connect automatically. In this way, you'll automatically connect to only the networks you want, even if more powerful ones are nearby.

Getting Connected

You should just connect to whatever is nearby when you turn on your system. But sometimes that doesn't happen. How would you know (besides the obvious lack of web page appearance)? Well, in the Network and Sharing Center, you would see a red x on the mini-map through the connection line. You will also see the Network Details say Not Connected. The globe will disappear from the network icon in the systray as well.

In the event you don't already have a connection, you can click Start and then Connect To, which displays the dialog box that allows you to choose the various connection options. You can go through the Network and Sharing Center by selecting Connect to a Network. Vista shows you all the available networks in your area from which you can choose.

If it's a wireless network that requires a Wired Equivalent Privacy (WEP) or Wi-Fi Protected Access (WPA) security key, you see the dialog box shown in Figure 7.3. Type the key and click Connect.

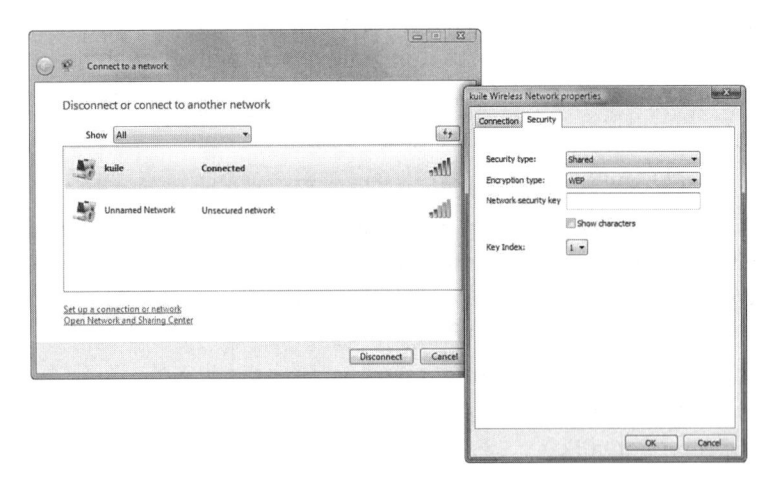

FIGURE 7.3
Including your WEP information.

Some wireless networks require security validation. Paul McFedries, in his book *Microsoft Vista Unveiled* (published by Sams), said the following:

> Some security keys are quite long (for example, a 128-bit WEP key has 26 hex digits). To ensure that you enter these long keys correctly, activate the Show Characters check box to enter the key in plain text. Just make sure no one in the vicinity is *shoulder surfing*— looking over your shoulder to see the key.

Ad-Hoc Wireless Networks

If you don't have a wireless access point, visiting friends can still access the Internet through your computer. So, let's say you have a laptop with integrated wireless connectivity but you don't use this because you connect through your LAN connection to your cable modem and are content with this arrangement. Now a friend comes over and wants to share information with you. Even more than that, he wants to access the Internet. What can you do? Well, you could buy a wireless access point. Or, you could configure an ad-hoc network.

To do this, you go through the Network and Sharing Center and select Setup a Connection or Network from the Tasks pane. You have a variety of options from which to choose. Look for the option to set up a wireless ad-hoc network and follow the steps in the wizard.

An ad-hoc network creates a temporary connection between your computer's wireless access and the wireless access of another computer within 30 feet. In this way you can share documents, play multiplayer games, or even share your Internet connection.

One thing you might want to know about ad-hoc networks is that IPv6 is a requirement.

What Is IPv6?

You are probably already aware that the global implementation of IP is version 4. When IPv4 was developed it was more than what was needed for the 1970s networking world. But it wasn't designed to handle what we have been throwing at it: millions of worldwide connected computers transporting data around the clock.

Because IPv4 was designed with 4-octet addressing (which handles only about 4.3 billion addresses), the number of addresses we can use is limited. Network Address Translation (NAT) has helped to ease the strain on the addressing problem, but IPv6 can support about 50 octillion IP addresses. That should keep us set for a while.

But IPv6 is more than a way to extend addressing schemes. True, it does provide a 128-bit address space. In addition, IPv6 streamlines header and addressing to support hierarchical routing infrastructures (making IPv6 routers faster). Security is also beefed up with IPv6 by enhancing protection against scanning attacks and requiring the use of the Internet Protocol Security (IPSec) for cryptographic protection of your traffic. You can learn a lot more about these and other features from "The Cable Guy" (a series of articles written by Joseph Davies, a technical writer in the Windows Networking and Device Technologies Group at Microsoft). For the purposes of this discussion, the article you should read is at http://www.microsoft.com/technet/community/columns/cableguy/cg1005.mspx. In addition, you can read the book *Understanding IPv6* by Joseph Davies, which can help you to start planning to transition to IPv6 internetworking and find out all about the next-generation Internet—from its features and benefits to its packet structure and protocol processes.

Bradley Mitchell, an industry professional specializing in networking software with a bachelor's degree from M.I.T., commented on IPv6 and Vista.

> The new Microsoft Vista operating system contains built-in support for the IPv6 network protocol. Some news outlets recently have suggested Vista IPv6 may cause Internet network traffic problems. It's true that some extra traffic to DNS servers will be needed to support IPv6 queries, but this by itself is no big deal. In the long run, IPv6 will become the standard for Internet Protocol support, which will help the Net continue to grow for many years to come.

IPv6 wasn't released with Vista; it has actually been included in earlier OS versions (Server 2003 and Windows XP had support for IPv6). The capabilities offered were limited and configuring the settings required using the command-line tools, but it did exist. So, how is the Vista version different? In the article "How Vista Will Handle IPv6" on http://www.windowsdevcenter.com, Mitch Tulloch gave an excellent overview of the differences.

> The key difference between the old and new platforms is that prior to Vista the TCP/IP networking stack of all Windows platforms was implemented as a dual-stack architecture. This meant that the driver for the IPv6 stack (Tcipi6.sys) was a separate networking component from the driver for the IPv4 stack (Tcpip.sys), so if you wanted IPv6 connectivity you had to install IPv6 protocol support from the Network Connections folder because in Windows XP and Windows Server 2003 only IPv4 is installed by default. It also meant that the IPv4 and IPv6 stacks each had their own separate transport layer so they implemented TCP and UDP separately. Additionally, each stack had its own separate framing layer to encapsulate IPv4 and IPv6 packets for transmission over different LAN or WAN media.
>
> In Vista (and Longhorn Server), however, a fundamental change has taken place, for the Next Generation TCP/IP stack is now implemented as a dual-layer architecture, not dual-stack. That means the two network layer components for IPv4 and IPv6 share the same transport layer components for TCP and UDP. It also means that IPv4 and IPv6 share a common framing layer at the bottom of the stack. And it means that IPv4 and IPv6 are both enabled by default—there's no separate protocol to install using the Network Connections folder—though it is possible to disable IPv6 support at the physical layer in Vista if you're in an all-IPv4 networking environment. But the idea is that we're not likely to remain in such pure IPv4 environments for long as more and more large

enterprises (and possibly whole countries like China, Japan, and South Korea) migrate their legacy IPv4 networks to IPv6, so leaving IPv6 enabled by default is probably a good idea.

In Vista now you also can configure IPv6 settings using the GUI and not just using `netsh` from the command line. Another change is that Teredo, an IPv4/v6 transition technology for supporting end-to-end communications through NATs using IPv6 global addresses, is enabled by default on Vista computers that are members of a domain. Still another enhancement in Vista is that IPSec over IPv6 now fully supports both data encryption and IKE, and instead of having to configure IPSec policies and security associations from the command line, now you can use the IPSec snap-in to do this more easily from the GUI. Finally, the new APIs of the Next Generation TCP/IP stack let developers write network-aware applications more easily, though consideration should be given to ensuring that applications are still compatible with down-level Windows platforms.

To learn more about IPv6, you can read the RFC posted on the Internet Engineering Task Force website at http://tools.ietf.org/html/rfc2460.

IPv6 and Ad-Hoc Networking

Microsoft has enabled IPv6 by default in Vista. There are several reason for this change, and instead of complaining about it, we should just get on board. Why? Well, let's consider the words of Brien M. Posey (www.brienposey.com), a technical author who has produced thousands of articles, tips, and whitepapers since 1995. He wrote an article called "Get Ready to Run IPv6 (Whether You Want to or Not)," which was originally posted on Windows Networking.com. You can also find it at http://searchnetworking.techtarget.com/home/0,289692,sid7,00.html, though. Here are some of the highlights:

The United States federal government has mandated that all federal agencies must make the transition to IPv6 by June of 2008. In an effort to make the transition easier for the government and for others, Microsoft has enabled IPv6 by default in Windows Vista. Since most people expect IPv6 to be the protocol of the future, Microsoft has based at least some of Vista's new networking features on this protocol.

When Microsoft created Vista's peer networking component, one of their goals was to make it easy for anyone to transition between corporate networks and ad-hoc networks. As such, the development team worked under the assumption that people other than IT professionals would want to use the peer networking feature and that external resources such as DNS servers and DHCP servers would not be available.

This is where IPv6 comes into play. IPv6 supports discovery of services in a way that makes ad-hoc collaboration possible. For example, let's assume that a group of people wants to form an ad-hoc network and communicate using the collaboration services. As the network is formed, one person in the group launches an application that is designed to integrate with the collaboration services. As soon as the collaboration services start, they transmit a multicast message to everyone on the ad-hoc network notifying them of the service's availability.

Obviously, there is a lot more to learn about IPv6 and over the coming months and years we will certainly see more information released by Microsoft on how IPv6 will be implemented in future products.

Windows Connect Now

We've been talking about wireless connections in this section, so we should mention that WCN has been improved over Windows XP SP2's version. WCN was designed to help make setting up a wireless network easier. Gabe Frost on the Windows Core Networking blog site http://blogs.msdn.com/wndp/ said:

> WCN is compliant with the Wi-Fi Alliance Wi-Fi Protected Setup protocol, and is purposed at simplifying the setup of new wireless networks and then getting PCs and devices connected to that network. For Vista general availability, a PC connected via Ethernet to a Vista logo'd wireless router (or any wireless router that implements Wi-Fi Protected Setup) is able to discover and configure the un-configured wireless router. Hopefully in a subsequent service pack, Vista will have the ability to configure an un-configured wireless router wirelessly. Once you unbox your shiny new wireless router and wire it to the Vista PC, go to Start, Network, where you'll see an icon for the wireless router. Double-click this icon to start the configuration process.
>
> Once your secure wireless network is set up, you can add additional PCs and devices just as easily. From Start, Network, click the Add a Wireless Device button. Any un-configured wireless devices that support Wi-Fi Protected Setup will be discovered here, but unfortunately, not Vista or XP PCs (hopefully this support will be added in a subsequent release). Select any of these devices, then your newly created profile, and the device will be automatically associated to the network. There are also many devices which support the USB version of WCN, such as the Xbox 360, Vista, and XP PCs. In this same screen, you can insert a USB key and push the newly created network profile onto it, then insert the USB key into any supporting PC or device to add it to the network. I love the idea of setting up an entire wireless network and associating all my PCs and devices without having to remember any of the settings; I'm sure you will, too.
>
> Incidentally, regarding WCN, Vista SP1 will allow a wireless PC (not just a wired PC) to configure the AP.

Function Discovery

With Windows XP, you would search for systems and a limited set of devices through Network Neighborhood. You would see the other computers on your network and any devices that had Universal Plug-n-Play support enabled, such as your router. The ability you had here was limited, although you could browse network file shares. The Core Networking Team focused on improving these features in Vista. Network Neighborhood is now Network Explorer, and more than a name change is involved, thanks in large part to the implementation of function discovery.

Gabe Frost
Windows Core Networking Blog
http://blogs.msdn.com/wndp/

In Vista's Network Explorer (the replacement to XP's Network Neighborhood), devices are discovered using function discovery. Function discovery can find devices using much more efficient, diverse, and robust protocols than were available in XP's Network Neighborhood. These protocols include NetBIOS, UPnP/SSDP, and Web Services Discovery (WSD). Further, additional providers can be added via a flexible function discovery platform, which means software developers can plug their own discovery methods in for a consistent user experience through the Network Explorer.

So how does this relate to Network Neighborhood? In Vista, you can access the Network Explorer by clicking Start, Network. The value of improved function discovery is experienced here. PCs, devices, and their respective services are displayed here in all their glory. In addition to the out-of-box high-resolution icons Vista provides for various device classes, Windows shell extensions can be defined (by the device maker, not the end user) for custom icons and actions (when you right-click or double-click the device). And, network connected devices requiring a device driver can be installed directly from the Network Explorer following a simple plug-and-play process (the same experience as installing a directly attached peripheral).

After you are connected to your network, you probably will want to see the other systems and their resources. Vista provides two ways to do this:

- Through the Network Center tasks pane, select Browse the Network.
- Select the Start orb and select Network.

You'll see the main network resources from Network Explorer. Details view shows you the resource name, type, category (workgroup name), and name of the network profile. You can double-click a resource to see what it contains.

Media Sharing with Windows Media Connect

Windows Media Connect (WMC) is a technique for sharing media content on (mostly in-home) networks. With WMC, which uses UPnP for discovery of devices, you can stream media files from your PC to a Digital Media Receiver such as the Xbox 360 or a digital photo frame.

Evolution of Windows Media Connect to Windows Media Player Network Sharing Services

Windows XP initially worked with WMC v1 and 2, but with Windows Media Player 11, XP upgrades to v3—and in Vista we are looking at v4. A new name is given to WMC, too. It's now called Windows Media Player Network Sharing Services (WMPNSS), which explains why we are covering it here instead of in Chapter 9, "Mastering the New Vista Apps," which covers various Vista applications, including Media Player 11.

The basic point of this feature is to allow your Vista system to become a streaming media server by using Vista's native UPnP networking support combined with Media Player 11's cataloging features.

James Bannon wrote an article titled "Media Sharing Made Easy with Vista" at http://apcmag.com/3192/media_sharing_made_easy_with_vista , where he said:

> Not all clients can connect to a Vista-based machine, though. Other Vista clients can, as can the Xbox 360. Check out the playsforsure.com website for a full list of compatible clients. Media sharing works for music files (WMA, MP3, and WAV), video files (WMV, AVI, MPEG-1, and MPEG-2), pictures (JPEG, JPG, and PNG), and playlists (WPL and M3U). According to the media sharing documentation, other file types MAY be sharable, "depending on how your computer is configured"—this basically means that if the content is accessible and Media Player can catalogue it, it should be sharable.
>
> Obviously, though, Microsoft isn't going to support anything beyond what it has explicitly stated. For content like DivX and XviD, streaming support is really dependent on the client. If the client is a Vista-based machine with the right codecs installed, then it should work fine. Clients like the Xbox 360 don't support DivX, though, and can't be made to, and other

> **NOTE:** Universal Plug and Play (UPnP) is a set of network protocols that is supported and developed by the UPnP Forum (http://www.upnp.org) to ensure devices can connect easily within both home and business networks with zero configuration. The goal is to allow devices from a variety of vendors to automatically configure themselves and discover the presence of other devices on the network and see their capabilities.

compatible hardware-based clients will have the same limitation. (You can work around this using one of the various methods of transcoding DivX video into Windows Media Video upon playback, though. Check out Transcode 360 (http://runtime360.com/blog/) and Easy DivX to Xbox 360 streaming (http://www.jakeludington.com/xbox/20060321_easy_divx_to_xbox_360_streaming.html).

Setting Up Media Sharing

Media Sharing in Vista isn't all that difficult to set up; you just have to follow the wizards. To start, open the Network and Sharing Center, expand the Media Sharing section, select Change, and then enable Share My Media.

On the Media Sharing page you can select the box Share My Media To with the default being Other Users of This PC. After you enable your media sharing, as other devices come online, your system detects them and prompts you to allow sharing with them.

You can also select the Settings option to configure what you want to share (see Figure 7.4). You can change how other users see the content shared out (for example, the default setting is under your username) and you can filter out content based upon media type, content ratings, and/or parental ratings.

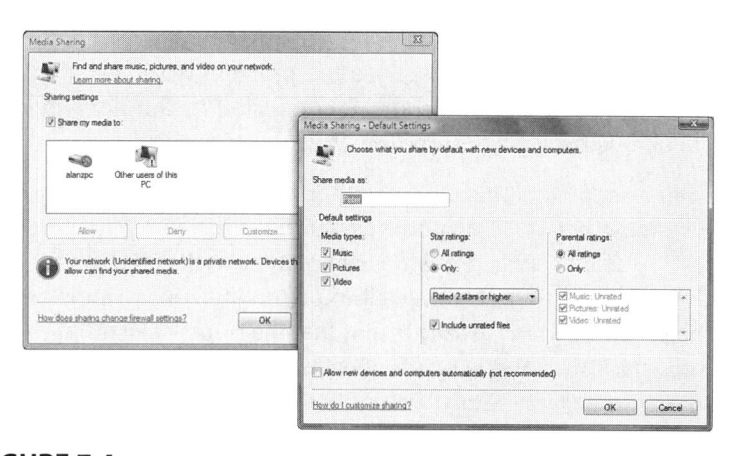

FIGURE 7.4
Configuring your Media Sharing settings.

After you have Media Sharing configured, your computer appears twice on your network (one for your system and one for your Windows media host). Users simply have to right-click the Windows media host and select Open Media Player.

James Bannon
Tech Writer for ACPMAG.com

The one downside with media sharing on Vista is that it's completely reliant on MP11, which means you have to catalogue your digital content in Media Player's library first. This affects how the content is viewed on the network—the library is populated and organized using metadata, so if you're like me and have organized your music into logical folder and filenames with little attention paid to metadata, the library could end up looking like the alley behind a dodgy pub. And that's how it will appear to every client on the network, which is no good at all. To make navigating through the collection anything less than a hair-pulling litany of frustration, you'll have to put some work into applying decent metadata and making the library look at least half-organized.

Network Diagnostics

John Henry is a famous American folk hero who battled in a man-versus-machine scenario against a steam hammer to prove which is better. In the end, he won, but he suffered a heart attack and died. Why bring it up here? Because modernization of network diagnostics requires that we let go of some of our standard methods (unless they are needed).

So, the trick here is to let your system try to diagnose the problem with your network first. You might be used to the XP repair tools and uninterested in letting Windows waste your time. In his book *Microsoft Vista Unveiled*, Paul McFedries writes:

Windows XP came with a Repair tool that did a pretty good job of repairing connectivity problems because most networking problems can be resolved by running the Repair tool's basic tasks: disconnecting, renewing the DHCP lease, flushing various network caches, and then reconnecting. However, all too often the Repair would report that it couldn't fix the problem, which usually meant that the trouble existed at a level deeper in the network stack than the Repair tool could go. In an attempt to handle these more challenging connectivity issues, Vista comes with a completely redesigned Network Diagnostics Tool that digs deep into all layers of the network stack to try to identify and resolve problems.

Initiating a Diagnostic

There are a variety of ways to use the Network Diagnostic Tool. From the Network and Sharing Center, you can select Diagnose and Repair from the Tasks pane. If you are having problems with a specific connection, you can select Manage Network Connects from the Tasks pane and then right-click the connection and select Diagnose (as shown in Figure 7.5). From the Network Connections windows, you can select a broken connection and select Repair This Connection.

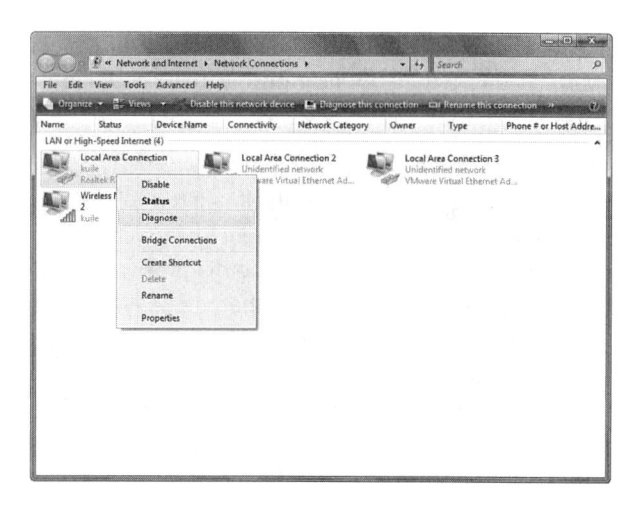

FIGURE 7.5

Diagnose network connections using the built-in tools.

The network diagnostics automatically run a set of troubleshooting tools that analyze all elements of the network stack and provide a systematic diagnosis of connectivity problems. It can then automatically resolve the problems it finds or at least provide simple solutions to walk you through. Furthermore, the network diagnostics data is saved in an event log to help you resolve these issues.

These tools are based on the Network Diagnostics Framework (NDF). Bob Kelly is the founder of AppDeploy.com (a resource focused on desktop management products and practices). He made a podcast called Network Diagnostic Framework (NDF) at http://www.realtime-vista.com. In it, he said the following:

> In previous versions of Windows there wasn't very much help as far as diagnosing network problems. It would tell you the cable is unplugged or not connected but you didn't get any intelligent diagnosis tools. One tool that did exist was the ability to repair a network connection which would basically just renew the IP address, clear the arp cache, clear and refresh net BT, clear the DNS cache, and then it would register with DNS. It would do the same things every time regardless of what the problem was, just a blunt-force repair that would resolve many problems but certainly not all. And it was

doing things potentially unnecessary. So in Windows Vista it is actually looking at the whole layer from the network card all the way up to the application, and then in the context of where it was launched, Network Diagnostics will go and determine at what point there is a failure and then recommend and provide simple buttons in cases where it is possible to resolve the problems. And this same functionality, because it is exposed through a certain framework, (there is an SDK available), vendors with just a couple lines of code can introduce repair buttons in their applications so that if a network connection problem is detected within their application they can leverage NDF to help the user resolve that.

To discuss the actual Network Diagnostic Framework itself a little bit, when it's launched it performs diagnosis based on the context from where it's launched so if you launch from IE the target URL is going to be considered in the diagnosis; if you right-click on a network and say Connect To, then it's going to use that media type as a basis for its diagnosis; and if you're in the network connections folder and you specify a network interface that you click to say Repair this, then it's going to focus on that one network interface. There are three different repair types that NDF supports. There is "automatic" where if it's able to, it will repair it automatically. Sometimes those automatic repairs are going to require administrative credentials but most of the time, problems can be resolved automatically. Then there is also "manual," like when there are times where you need to plug in a network cable or something to that effect. It will be a manual instruction you receive. And then in cases where there are very complex steps [and] a more detailed explanation is necessary, you'll receive help topic links.

There are a couple of scenarios where this would display itself. A cable modem intermittently stops switching network traffic, you call the ISP for support and they are going to tell you to reboot your cable modem. You would probably do that on your own but think of your brother or your aunt or somebody calling you for help all the time. They can go ahead and have NDF tell them "Power off" the cable modem, wait a minute, power it back on. It will tell them that for you, so you don't have to handle those support calls. Of course, that converts into dollars and cents when you talk about an Enterprise environment where these features are surfacing themselves but for you and I at home, at this stage, until you get Vista in the workplace this can help you to not have to support your relatives and friends quite so much.

Here is another scenario: A person goes on a plane, they turn off their wireless radio in their laptop, and then when they land they don't remember to turn it back on. So, instead of being frustrated and trying to figure out what the heck is going on, NDF will pop up and say, "hey, turn your wireless radio back on."

Another common error that occurs when you're browsing the Internet is that a web page will not load. An error message indicates the failure to complete the task (such as `Page cannot be displayed` or `Server is not available`) and prompts you to run Network Diagnostics. Within a few moments, a Network Diagnostics dialog box displays a description of the actual error and provides a recommendation on how to fix it (as shown in Figure 7.6).

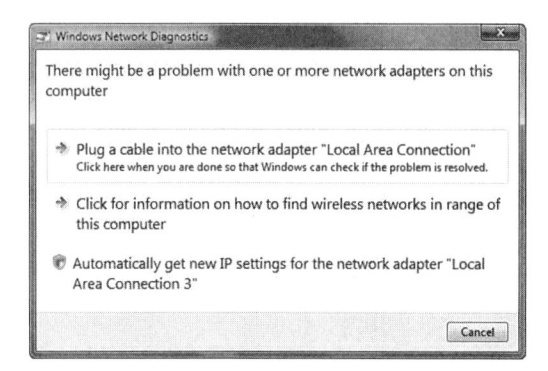

FIGURE 7.6
Windows Network Diagnostics results.

Command-Line Tools

As much as we would like to promote the new diagnostic tools, there are times when you need to (or want to) perform your own diagnostics using the command line. Here are some of the best tools for the job.

- Hostname—Use this to find out the name of your computer.
- ipconfig—Use this to see the IP address of your computer. It's especially useful when that address was provided through a DHCP server and wasn't manually configured within your network options.
- ipconfig /all—This shows you more detailed information about your network connections, including the media access control (MAC) address of each adapter.
- ipconfig /release (/renew)—When working with a DHCP server, this lets you release the address you currently have and request a new one. The DHCP configuration for all adapters will be renewed. To renew the IP address for a specific adapter, type the adapter name that appears when you type ipconfig at the command prompt.
- ping—This allows you to test other systems to see whether they are capable of responding. The ping command uses Internet Control Message Protocol (ICMP) to send

a packet of data to a remote host and then waits for the host to bounce the packet back. When you're having a network connection problem, you can ping your own system (using the loopback 127.0.0.1 or the IP address of your system), ping another system on the same subnet, then ping your side of the router, ping the other side of the router, and perhaps ping another system you know of (such as your DNS server and so forth). You can also ping using the DNS name. If an IP address is returned and you can ping the address, your DNS servers are functioning just fine.

- `nslookup`—This shows you Domain Name System (DNS) servers. This command-line tool helps you troubleshoot DNS issues.
- `arp`—This resolves TCP/IP to MAC address. The MAC address is a hexadecimal address that is burned into the card by the company that produces the card. TCP/IP addresses allow you to have some semblance of order within your network, although the cards themselves are using MAC addresses.
- `tracert`—This verifies that router paths exist between your system and a remote system. It reports the number of hops required to reach the destination and the router for each hop.

Tim Rains (http://blogs.msdn.com/tim_rains/default.aspx) is a Microsoft developer who created a tool (both command line and GUI) you might be interested in. It is used to detect network sniffers running on Windows systems.

Vista Master I have developed a tool that can detect *managed* Windows systems that have network interfaces running in promiscuous mode—a key indicator that a network sniffer is running on the system. I use a host-based detection technique instead of a network-based detection technique in order to make this tool as accurate as possible.

You can find the command-line version (promqry) and the GUI version (promqryUI) from the download center at www.microsoft.com. You should also check out Tim Rains's blog site because he includes a list of all his

> **TIP** Sometimes you might `ipconfig` your system and see that you received an IP address. However, if the IP address is 169.254.x.x, you should know that the computer was not able to receive an IP address from the DHCP server and so gave itself what is called an *automatic private IP address (APIPA)*. I had a personal experience in which one of the servers was not showing up on the network at the Newark airport for Continental Airlines. They called me in to investigate the problem, and it turned out to be something as simple as the DHCP server in Houston not giving out addresses. What made it difficult to diagnose was the fact that DHCP leases addresses so other systems appeared fine because their leases hadn't expired yet. But given enough time, none of the systems would have been able to contact Houston. Not to be corny, but the call could be made in earnest, "Houston, we have a problem!"

favorite command-line tools and their locations to download, as well as information on what they do and how to use them.

Windows Meeting Space: Virtual Meetings, Real-time Collaboration

You might remember NetMeeting, which enables you to share local programs or documents with any number of remote users and collaborate together. Windows Meetings Space replaces NetMeeting with an entirely new application based on several new features available in Vista, including IPv6.

A few things are required to even begin working with WMS. You need to configure your Firewall settings to work with it, and you need to enable file replication and People Near Me.

People Near Me

To use Windows Meeting Space, you must first sign in to People Near Me. You do this either by starting Windows Meeting Space or directly via the Control Panel. For the latter, you have two choices:

- In Category view, click Network and Internet, and then click the Sign In link below the People Near Me icon.
- In Classic view, double-click the People Near Me icon.

In the People Near Me dialog box that appears, display the Sign In tab and activate the Sign In to People Near Me option. Before you click OK, you might want to take a look at the Settings tab (shown in Figure 7.7), which enables you to change the name and picture that other people see and to control various other People Near Me options.

You can configure People Near Me to work with only trusted contacts. A trusted contact is one who has sent you her contact information in an email message or given you the information on a disk or another type of removable media. A trusted contact's information always includes a certificate. For you to ensure that you can be on someone's trusted contact list you have to send her your contact information. You can do this by going to your Windows Contacts, right-clicking your personal contact, clicking Copy, and then pasting it into an email message for the other person. Do not convert it into a vCard.

> **NOTE** For meetings within the local subnet (People Near Me), you don't need to have a formal IPv6 infrastructure in place. For this reason and others, you can only hold WMS sessions with Vista systems at this time.

FIGURE 7.7
The People Near Me settings.

Starting Windows Meeting Space

When you're signed in to People Near Me, you can launch WMS from the Start orb by typing **Meeting Space** in the Search pane. The first time you do this, the Windows Meeting Space Setup dialog box appears. It asks Do You Want to Enable File Synchronization and People Near Me, and to Allow Windows Meeting Space to Communicate Through Windows Firewall?" If you click Yes, the changes are made automatically.

You might want to know which changes were made to your firewall. To see these, open your standard Firewall (not the Advanced one) and look at the Exceptions settings. You should see a list of three new exceptions. These include Windows Meeting Space, Windows Peer to Peer Collaboration Foundation, and Connect to a Network Projector.

When you have the Windows Meeting Space before you, it's time to start or join the meeting. If you want to start your own session, click Start a New Meeting (see Figure 7.8). Windows Meeting Space prompts you to enter a meeting name and password and then starts the new meeting.

> **Mitch Tulloch**
> *President of MTIT Enterprises*
>
> If you want to know which TCP and UDP ports have been opened for these three exceptions, open Windows Firewall with Advanced Security (under Administrative Tools in Control Panel), select either Inbound Connections or Outbound Connections, and use Filter By Group to select the exception you want to examine. Note that some additional services have also been started at this point, and using the sc query command before and after you start Windows Meeting Space for the first time, shows that the following services have now been started: Peer Networking Identity Manager (ptpimsvc), Peer Networking Grouping (p2psvc), and Peer Name Resolution Protocol (PNRPsvc).

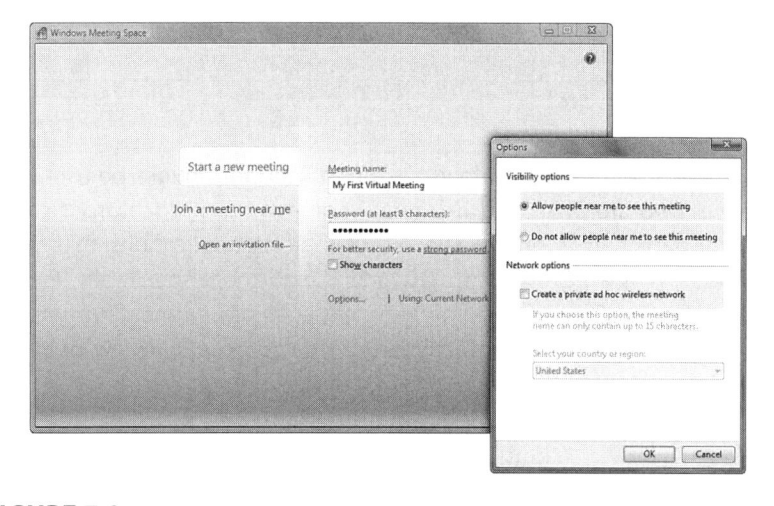

FIGURE 7.8
Configuration options for Windows Meeting Space.

As you can see in Figure 7.9, your meeting space is crisp, offering a clear way to invite others, offer handouts to your audience, and share an application with others. When you share handouts, these are copied to each participant's computer. In doing so, people can edit the handouts and these edits are sent to the copies that others have, but they do not change the original file.

Eric Lee, who was a developer on the Visual Studio Team, saw potential for Windows Meeting Spaces in a variety of fields, including extreme programming.

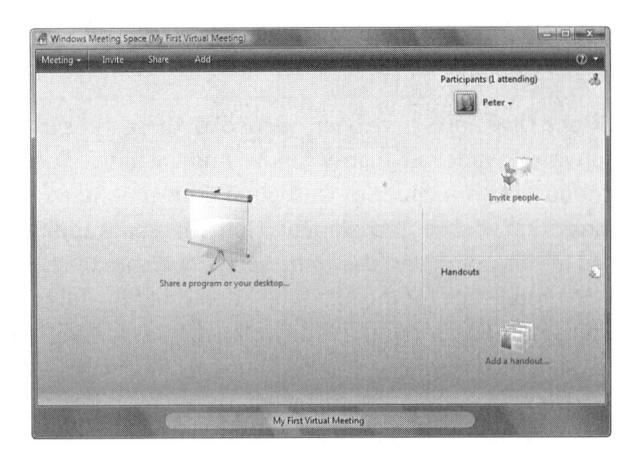

FIGURE 7.9

Your Meeting Space is easy to work with.

> **Vista Master**
> I've been playing with a feature in Windows Vista that I thought might be useful for development teams who are practicing Extreme Programming. The feature is called Windows Meeting Space and is one of the out-of-the-box applications that takes advantage of Windows Vista Peer-to-Peer networking and more specifically, People Near Me. Windows Meeting Space struck me as an easier to use netmeeting/netsharing/livemeeting technology. It seems perfectly suited for a quick code review, or paired programming session.

How do we get others to join us in our meeting? Well, people can view the WMS interface, see the list of available meetings, and select your meeting. You can also email them an invitation and use an invitation file that is shared or transferred.

You can choose to share out a single application, rather than your entire desktop. Others can see what you are doing, but they will not be able to take control of your desktop or application unless you explicitly give them permission.

Deb Schinder (MCSE, MVP for Security) is a technology consultant, trainer, and writer who has authored a number of books on computer operating systems, networking, and security (http://www.shinder.net/). She gave a few additional points for us to consider about Meeting Spaces. In an article on this Vista feature, she said there are built-in security mechanisms:

You can select to receive invitations only from trusted contacts (those who have provided digital certificates verifying their identities) and require participants to enter a password before being allowed to join a meeting. All Meeting Space communications are encrypted so that only authorized persons can see the shared desktops, applications, and files....

Windows Meeting Space lets you configure visibility options. If you make a meeting invisible, Vista users near you won't be able to see it in the list of available meetings and will have to be explicitly invited to join.

Chapter 8

SYSTEM RECOVERY AND DIAGNOSTIC TRICKS

Backup and Restore Center

Computers die. It's true. They overheat; they get old and run down. A lightning strike creeps up the wires into your box. They call them *terminals* for a reason. It's because their lifespan is terminal (okay, not really, but you take my point). The difference with a computer is that you have the ability to back up your data, settings, and preferences and restore them to the same machine with new hardware or an entirely new machine.

IN THIS CHAPTER

- Backup and Restore Center
- The System Rating
- Windows System Assessment Tool
- Problem Reports and Solutions
- Reliability and Performance Monitor
- Memory Diagnostics Tool
- ReadyBoost and SuperFetch
- Vista Recovery: Advanced Boot Options, WinRE, and WinPE

The Backup and Restore Center

Even novice users can open the Backup and Restore Center (shown in Figure 8.1) and work their way through the wizards. To find it you can type **Backup and Restore Center** from the Start orb search pane, or you can open the All Programs folder, go to Maintenance, and select it from there to start the wizards.

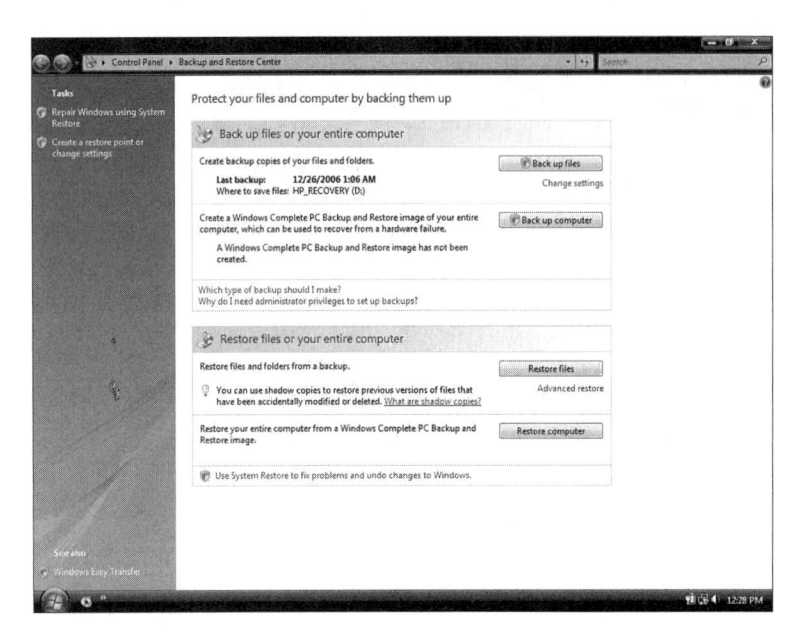

FIGURE 8.1
The Backup and Restore Center is an easy console for novice users to work with.

From within the center you can do the following:

- Back up your data files (or schedule your files to be backed up at regular intervals to ensure data protection).
- Perform a Windows CompletePC Backup image (which creates a snapshot of the entire system, including files). CompletePC Backup is available in the Business, Enterprise, and Ultimate versions of Vista.
- Restore your files or entire PC from the backups you've created.

There are some improvements of the backup program in Vista besides ease of use. Mitch Tulloch, a Microsoft MVP and president of MTIT Enterprises (www.mtit.com), says that choosing "where you want to store your backup files.... This is the biggest improvement in the Windows Vista version of Windows Backup over the Windows XP version of the same tool." You can back up files to another drive on your system, to a removable drive (such as USB), a CD, a DVD, or even to another system using a shared folder on that other system. Keep in mind that you need to include the proper credentials on the other system if you use a network location.

Before you go backing up your complete system, it would be good to know what the caveats are. When you restore your CompletePC backup, you are pretty much overwriting the drive, which can be destructive to the existing contents, so keep that in mind before you decide to test this on your home system just for fun (although reports show that the process works quite smoothly, much like restore CDs that have been included PCs). It's an emergency tool. Also, be sure you have enough disk space for the backup. Compression varies depending on the type of data you backup, so until you get a handle on how much backup space you need, assume a 1:1 backup (meaning if you have 1 GB of data to backup, make sure you have that amount of space available for your backup). With a CompletePC backup, because of the way it works, you cannot save the image to the same hard drive that holds the location of the system files. You'll need another drive (formatted as NTFS) or a bunch of DVD's (the more data, the more DVD's).

Accessing Backups with Virtual PC or Virtual Server

Keep in mind that a CompletePC backup saves its data to a virtual hard disk file (.vhd extension). This is the same format used by Virtual PC and Virtual Server. Now the coolest part about this is—you guessed it—you can mount the virtual disk! Note, this doesn't mean you can boot up the VHD file, just that you can access the information off of it from an existing virtual machine.

Daniel Nerenberg
www.thelazyadmin.com

Ever wish you could grab just one file from a PC backup rather than having to restore the entire backup? Now with Vista CompletePC Backup you can! Using Vista CompletePC Backup, you can now create full backups of your entire hard drive to external media—for instance, a USB hard drive. To browse to the folder you specified, you need to drill down to the folder that contains the VHD file. Now that you know where the VHD is located, you need to open it. Using either Virtual PC 2007 or Virtual Server 2005, you can add the VHD to the list of hard drives installed on a virtual machine (VM) you have already created (a VM install on XP or Vista works best). Now turn on your VM as usual. When the VM is running, you should see the backed-up data listed as a new drive in your VM's hard drive list. You can pick and choose the files you need to recover.

Note: You need to ensure that the account you are using to run Virtual PC or Virtual Server has read/write permission on the VHD file. If the account does not, you might not see the drive and will not be able to mount it in Windows.

After your VM is up and running, you can see the backed-up data listed as a drive by going through My Computer (or Explorer). Philip Colmer (http://pcmusings.spaces.live.com/) says, "If you've got Virtual Server 2005 installed, there is also a command (vhdmount) that allows you to mount a VHD file as a virtual drive within a running system, so you don't need to start up a virtual environment."

Here is a story that demonstrates the real-world side to these solutions:

Bryant Likes, MVP
Senior Solution Developer for Avanade
http://blogs.sqlxml.org/bryantlikes

When I upgraded from Vista Pre-RC1 to RC1, I used the built-in backup program to back up my files. It worked very well for me so when I was upgrading from the Sept CTP to RC2, I decided to use it again. I also put a little more confidence in it and didn't do a completely thorough job of backing up my files (besides the full backup, that is). So, when I realized that I forgot to back something up, I fired up the backup program and pointed it to my Sept CTP backup. However, the tool complained that there were no backup sets on the drive. Hmmmm. I wasn't able to get the restore to ever recognize the backup set, but I did find that Microsoft is storing the backup as a VHD file. Those of you familiar with virtualization will know that that is a virtual hard disk. So, with some help from the Virtual PC guy (http://blogs.msdn.com/virtual_pc_guy/default.aspx), I was able to mount the VHD using Virtual Server R2 SP1 Beta 2's VHDMount utility (yes, that really is the product's name). So I now have a drive on my Vista RC2 machine that contains all the files from my Sept CTP machine and I can browse them and restore them at my leisure. Whoever made the call to back up to VHD, I owe you a beer. Great choice!

The "Virtual Machine Guy" is Ben Armstrong, program manager of the Virtual Machine Team (http://blogs.msdn.com/Virtual_PC_Guy/). He has some great advice to give. One cool trick he offers is to make some Registry changes using a .reg file that enables you to double-click a VHD file to mount it and right-click it to unmount it using the vhdmount tool from your OS (keep in mind that you need to download the tool for your Vista system, although it is installed automatically on systems running Virtual Server 2005).

Virtual Server 2005 R2 SP1 Beta 2 includes vhdmount, a tool that enables you to mount a virtual hard disk directly on your host operating system. Although vhdmount is provided as a command-line tool, a very small amount of work lets you mount VHDs by just double-clicking them. You can create a .reg file with the following contents:

```
Windows Registry Editor Version 5.00
[HKEY_LOCAL_MACHINE\SOFTWARE\Classes\Virtual.Machine.HD]
```

```
[HKEY_LOCAL_MACHINE\SOFTWARE\Classes\Virtual.Machine.HD\shell]
@="Mount"
[HKEY_LOCAL_MACHINE\SOFTWARE\Classes\Virtual.Machine.HD\shell\Dismount]
[HKEY_LOCAL_MACHINE\SOFTWARE\Classes\Virtual.Machine.HD\shell\Dismount\com
mand]
@="\"C:\\Program Files\\Microsoft Virtual Server\\Vhdmount\\vhdmount.exe\"
/u \"%1\""
[HKEY_LOCAL_MACHINE\SOFTWARE\Classes\Virtual.Machine.HD\shell\Mount]
[HKEY_LOCAL_MACHINE\SOFTWARE\Classes\Virtual.Machine.HD\shell\Mount\command]
@="\"C:\\Program Files\\Microsoft Virtual Server\\Vhdmount\\vhdmount.exe\"
/p \"%1\""
[HKEY_CLASSES_ROOT\.vhd]
@="Virtual.Machine.HD"
```

Then if you double-click the `.reg` file (to load it into your Registry), you will be able to double-click a VHD to mount it and right-click it to dismount it.

Backup Status and Configuration

The Backup and Restore Center is the simple way to protect your data. But if you want to make some changes to the process, you need to use the Backup Status and Configuration tool found by selecting Programs, Accessories, System Tools (see Figure 8.2).

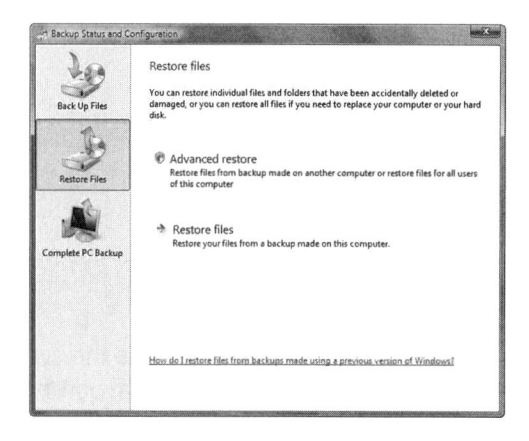

FIGURE 8.2
Backup Status and Configuration options.

It's from within the BSC options that you can choose which disk or network drive to back up to. You can also choose the types of files you want backed up regularly (Pictures, Music, Videos, E-mail, Documents, TV shows, Compressed Files, Additional Files, and so on). And the cool side to all of this is that you can schedule your backup to occur whenever you like.

The System Rating

If you open Control Panel and select System, you are greeted with some basic information about your system, including the version of Vista, the processor and memory settings, and even the Product ID (as shown in Figure 8.3).

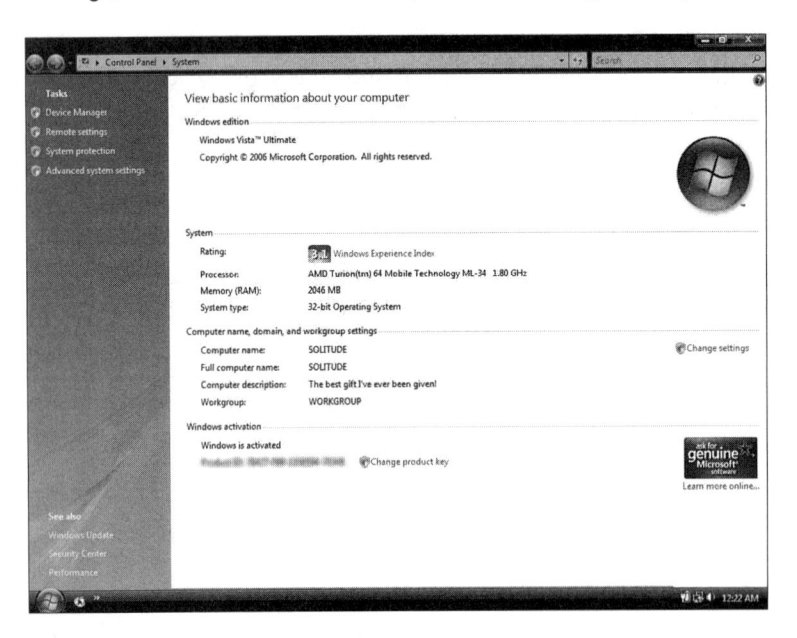

FIGURE 8.3
System information at your fingertips.

One of the more important pieces of information included in System Info is the system rating. This is calculated by Vista on a per-system basis, and it can be changed based on different hardware and configuration changes you can make to your system.

The rating (called the Windows Experience Index) is based on five ratings that are given to your system in the following categories: Processor, RAM, Graphics, Gaming Graphics,

Chapter 8 System Recovery and Diagnostic Tricks

and Primary Hard Disk. The final rating is not, as you might expect, a compilation of all the ratings; it's actually the lowest of the subcomponent scores.

You'll find a good explanation of the level indexing at http://news.softpedia.com/news/Windows-Experience-Index-Calculate-the-Vista-PC-Score-41047.shtml. In general, the levels indicate the following:

Level 1 = Vista capable (just barely)

Level 2 = Upgradeable (target) system

Level 3 = Value end machine

Level 4 = High end

Level 5 = High performance/gaming

Level 6 = Not yet defined

Keep in mind a couple of things regarding this score: First, it's usually wrong when you first look at it. Run it again! Select the link for the Windows Experience Index; then you can see the five subcomponents shown in Figure 8.4. Select the option Update My Score.

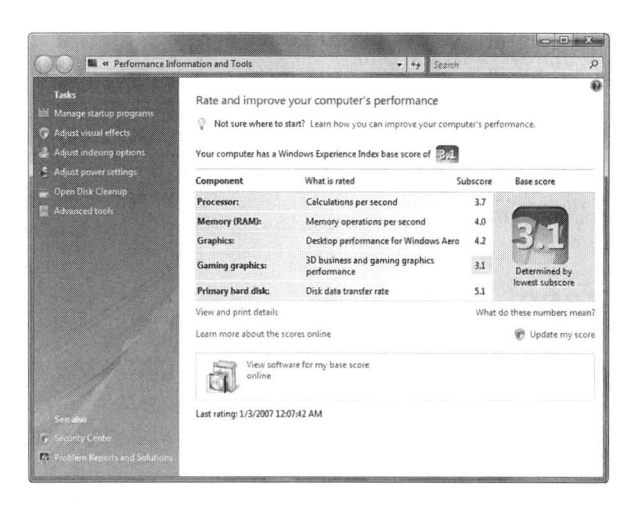

FIGURE 8.4
Rerunning the WEI—second time's a charm.

A big reason for this recommendation is that all the Vista gurus are up in arms over it. Mitch Denny ran the test on his "Ferrari 1000" and came up with an initial reading of 2.8. Ed Bott says he received the same score on his "Ferrari 5000." Keep in mind that it's because of the lowest rating that came from Aero settings on those systems. After readjusting a few settings and making sure they had the latest drivers and updates, they re-ran the tests and they got better scores. The highest rating possible is a 5.9 (for now, obviously Microsoft can alter the settings as hardware improves).

What does that mean? Should we be going crazy to meet these numbers? Well, it depends on how your system is actually performing. The Microsoft help files tell you that a system with a base score of 3 will run Aero and function nicely. But others have run Aero with a lower base score. It's all in the details, and it all depends on what you are looking for.

Alan Wright
Hardware guru

You can alter the results of the WEI if you know how. You can find the XML file (its location is mentioned in the following section) and actually change the numbers. You should first save the original, make the numbers what you like, and then take another look at the tool. Sometimes it works; sometimes it doesn't. But it's fun to try to tweak the numbers.

One odd site on the Net for those who like to compete over these things lets you compare your WEI score to others. Some of these scores seem a little too good to be true, but check it out at http://www.shareyourscore.com/.

But as a Vista Master, you might want to know how the test is performed. When you kick off the update of the score, you can see that it asks for permission to run the Window System Assessment Tool (WinSAT).

Windows System Assessment Tool

For the most part, when you install an OS like XP, you get XP in all its glory, regardless of the box on which you are running it. So, although the underlying DLLs might be different, the OS options should be the same, right? Or should they? Does it really make sense that two systems, one of which is a $200 cheap-o box with cheesy hardware, should be put in the same position to handle the OS features of a mega system? Well, Vista has an underlying tool that helps to differentiate between the two. It's called WinSAT.

When you first install Vista, but before the first login, WinSAT runs its testing process to see what your individual system can handle. It takes that information to determine which operating system features should be enabled or disabled by default. For example, if your system cannot handle Aero, the settings on your OS reduce to Vista Basic mode.

One of the benefits to WinSAT that was discussed at the Microsoft Meltdown Conference in 2005 is that game developers can use the API to focus on the performance for their games as a result of the tests. The game can be developed so that, during installation, the WinSAT tool is run to tell the game which features should be enabled/disabled depending on your hardware. Logically, users who want to tweak their own games can do so, but at least initially the game will perform to the best of your system's ability because WinSAT has informed the game of where that level is.

Phillip Colmer
http://pcmusings.spaces.live.com

> Many bloggers have written about the location of the WinSAT data store. The best of these blogs came from Tony Campbell on the http://vista.beyondthemanual.com blog site. He says, "The WinSAT utility creates its output in the system directory: %systemroot%\Performance\WinSAT\DataStore. Each time you run WinSAT, a new XML file is generated in this folder with the date of the assessment at the beginning of the filename—for example, 2007-01-01 12.00.00.000 Assessment (Formal).WinSAT.xml. In addition, a file exists in this directory with the word *Initial* inside the bracketed part of the filename. This is the system performance assessment carried out when Vista was first installed on your PC.
>
> Keith Combs (a technical evangelist with Microsoft for more than six years, http://blogs.technet.com/keithcombs) tipped us off from his blog site that we "should definitely take a close look at the information inside that file. We only present part of the information in the UI."
>
> When you open the XML file, you can see the extensive level of tests that were performed and, instead of just a simple numerical response, literal response times for the tests run. The average user would never know what to do with all this, but it's cool to know what is happening on your system.

Problem Reports and Solutions

Found in the Control Panel (or by typing **wercon.exe** in the Search pane), this is a new tool in Vista to help you find solutions to your problems (as the name implies). So, when a program closes down unexpectedly it is recorded into a log that you can then request additional information about.

When you open the tool you see a list of tasks you can perform, including the following:

- **Check for New Solutions**—Sometimes (many times) your problem doesn't have a solution, so you can wait until a later time to try again. This will recheck all the problems you have listed in the log and see whether an update to the solutions is offered.

- **See Problems to Check**—Shown in Figure 8.5, you can see all the problems your system has had, the date, and any additional details that might be available. This option enables you to select check boxes for the solutions you want checked as opposed to checking for solutions to all the problems in the log of problems.

- **View Problem History**—Shows you a list of problems Windows has detected up to that point.

- **Change Settings**—You can have Windows automatically check for solutions to problems, or it can prompt you first. You have a variety of "consent levels" from which to choose. You can configure advanced settings, such as the ability to block reports being sent regarding certain applications.

- **Clear Solution and Problem History**—This is a quick way to erase all the recorded problems. After you've made the necessary changes or fixes, you might want a clean slate to start from.

> **TIP**
> One consent level you cannot configure through the Control Panel interface is the Send All Data option, which can be configured only through Group Policy settings. If this setting is configured within Group Policy, all the data is sent without prompts. You can also use Group Policy to completely disable sending these reports from your network systems. Or you can use Corporate Error Reporting.

The Problem Reports and Solutions tool uses a web browser control to help users control information sent back and forth between their systems and Microsoft, but Windows Error Reporting does the underlying work to request solutions. Those solutions can include instructions for fixing the problem, or a *workaround*; it could also include a link to the Windows Update website or to a Microsoft Knowledge Base article.

What Is Corporate Error Reporting?

Consider a scenario larger than just one system (for home users), such as an office with hundreds of systems with which you want to use the Windows Error Reporting (WER). The interface from Control Panel is great for a couple of systems, but analyzing data one system at a time would take forever. Event Viewer is helpful, and you can compile multiple logs, but Corporate Error Reporting is a better way to see the application errors on your network.

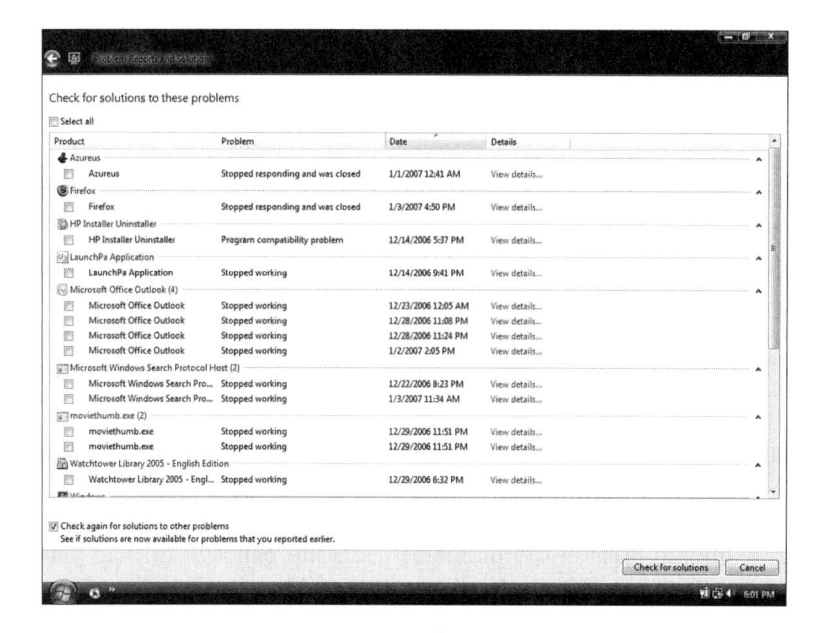

FIGURE 8.5

See which problems you want to check with Microsoft about solutions.

To set this up, you use Group Policy to redirect your error reports to an intranet server using the Corporate Windows Error Reporting GP setting. Then you need to get the analysis programs from Microsoft so you can gather and filter through the many errors you will receive before sending it to Microsoft.

To learn more about Corporate Error Reporting, check out the website http://www.microsoft.com/resources/satech/cer/.

Microsoft organized the error reports into *bucket* categories. With user-mode crashes, these buckets are defined by the name and version of the application, along with the module name and version. With kernel-mode crashes, the bucket includes the stop codes and associated parameters. You can discover the bucket associated with your particular application problem by going through Event Viewer, opening the application logs, and then finding the application crash that relates to your problem. The event includes the bucket number, which Microsoft keeps track of.

Microsoft keeps track of the buckets. Chris Pratley (Microsoft program manager; http://blogs.msdn.com/chris_pratley) discusses how this works on his blog site.

> *Chris Pratley*
> *Microsoft Program Manager for the Office Team*
> *http://blogs.msdn.com/chris_pratley*
>
> When you report the crash, if that is a crash that someone else has already had, we increment the count on that "bucket." After a while, we'll start to get a "crash curve" histogram. On the left will be the bucket with the most "hits." On the far right will be a long list of "buckets" so rare that only one person in all those millions had that particular crash and cared to report it. This curve will then give you a "top N" for crashes. You can literally count what percentage of people would be happier if we fixed just the top 10 crashes.

An article was posted in the October 9, 2006 issue of the *New York Times* by John Markoff called "After a Debugging Race, Will Vista Measure Up?" In it he described the concepts of the 80/20 rule, which basically says that fixing 20% of the coding problems Microsoft gets eliminate 80% of the problems users are exposed to. The point is clear, though, that Error Reporting has assisted in significantly reducing the number of bugs in Vista and Office 2007 software. So, this is one set of features to be thankful for.

Keep in mind that error reporting is a submission tool that should be used in order to help fix existing problems and to create service packs and other updates. Although users may not get a personal response, the information they submit is included in a database for fixes and updates.

Reliability and Performance Monitor

"It is an immutable law in business that words are words, explanations are explanations, promises are promises but only performance is reality." What Harold S. Geneen, CEO of ITT from 1959 to 1977, was trying to say is that "talk is cheap," but performance stands on its own. The question for computer users is how do we determine whether our computers are performing up to par.

Each computer has a baseline. A *baseline* is the optimum, standard way of operating for a computer under its current set of hardware and software. Once you know your system's baseline, you can watch to see whether time or a new application takes a toll on the system's performance and reliability. But literally "seeing" that happen requires a good performance monitoring tool. Vista includes a new version of its Performance Monitor of old.

Reliability Monitoring

What is your standard method for determining the reliability of your system? Most of us determine a system's reliability by how long it has been since it has blue-screened on us or forced us to reboot. Not a truly "technical" way to assess reliability, huh?

So, it is with open arms that sys admins welcome the new reliability monitor. To open it, you can type `perfmon.msc` into any Search field or go to your Administrative Tools and select the Reliability and Performance Monitor.

The main goal of the reliability monitor is to keep track of reliability events that have been defined as changes to your system that could alter the stability or other events that might indicate system instability. Events monitored include:

- Windows updates
- Software installs and uninstalls
- Device driver installs, updates, rollbacks, and uninstalls
- Application hangs and crashes
- Device drivers that fail to load or unload
- Disk and memory failures
- Windows failures, including boot failures, system crashes, and sleep failures

Figure 8.6 shows a system that is becoming more unreliable over time. You can literally watch as your Vista decays. Using the monitor, you can see what is causing the instability. Is it an application or a set of applications? Did it begin with the addition of something new?

The System Stability Chart gives you a visual on how reliable your system looks over time. You are given an overall stability index score: 10 is perfection; 1 is the lowest. The Reliability Monitor retains up to a year's worth of data so you can really see how your system has been performing.

If you see a drop in the stability, you can check the date the drop began and then see if it was one of the following that caused the instability: Software (Un)Installs, Application Failures, Hardware Failures, Windows Failures, or Miscellaneous Failures.

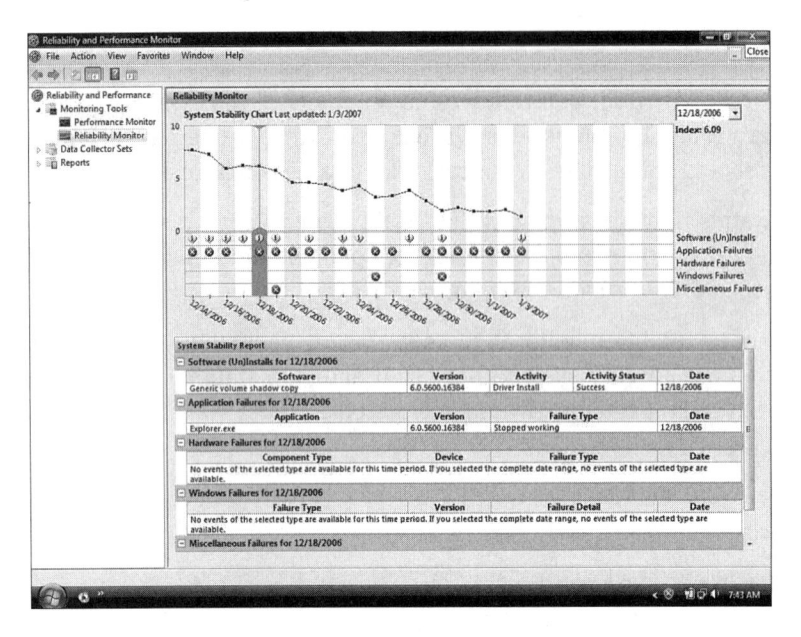

FIGURE 8.6
Reliability Monitor lets you see if your system is something you can depend on.

Many have questioned the validity of the Reliability Monitor. Some of the questions asked by prominent writer Ed Bott include:

> If my Stability Index slips below 5, is it time to do a complete reinstall? Is it really fair to conclude that my overall system stability dropped from a perfect 10 to 8.17 because Explorer crashed twice on May 25, or that it then slid all the way down to 5.77 the next day because OneNote 2007 Beta 1 stopped working twice (and hasn't failed since)?

> The monitor, especially that line chart, needs to be taken with a grain of salt. Its real strength lies in an organized way to see system performance decline based upon specific, recorded situations.

Resource Monitor

The Resource Monitor isn't a different tool, actually. When you first open the Reliability and Performance Monitor, you are presented with real-time views of your CPU, disk, network, and memory in four charts. You can

> **NOTE:** You can stop the Resource Monitor by clicking the Stop button on the toolbar. You can also quickly navigate to any of the more detailed lists by putting your cursor over a chart (it forms a target icon) and clicking in the chart.

click down arrows next to each category to see a more detailed list of what is being done by any one of those resources at that moment (see Figure 8.7).

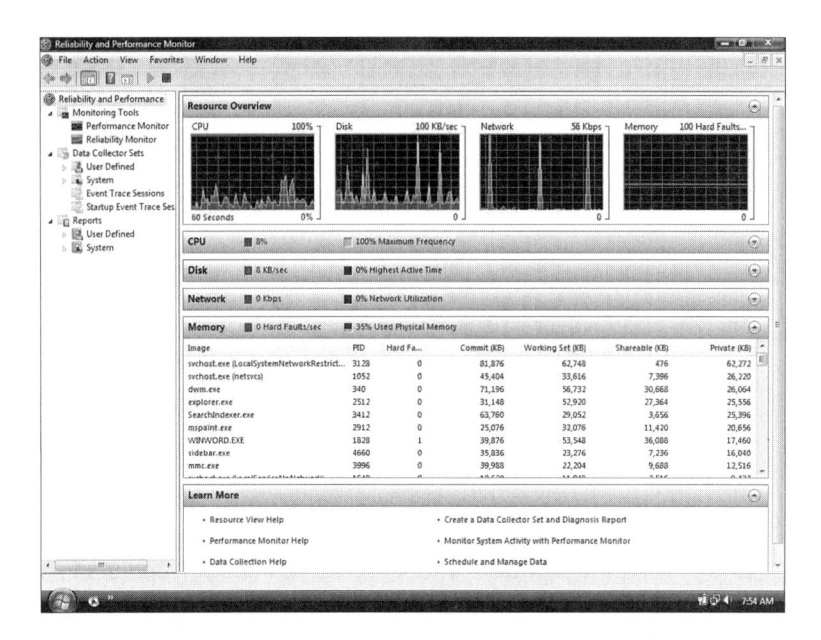

FIGURE 8.7
Resource Monitors let you see your system activity at that moment for CPU, disk, network, and memory.

Performance Monitor

This tool shows you a visual representation of your system so you can inspect a variety of components, beyond what the Resource Monitor shows you. Initially, you won't see more than the % Process Time initially displayed. You can add more performance metrics, called *counters*, by clicking the + sign. When you first see the number of possible counters and instances, you can see that the task of choosing which items to monitor can be overwhelming (see Figure 8.8). Any given system has roughly 85 different performance objects (you can monitor the local system or a remote one). Each of those objects contain counters (there are way too many to know them all). After you have all your counters set up, you can make changes to the way they are displayed. For example, you can change the line colors for each counter to make it easier to determine which line you are watching. You can change the format of the display from a graph to a histogram to a report (numeric display).

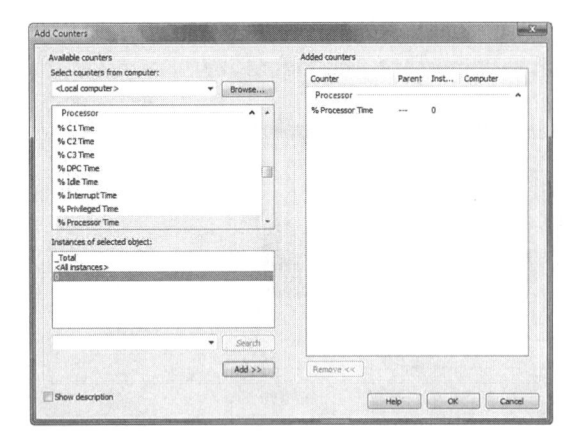

FIGURE 8.8
Adding counters to your performance monitor can be a daunting task.

Baselines and Bottlenecks

Before you can truly know the performance of your system, you need to be able to compare it to something. A *baseline* is a collection of performance data for your system over a set period of time that indicates where your system normally performs under normal working conditions. Without a baseline you have nothing with which to compare your system. You need to compare it to itself at a better time in its past, if that makes sense. When you do see items in the future that indicate your system is running more slowly, these are called *bottlenecks*, because they are tying up your system's traffic in some way. You need to eliminate bottlenecks.

John Kellett (http://www.johnkellett.co.uk) gives the following advice about creating your baseline:

> You may want to take a baseline reading with Performance Monitor before installing an application, install the application, and then take the reading again using the same Performance Monitor counters while the application is in use. Taking the baseline reading itself has been known to throw up a few issues. If your system has decent hardware and a user that doesn't really push it to the limit, I would be expecting the system to be pretty much flatlining. If one counter is a lot higher than you are expecting, then you can troubleshoot this before going any further.

Keep in mind that even though you technically can monitor and perform a baseline remotely, because of the congestion on a network for remote monitoring, Microsoft recommends that you perform baselines locally. In addition, you should log across multiple days at multiple time intervals to really see the performance. Finally, you should check the system's baseline at regular intervals (once a month or every other month) to see how it's doing. Keep in mind that, for larger networks, you might want to obtain third-party monitoring solutions.

Important Objects and Counters to Monitor

We already mentioned that you have many options from which to choose when using Performance Monitor. That's why we went to the masters to ask them which ones are the most important ones to know.

Richard Brucrew of Sebring, Florida, remembers some of the important ones that were important according to the Microsoft exams to be an engineer. Here are some of the exam objects and counters:

Memory

- **Pages/sec**—Over 20 pages/sec could indicate too little RAM. This counter shows the transfer of data from the physical memory in your system to your pagefile. When these counters are too high it indicates a memory shortage. What's the solution? Adding more memory to your system might be your first thought, but before doing that you should consider stopping unnecessary services and background applications that might be using up your memory.

- **Available Bytes**—This should be more than 4MB. If it drops under 4MB, this indicates a memory issue. This setting monitors the amount of memory that is available after the working sets of applications and the cache have been served.

Derek Melber
Independent technical trainer and consultant
From Windows XP Professional Exam Cram, 1st Edition

Memory is often the first performance bottleneck in the real world. The counters related to processor and hard drive utilization might be well beyond their thresholds simply because inadequate memory is causing paging, which impacts those two components.

Processor

- **% Total Processor Time**—A continuously high value can indicate a bottleneck. Anything over 80% for extended periods of time should give you cause to worry. Make sure, though, this isn't during the running of some of those elaborate screensavers (they take up a lot of processor time when running) and that your memory isn't the main cause for the problem.

- **Processor Queue Length**—This should be less than 2, on average. This measures the number of threads waiting in the queue to be processed.

Disk

- **Logical Disk: % Free Space**—Lets you see how much space you have left on your disk.
- **Physical/Logical Disk: % Disk Time**—This counter shows the amount of time spent reading and writing requests. Anything from 50% to 100% indicates a bottleneck.
- **Physical/Logical Disk: Disk Queue Length**—Similar to the processor queue, this should be under 2 for read/write requests that are pending.

> **TIP:** Although a high processor time can indicate the need for a faster processor, you should check the queue length, too. If this is above 2 on average, you might consider adding a second processor or trying to remove pressure from your system by moving certain processes to other systems.

> **TIP:** Where do you turn next? To Guy Thomas, Microsoft MVP). He has a lot of information on his site regarding performance counters. He has an ebook titled *The Art and Science of Performance Monitoring* that is worth downloading from http://www.computerperformance.co.uk/ebooks.htm.

Data Collector Sets and Reports

Although the real-time view of your system is fun to watch for about a minute, to really collect data and manage it for future comparison you need to know about data collector sets and reports, which are new to Vista.

Data Collector sets allow you to put together a collection of alerts and thresholds that allow you to monitor your system immediately or over a period of time. Data collector sets can contain the following types of data collectors: performance counters, event trace data, and system configuration information (including Registry key values). You can create a data collector set from a template, from an existing set of data collectors in a Performance Monitor view, or by selecting individual data collectors and setting each individual option in the data collector set properties.

Nathan Greal
Network admin and Internet blogger

The library of data collector sets you can configure may seem a bit overwhelming. Start off by setting your performance counters and then saving that as a data collector set. Then you know exactly what you are monitoring. You'll graduate over time to the bigger items.

Performance logs are created with a .blg extension and are kept in the Peflogs folder by default. You don't open them from the folder, but from within Performance Monitor itself. If you want to convert these .blg files to other types or you review your logs frequently to see recent data, we recommend that you use limits to automatically segment your logs. You can use the `relog` command to segment long log files or combine multiple short log files. Type **relog /?** from a command prompt to learn more about this tool.

System Diagnostics Report

Data collector sets are absolutely incredible. Diagnostic capability in Vista is much better than in previous versions. Previously, we mentioned that you can set counters, save these as a data collector set, and view your log files. This has been available for some time. But moving to the next level, you can configure a more granular view of your system. To prove it, there are system data collector sets that really impress us.

Nick White, Microsoft product manager for Windows Client, has this to say about Vista's diagnostic capabilities:

To see a quick system checkup, you can do one of the following:

- The simple method is to open Control Panel, go through System and Maintenance, and then click Performance Information and Tools (or you can go through the System applet and select the Windows Experience Index). In the Tasks pane you can select Advanced Tools. Many items are available that you might consider for later reference (quick links can be found to several performance tools, and you might also note some performance issue tips at the top to help you fix some of your performance problems). Locate the Generate a System Health Report option and then wait one minute while the test runs. You'll notice that, even though you went through a different path, you are still using the Reliability and Performance Monitor to run the report.

- Another way to run the same report is to do it from the Reliability and Performance Monitor itself. Open the tool; then from the system data collector sets, you'll notice four preconfigured tests. Select System Diagnostics, right-click, and select Start. Then, under Reports, open System Diagnostics and select the report that is running (the latest one). You will see that it's the same as the previously mentioned method.

- The simplest method to run the test is to open a command prompt (elevated ornonelevated—it asks you for permission to proceed if it is nonelevated) and then type **perfmon /report**.

> **TIP** One of my favorites, as with many others here internally at Microsoft, is the ability to create a System Health Report. This report will help you diagnose your system's health and provides possible solutions [to] issues that may be affecting your PC's health.

You might wonder why you should use this complicated way when you could use the simple Control Panel method. It's a fair point; however, the Control Panel method doesn't give you the other three preconfigured tests—namely, LAN Diagnostics, System Performance, and Wireless Diagnostics. These are also great to work with from the new diagnostics tools to see how your system is doing.

> **NOTE:** If you wanted to run a different data collector set, you could type **perfmon /report "Name of Data Collector Set"** to start it.

System Information Tool

In scouring the world for Vista Masters, we gathered together a few additional tools and tricks for you to use. First is System Information (located under Accessories, System Tools). D. David Dugan, the president of DD&C (http://www.dugancom.com), an IT consulting and solution providing organization, has written several posts regarding the importance of the System Information tool (`msinfo32.exe`). This free tool will really surprise you with the level of detail regarding your system's hardware configuration, the components in your system, and the software installed (including drivers and the services that are running). If you aren't sure whether this tool has value for you, just open it one time. Just once and you will clearly see the level of immediate information that is placed before you...and you'll love it.

You'll notice a high volume of Vista tips and tricks sites on the Web, and most of them will offer the same information. Computer Power User (http://www.computerpoweruser.com) gave us this tip that was worth repeating:

> **Vista Master:** Vista users have a hidden resource, systeminfo, that gives them a quick, comprehensive snapshot of their installed hardware and even minutiae such as the original installation date of the OS, BIOS version, installed and available memory, and much more. To bring up systeminfo, click Start, Run; type **cmd** in the Open field; and click OK. At the command window prompt, type **systeminfo** and press Enter.

What's New in Task Manager

Task Manager, for many of us, is our go-to guy for problems. You have a problem; you go to Task Manager—it's almost ingrained in us. You'll see quick and dirty information about your processes, CPU usage, memory, network, and so forth. So any changes that can benefit us are worth considering.

For one thing, the first time you start it you'll see that you can see just your computer's processes. You can also choose to see processes from all the users of the system. One thing you'll notice right away is the new Description aspect to the Processes tab (see Figure 8.9).

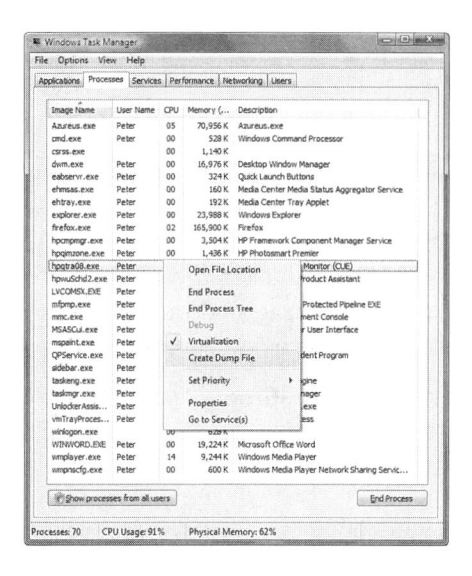

FIGURE 8.9
The new Task Manager adds a Description column and a Services tab.

One of the new features of Task Manager is the capability to create a minidump file of an application that is running. You can right-click an application or process that is running and select Create Dump File (refer to Figure 8.9). You will be presented with a dialog box that shows you where that file has been written. You can use this feature to discover why a particular application might be crashing so often; conversely, if a process has already crashed and is no longer responding, you can try to discover the cause.

After you have the dump file, you need to install the symbols for Vista (which you can get at http://www.microsoft.com/whdc/devtools/debugging/symbolpkg.mspx) and then install the latest debugging tools (which you can find at http://www.microsoft.com/whdc/devtools/debugging/default.mspx). Then, as Mitch says, "Then, I can run the Windows Debugger (WinDbg), load the symbols, open the crash-dump file, and try to determine what went wrong."

> **NOTE:** Mitch Tulloch, a Microsoft MVP and president of MTIT Enterprises (www.mtit.com), gave some great pointers on using the new Task Manager in an article in Windows Networking.com (http://www.windowsnetworking.com/articles_tutorials/Managing-Processes-Tasks-Windows-Vista.html).

Obviously, that sounds a lot simpler than it really is. Reading dump files is a specialized talent that requires a bit of study and research on the Web. But there is a starter article for beginners at http://www.microsoft.com/whdc/devtools/debugging/debugstart.mspx.

What Else Can Task Manager Do?

There's still more that you can do with Task Manager. For one thing, it now has a Services tab. From here, you can see all your services, some descriptive information regarding them (description and group information), and whether they are running. You can stop or start services from here. So, now you don't have to open your Services console to simply stop or start a service. You will still need to use that console if you want to do any permanent service adjustment (disabling a service, for example).

You can also right-click an application and select the Properties option, which is new in Vista. This allows you to go the properties of that particular executable so you change things such as the Compatibility options or other aspects of the program.

Process Monitor v10.21

Some of you might already be using tools created by Mark Russinovich, such as Filemon and Regmon. These are some of the most popular tools Sysinternals has offered the world. Microsoft acknowledged the strength of these tools and has acquired Mark's abilities with his tools. They are still offered freely on the Microsoft site at http://www.microsoft.com/technet/sysinternals/.

Filemon and Regmon had some limitations, such as a lack of detailed event information, limited filtering, poor scalability, and no insight into process events. Process Monitor, on the other hand, offers all those features. It has been likened to putting Windows under an x-ray machine. The tool is free on the Microsoft TechNet site. Learning to use it may take some time, though.

You'll never have the advantage of Mark Russinovich sitting in your living room and explaining to you the inner workings of his tools, but here is the next best thing: a set of videos Mark made with David Solomon that are absolutely incredible. You can get them from the Microsoft site, or the Solomon site at http://www.solsem.com/videolibrary.html.

If the videos seem a bit pricey for you (although they're worth every penny), you can check out their book, *Microsoft Windows Internals, Fourth Edition: Microsoft Windows Server 2003, Windows XP, and Windows 2000 (Pro-Developer)* (hardcover; ISBN 0-7356-1917-4).

Memory Diagnostics Tool

It's a fact of life that memory problems are hard to diagnose, and it's frustrating if you are the one dealing with them. Microsoft used to make the memory diagnostics tool available as a separate download for those in the know, but now it's included in the Vista OS.

In fact, two tools are running in the background to address memory issues with Vista. The first one is titled Resource Exhaustion Detection and Recovery (RADAR), runs completely in the background, and monitors the system-wide virtual memory commit limit. That is to say, it basically keeps track of all your virtual memory on the system, so it can tell when your virtual memory is running low and also identifies which programs are using the most virtual memory. When it detects a shortage of virtual memory, it displays a warning and lists the highest-level offenders for you to shut down. This is a nice enhancement from earlier times where you had to start shutting down programs to conserve virtual memory but couldn't be sure which ones were the culprits.

> **TIP** If you want to see RADAR in action, you can use Performance Monitor. RADAR divides the current level of committed virtual memory by the commit limit, which is the maximum size of the paging file. When the percentage reaches 100%, RADAR warns you. However, you can set the Memory object in Performance Monitor to track the % Committed Bytes in Use counter and the Committed Bytes and Commit Limit counters. This gives you a visual representation of what RADAR works with in the background.

> **TIP** Sometimes you might be surprised if your memory gives you a problem. Kerry Brown, Microsoft MVP, says, "Get a second opinion here http://www.memtest.org/."

The other tool is Memory Diagnostics, which also runs in the background (if it discovers a problem, it runs diagnostic tests, which is added to the event logs), but you can kick start it if you think your system is having memory issues. You can run the tool from the Administrative tools or from a command prompt: MdSched.exe. You'll have to restart the computer for the test to be run, so be sure you save your work before the test.

To get a more detailed look at the tool, you can download the User Guide from http://oca.microsoft.com/en/windiag.asp.

But what if you cannot even install your OS or boot to your OS to run this tool?

Parveen Patel
Developer on the WinRE team blog
http://blogs.msdn.com/winre/default.aspx

> Running Windows Memory Diagnostic without installing Vista. I have gotten multiple queries on this. Yes, it is possible to run Windows Memory Diagnostic without installing Vista!

You can do it through the Windows installation disc. To run memory diagnostic, insert the installation disc in the computer and reboot. When you get the prompt Press any key to boot from CD or DVD, press and hold the spacebar or tap it multiple times. This should bring up the Windows boot manager menu that lists Windows Memory Diagnostic as an advanced tool. Hit the Tan key to select Windows Memory Diagnostic and then hit Enter to run it.

After Memory Diagnostic is done, the machine will continue booting into the installation disc.

The System Recovery Options (shown in Figure 8.10) have a variety of tools, including Memory Diagnostics. By using this tool, you just might find out why Vista isn't installing.

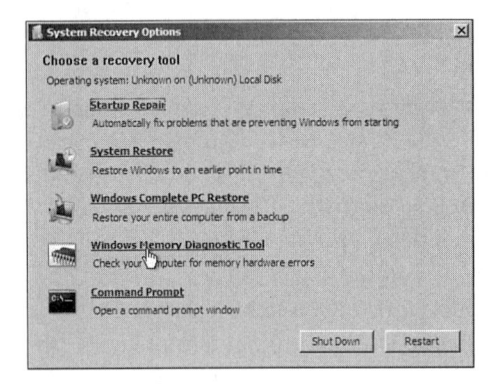

FIGURE 8.10
System Recovery options using the DVD.

We are discussing Memory Diagnostics, but you'll note that Figure 8.10 shows several other important recovery options you might need at any given time to restore your system or bring it back from a major issue. One of those is Startup Repair. In the event your system cannot start, try this option. The Startup Repair Tool (SRT) looks through startup logs and runs a set of diagnostics to determine the failure's cause. It could be incompatible or corrupted device drivers, missing or corrupted startup configuration files, or even corrupted disk metadata. SRT attempts to fix the problem. If it does, it writes to a log file to let you know what the cause was. If it cannot, it tries to use the Last Known Good Configuration as a last resort. If this doesn't work, it writes the diagnostics information to a log and offers to assist you in trying to fix the problem yourself.

The SRT log is located at %WINDIR%\System32\LogFiles\Srt\SrtTrail.txt.

Parveen Patel
Developer on the WinRE team blog http://blogs.msdn.com/winre/default.aspx

In this post, we describe how to use Startup Repair to repair a missing file that is preventing Windows Vista from booting. The goal is to familiarize yourself with Startup Repair so that you can use it when you or your customers need it. We really hope no one will need to use it :); but if you do, this knowledge might come [in] handy.

Warning: Try this at your own risk. If things don't work as planned, you might not be able to boot into your Vista installation or might even lose your data.

Preparation: Before we try to make Vista unbootable, please make sure that your machine has a good restore point. The restore point is not needed for file repair, but would be useful if things go wrong. To create a restore point: search for System Restore in the search box from Vista's Start button, click on Open System Protection, click Create. And then follow the instructions to create a restore point.

Making Vista unbootable: To demonstrate how to use Startup Repair to repair a file we will move the `%windir%\system32\winload.exe` file, which is a must-have for booting Vista. We cannot easily delete this file from Vista itself, so we'll use WinRE to delete it, as follows:

1. Boot into Vista installation DVD.
2. Choose your language settings and click Next.
3. Click Repair Your Computer.
4. Choose your operating system and click Next. This should bring up System Recovery Options.
5. Click on Command Prompt.
6. Once on the command prompt move the `winload.exe` file from your Vista installation. For example, if Vista is installed on C:, run

   ```
   move C:\Windows\System32\winload.exe
   C:\Windows\System32\winload.exe.backup
   ```
7. Now restart your computer using the Restart button on System Recovery Options.

Your Vista should now fail to boot! It should instruct you to use Repair Your Computer from the Vista installation disc.

Repairing your computer: To repair your computer using Startup Repair follow these steps:

1. Boot into Vista installation DVD.
2. Choose your language settings and click Next.
3. Click Repair Your Computer.
4. Choose your operating system and click Next. This should bring up System Recovery Options.
5. Click on Startup Repair.

Startup Repair should now start diagnosing your system to identify the root cause of the failure. Once it has identified the root cause, it would automatically start repairing your computer. If you are curious to know what Startup Repair did, you can click on the details link and see which tests Startup Repair ran to diagnose the problem.

After Startup Repair has finished the repairs, click Finish to reboot your computer.

Your computer should now be able to boot normally into Vista!!

Note: If your computer cannot boot into Vista even after repairs, then go back to System Recovery Options and run System Restore.

That's it! This is how you use Startup Repair for most unbootable situations.

ReadyBoost and SuperFetch

We've talked enough about discovering performance inhibitors; now let's get into the performance enhancers: ReadyBoost and SuperFetch.

ReadyBoost

Every Microsoft Engineer knows the one magic trick Microsoft encourages toward better performance and a stable OS is more RAM. Logically, this is not always an easy thing to achieve. Sometimes, for example, you might find yourself as one tech did (whom we shall name Charlie), needing more memory to install a virtual server on his system. He needed the memory immediately but couldn't get it where he was (in the middle-of-nowhere Florida visiting parents). ReadyBoost could have been Charlie's solution if he were running Vista, but he wasn't. Sorry Charlie.

ReadyBoost allows you to add "memory" to your system by adding a USB 2.0 keychain drive (you can use SD cards, too) to your system. You might be wondering why we used quotation marks back there: You are not actually adding memory to your system; in actuality you use memory from your flash drive and allow it to work like a virtual cache for your hard disk. Vista can use some or all of that drive as added memory. Although hard disks are faster for large sequential I/O, ReadyBoost improves performance on the smaller random I/O.

No doubt you have questions, as many did when this was first released. Tom Archer posted a list of Q&A with Matt Ayers (the program manager in the Microsoft Windows Client Performance Group, which basically owns the ReadyBoost feature) at http://blogs.msdn.com/tomarcher/archive/2006/06/02/615199.aspx.

You can read the entire discussion at the site, but here are the highlights (and we'd like to thank Tom Archer for sharing them with the world):

First, you should know that not all USB devices will work (which you may have already discovered if you tried using ReadyBoost with your keychain USB). Performance-wise, Matt Ayers says you need 2.5MB/sec throughput for 4KB random reads and 1.75MB/sec throughput for 512KB random writes. You can use up to 4GB of flash with ReadyBoost (which turns out to be 8GB of cache thanks to the compression). The reason for the 4GB limit is that FAT32 is being used. The smallest size is 256MB, but the recommendation is that you use at least a 1:1 ratio with your system's memory, with 2.5:1 being the high end.

If you remove the drive, nothing bad happens. Because all pages on the device are also on disk, nothing is lost. As for security, everything is AES-128 encrypted.

Make sure your drive is ReadyBoost capable; otherwise, you will find yourself frustrated that it doesn't work like you hoped.

SuperFetch

Improving performance requires getting over the disk I/O bottleneck. Windows XP has a technology called Prefetch, and this is the next generation of that feature—hence the name SuperFetch. These technologies improve memory management by keeping track of which applications you use most often and keeping them ready to load in

> **NOTE** It's good to note trends in the vernacular of computer geeks over the years. In recent years with storage becoming a central player, we heard words like *ubiquitous* and *heterogeneous*. The word for 2007 seems to be *heuristic*. Instead of using it in the wrong context or nodding in agreement when it's tossed out in conversation, let's just put a definition on it. One online dictionary defines it this way: "A computational method that uses trial and error methods to approximate a solution for computationally difficult problems."
>
> Sounds a little iffy for a solution to a computer speed problem, right? Well, it's not a perfect science. It's what you might call an educated guess about what you're going to use. Suse Linux kernel developer Andrea Arcangeli says, "In many cases, preloading new memory means flushing away an existing cache." So it's not a risk-free, perfect arrangement.

memory. It also reorganizes data and applications on your hard disk to make them more available for loading into memory if it notes the need.

Jim Allchin, co-president of the Platform and Services Division, says, "We redesigned the memory manager in Windows Vista so that if you give the system more memory, it uses that memory much more efficiently than previous operating systems via a technique called SuperFetch—part of Windows Vista's intelligent heuristic memory management system."

SuperFetch uses an intelligent prioritization scheme that not only determines which applications you use most often, but also the time of day you use them. So, if every morning you start with your Firefox browser, that is preloaded in the morning for you. If you go to lunch at noon every day and start work again at 1 p.m., SuperFetch can have your applications ready for you at that time. This solves one of the problems we always had in previous Windows versions—the fact that leaving the OS idle for any period of time made the OS think it should just begin working on its background processes. But with SuperFetch, it knows to keep your applications ready.

To truly understand this technology, it would be good to ask "why" our post-lunch XP boxes were so sluggish. With an OS that uses demand paged virtual memory, when more physical RAM is needed, data gets flushed to the pagefile. So, when a person goes to lunch and another process starts to run on the machine during that time, all the person's applications and data are pushed to the paging file. So, we understand why it's pushed out, but when those other processes finish, nothing automatically calls that information back. When you sit down and start working, the system is sluggish because it's being forced to swap the data back into physical memory. SuperFetch foresees this problem and tries to be proactive about putting the applications you need back into physical memory.

You don't configure SuperFetch; it works all on its own. A folder called Prefetch is located under the `C:\Windows` directory, and some have suggested making changes to this folder, but read the following note.

Where Is My Memory?

One of the complaints users have with SuperFetch (due to a lack of understanding) is that they remember how much available memory they had under XP's memory manager, and now in Vista, when they check out their available or free memory, it's next to nothing. Why is that?

Jeff Atwood addresses this on this site www.codinghorror.com. He explains the need to consider your memory as a cache, not as a resource. A cache that is empty isn't doing you any good, so Vista is trying to fill it with as much preemptive material as it sees fit using SuperFetch. Jeff says, "The less free memory I have, the better; every byte of memory should be actively working on my behalf at all times."

At the same time, Jeff makes a good comment in his article that one downside involves gaming. Some games rely on free memory that SuperFetch sees as available and takes. There are different opinions on whether all this is true, with arguments on both sides, but for us, we just want to know if we can disable SuperFetch if we want to.

Fortunately, SuperFetch can be disabled in a couple of ways. The easiest is to go into the Services tab through Administrative Tools and disable or temporarily stop the SuperFetch service.

You can also disable this in the Registry. Open the Regedit and check the value of `EnablePrefetcher` and `EnableSuperfetch` in the Registry under the `HKEY_LOCAL_MACHINE\SYSTEM\CurrentControlSet\Control\Session Manager\MemoryManagement\PrefetchParameters` Registry key.

> **NOTE**
>
> Mythbuster: It's not often you can crush a myth that has been propagating for years (no, we aren't talking about the whole Bill Gates will give you thousands if you respond to this email myth). What we are talking about is the myth that you can clear out your Prefetch folder (in XP or Vista) or add a Registry key that enables SuperFetch for XP. The biggest advocate against this myth is tech guru Ed Bott, and you can read his tirade against it in his archives at www.edbott.com.
>
> At `C:\windows\prefetch`, you see a set of files with names that are related to your programs and with a `.pf` extension. This information was used and is used by Windows in fetching technology to improve performance. Some have said clearing this out improves performance. The basic answer is this: Don't clean out the Prefetch folder because it will not improve performance, even though some tips on the Web say otherwise. Windows manages the folder just fine and will only cause more work because Windows will just replace that information. As for adding a Registry key to XP, from the highest sources, this is not accurate.

Here are the descriptions of these values:

  0 = Disabled

  1 = Application launch prefetching enabled

  2 = Boot prefetching enabled

  3 = Prefetch everything enabled (optimal and default)

The recommendation is that you ensure that it's set to 3 and leave this alone…but tweakers love to tweak.

Vista Recovery: Advanced Boot Options, WinRE, and WinPE

The last thing you want to happen is for your system to not boot. Performance is a great thing to worry about right up to the day your system shows you a black screen with an error message instead of the colorful login screen. With a lump in your throat, you sigh with relief because you know you have a CompletePC backup...or do you? Before you go for the backup, you should try to fix your problem. Start with Advanced Boot Options.

Advanced Boot Options in Vista

By pressing F8 upon bootup, you can see the Advanced Boot Options available to help you to handle a particular crisis. Knowing how each works can enable you to make an informed decision about which tool is going to get your system up and running the fastest. Here are your choices:

- **Safe Mode**—Loads a minimal driver set and set of services.
- **Safe Mode With Networking**—This loads safe mode settings but also loads network connections, allows logon scripts to run, allows security settings and Group Policy settings (for system that connect to a domain) to be applied. If you know it's not a network problem that is preventing your system from booting, this mode can be helpful to allow you access to other resources (and to back up your system if you haven't done so already).
- **Safe Mode with Command Prompt**—Boots up your system but with a command prompt instead of the GUI. Why would you use this? Well, if you believe the system will not start due to a problem regarding a process started through the Explorer shell, this prevents the Explorer shell from executing in the first place.
- **Enable Boot Logging**—Creates a log file that lists all the services and drivers that load (or do not load, as the case may be). This log file is called Ntbtlog.txt and is located in the Windows folder. The modes listed previously also create boot logs, but this one does it without going into a safe mode.
- **Enable Low-resolution Video (640×480)**—This used to be called VGA mode in XP. Useful for problems you encounter with video drivers or incorrect video display settings, it provides a standard (ugly), stable (low-resolution and refresh rates settings), VGA driver to allow you to see your screen so you can fix your problem.
- **Last Known Good Configuration (Advanced)**—The last time you logged on successfully, your Registry took a snapshot and saved it. In the event you did something to your system and it prevents you from logging in again, not to worry—just use the last known

Chapter 8 System Recovery and Diagnostic Tricks

good to go back in time to your last logon. However, if you are able to log in after a poor installation of a driver or service, this option will not help you in the least. So, if you know something isn't right, don't log in first and then see whether you are right. Instead, go with your gut feeling and last known good. It doesn't solve problems caused by corrupted or missing drivers or files—that requires WinRE, which is discussed later.

- **Directory Services Restore Mode**—This setting applies only to domain controllers, so you don't need this for your desktop OS.
- **Debugging Mode**—This enables Vista to send debugging information through a serial cable to another computer for troubleshooting the kernel and other analysis of the system.
- **Disable Automatic Restart on System Failure**—This is useful for when your system is in a loop of restarting because it stops the blue-screen restart loop so you can troubleshoot the cause of the problem.
- **Disable Driver Signature Enforcement**—Allows drivers with improper signatures to be installed. This setting does not continue with multiple reboots. You use it; you install the driver you need; and when you reboot, the Driver Signature Enforcement is enabled again.
- **Start Windows Normally**—Starts the system normally, as you might have guessed.

Nick Peers, the freelance journalist (http://www.nickpeers.com) says:

> A damaged Registry can lock you out of your system and important files. The Registry is a massive database that contains all your system and program configuration and is central to the way Windows works. If it becomes damaged (or corrupt) in any way, you may find yourself unable to boot into your system. The simplest thing to try is Last Known Good Configuration. This replaces the Registry with the version that was used the last time Windows successfully loaded. In most cases this will fix the boot problem, although you'll find any changes made to the Registry since that copy was made are lost.

Nick is correct, but if you really find yourself in trouble, your next step is the Windows Recovery options.

The Windows Recovery Environment

For those of you familiar with the Recovery Console in XP, it has been replaced by the Windows Recovery Environment (WinRE). WinRE is a recovery platform based off the Windows Preinstallation Environment (WinPE), the core deployment foundation for Vista. WinRE has two primary functions, that of diagnosing problems using the Startup

Repair tool (discussed earlier in this chapter) and providing a platform for advanced recovery tools, according to the WinRE team. You can read their postings at http://blogs.msdn.com/winre/ for some great information.

Using the WinRE is easy enough. You boot up your Vista installation disk (or ISO). You will be asked to select a language, time, and so forth. When you see the button labeled Install, you can look to the bottom-left corner for the option to Repair Your Computer. This takes you into the System Recovery Options (that we mentioned earlier for memory diagnostics and Startup Repair).

Windows PE 2.0

The Windows Pre-installation Environment (WinPE 2.0) is a tool that enables you to boot the PE operating system, which is a mini-OS that allows you to handle installation, diagnostic troubleshooting, and recovery solutions for Vista. Some say WinPE is super-DOS. It's not DOS; it's more like Son-of-DOS, so call it SOD if you like.

When you load the WinRE options of the Vista DVD, it is actually running WinPE as the underlying OS. The same is true when you start the installation from the DVD. But you can actually make your own boot CDs or boot from a USB flash drive.

To begin, you should download the Windows Automated Installation Kit (Windows AIK) from Microsoft. Be sure you obtain the one from the final Vista release (in the event you are downloading or borrowing the kit from another source). The Windows AIK includes tools you need for deployment, as well as ones for creating the boot environment for WinRE. One of the most important tools you will need is imagex.exe, a command-line tool used for capturing, modifying, and applying installation images.

There is quite a bit of documentation to go through to fully understand the new deployment and troubleshooting tools, but it is worth it to keep your system humming along. But to understand the following discussions, you need to at least understand the basics.

The Basic Tools of WinPE

After you install the Windows AIK, the tools you need will be in those folders. If you don't want to remember all the paths, you can make a quick edit in your system's environment variables to include the paths. To do this, open your System properties, select the Advanced tab, and click the Environment Variables button. For the system variables you want to add to the path variables, be

> **NOTE:** You can also get the Windows AIK by obtaining the Business Desktop Deployment 2007 Kit. The BDD 2007 includes the Windows AIK along with other necessary deployment tools and documentation.

Chapter 8 System Recovery and Diagnostic Tricks   **291**

sure to include the paths you need. For the following examples, you add the following two paths:

```
C:\Program Files\Windows AIK\Tools\PETools
C:\Program Files\Windows AIK\Tools\x86
```

Some of the tools mentioned include the following:

- **CopyPE**—Run the `copype.cmd` script to automatically create a local Windows PE build directory. The script is located in the PETools folder. The script requires two arguments: hardware architecture and target location:

  `copype.cmd <arch> <destination>`

  Where `<arch>` can be x86, amd64, or ia64 and `<destination>` is a path to a local directory. For example

  `copype.cmd x86 c:\winpe_x86`

  (Don't create the folder ahead of time because the tool creates the folder for you.)

  The script creates the following directory structure and copies all the necessary files for that architecture:

  `\winpe_x86`
  `\winpe_x86\ISO`
  `\winpe_x86\mount`

- **imagex**—This tool is the mega-tool. It is "the" tool for creating and reconfiguring, as well as applying, `.wim` files. Some have compared this tool to an advanced `.zip-ping` tool, and it is in some ways. You can take files, or your entire system, and pull it into one `.wim` file. You can also compress that file. It looks at the `.wim` file as a directory so you can add to it any parts that are missing. One example of the capabilities of imagex can be seen just by looking at the `install.wim` for Vista. For starters, it's a 2GB+ file that expands out to be about 8GB. That speaks volumes for imagex's capabilities. OEMs can use this to open their Vista images, input their own Welcome Center information and other restore features, and close them again.

- **PEImg**—After you use imagex to expand a Windows PE structure, you can use PEImg to make changes to Windows PE, such as installing packages, drivers, and language packs.

- **OsCDimg**—Lets you take your `.wim` files and make them ISO files. After they're in ISO format they can be burned onto a CD to make them bootable.

- **Diskpart**—This is a command-line tool for disk management. You use this tool in preparing your keychain drive for it to be a bootable tool later.

There are other tools to consider that you can learn more about through the Windows AIK.

Creating a Windows PE Boot CD with Windows Vista and Windows AIK

Section by Mario Szpuszta (mszCool)
Microsoft Developer
http://blogs.msdn.com/mszCool

About two months ago I discovered the Windows Automated Installation Toolkit (Windows AIK or just WAIK) to be able to work with different demo images for the sessions I did at TechEd Europe with physical machines instead of the (still much slower) Virtual PC images. The WAIK includes imagex.exe, which is a tool that allows you to create images of a partition of your machine and package them into the new Windows Imaging Files (WIM).

The first steps involve using WAIK and imagex.exe. These files can be used for centralized deployment via the Windows Deployment Services (successor of Remote Installation Services). But in my case I used it to image and restore different types of demo images for my physical machines as I did not want to work with the slower VPC counterparts at a conference such as TechEd Europe. Therefore, I created two partitions on my developer machine, one with my primary OS-instance (Vista joined into our working domain for email, etc.) and a second partition for my different demo images. On the second partition I installed Windows Server 2003 with everything I needed for my demo sessions (different images, detailed steps, see below) and then I created a WIM-image from the Vista OS instance using imagex.exe from the WAIK as follows:

```
imagex /capture D: M:\WindowsImages\Windows2003_OfficeDev.wim "Windows Server 2003 Office Development"
```

This command captures everything on drive D: into a WIM file stored on my external hard disk M:. Then I tried the demos for the session and to get the original situation again I just restored the image as follows:

```
format D: /q
imagex /apply M:\WindowsImages\Windows2003_OfficeDev.wim 1 D:\
```

To get the complete picture, here is what I did for TechEd, where I required, for example, one image for SharePoint 2007 Office Development, one image for Windows Vista for WPF and Composite UI Application Block Development, and a third one for plain old Office 2003 development (during the beta stage of Office 2007 and especially VSTO 2005 SE installing Office 2003 and Office 2007 side-by-side was not supported…right now fortunately this is supported and works really fine, therefore I have tried the imaging stuff on several machines already):

1. First I created a basic install of Windows Server 2003 on my second partition D:.

2. Then I installed my main Vista partition for regular work (email, development in our office, etc.).

3. On my main Vista instance I installed the WAIK.

4. Then I have created the first image of the Windows Server 2003 partition using `imagex /capture`.

5. Afterwards I installed everything for Office 2003 development on this Windows Server 2003.

6. Now I captured this Office 2003 development workstation using `imagex /capture`.

7. Next, I restored the original Windows Server 2003 instance using `imagex /apply`.

8. On the restored instance of Windows Server 2003, I installed everything for Office 2007 development.

9. I imaged the Office 2007 development workstation using `imagex /capture` again.

10. Now I had my demo images as WIM images available and could switch between Office 2003 and Office 2007 (beta at that point of time) within 15 minutes by restoring the appropriate image via `imagex /apply`.

With that, management of my demo partitions became really fairly easy and I was not forced to use Virtual PCs but still remain with the same advantages such as restoring an original stage of my machines very quickly.

The next step was fairly obvious. At home I used the days between Christmas and New Years to get my IT infrastructure done, at home. And of course I wanted to have a very smooth way of restoring my test servers and workstations quickly if something went wrong. So my idea was creating WIM images for each of the servers and either deploying them via Windows Deployment Services from my PDC or just from external hard disks. But I didn't want to have two OS instances on each machine (one for imaging and image restore and the other one for "productive work"). So I required a CD-bootable version of Windows to be used as imaging and restore OS-instance with imagex.exe installed. Finally, the WAIK includes all the tools for creating Windows PE instances which are bootable from either CDs, DVDs, or USB sticks (!!).

I thought before the new year starts, right now I need to try something risky with my home machine. After searching a while I've found…the steps are so simple that I was completely surprised:

1. Download and install WAIK (obvious).

2. Open the Windows PE Tools Command Prompt.

3. Create a directory for the template of your Windows PE image (e.g. `C:\WinPE` as I use it here).
4. Next switch to `C:\Program Files\Windows AIK\Tools\PETools`.
5. Execute `copype x86 C:\WinPE`.

   Now copy anything (tools, programs, etc.) you want into the ISO directory of your Windows PE template directory (in my case, `C:\WinPE`). You can create any subdirectory you want within the ISO subdirectory such as "Imaging" in the example below where I copy the imagex.exe tool to the Imaging directory of my ISO template directory as follows:

   ```
   copy "C:\Program Files\Windows AIK\Tools\x86\imagex.exe"
   c:\WinPE\ISO\Imaging
   ```

6. Then switch to `C:\Program Files\Windows AIK\Tools\PETools\x86`.

   Now apply the original Windows PE boot image:

   ```
   imagex /apply winpe.wim 1 c:\WinPE\mount
   ```

7. Using the peimg.exe tool you can install either additional drivers by specifying an INF file, or prebuilt packages such as MDAC, MSXML, or Windows Scripting support (see the following table). Examples:

   ```
   peimg /install=WinPE-XML-Package C:\WinPE\mount
   peimg /install=WinPE-Scripting-Package C:\WinPE\mount
   ```

Package Name	Description
WinPE-HTA-Package	HTML Application support
WinPE-MDAC-Package	Microsoft Data Access Component support
WinPE-Scripting-Package	Windows Script Host support
WinPE-SRT-Package	Windows Recovery Environment component
WinPE-XML-Package	Microsoft XML (MSMXL) Parser support

8. After the "mount" directory has been prepared (using `peimg.exe` with the `/prep` switch), you can create a WIM image for your ISO template directory as follows:

   ```
   imagex /capture /boot /compress max "C:\WinPE\mount"
   "C:\winpe\iso\sources\boot.wim" "mszCool PE"
   ```

9. Next you need to create the ISO image that you can burn onto a CD using any tool you want (such as Nero):

   ```
   Oscdimg -n c:\winpe\ISO c:\winpe\mszCool_winpe.iso -n
   -bc:\winpe\etfsboot.com
   ```

10. Using the OSCDIMG.EXE tool, you have created a ready-to-use ISO image that you can burn onto a CD. That CD is then a bootable version of Windows PE. From within this CD-booted instance, you can image and restore any partition on your computer you want—for free.

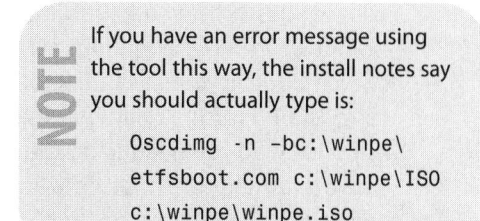

> **NOTE** If you have an error message using the tool this way, the install notes say you should actually type is:
>
> ```
> Oscdimg -n -bc:\winpe\
> etfsboot.com c:\winpe\ISO
> c:\winpe\winpe.iso
> ```

As I wanted to have some fun and risk on the second-to-last day of this year, I just tried this on my home workstation by imaging and restoring my primary OS instance partition (which is the boot partition as well)…and it just rocks…it only took about 40 minutes including all the Internet search on how-to create such a Windows PE images.

Bootable USB Keys

Mario Szpuszta mentions in the previous section the capability to use Windows PE from a CD, DVD, or USB Flash drive. James O' Neil (another Microsoft developer) has some excellent advice on how to make this happen at http://blogs.technet.com/jamesone/default.aspx.

To make a USB key bootable using the Vista/Windows PE version, you need to use the Diskpart commands. Here are the commands:

1. `Select disk 1` (or the number of your USB key, be careful!)
2. `Clean` (like I said, be careful! This erases the disk.)
3. `Create partition primary`
4. `Select partition 1`
5. `Active`
6. `Format fs=fat32`
7. `Assign`
8. `Exit`

Having done that, you copy the ISO folder to the USB key

That's it. Now you have your universal tool for imaging and repairing Vista.

Now at this point you have a disk which will try to boot using BootMgr in the style of Windows PE/Vista/Longhorn server. Several people have asked about making a key which boots in the style of Server 2003/XP/Windows 2000/Windows NT. I can't make the Vista/PE version of diskpart run on Windows XP, and the older version won't prepare a USB key. So you need to do this from Vista or the Vista build of Windows PE. Once the drive is formatted, it has a Vista Boot sector—this won't boot NT/200x/XP operating systems. You need to use the BootSect utility:

`Boosect /nt52 E:`

This stamps a Window 2003 Server boot sector (one which uses `boot.ini`) onto drive E:. I haven't tried it, but you should be able copy NTLDR, BOOT.INI, and NTDETECT.COM onto a USB key as a way of starting a machine suffering from a corrupt boot environment.

Chapter 9

MASTERING THE NEW VISTA APPS

Internet Explorer 7

In terms of market share, Microsoft has been taking a decent loss to Mozilla's Firefox browser over the past couple of years. Many Vista masters admit that Firefox is the first thing they installed after installing Vista. But IE7 takes a shot at redeeming itself.

The security enhancements (such as protected mode and the phishing filter) to IE7 have already been discussed in Chapter 4, "Security Enhancements," but we want to highlight some of the other features at this time. For example, one thing we like about IE7 is that it finally includes tabbed browsing. But the feature we really like is that there is always a tab waiting for us. You can press Ctrl+T in both Firefox and IE7 to open a new tab, but it's nice to have one sitting on the tab bar whenever we need it.

IN THIS CHAPTER

- Internet Explorer 7
- Windows Mail
- Windows Contacts and Calendar
- Windows Photo Gallery
- Windows Movie Maker
- Windows Media Player 11
- Windows Media Center
- Windows DVD Maker
- A Few More Media Tips

Quick Tabs

Another cool feature of IE7 is the Quick Tabs feature. This enables you to see all your open tabs in mini windows, as shown in Figure 9.1. Quick Tabs provides a thumbnail view of your tabs so you can visually identify which pages you are working with, something that becomes more difficult as you open more tabs because you cannot see all the tabs. Firefox has the same type of button to list tabs but not a Quick Tabs option as of the time of this writing.

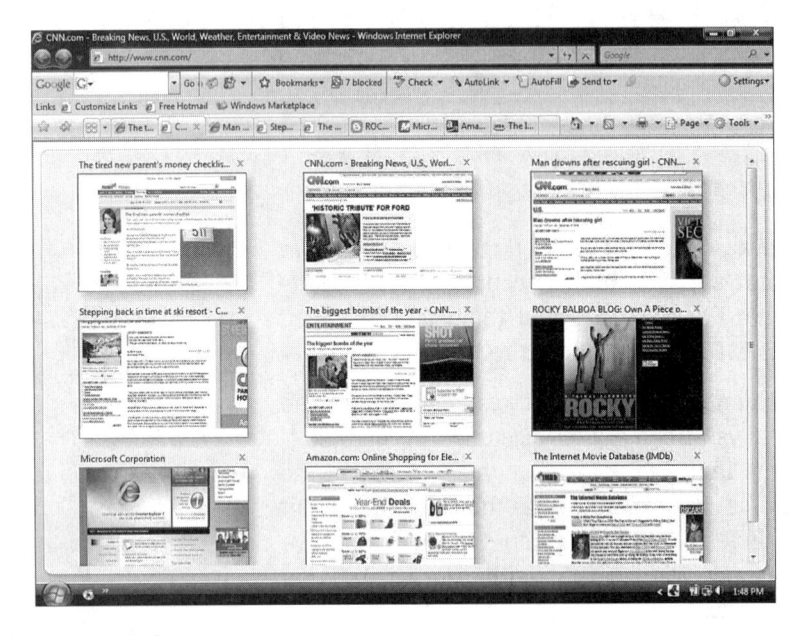

FIGURE 9.1
Quick Tabs can be access using the Quick Tabs button or by pressing Ctrl+Q.

To customize your Tab settings, click Tools, Internet Options, and then click the Settings button in the Tabs section. One of the options you should note that is set on by default is Open New Tabs Next to the Current Tab.

One of the benefits to this feature is that new tabs aren't appended to your ever growing collection at the very end. For example, if you have 30 tabs open and the first tab is your Google page, opening a link off of that page could open the tab right next to your Google page, or all the way at the end of your 30 other tabs. This would cause you to scramble from one end of your tabs to the other just to find the new tab, if not for this option to open tabs next to the current one.

Tab Groups: Grouped Favorites and Multiple Home Pages

With IE7, you can open a collection of tabs and then select an option to Add Tab Groups to your Internet Favorites. This enables you to select that group with one click and open all the grouped sites once.

You can also set up more than one home page to open when you start IE. To do this, go to the General tab of Internet Options and enter the URL for each page you want to appear, as shown in Figure 9.2.

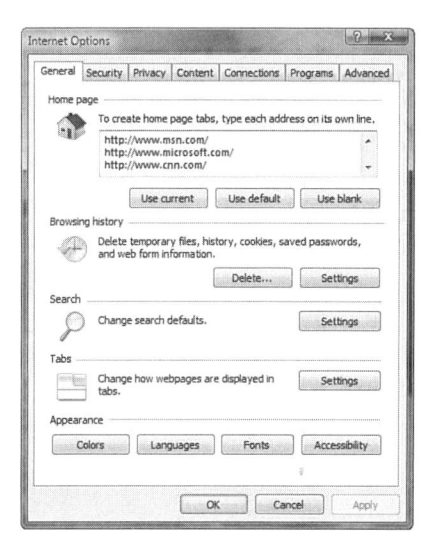

FIGURE 9.2
Creating multiple home pages.

From the Tabbed Browsing Settings, you can select the option to open only the first home page when IE starts. This is a nice features if too many pages open at once is distracting for you. You can still open all the home pages by clicking the Home button on the toolbar.

When you close your Internet Explorer, it asks whether you want to open all the same tabs the next time you open the browser. This is great for situations in which you have a lot of research available and need to shut down for some reason but don't want to lose all the pages you've been viewing.

Increasing the Number of Tabs

Sandi Hardmeier, a Microsoft MVP since 1999 who specializes in Internet Explorer and Outlook Express, has a great site for learning all the latest IE7 tricks (http://www.ie-vista.com). She mentions some problems you might have if you open an abnormal amount of tabs in your work (let's say 50+). You can experience various problems with tabs not opening and other odd happenings. You can fix this by editing the Registry.

The key to use is as follows:

HKEY_LOCAL_MACHINE\System\CurrentControlSet\Control\Session Manager\SubSystems\Windows

There you'll find a DWORD very similar to the following:

```
%SystemRoot%\system32\csrss.exe ObjectDirectory=\Windows SharedSection=
1024,3072,512 Windows=On SubSystemType=Windows ServerDll=basesrv,1
ServerDll=winsrv:UserServerDllInitialization,3 ServerDll=winsrv:
ConServerDllInitialization,2 ProfileControl=Off MaxRequestThreads=16
```

Change the `3072` in the `Windows SharedSection=` part of the DWORD to 4096 or even 5120. This portion of the registry key relates to how the desktop heap is allocated, specified in KB. By increasing the size you give IE more room to work with in your OS. For more information on what the Desktop Heap is you can read http://blogs.msdn.com/ntdebugging/archive/2007/01/04/desktop-heap-overview.aspx

Additional IE7 Features

Some of the additional improvements for IE7 include the following:

- **Printing Settings**—It was frustrating in the past to print certain web pages because the right side of the page was often cut off. Many users got around this by copying what they wanted into a Word document and then printing it. You could also change the mode to Landscape, but that workaround uses more paper. IE7 has a Shrink to Fit setting that ensures the page can print on any size paper. The Print Preview window also enables you to manipulate your print settings.

- **Search Toolbar**—To the right of the Address bar is the new Search bar, which is not new in browsers but is new in IE. It has search providers from which you can choose, and you can add extra ones if you like. For example, Eric Law of Microsoft has a site that includes additional providers at http://www.fiddlertool.com/ie7/searchbuilder.asp. You can also check out Next Venture Partners, who have a site at www.opensearchlist.com with hundreds of available search engines to try.

- **Zoom**—Another great feature that enables you to increase the size of both the text and graphics of a page. You can increase or decrease by pressing Ctrl +/- or return to 100% by pressing Ctrl+0.
- **Supports RSS Feeds**—RSS feeds, which have become extremely popular for allowing users to subscribe to content updates of all kinds on the Internet, are a nice addition to IE7. Some great information is provided by Sandi Hardmeier (our IE guru mentioned previously) at http://www.ie-vista.com/rss.html. You can learn more about connecting to web feeds and adjusting subscription settings.
- **Delete History**—Again, this is not a new feature to browsers but one sorely needed for the quick deletion of cookies, history, and so forth. Now all the options are in one location under Tools, Delete Browsing History, which displays all your options, as shown in Figure 9.3.

FIGURE 9.3
Your super-console for deleting history and more.

Windows Mail

Outlook Express—the standard free email program in previous Windows versions—has been renamed and revamped into Windows Mail. The majority of the features work exactly the same, although it's visually different so that it fits in with the Vista theme.

New Features of Windows Mail

When you open Windows Mail you might notice a few options for Windows Contacts and Windows Calendar that, upon first glance may give the impression of integration between the applications. Don't let the buttons fool you; those are shortcuts to the other tools, not true integration (which is what Microsoft originally promised).

Here is what Windows Mail does have:

- **Phishing Filter**—We discussed this earlier in Chapter 4 regarding IE7's new security filter. Any time Windows Mail thinks you have received an email that is a phishing scam, it alerts you immediately. To adjust your phishing options, select Tools, Junk Mail Options, and then select the Phishing tab. For example, you can move phishing email to the junk mail folder.

- **Junk Mail Filter**—The filtering in Windows Mail includes top-level domain and encoding blocking. You can access these settings by selecting Tools, Junk Mail Options (shown in Figure 9.4), and you can turn off the settings, turn the filter on low or high, or select Safe List Only, where you configure a safe senders list to lock out all other types of emails. The International tab contains the top-level domain options (where you can filter out emails from other domain extensions) and the encoding blocking (where you can filter out different languages from coming into your Inbox).

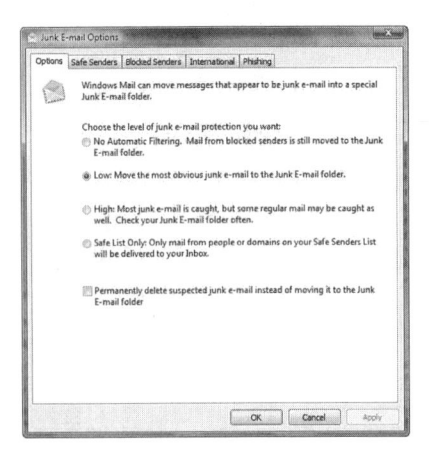

FIGURE 9.4
The Junk Mail Filter settings.

- **Email Stored As Individual Files**—Outlook Express uses `.dbx` files, whereas Vista uses `.eml` files. An `.eml` file is basically a raw POP3 email saved as a file with the `.eml` extension. This is a great change that enables easier real-time searching of your messages and causes fewer corruption issues because, if a file becomes corrupted, it affects only that single email rather than the entire store.

- **Improved Search**—Using the WordWheel in the upper right-hand corner gives you the ability to start typing in and it will search the headers and the body, a full index search as you type. To quickly bring yourself into the search just type Ctrl+E and it will bring you right to the WordWheel.

- **Integrated Spell Checking**—Outlook Express requires you to install a stand-alone spellchecker, such as Microsoft Office or another Office standalone application to gain spell-check features, but Windows Mail has those features included. It also includes a variety of languages to check your spelling in.

Backing Up Your Windows Mail

If you want to back up your message store, you will most likely find it located under %UserProfile%\AppData\Local\Microsoft\Windows Mail\. However, in the event you need to locate this folder, you can find it by selecting Tools, Options, Advanced Tab Settings. Under Maintenance and Troubleshooting, select the Store folder (see Figure 9.5).

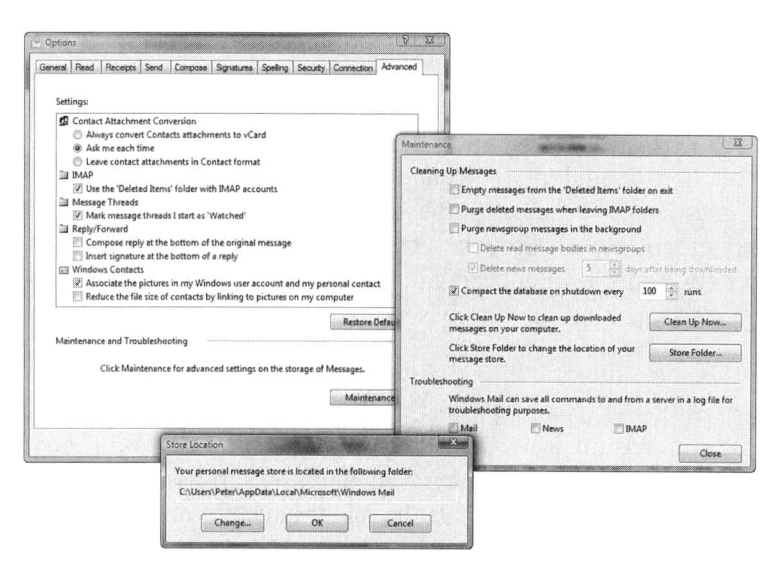

> **NOTE**
> Windows Mail's junk email filter uses Bayesian junk mail filtering, which ties to filter mail in the same way our eyes work. Our eyes can quickly look at an email and determine whether it is spam. The Bayesian filter works the same way by scanning an email and assigning a score, which helps determine the probability of the email being spam. One of the benefits to a Bayesian filter, as opposed to other scoring content-based filters, is that it adjusts itself based on your specific email content, as opposed to a preconfigured list. So, if you receive emails that contain words that might normally be thought of by a filter as spam, and yet those words are part of your everyday business vocabulary, the filter learns over time that you don't want those emails categorized as spam.

FIGURE 9.5
Maintenance settings and the location of the message store.

Along with the file backup, you can export three Registry keys that contain the settings and rules for Windows Mail. They are as follows:

- HKEY_CURRENT_USER\Software\Microsoft\Windows Mail (This key contains your Windows Mail configuration information and is the most important to back up.)
- HKEY_CURRENT_USER\Identities (Not really an important key, this feature has been removed from Windows Mail, but it's for legacy purposes.)
- HKEY_CURRENT_USER\Software\Microsoft\IAM (Contains the account information on your Default LDAP, Mail, and News accounts.)

To restore the backup, you restore the Store Root directory in the location that is listed in the Registry key and then restore all the files and folders backed up into that directory. You should also restore the Registry keys so the settings are exact.

Rodrigo Lobato, an avid Mozilla Thunderbird user, wanted to move his message store into Windows Mail. To do this, he says:

> **Vista Master** You can search online for a variety of different converters. For example, for Thunderbird I recommend a tool at broobles.com called IMAPSize (http://www.broobles.com/imapsize/th2outlook.php) that converts your mbox format to .eml format. Or for Outlook Express, which uses .dbx files you can use a tool like DBXpress (http://www.oehelp.com/DBXpress/Default.aspx). After the files are in .eml format, you can then use Windows Explorer to drag and drop the messages into your Vista store.

Windows Contacts and Calendar

For the standard home user or student, the contacts and calendar features of Vista are enough to keep life in order. For business purposes, though, you would probably want to use a higher-level organizing application such as Outlook 2007 or Goldmine. But, out-of-the-box, the new Windows Contacts and Windows Calendar applications are solid tools. That said, keep in mind that there is nothing stellar about them.

Windows Contacts

You can open Contacts in several ways, including via the Start menu's All Programs folder or through the Windows Mail application. You might be surprised that the application opens inside an Explorer shell. It shows the folder structure on the left and the Contact information in the middle with a preview pane on the right, letting you easily see your contact information. Adding and editing contacts is simple through the standard, well-labeled tools. From within Contacts, you can select the Email option to take you directly into a window for composing an email to that person. That should come in handy.

You can import and export your contacts, but the functionality is limited (as it has been in previous contact applications in Windows). You can only import CSV, LDIF, vCard, and Windows Address Book files. In addition, you can only export to CSV or vCard files. True, other applications usually allow you to export to CSV so you can then import these, but it's somewhat disappointing that more options aren't included.

> **TIP** Chris Lanier blogged about a cool tool that integrates with your Vista contacts, called Big Screen Contacts from Mobilewares (http://www.mobilewares.net/mce/bschtm.htm). The interface is the Media Center UI and works with the Media Center Remote Control. It's an interesting application, but more importantly, it highlights the capability of developers to work with Contacts. Other applications for Palm and so forth easily sync with the Contact tools.

The following are the points a Vista Master should be aware of:

- **Search**—Because your contacts are data types that can be indexed and searched, you can select the Start orb, select the Search pane, and type the contact you are looking for; this locates your contact.

- **Sidebar Gadget**—If you are a fan of gadgets, you can include contacts right on your desktop so your address book is always available.

Windows Calendar

One of the features missing from Outlook Express is a calendar. Users who are used to working in Outlook (with their calendars) are disappointed with that fact if they find themselves forced into using Outlook Express. Of course, there are ways to get around this. One option is to install a third-party application as a side calendar; another is to find a calendar that integrates with Outlook Express, such as OEComplete from www.cellarstone.com. But most of us don't want to go through the hassle. That's why many users are happy to have a calendar included in Vista (see Figure 9.6).

Using the calendar isn't difficult—a simple three-paned interface includes a little calendar, an active calendar in the center, and a details pane on the right. However, there are a few extra features you should know about:

- **iCalendar Standard**—This is an approved cross-platform standard for calendar exchange. This enables you to share your calendar or send meeting requests through email using standard (.ics files) without having to worry if the other person is using the same OS or application as you. A majority of software developers support it, including Apple's iCal, Google Calendar, Lotus Notes, Mozilla Calendar (and Sunbird), and so forth. For example, you can schedule a meeting and then in the Details pane scroll down and add Attendees by inserting their email addresses. You won't have to worry that they won't be able to open the `.ics` file that will be sent.

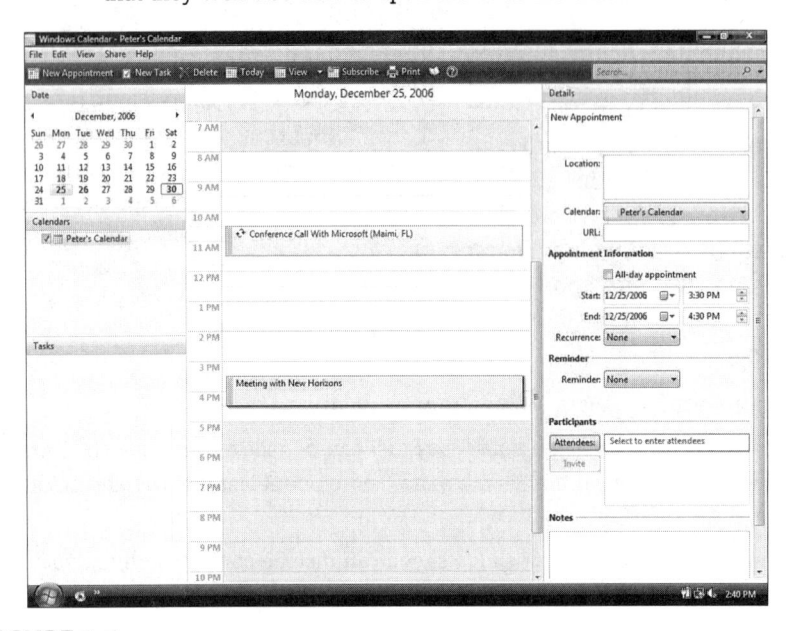

FIGURE 9.6
Windows Calendar has three panes and is easy to use.

- **Multiple Calendar Support**—You might have the need to keep different calendars for different reasons. For example, one for family events, such as reunions and birthdays, and one for business appointments. You can use Windows Calendar to create additional calendars in one location and create calendar groups, too. Notice in Figure 9.7 that you can include or remove a calendar by deselecting the check box.

- **Calendar Sharing**—You can share your calendar with others on your computer—for example, with other family members. This can help you keep track of the busy schedules everyone has. You can clearly see, in different colors, other family members' upcoming games, tests, and so forth and can adjust your schedule (or theirs) accordingly.

> **TIP**
> A TV fanatic (who asked not to be named) recently pointed out to me that you can search online for iCalendar websites and then subscribe to those calendars. One of the recommended sites is called iCalShare at http://icalshare.com. If you check out the Top Calendars, you will notice that the FIFA World Cup schedule is still available. There are thousands of calendars to choose from, or you can add your own by publishing your calendar to one of the many calendar sites.

- **Subscribe or Publish Your Calendar**—During the 2006 World Cup, people from all over the world were trying to keep up with which game was being played in which city between which teams. Having the ability to subscribe to calendars that have been published by others (thanks to the iCalendar standard in place, as mentioned previously) makes this easier to do.

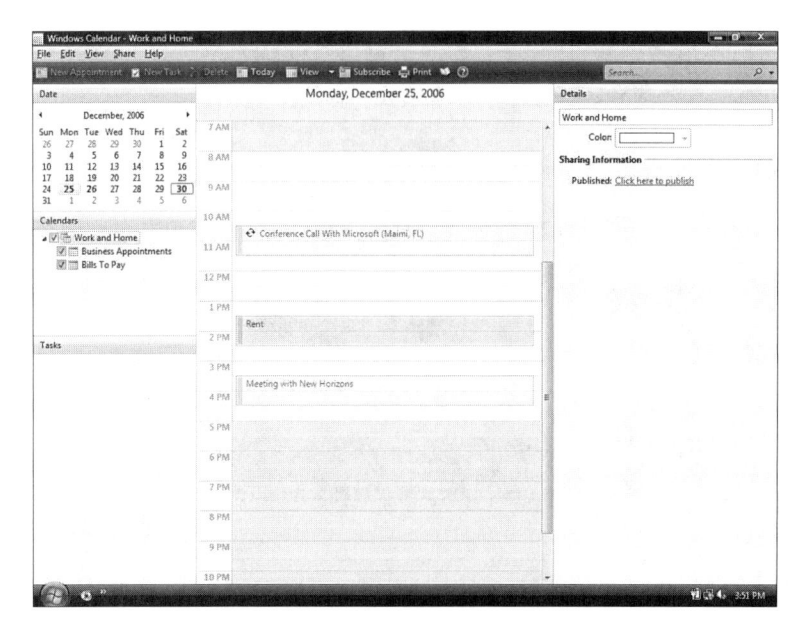

FIGURE 9.7
Multiple Calendars and Calendar Groupings help to organize all aspects of your life.

Windows Photo Gallery

Open your Windows Photo Gallery (shown in Figure 9.8), click through the features for a couple of minutes and you are bound to say, "Hmmm…well done!" Are there better photo managers? Perhaps. But this one is free, it's integrated with the OS, and it's filled with features we need (especially if we plan on getting more organized with our picture metadata). The Windows Photo Gallery blog site is located at http://blogs.msdn.com/pix/

Windows Photo Gallery includes some great ways to organize our ever-growing photo/video archives. You can import your photos and add tags to them so you can easily search for them at a later time. You can even use stars to rate your photos and then search for photos based on the number of stars. You can also search by the year, month, or day a photo was taken. You can perform some minor editing of your photos (including red eye removal, resizing, and cropping your images).

FIGURE 9.8
Working with the Windows Photo Gallery.

Nick White
Microsoft Windows Client Product Manager
http://windowsvistablog.com/blogs/windowsvista/archive/2006/10/16/managing-your-photos-with-windows-vista.aspx

Windows Vista allows for extensive file tagging to organize files, and Windows Photo Gallery takes full advantage of this. Add captions to your photos or tag the files themselves very easily in Windows Photo Gallery. All you have to do is click Info on the top toolbar after selecting the desired photo to which you'd like to add information. You can add as many tags as you'd like to any given photo. After you add tags and a caption to your photo, those settings stick with that specific photo in Windows Photo Gallery and throughout Windows Vista. If you browse to that photo in Windows Explorer, Windows Vista's enhanced shell will display the tags, ratings, and captions you've set in Windows Photo Gallery. Tagging your files also provides faster search results for the specific types of photos you're looking for.

This enhanced metadata structure, along with comprising traditional photo information such as filename, file size, file type, date last modified, and so forth, has added data fields for Tags, Date Taken, Rating, Caption, Image Resolution, Camera Make/Model, Shutter Speed, and more. Keep in mind that your camera adds some of that information automatically (such as the shutter speed and date taken) although you can alter this information. But other portions are added by the user, which means users need to increase their understanding of metadata and the need to work with their photos if they want to take advantage of these tags' search capabilities.

The goal here is to make the metadata an integral part of the files. And that metadata can be accessible to other applications because Microsoft has agreed to base its system on XMP (developed by Adobe as a framework for embedding metadata within files). In addition, EXIF and IPTC are supported for legacy metadata reads on the photos. If a photo doesn't have XMP data included, Vista looks for EXIF or IPTC. If you make changes to a photo that includes EXIF or IPTC formats for metadata, Vista writes those changes to both the XMP system and the legacy format for compatibility.

A blog site discusses digital imaging and the Windows Photo Gallery from the Microsoft development team is located at http://blogs.msdn.com/pix/default.aspx.

Free Photo Tools That You Will Love

Microsoft (or sometimes people who work with or for Microsoft) creates some great tools to play with that will help to add to your digital photo experiences. Here they are:

- **Photo Story 3.0**—Lets you create slideshows using your digital photos. With a single click, you can touch up, crop, or rotate pictures and add stunning special effects, soundtracks, and your own voice narration to your photo stories. Then, personalize them with titles and captions. Small file sizes let you easily send your photo stories in an email. You can even watch them on your TV, a computer, or a Windows Mobile–based portable device. Go to http://www.microsoft.com/windowsxp/using/digitalphotography/photostory/default.mspx or http://www.windowsphotostory.com/.

- **Microsoft Photosynth**—Photosynth takes a large collection of photos of a place or an object, analyzes them for similarities, and displays them in a reconstructed three-dimensional space. These photos might come from the same person or multiple people at multiple times of the same location. Learn more at http://labs.live.com/photosynth/. One of the coolest aspects to Photosynth (for you video game addicts) is the ability to move through your 3D photo space like you are moving in a game (such as *Half Life 2*).

Windows Movie Maker

If you have never worked with this tool (toy) in Me or XP, you might find that you really like Windows Movie Maker. The tutorials included within the help files make it easy to learn.

The latest version of Windows Movie Maker (WMM) is 6.0, and it's not very different from its predecessors (it has 20 or so new effects and a few new transitions). There are a few new features you should be aware of, though, starting with the capability to import and publish Windows Media Video (WMV)-based High Definition (HD) formats (though only in the Home Premium and Ultimate editions; Home Basic does not support HD). You can also import and edit shows that have been recorded through the Media Center DVR-MS format.

> *Paul Thurrott*
> *Windows Supersite*
> *http://www.winsupersite.com/reviews/winvista_05g.asp*
>
> My favorite WMM 6 feature, however, is its new capability to import and edit Media Center–recorded TV shows, which are stored in the oddball DVR-MS format. Just importing such a file and exporting it as a standard WMV file can save massive amounts of space: Whereas a 30-minute recorded TV show can often take up 2GB of storage space, a high-quality WMV file with the same resolution (720 x 480) takes up less than 700MB. A VHS-quality version (640 x 480) offers even better space savings, coming in at around 240MB. And if you can take the time to edit out commercials, you'll save even more space. Finally! (Note that you cannot edit or transcode TV shows that are protected with Broadcast Flag technology. This includes all HBO and Cinemax shows, for example.)

You can also export movies to the new Windows DVD Maker, which we discuss later in this chapter.

There are some great tutorials on advanced Movie Maker from John "PapaJohn" Buechler (http://www.papajohn.org/), and if you really want to improve your Movie Maker clips, check out the forum at http://www.windowsmoviemakers.net/. It includes tips, tutorials, add-on tools, and so forth.

Windows Media Player 11

The new Media Player has a streamlined interface that fits in nicely with Vista. Even more so, it's still your one-stop-shop for playing digital music, audio CDs, and Internet radio; watching digital movies and DVDs; synching up to external devices; burning files to disk; and much more.

Here are some of the new features:

- **Streamlined Interface**—Classic menus are turned off by default (although you can right-click the frame of the player and turn them back on). Activity tabs enable you to quickly select what you need (Library, Rip, Burn, Sync). It also has cooler-looking playback controls (as you can see in Figure 9.9).

FIGURE 9.9
Windows Media Player 11 has an easier interface.

- **Instant Search**—The search capabilities are once again an important aspect to Vista's features. As-you-type searching enables you to quickly search for both document names and metadata so you can rapidly get the results you need.
- **Network Sharing**—Just like sharing a folder for users to access your data, you can share your media with others from within the Media Player. This enables you to share your media with other devices on your network such as an Xbox 360 using Windows Media Connect (WMC), which has been embedded within the player.
- **MTV's URGE**—In WMP 10, Microsoft promoted the Digital Media Mall that allowed for a large array of online music stores. These are still available for WMP 11, but the big push is for the new MTV URGE service. URGE gives you access to more than two million

songs from every genre and exclusives from MTV, VH1, and CMT. The iPod, with iTunes as a service, has been dominating the world market. But the URGE service is prepared to go up against it. You can learn more about URGE from its launch site at www.urge.com. One of the primary questions on the URGE website FAQ section is, "Does URGE work with an iPod?" And the response: "Music you download or purchase from URGE is in Windows Media Audio (WMA) format and protected by the Windows Digital Rights Management (DRM) software, which is not compatible with the iPod. Apple has currently only made the iPod compatible with another format called AAC. If you use URGE to rip CDs, you can save your files as MP3, WAV, or WMA (unprotected), all of which will play on an iPod."

> **TIP:** Rich Hanold loves the network sharing feature of WMP 11. It reminds him of the features he has in iTunes, but with the more familiar feel that comes from using Microsoft Media Player. To turn it on, he says you can do one of two things. "Go into your Options and go to the Library tab. Select the Configure Sharing option and follow the prompts. You can also select the Library tab and choose Media Sharing."

- **Stacking**—Albums that share the same characteristics (artist, album, genre, year, or rating) are shown in *stacks*, providing you with a visual reference that mimics a stack of CDs or records.

Just to make it clear, this section isn't saying that the Windows Media Player is the best tool out—most would say it's not. Apple's iTunes is an excellent alternative even if you don't have an iPod. One of the main complaints about the new player is a lack of integrated support for podcasts. Aaron Coldiron, a Microsoft Product Manager, said at the Podcast and Portable Media Expo in 2006 that plug-ins and podcasting tools for Vista will likely come from third-party developers. Although Microsoft has no plans to build a podcast aggregator into Vista, "the company is thinking about it," Coldiron said. "It's on Zune's list of features."

You might or might not have noticed that video in Vista plays smoother than in XP. What accounts for the increased performance? David Solomon, author of the *Inside NT/Windows 2000/Windows 2003 Series* from Microsoft Press, explains a few reasons.

Vista Master: For one thing, the Multimedia Class Scheduler boosts the priority of Media Player threads, which provides glitch-free audio and video. In addition, prioritized I/O and I/O bandwidth reservations keep the I/O pumping.

The Multimedia Class Scheduler Service (MMCSS) is a new system service in Windows Vista that runs in a svchost process through the `Mmcss.dll` used by Media Player.

MMCSS enables multimedia applications to ensure that their time-sensitive processing receives prioritized access to CPU resources. You can read more about these features at http://msdn2.microsoft.com/en-us/library/aa830526.aspx.

Windows Media Center

Media Center was an available application for Windows XP Media Center Edition (which was only on OEM systems as a preinstalled OS). Vista users will appreciate that for the Home Premium and Ultimate editions Media Center is included.

Some people like to use Media Center in lieu of Media Player on their systems because they like the interface. But the true value of Media Center is that it gives you the ability to leave the computer in the office, but over the network, view your media on up to five TVs using Media Extenders—or even on your Xbox360, which has a media extender already built in. You can even search for and purchase an MCE remote control that works with both your TV and your Media options.

Aside from the obvious changes (mild though they are) in the interface, one of the more eagerly awaited features is the support for CableCARD-equipped hardware, which enables you to record and play back HDTV. In March 2006, Engadget's Stephen Speicher had a great interview with Microsoft's Joe Belfiore (who runs the eHome division that produces Media Center) at http://www.engadget.com/2006/03/02/the-clicker-a-sitdown-with-microsofts-joe-belfiore-part-i/.

For those of you who really want to design and build the ultimate Media Center environment, you'll need all the approved dfMCE equipment. Chris Lanier (http://msmvps.com/blogs/chrisl/default.aspx) provides a link to the Microsoft site where you can download a list of components that are dfMCE compliant. This includes DVD decoders, graphics cards, TV tuners, remote controls, and wireless routers. The document from Microsoft is "Designed for Media Center Edition Master List."

One of the best sites available for improving your MCE experience is the Tweak MCE site at http://www.tweakmce.com/. Another great site for learning more about Media Center is the Media Center Show at http://mediacenter.thepodcastnetwork.com/, hosted by Ian Dixon.

Here is a list of some other tools provided by Dana Cline (MVP) that you might want to work with (http://www.mediacenterstuff.com/downloads.htm):

- **Crunchie**—A utility to convert `dvr-ms` files to `divx`.
- **MCESync**—A utility to copy `dvr-ms` files to or from a Media Center's Recorded TV directory for viewing or archiving.

- **MCECustomizer**—An add-in to allow additional customization of Media Center.
- **MCE Test File**—A `dvr-ms` file of one-minute duration, provided for development purposes.

Windows DVD Maker

XP didn't include a DVD burning solution (with the exception of the Media Center Edition, which allows you to burn DVDs), although a CD burning solution was included. Vista goes to the next level and enables DVD burning directly from several applications, including the following:

- Windows Photo Gallery
- Windows Media Player
- Media Center
- Windows Movie Maker
- Windows DVD Maker

DVD Maker enables you to create DVD menus and scene selections as opposed to just burning data onto a DVD. The DVD Maker isn't a fancy tool; it's nowhere near the level of a third-party-purchased DVD creation tool, but it is functional and simple for new users.

DVD Maker is meant to go up against Apple's iLife application with iDVD (although DVD Maker is not quite at the same high level as iDVD). Only the Home Premium and Ultimate Editions include the DVD Maker application.

The interface is pretty simple, as shown in Figure 9.10, allowing you to add your content (movies and photos), make up a disk title, and then choose your theme (20 themes, called *menu styles*, are provided). You can change the fonts used, the scene button options, the background music, and so forth. KJ, of "2010" says:

> You don't have to settle for the themes they have given you. You can take those themes and build off of them by creating Custom Styles. To do this you just select the Customize Menu button; make your changes to the Font, the Video and Audio settings, and the Scene button selections; and choose Save As New Style. Give it a name and you will now have the Custom Styles option along with the Menu Styles options.

The Windows DVD Maker supports the NTSC and PAL TV formats. It also includes options for both the 4:3 output resolution and the 16:9 widescreen, which you can alter from the Options settings shown in Figure 9.11. You can also change the speed for writing to DVD. Galan Bridgman, a Microsoft MVP, says, "For higher compatibility and longer-lasting DVDs, you'll get better results with a burn speed no higher than 4x," in the article http://www.microsoft.com/windowsvista/community/dvdmaker.mspx.

FIGURE 9.10
DVD Maker has a simple interface, but for most, it's all you need.

FIGURE 9.11
Option settings for the DVD Maker applications.

John "PapaJohn" Buechler (http://www.papajohn.org/) gives some tips online regarding the temporary files that are created by DVD Maker. He says:

> The temporary files created by DVD Maker and used to produce the disc are in the folder of your choice (Options, Temporary file location). They are not the same as the files that end up on the disc. During the first 5% of the disc-making process, DVD Maker generates the custom images (BMPs), audio (AC3), and videos (MPEG-2) used in the menu animations. They are easy to copy and make great special features for other projects—get them before the temporary files are deleted as DVD Maker closes.

For more information on Windows Vista DVD Maker, check out Mark Coffman's blog site at http://www.windowsdvdmaker.com/.

A Few More Media Tips

There are always going to be more tricks to using Vista. The online user forums are filled with people who want to complain, praise, discuss, help, plead for help, vent…AND provide tricks about Vista. These two are pretty good to round out this chapter.

Volume Control

Don't you hate it when you are listening to a great song and you get an IM at the same time and hear that stupid ding sound? Well, Lester Lobo talks about fixing this at http://blogs.msdn.com/llobo/default.aspx.

> Click on the audio icon in the tray and open the mixer. You will see sound adjustments for several devices. You can customize the sound level on the IM in the audio control. Ain't that sweet?

This is called *per-application volume control*. As shown in Figure 9.12, you can use a volume control slider to alter the sound for every running program that produces audio output. When the program is closed, its slider is removed from the mixer options. Even though you might close a program, the volume control remembers what settings you had for that application. This means the next time you open the same application, it has the same volume settings—which is great because it means you don't have to keep configuring sound each time.

Troubleshooting your audio can be done with this tool, too, because a green meter shows the sound for each device. So, if you see that a program is producing audio output and the green meter is responding but you still don't hear any actual sound, the problem is not with the application. Maybe your speakers are turned down or unplugged.

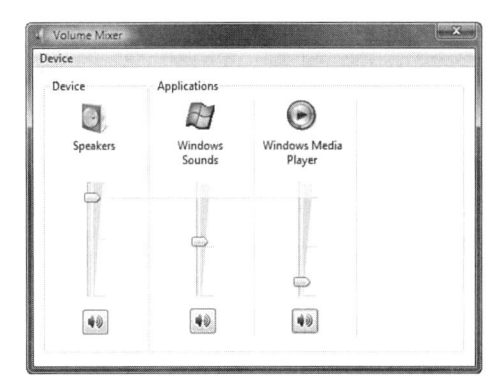

FIGURE 9.12

Per-application volume control allows you to control volume for each program with audio output.

The Snipping Tool

In the past (and present), we used the Print Screen method of obtaining screenshots. Otherwise, we used to have to find and download tools that enabled us to take a screenshot of certain parts of our systems (especially those of us who put together presentations). Vista includes a tool that lets us do a few types of snaps.

You can find the Snipping Tool either via Start, All Programs, Accessories, Snipping Tool or by simply typing Snip into any Search window. You can capture the entire screen, the active windows, a rectangular location of your choosing, or (our favorite) a freestyle selection, shown in Figure 9.13. You can then save the capture as HTML, JPG, GIF, or PNG. And you can even email the file.

Joseph Fieber
Founder of ITsVISTA.com

That's not all. Beyond just capturing and saving part of your screen, you can annotate or highlight parts of the capture with the pen and highlighting tools.

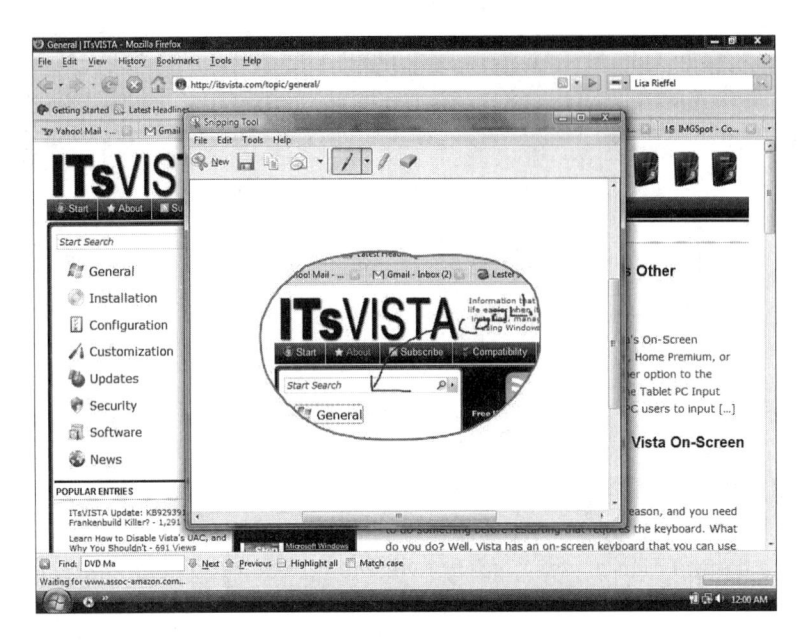

FIGURE 9.13
The Snipping Tool enables you to take freeform shots, mark them up, and even highlight portions.

Chapter 10

GROUP POLICY POWER

Group Policy Enhancements

Group Policy has some changes coming down the pike in Windows Vista. That would seem inevitable and quite logical. The changes include additional policy settings, a change in the structure, and more. We won't even fully appreciate all the changes until the next version of Windows Server (code-named Longhorn) is released. But Vista offers us a glimpse into the future.

Group Policy is a mammoth subject to discuss, requiring entire books on the subject. We are going to assume that you already know the basics. Group Policy is the primary configuration management technology used in connection with Active Directory to control a system's security, desktop, software deployment, and more.

IN THIS CHAPTER

- Group Policy Enhancements
- ADMX Files
- Network Location Awareness
- Multiple Local GPOs: Some Animals Are More Equal
- New Group Policy Settings
- Group Policy Tools: Carpenters Have Toolbelts, GP Admins Have USB Keychains

For those who love working with the Group Policy Management Console (GPMC), which originally was available as a download for XP and Windows Server 2003, the GPMC is built in to Vista. Thus, all you have to do is type `gpmc.msc` from the Search pane.

> **NOTE:** Even home users can take advantage of policy knowledge because each computer has a local policy users can configure manually. Group Policy involves the larger, enterprise solution of making changes to a system without physically going to that machine and changing the local policy. If you do want to access your local policy, you can access it through the Group Policy Object Editor snap-in by going to the Start orb and typing `gpedit.msc` in the Search pane.

Number of Policies Increased

The number of policies you can use has been increased; in fact, they've almost doubled. Danny Kim, CTO at FullArmor Corp. in Boston, says, "XP SP2 has between 1,200 and 1,500 settings. In Vista, there are about 3,000. There has been a soft mandate within Microsoft that all product groups should Group Policy-enable their products. And about 80% of the new settings are security related."

This is great news. The more policies, the better control we have. We will no doubt see these numbers increase in the future. To be a bit more specific, Michael Pietroforte, a systems administrator for 15 years and lead administrator for the IT department of the University of Munich, Germany says:

> **Vista Master:** If you compare the Excel tables containing all settings, you can calculate the number of new settings that were introduced with Vista. There are 1,671 settings for Windows 2000/XP/2003. Vista adds 824 new settings. So, all in all, we have now 2,495 switches to tune Windows. It is getting more and more difficult to have Group Policy under control.

You might wonder what he means by an Excel table, but if you visit the Microsoft download center and search for VistaGPsettings.xls, you will be provided with an extensive list of 2,495 policy settings and a list of important information. Here is an example of what the list provides for each policy setting:

Filename	`ActiveXInstallService.admx`
Scope	Machine
Policy Path	`Windows Components\ActiveX Installer Service`
Policy Setting Name	Approved Installation Sites for ActiveX Controls
Supported On	At least Windows Vista

Explain Text	The ActiveX Installer Service is the solution to delegate the install of per-machine ActiveX controls to a Standard User in the enterprise. The list of approved ActiveX install sites contains the host URL and the policy settings for each host URL. Wildcards are not supported.
Registry Settings	`HKLM\SOFTWARE\Policies\Microsoft\Windows\AxInstaller!ApprovedList, HKLM\SOFTWARE\Policies\Microsoft\Windows\AxInstaller\ApprovedActiveXInstallSites`
Reboot Required	No
Log Off Required	No
Active Directory Schema or Domain Requirement	None

If it seems a little confusing regarding how you will get Active Directory to know about and work with the new policies, Darren Mar-Elia (CTO and founder of SDM Software, Inc., a startup focused on delivering innovative Group Policy management solutions; www.sdmsoftware.com) says:

> All the changes happen by using a Vista system to manage GP. Once you start introducing Vista to your environment, you should start managing GP from Vista systems going forward. Really the Vista settings are a superset of what is in XP, so you can create a GPO on Vista that impacts XP and Vista, but the new Vista-specific stuff will just be ignored by XP, 2003, etc. Longhorn is not required at all to get most of this, although you do have to make some AD schema changes pre-Longhorn to be able to use all the GP functionality that Vista supports.

So, your domain policy administration workstation needs to be running Windows Vista. Windows Vista can be used to manage all the operating systems that support Group Policy (from Windows 2000 and up).

ADMX Files

You might have noticed the filename of the previously mentioned policy is an ADMX file. This is a new feature in Vista Group Policy. To truly appreciate how it benefits us, we need to understand how ADM files work.

ADM files are templates (administrative templates) located by default in the folder `%windir%\inf`. Some examples of ADM files include `system.adm` (for operating system settings) and `inetres.adm` (for IE settings). When you open the GP Object Editor or Management Console, you see the templates on your machine. When you create a policy change, a `registry.pol` file is created in the Group Policy Object (GPO) container with all the Registry settings defined according to the template file. The machine that receives the policy doesn't need all those ADM files at all. It has a Registry and can apply the changes.

In Figure 10.1 you can see an example of the ADM format.

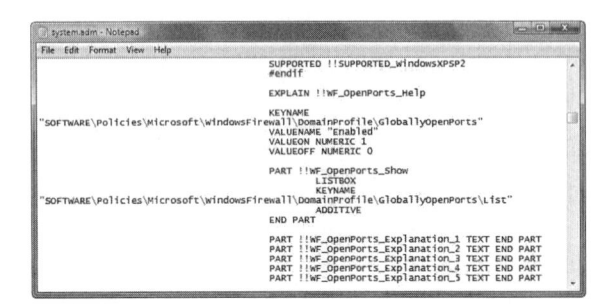

FIGURE 10.1
A Notepad view of an ADM file.

With ADM files, if you master the obscure syntax, you can create your own Registry policies and configure your clients in your own way. However, Vista changes the syntax completely to XML and the files are now ADMX files, found in the `%Windir\PolicyDefinitions` folder.

> *Jakob H. Heidelberg*
> *MCSE:Security/Messaging, MCDST, MCT, and CCNA*
> *System Consultant for Interprise Consulting A/S, a Microsoft Gold Partner*
> *Contributes to it-experts.dk.*
>
> The new ADMX/ADML files take over from where ADM files left. They are still just templates and only there for the administrators creating and modifying group policies, local as well as domain based. The managed "end users" and "end machines" will have no awareness as to whether the policy settings were configured from Vista (using ADMX/ADML files) or Windows 2000/2003 (using ADM files)—we still just edit and populate the `registry.pol` file. This is the reason why ADM and ADMX/ADML files can coexist. You will not notice the presence of ADMX files during your day-to-day policy administration tasks.
>
> So you might ask why we now have both ADMX and ADML template files! Well, the reason for this is that ADM files only supported a single language—now we get true

multilingual support. On a French Windows XP the French ADM files were included and on a Danish Windows XP the Danish ADM files were included—you could not have both. ADMX files are language-neutral and don't include policy descriptions etc. like ADM files did. Instead they reference to ADML files, which are language-specific files: one ADML file is required per language, making the ADMX files multi-lingual without much effort.

ADMX and ADML files take advantage of an XML-based format—this should make them easier to read, write, and understand (however, I still think it's hard to make your own files by hand). Maybe it's now easier to create Administrative Templates for developers or third-party group policy tools, but not for a normal human being. I actually don't believe we have an easier job with XML in the good old Notepad. Unfortunately, you won't find much information these days on how to create/customize your own ADMX templates. This seems to be a "secret" for now, but you can use a utility such as XML Notepad 2006 v1.0 to view and edit the content; also Visual Studio supports and "understands" the XML format by the use of Intellisense (the technology that helps the developer while programming, showing the available classes, methods, properties, syntax, etc.). You can also use other XML tools or programmatic XML libraries (e.g. the .NET Framework) to create/modify ADMX files—just remember that "best practice" is still to leave the default ADMX files untouched and create your own customized versions. You can see the ADMX Schema reference online.

In Figure 10.2 you can see an example of the ADMX format.

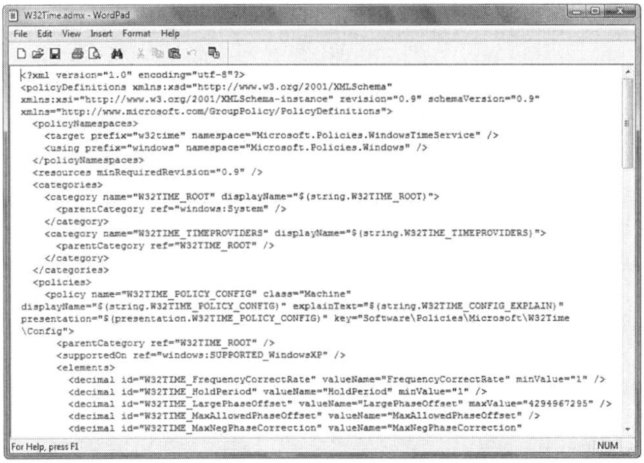


```
<?xml version="1.0" encoding="utf-8"?>
<policyDefinitions xmlns:xsd="http://www.w3.org/2001/XMLSchema"
xmlns:xsi="http://www.w3.org/2001/XMLSchema-instance" revision="0.9" schemaVersion="0.9"
xmlns="http://www.microsoft.com/GroupPolicy/PolicyDefinitions">
  <policyNamespaces>
    <target prefix="w32time" namespace="Microsoft.Policies.WindowsTimeService" />
    <using prefix="windows" namespace="Microsoft.Policies.Windows" />
  </policyNamespaces>
  <resources minRequiredRevision="0.9" />
  <categories>
    <category name="W32TIME_ROOT" displayName="$(string.W32TIME_ROOT)">
      <parentCategory ref="windows:System" />
    </category>
    <category name="W32TIME_TIMEPROVIDERS" displayName="$(string.W32TIME_TIMEPROVIDERS)">
      <parentCategory ref="W32TIME_ROOT" />
    </category>
  </categories>
  <policies>
    <policy name="W32TIME_POLICY_CONFIG" class="Machine"
displayName="$(string.W32TIME_POLICY_CONFIG)" explainText="$(string.W32TIME_CONFIG_EXPLAIN)"
presentation="$(presentation.W32TIME_POLICY_CONFIG)" key="Software\Policies\Microsoft\W32Time
\Config">
      <parentCategory ref="W32TIME_ROOT" />
      <supportedOn ref="windows:SUPPORTED_WindowsXP" />
      <elements>
        <decimal id="W32TIME_FrequencyCorrectRate" valueName="FrequencyCorrectRate" minValue="1" />
        <decimal id="W32TIME_HoldPeriod" valueName="HoldPeriod" minValue="1" />
        <decimal id="W32TIME_LargePhaseOffset" valueName="LargePhaseOffset" maxValue="4294967295" />
        <decimal id="W32TIME_MaxAllowedPhaseOffset" valueName="MaxAllowedPhaseOffset" />
        <decimal id="W32TIME_MaxNegPhaseCorrection" valueName="MaxNegPhaseCorrection"
```

FIGURE 10.2

A WordPad view of an ADMX file.

A Conversion Tool from ADM to ADMX

Some of you administrators might be wondering if you have to rewrite your existing templates to migrate to ADMX. Not if you use the free ADMX Migrator, which you can find on the Microsoft Download Center (http:// www.microsoft.com/downloads/). This tool is used to convert your ADM files to the new ADMX style.

With ADM you had to create more than one file to support multiple languages, however, ADMX includes multiple support. In addition, you will have a single centralized datastore for your files. This helps to prevent having several versions of the same file (which would occur frequently with ADM files). ADMX files are stored in one location that is replicated. This saves you space on your Domain Controllers and makes management of the files much easier.

With the ADMX Migrator you are also given an ADMX editor that provides a GUI for creating and editing your templates. Rather than manually working with your files you can choose settings from menu options.

The Central Store

Derek Melber, Director of Education and Compliance Solutions, DesktopStandard Corp., in an article at http://www.windowsecurity.com says, "One of my favorite features of Vista is the introduction of the ADMX central store. This will provide a centralized method for updating, storing, and managing ADMX files. ADMX files will no longer need to be stored in each GPO. Instead, each GPO will look to the central store for the ADMX files. This will save space on domain controllers and will allow for easier management of these files."

Why is this so interesting? Well, current implementations of domain-wide Group Policies store ADM files in the SYSVOL folder in `%SystemRoot%\SYSVOL\sysvol\domain name\Policies\{GPO_GUID}\Adm`, where `{GPO_GUID}` is a folder named after the globally unique identifier (GUID) of each individual GPO. So, if you have 25 or so GPOs for your domain (or more if you have a larger company) you have 25 copies of each of your ADM files in your SYSVOL folder, which now has to be replicated. (For every GPO, this takes a minimum of 4MB.)

Mitch Tulloch
President of MTIT Enterprises
http://www.mtit.com

This adds unnecessarily to the replication traffic when the File Replication Services (FRS) replicates the contents of SYSVOL between domain controllers in your domain. In Longhorn Server, however, you'll be able to store a single copy of each ADMX file in

SYSVOL and replication traffic will thus be reduced, which is good. Of course, this only works if your client machines are running Windows Vista since earlier versions of Windows don't support ADMX files.

Longhorn Server enables you to store all ADMX files in SYSVOL `%systemroot%\sysvol\domain\policies\PolicyDefinitions\`, as opposed to storing ADM files within each GPO. But keep in mind that the Central Store (CS) doesn't require Longhorn. The CS can be added to the SYSVOL of a Windows 2000/2003 domain and works just fine. Group Policy uses Active Directory to organize and deploy settings and uses the SYSVOL folder to store and replicate the data, but deep down, Group Policy is a client-side architecture.

The CS has no tool available to create this folder on your domain controllers. Jakob H. Heidelberg, in an article titled "Managing Windows Vista Group Policy (Part 1)" at http://www.windowsecurity.com says:

> There is no user interface to create and populate the Central Store in Windows Vista, but the process is very simple and has to be done only once per domain. All you have to do is to create the Central Store folder, preferably on the primary domain controller (PDC Emulator) because both GPMC and GPOE connect to the PDC by default, copy all ADMX files to the directory, create a subfolder for each language, copy ADML files to these directories, and let the File Replication Service (FRS) do its job replicating the content to all DCs.

Additional Points to Remember

With ADM files, if you wanted to add new templates, you would use the Add/Remove Templates dialog box from the GP Object Editor. This is still possible with ADM files, but with ADMX files you don't have this option. The new GP Object Editor reads and loads all ADMX files from the CS (or local directory) upon startup. If you want to add customized ADMX files, you just copy the file into the local directory or CS and restart the GP Object Editor.

Here are a few more points to remember:

- Group Policy tools like GPOE/GPMC adjust their display language according to the administrator's configured operating system (OS) language. Windows Vista has a language fallback mechanism that steps into action if no language file is available for the user's OS language; English is the default fallback language, and therefore a language file from the US-EN folder is preferred. If the English ADML file is missing too, the policy settings show up under Extra Registry Settings without any text and explanation.

- Keep in mind too that the file location of Administrative Templates changed with Windows Vista. Earlier Windows versions, located ADM files in the directory %WINDIR%\inf, In Vista, ADMX files are placed within %WINDIR%\PolicyDefinitions, and corresponding ADML files are located in %WINDIR%\PolicyDefinitions\<LanguageFolder>. The <LanguageFolder> might be named \EN-US for U.S. English, \FR for French, and so on.

Network Location Awareness

There were and are many reasons a policy you create now doesn't apply on a system for a long period of time. On your regular network a policy is set to apply for the computer only at machine startup (for computer setting) or at user logon (for user settings) and then every 90 minutes (with a 30-minute offset time) as a refresh interval. You could also physically go to the machine and force an update. But unstable network environments, VPN connections, and systems that never shut down or reboot (simply hibernate or standby) could all interfere with the process. Really, the process could be frustrating to force a standard policy to apply quickly.

One of the policy application features was Slow Link Detection (SLD), which used the Internet Control Message Protocol (ICMP) to determine whether a slow connection existed between the DC and the system (slower than 500Kbps by default). However, sometimes routers filter ICMP (Ping/Echo request) or firewalls don't allow these messages to pass through, resulting in policies never being applied because the fact that a slow or fast link was involved couldn't be confirmed.

This is where Network Location Awareness (NLS) version 2.0 comes in. NLS constantly monitors the network condition and responds to changes in both network conditions and resource availability. Danny Kim, CTO at FullArmor Corp. in Boston, says:

> Before, Group Policy would only refresh when you logged in. People were asking for a more timely mechanism. If I have a security setting that I want to push to the desktop, I don't want to wait for 90 minutes or so for those [settings] to apply. If a client is attached to the network and it detects a network change—for example, if a user changes his context from networked to wireless—Group Policy will refresh right away.

Here are some of the benefits that come with NLS, according to Derek Melber in an article titled "Group Policy Changes in Vista" posted at www.windowsecurity.com:

> When a computer is booting, the time that is spent trying to apply policy even though the network is not yet available can be daunting. Vista will provide indicators to Group Policy applications as to whether the NIC is enabled or disabled, as well as indications as to when the network is available.

Vista will introduce the ability for a client to detect when a domain controller is available or when one becomes available again after a period of being offline. This is ideal for remote access connections, such as dial-up and VPNs.

There will no longer be a reliance on ICMP (PING) for determining the connection speed to the computer. This was needed for slow network connections, but if ICMP was disabled for security reasons, the computer would reject the PING request, causing Group Policy application to fail. Now network location awareness handles the bandwidth determination, allowing policy refresh to succeed.

So you can see how NLA will benefit us with GP application. The improvements ensure that policies will be applied when DCs are available, over VPN connections, through firewall settings, when systems recover from hibernations, when you move in and out of a wireless network, when you dock your laptop, and more.

This enhancement will also improve security because policies will be applied quickly, so if you've made a change to security aspects of your network, those changes will be applied more quickly and reliably.

Multiple Local GPOs: Some Animals Are More Equal

In pre-Vista systems you get a single local group policy to configure. This can be frustrating when you're trying to disable something for users (such as the Run command) but don't want it disabled for the local admin. If you've ever configured kiosk machines, you no doubt found yourself fighting with the local policy, changing the policy, making your changes, and then reenabling the policy.

Vista has Multiple Local Group Policy Objects (MLGPO) for our non-AD environment where we can configure different policies between users and administrators. So, we have the Default Local GPO (which includes Computer and User Configuration settings), a Local Group Membership GPO (which includes either Admins or Non-Admins, with non-admins being anyone who isn't an administrator of the local system), and a Local Users GPO (which involves specific users of the system). The policies apply in that order, too: Default Local GPO, then Group Membership GPO, and then specific Local Users GPO.

> **NOTE** In the event you want to stop processing all local policies, you can configure a new policy setting—Computer settings\Administrative Templates\System\Group Policy\Turn off Local Group Policy objects processing—for domain users and computers.

If multiple policies exist, multiple policies apply in that order with the last one applied being the strongest and resolving any conflicts between the policies. In the end, however, regardless of what the resultant set of policies are on the local side, any Active Directory policies take precedence. The last processed policy wins. So, in a domain situation, the policies apply Local GP, Site, Domain, and then OU.

Creating These Alternative Policies

You need to start from the Microsoft Management Console and add the Group Policy Object Editor Snap-in. Note that this isn't the same as opening the policy with `gpedit.msc` because that opens the actual local policy itself. You are looking to configure a different policy. When you add the GPOE snap-in, you see the Group Policy Wizard begin.

If you select Browse, the dual-tabbed Computers/Users dialog box opens, where you can select individual users to configure or the Administrators/Non-Administrators policies (see Figure 10.3).

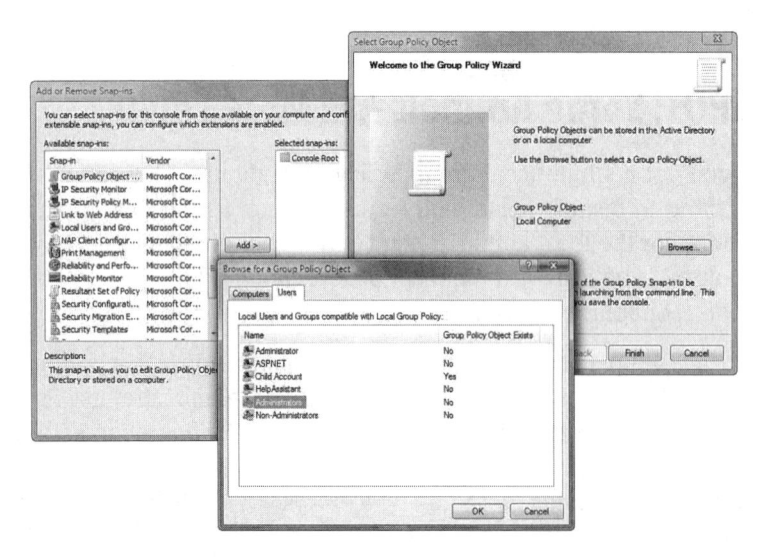

FIGURE 10.3
Creating new MLGPOs.

You can select the user or group (admin or non-admin) to work with; then you will have the MMC console with user configuration options that you can configure. However, you can also add other snap-ins, as shown in Figure 10.4. This enables you to configure your policies all from one console. You can add all your users and groups into one console and save that console for later use, so you can easily access and configure your machine.

> **NOTE**
> You might notice in Figure 10.3 that user Child Account already has a policy configured. That was odd at first because I didn't remember creating one. However, when I set up Parental Control for that user, an individual user policy object was created behind the scenes.

To see the location of the Local GPO, go to %WINDIR%\System32\GroupPolicy. To see user- or group-specific GPOs, go to %WINDIR%\System32\GroupPolicyUsers where you will see the policies within folder structures named with the Security ID (SID) of the user or group.

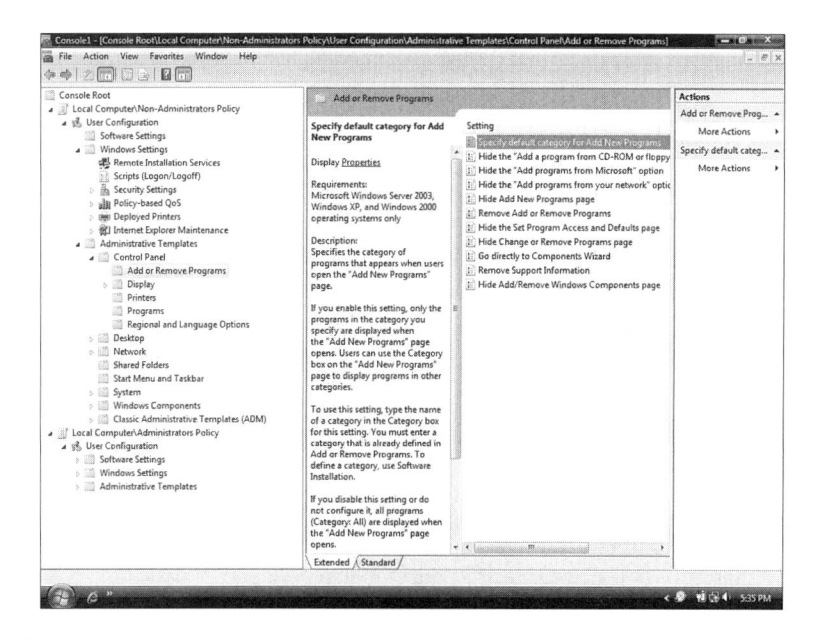

FIGURE 10.4
Create a super console that includes all the users or groups you want to be able to quickly configure.

New Group Policy Settings

We mentioned at the outset of this chapter that there are 800 new policy settings. Microsoft is pushing for even more aspects to be Group Policy controlled. In Vista, though, which ones make the top 10 list of people's favorite choices? Here are the most talked about options.

Power Management

Power Management settings are located in

    Computer Configuration\Administrative Templates\System\Power Management

For home users, Vista's power management features may not cross your mind as something of vital importance to using Windows. But to businesses, in particular, power management is crucial to controlling costs. As Mitch Tulloch, President of MTIT Enterprises (http://www.mtit.com) says:

> Simply being able to configure power management settings using Group Policy could save you around $50 per year per desktop computer on your network, and in a medium or large network that can add up to substantial savings.

Derek Melber
Director of Education and Compliance Solutions at DesktopStandard Corp

> The reasons for controlling power can provide an immediate impact for companies, since both Microsoft and the EPA have tested and reported that you can save over $50 per computer, per year by establishing power management settings on desktops. The idea is simple: There is no reason to have the computer in a full power state when the end user is not even at work. Before Vista, companies had to look at products from DesktopStandard and Full Armor to control power for Windows 2000 and XP.

Blocking Device Installation

These settings are located in

    Computer Configuration\Administrative Templates\System\Device Installation

This allows you to restrict devices from being installed on computers within your network. With this level of control you will be able to establish and enforce policy settings that can block access to USB drivers, CD-RW or DVD-RW drivers and other types of removable media.

Danny Kim, CTO at FullArmor Corp. in Boston, says:

> I can create a policy that says whether or not you can put a USB hard drive in your machine. I can set it up so it's only read access. Lots of corporations want people to use USB storage devices but don't want them to take data out. Coupled with the intelligent firewall [in Vista], you can really block Internet access so machines are only used in the context and domain that you like.

Derek Melber
Director of Education and Compliance Solutions at DesktopStandard Corp

Most IT professionals that work in the area of security for their company are very concerned about removable media devices. These devices pose a looming threat to the desktop and the network as a whole. Without control over the installation and use of these devices, users can introduce viruses, worms, and other malicious applications using these media.

Regarding power management and blocking device installation, Jeremy Moskowitz, a true master of Group Policy (http://www.gpanswers.com), wrote the following for Microsoft's *Technet Magazine* (http://www.microsoft.com/technet/technetmag/issues/2006/11/VistaGPO/default.aspx):

With the additional Power Management settings in Windows Vista, an administrator can elect to turn off or place an inactive video display monitor into a low-power "sleep" mode. Studies published on the Environmental Protection Agency's Energy Star website have shown that controlling monitor power use can result in savings of $10 to $30 USD per monitor annually. That savings can really add up when you've got hundreds or thousands of monitors in your company.

As for Removable Storage Management, consider this scenario: An administrator wants to allow students to use their USB flash drives to access term papers, homework, or other documents on any campus kiosk workstation. However, due to possible misuse, as well as potential security risks, the students should not have write access to the USB drives at the campus kiosk workstation—unless, of course, it is a school-approved USB drive. This type of device management granularity is possible using Windows Vista Group Policy settings.

Security Settings with Advanced Firewall

These settings are located in

```
Computer Configuration\Windows Settings\Security Settings\
Windows Firewall with Advance Security
```

Two security-related technologies, IPSec and Firewall, have been combined in Group Policy to allow you to leverage both together. Protection can be gained for server-to-server communications over the Internet, controlling which resources a computer can access on the network based on the computer health, and resource access based on regulatory requirements for data privacy and security.

Printer Assignment Based on Location

These settings are located in

```
Computer Configuration\Windows Settings\Deployed Printers and
User Configuration\Windows Settings\Deployed Printers
```

Managing printers has become more difficult with more laptop users who move from one location to the next throughout your network. Vista Group Policies allow you to configure printers based on Active Directory site locations. So, when a user moves to a new location, the Group Policy updates the printers for that location based on the site, which is usually arranged by geographical or physical topology.

A great article from Jeremy Moskowitz is located in the Microsoft *TechNet Magazine* at http://www.microsoft.com/technet/technetmag/issues/2006/08/ManagePrinters/default.aspx.

Controlling Windows Defender Through Group Policy

These settings are located in

```
Computer Configuration\ Administrative Templates \ Windows Components \
Windows Defender
```

Windows Vista by default comes preinstalled with the Windows Defender antispyware application. And a benefit to us is that it is configurable through Group Policy.

Delegating Printer Driver Installation to Users

These settings are located in

```
Computer Configuration\Administrative Templates\System\Driver Installation
```

Administrators can now delegate to users the ability to install printer drivers (and other device drivers) through Group Policy. This doesn't give users carte blanc to install any drivers. You need to specify through a list of device setup class GUIDs which drivers a user can install on the system. The drivers must be signed according to the Windows Driver Signing Policy or be signed by publishers already in the Trusted Publisher store.

User Account Control

These settings are located in

```
Computer Configuration\Windows Settings\Security Settings\Local
Policies\Security Options
```

The settings located under this policy heading allow you to configure your User Account Control settings and the prompts you receive. The settings include the following:

- User Account Control: Admin Approval Mode for Built-in Administrator Account
- User Account Control: Behavior of the elevation prompt for administrators in Admin Approval Mode
- User Account Control: Behavior of the elevation prompt for standard users
- User Account Control: Detect application installations and prompt for elevation
- User Account Control: Only elevate executables that are signed and validated
- User Account Control: Run all administrators in Admin Approval Mode
- User Account Control: Switch to the secure desktop when prompting for elevation
- User Account Control: Virtualize file and Registry write failures to per-user locations

You'll notice that most of these options relate to elevation prompts. You will be able to determine whether you want to be prompted for consent or credentials or have the prompts turned off altogether (which somewhat defeats the purpose of UAC).

The UAC team blogged about the settings and other information on their blog, which is still running, but has discontinued blogging. See http://blogs.msdn.com/uac/archive/2006/01/22/516066.aspx.

Tablet PC Policies

These settings are located in\
```
Computer Configuration (or User Configuration)\Administrative
Templates\Windows Components\Tablet PC
```
These setting give you control over all the new pen settings and flick behaviors. You can also determine which accessories can and cannot run on the Tablet PC.

Wireless and Wired Policies

Craig Pringle (http://www.pringle.net.nz/Blog/default.aspx) says, "If you are looking at deploying Vista into your corporate environment and you have an Active Directory based domain you can now use Group Policy to configure wireless networking settings on the clients. To do this you need to extend the schema to accommodate the additional attributes required by the policies."

Wireless and wired clients running Microsoft Windows Vista support enhancements that can be configured through Group Policy settings and are supported by domain controllers running Windows Server code-named Longhorn (currently in beta testing).

To support these enhancements in a domain running Windows Server 2003 or Windows Server 2003 R2, the Active Directory schema must be extended. To learn more about how to extend the Active Directory schema to support these new features, consider this article: http://www.microsoft.com/technet/network/wifi/vista_ad_ext.mspx.

Microsoft says the following about enhancements to Group Policy–based configuration:

- **Wired LAN settings**—Unlike Windows XP, Windows Vista now supports the configuration of IEEE 802.1X-authenticated wired connections through Group Policy.
- **Mixed security mode**—You can now configure several profiles with the same SSID with different security methods so that clients with different security capabilities can all connect to the same wireless network.
- **Allow and deny lists for wireless networks**—You can configure a list of wireless networks to which the Windows Vista wireless client can connect and a list of wireless networks to which the Windows Vista wireless client cannot connect.
- **Extensibility**—You can import profiles that have specific connectivity and security settings of wireless vendors, such as different EAP types.

To extend the AD Schema to support the new Vista features, you have to follow the instructions located on the Microsoft site. At the time of this writing they were located at http://www.microsoft.com/technet/network/wifi/vista_ad_ext.mspx.

Windows Error Reporting

These settings are located under both the Computer Configuration settings and the User Configuration settings in

```
Computer Configuration\Administrative Templates\Windows Components\Windows
Error Reporting
User Configuration\Windows Components\Administrative Templates\Windows
Error Reporting
```

This disables Windows Feedback only for Windows or for all components. By default, Windows Feedback is turned on for all Windows components.

Jeremy Moskowitz gave a quick overview of the changes in error messages and troubleshooting within Vista in an article titled "More Powerful Group Policy in Windows Vista" for *TechNet Magazine* at http://www.microsoft.com/technet/technetmag/issues/2006/11/VistaGPO/default.aspx. He says the following:

Windows Vista has an entirely new Event Log system. The Group Policy engine leverages this new Windows Eventing 6.0 system (commonly known as the Event Log) and splits events into two particular logs. The familiar System log (which is now seen as an

Administrative log) contains Group Policy problems. If an error with the Group Policy engine occurs, it should appear in the System log, listed as coming from the Group Policy Service (not the Userenv process).

A new Applications and Services log (which is an Operational log), is specifically for Group Policy, and stores operational events. This essentially replaces the cumbersome `userenv.log` troubleshooting file, as each step from the Group Policy engine is listed here for easy reading.

Group Policy Tools: Carpenters Have Toolbelts, GP Admins Have USB Keychains

We need tools to better manage Group Policies. Microsoft knows it; otherwise, they wouldn't have purchased several companies that were making these tools on the outside and then released them to us. Several products purchased from a company called DesktopStandard include GPOVault and PolicyMaker.

Derek Melber explains what each one does in an article from Redmondmag.com titled "Opening Up New Vistas in Group Policy":

- **GPOVault**—GPOVault is a change-management solution that is a snap-in to the GPMC. Some of GPOVault's capabilities include offline editing, auditing, roll-back and roll-forward, templates, delegation, and workflow. You can obtain your copy of GPOVault in the new Desktop Optimization Pack for Software Assurance (DOPSA) package. GPOVault is called Advanced Group Policy Management (AGPM) in DOPSA and is accompanied by three other products in the package.

- **PolicyMaker**—PolicyMaker was the primary reason Microsoft wanted to get its hands on DesktopStandard. PolicyMaker is still available today in the same form it was before the acquisition, but it won't be available from Microsoft for about a year. At that time, it will be delivered as part of either a service pack or add-on pack, or possibly another form of distribution. It has not yet been decided whether the new implementation of PolicyMaker will be backward compatible with Windows 2000 and Windows XP. Regardless, if you have not seen the settings, features, and overall benefits PolicyMaker provides for controlling your desktop, you should download it soon.

For some additional tools in managing Group Policies, check out http://www.gpoguy.com/Tools.htm from Darren Mar-Elia (CTO and founder of SDM Software, Inc., a startup focused on delivering innovative Group Policy management solutions).

The tools he provides include the following:

- Registry.Pol Viewer Utility
- AD, DNS, FRS Event Log Settings ADM File
- GPO Logging ADM File
- Command-line Remote GPO Refresh
- Group Policy Software Installation Viewer Utility
- GPO Editor Clipboard Utility
- GP Time Utility
- WMI Filter Validation Tool

All the tools are discussed on the website. Darren is currently advertising a very cool new tool on the site. Get the new GPHealth Reporter tool from SDM Software! The tool reports on Group Policy processing health on a given XP, 2003, or Vista system. You can download a free 10-day trial copy at SDM Software (www.sdmsoftware.com/products).

One great location for GP tools is www.gpanswers.com. http://www.gpanswers.com/toolbelt/ has a Zip file you can download and open to find an ISO file. When you mount the file, you will be surprised at how many great tools and documents there are. We have Jeremy Moskowitz to thank for these.

You might have already noticed (hopefully by this point in the book you have) that almost every Microsoft department has a blog these days. Group Policy is no different: http://blogs.technet.com/grouppolicy/default.aspx. Mark Williams, the Microsoft program manager for the Group Policy Team, has announced several tools (including the ADM to ADMX Converter mentioned earlier). Another new tool is the GPLogView. Mark says, "The tool is a quick and easy way to look at the events we report. This allows you to focus on Group Policy events specifically without having to filter them out of the full set of events collected across the operating system. GPLogView also allows these reports to be saved to your choice of text, HTML, or XML file."

You can download it from the blog. Don't forget to scan the earlier blog entries for some of the in-depth articles on Group Policy in Vista. The detailed review of the Defender policies is worth investigating.

In addition to a variety of tools (both command-line and GUI), Group Policy Administration Suites are available (that's a fancy name for third-party software that costs a bundle to do what you want in an easier way). These include the following third-party developers (which is by no means exhaustive): Centrify, Configuresoft, DesktopStandard, FullArmor, NetIQ, Quest Software, ScriptLogic, Special Operations Software, and Symantec BindView.

Index

Symbols

$ (dollar sign), hidden folder shares, 124-125
% Total Processor Time counter (Performance Monitor), 275
4SysOps.com website, 134
80/20 rule, 270

A

access control. *See* User Access Control (UAC)
Access Control Entries (ACEs), 196
Access Control List (ACL), 138, 196
  integrity ratings versus, 141
accessing
  backups with Virtual PC/Virtual Server, 261-263
  local policy, 320
accounts. *See* user accounts
ACEs (Access Control Entries), 196
ACL (Access Control List), 138, 196
  integrity ratings versus, 141
ACT (Application Compatibility Toolkit), 148
actions in Task Scheduler, 112
Active Directory schema, extending, 334
ActiveX controls, 158
ActiveX Opt-in (Internet Explorer), 158
Activity Reporting, 86
  enabling/disabling, 85
ad-hoc wireless connections, 241-244
Add Hardware applet, 56-58
add-ins
  Excel 2007, 223
  Internet Explorer, 157-158
adding
  metadata
    to files, 49-50
    to folder display, 49
  Run command to Start menu, 18

Address Bar, as breadcrumb bar, 39
address space layout randomization (ASLR), 137
ADM files, 321-322
    converting to ADMX files, 324
Administrative Approval Mode, 143
Administrative tab (Regional and Language Options applet), 73, 74
administrator access tokens, 147-148
Administrator Approval Mode
    disabling, 150-151
    elevating Command Prompt to, 19-21
administrators
    changing elevation prompts, 151
    UAC (User Access Control) and, 144
Adminpak, 133
ADML files, ADMX files versus, 322
ADMX files, 321-326
    ADML files versus, 322
    central store, 324-325
    converting ADM files to, 324
ADMX Migrator, 324
Advanced Boot Options, 288-289
Advanced Firewall settings (Group Policy), 331
advanced settings of Windows Firewall, 174-178
Advanced tab (System window), 128
    Performance section, 128-129
    Startup and Recovery section, 130-131
    User Profiles section, 130
    virtual memory, 129-130
Advanced tab (Windows Firewall), 172-173
Aero interface, slowing animations, 23-24
AIS (Application Information Service), 145
Allchin, Jim, 286
allowing (in Parental Controls)
    applications, 87
    Web sites, 87-88
Analysis ToolPak (ATP), 222-223
Analysis ToolPak VBA, 223
animations, slowing, 23-24
APIPA (automatic private IP address), 252
applets
    Add Hardware, 56-58
    AutoPlay, 58
    Color Management, 78-80
    creating customized folder for, 55-56
    Date and Time, 59
    Default Programs, 59-60
    defined, 52
    Device Manager, 60-61
    Folder Options, 62, 64-65
    grouping, 52
    Indexing Options, 80-81
        advanced options, 81-82
        Modify button, 81
    iSCSI Initiator, 65-66
    Offline Files, 82-83
        performance improvements, 84
        resolving errors/conflicts, 84-85
    Parental Controls, 85-88
    Pen and Input Devices, 67-68
    Power Options
        comparison of options, 89-90
        configuring, 91-92
        Group Policy settings, 92-93
        Hibernation mode, disabling, 90-91
        Sleep Mode, shortcuts for, 91
    Printers, 68-71
    Regional and Language Options, 72-74
    running as commands, 53-55

Speech Recognition, 93-94
  advanced options, 96-97
  listening, starting, 94
  Speech Reference Card, 95
  Speech Tutorial, 95-96
  starting, 94
  Voice Recognition Training, 96
Sync Center, 74-75
Tablet PC Settings, 97-99
Text to Speech, 75-76
User Accounts, 105-108
Windows SideShow, 76
Windows Update, 76-77
Application Compatibility Toolkit (ACT), 148
Application Information Service (AIS), 145
applications
  allowing/blocking in Parental Controls, 87
  excluding from Windows Defender scans, 163
Applications and Services log, 335
appointments
  tips, 232
  Vista sidebar gadgets, 231
Arcangeli, Andrea, 285
Archer, Tom, 285
Armstrong, Ben, 4, 262
arp command, 252
The Art and Science of Performance Monitoring (Thomas), 276

ASLR (address space layout randomization), 137
associating devices to wireless networks, 244. *See also* file associations
AT command, 114
Atkinson, Cliff, 230
atomic transactions, 184
ATP (Analysis ToolPak), 222-223
Atwood, Jeff, 2, 286
audit privilege use setting (UAC), 148-149
audit process tracking setting (UAC), 148-149
Aurora boot screen, enabling, 16-17
Authenticated Bypass (Windows Firewall), 174
authentication, 141
author, searches by, 44
AutoHotkey, 14
automatic private IP address (APIPA), 252
automatic wireless connections, 239
AutoPlay applet, 58
AutoRuns, 166-167
availability of printers, 71
Available Bytes counter (Performance Monitor), 275
Ayers, Matt, 285

B

Backup and Restore Center, 260-261

Backup Status and Configuration, 263-264
backups
  accessing with Virtual PC/Virtual Server, 261-263
  Backup and Restore Center, 260-261
  Backup Status and Configuration, 263-264
  of recovery keys, 199-200
  of usernames/passwords, 106
  of Windows Mail, 303-304
backward compatibility. *See* compatibility
Ballew, Joli, 3
Bannan, James, 4, 32, 246
Barrett, Ronald, 3, 49, 129
Bart PE, 87
baselines, 270, 274-275
basic disks, 186
  converting to dynamic, 188-189
  creating partitions, 190
Bayesian junk mail filtering, 303
BCD (Boot Configuration Data), 27
  editing, 28-31
BCDEdit, 28-30
BDD 2007 (Business Desktop Deployment 2007 Kit), 134, 290
Belfiore, Joe, 313

Beyond Bullet Points (Atkinson), 230
Big Screen Contacts, 305
Bilworth, Bill, 230
BitLocker, 201–202
    articles on, 204
    disadvantages, 204
    installing, 202–203
    recovery keys, 204
Bitmap Differential Transfer, 84
.blg file extension, 277
blocking
    applications in Parental Controls, 87
    device installation, 330–331
    Web sites in Parental Controls, 87–88
blocks. *See* sectors
blog editor, Word 2007 as, 219–220
blue files, 192
"blue screen of death," 131
Boolean filters in searches, 45
boot CDs, creating WinPE boot CDs, 292–295
Boot Configuration Data (BCD), 27
    editing, 28–31
boot problems. *See* system recovery
boot process
    Advanced Boot Options, 288–289
    dual booting, 31–32
    removing Windows Vista from, 32–33
    Windows Vista, 27–28
    editing, 28–31
    Windows XP, 26–27
boot screen, changing graphic of, 16–17
Boot tab (System Configuration tool), 34–35
boot.ini file, 26–27
bootable USB keys, creating, 295–296
bootmgr.exe file. *See* Windows Boot Manager
Boswell, Bill, 201
Bott, Ed, 3, 213, 227, 265, 272, 287
bottlenecks, 274–275
Bourgoin, Michael, 3
breadcrumb bar, 39
Bridgman, Galan, 314
Brondel, Scott, 235
Brown, Kerry, 281
browsers, Parental Controls and, 87. *See also* Internet Explorer 7
Browzar, 87
Brunelle, David, 206
buckets (Corporate Error Reporting), 269–270
Buechler, John, 310, 316
building blocks (Word 2007), 217–218
Building Blocks Organizer (Word 2007), 217–218
burning DVDs. *See* Windows DVD Maker
Business Desktop Deployment 2007 Kit (BDD 2007), 134, 290

C

CableCARD-equipped hardware, Windows Media Center support for, 313
cache, memory as, 286
Calendar (Outlook 2007), tips for, 232. *See also* Windows Calendar
Campbell, Tony, 3, 267
canonical names of Control Panel applets, 54–55
CardSpace, 159–161
CDs, AutoPlay applet, 58
cells, filling by dragging, 226
central store, ADMX files, 324–325
Certification Manager, backing up recovery keys, 199–200
character sets in URLs, 156
check boxes, selecting files, 42–43
Chinese, translating, 219
chkdsk utility, 193

Clark, Quentin, 182–183
classic menus in Windows Explorer, 41
Classic view (Control Panel), 51–52
Clayton, Steve, 12
Cleanup. *See* Disk Cleanup
clearing Prefetch folder, 287
ClearType, 216
CLFS (Common Log File System) API, 185
Cline, Dana, 313
clock, viewing multiple time zones, 21
Coldiron, Aaron, 312
collaboration (Excel 2007), 224–226. *See also* Windows Meeting Space
collectors, configuring for subscriptions, 119
Colmer, Philip, 262
color
  changing to signify elevated command prompt, 20
  in Outlook 2007, 231–232
  sorting by (Excel 2007), 221
Color Management applet, 78–80
Color Policy Database (CPDb), 80
color profiles
  installing, 79
  in Windows Photo Gallery, 78

columns, number of (Excel 2007), 221
Combs, Keith, 267
Comer, Douglas, 57
command line (Diskpart utility), 188
command prompt
  creating user accounts, 104–105
  elevating to Administrator, 19–21, 140
  Hibernation mode, disabling, 91
  Task Scheduler options, 114
command-line parameters (Windows Defender), 163
command-line tools for troubleshooting networks, 251–253
commands, running applets as, 53–55
Common Log File System (CLFS) API, 185
Comodo Personal Firewall, 180
compatibility
  Office 2007, 225
  Upgrade Advisor, 57
CompletePC Backup, 260–261
  accessing with Virtual PC/Virtual Server, 261–263
compression of disks, 192

Computer Management console
  Event Viewer, 116
    custom views, creating, 117–118
    subscriptions in, 119
    Task Scheduler and, 117
    XML in, 118–119
  services, managing, 119–120
  Shared Folders, 123–124
  Task Scheduler, 111
    AT command, 114
    importing/exporting tasks, 114
    scheduling tasks, 112–113
    schtasks.exe command, 114
    scripting, 114
    tips for, 115–116
    triggers and actions, 112
  tools in, 109–110
  user accounts
    advanced settings, 108–109
    creating, 103–104
Computer Name tab (System window), 127–128
Computer Power User website, 278
conditional formatting in Excel 2007, 226–227
Conditional Sum Wizard, 223
configuring
  collectors for subscriptions, 119
  DPI settings, 22–23

chkdsk utility

media sharing, 247-248
memory dumps, 131
People Near Me, 253-254
Power Options, 91-92
source systems for subscriptions, 119
Start menu, 17-19
with System Configuration tool, 33
   Boot tab, 34-35
   General tab, 34
   MSCONFIG Cleanup tool, 37
   Services tab, 35
   Startup tab, 35-36
   Tools tab, 36
UAC (User Access Control), 150-152
virtual memory, 129-130
wireless routers, 244

conflicts in offline files, resolving, 84-85

Conger, Jason, 107

connection security rules (Windows Firewall), 179

connections to shared folders, 125-126. *See also* networks

contacts, importing/exporting, 305. *See also* Windows Contacts

context menus. *See* right-click menus

contextual nature of ribbons, 211

Control Panel applets
   Add Hardware, 56-58
   AutoPlay, 58
   Color Management, 78-80
   creating customized folder for, 55-56
   Date and Time, 59
   Default Programs, 59-60
   defined, 52
   Device Manager, 60-61
   Folder Options, 62, 64-65
   grouping, 52
   Indexing Options, 80-82
   iSCSI Initiator, 65-66
   Offline Files, 82-85
   Parental Controls, 85-88
   Pen and Input Devices, 67-68
   Power Options, 89-93
   Printers, 68-71
   Regional and Language Options, 72-74
   running as commands, 53-55
   Speech Recognition, 93-97
   Sync Center, 74-75
   Tablet PC Settings, 97-99
   Text to Speech, 75-76
   User Accounts, 105-108
   Windows SideShow, 76
   Windows Update, 76-77
Classic view, 51-52
expanding from Start menu, 52-53
Home view, 52
searching, 48

converting
ADM files to ADMX files, 324
basic disks to dynamic disks, 188-189
email messages for Windows Mail, 304

copying
folders from user accounts, 103
Regional and Language settings, 73-74
with Robocopy, 112

CopyPE tool, 291

Corporate Error Reporting, 268, 270

counters (Performance Monitor), 273-276

CPDb (Color Policy Database), 80

crashes
Corporate Error Reporting, 270
recovery. *See* system recovery

Crunchie, 313
cumulative permissions, 196-197
custom Control Panel folder, creating, 55-56
custom themes, creating in Windows DVD Maker, 314
custom views for Event Viewer, creating, 117-118
customizing
　network settings, 238-239
　Office 2007 user interface, 211-212
　Quick Access toolbar, 211-212
　Welcome Center, 9-10

D

damaged Registry, 289
data collector sets, 276-277
　for system diagnostics reports, 277-278
Data Execution Prevention (DEP), 129
Data Platform Vision, 184
data protection, 142
Data Sources (ODBC), 133
Date and Time applet, 59
Davies, Joseph, 241
DBXpress, 304
Debugging Mode (Advanced Boot Options), 289
Default Programs applet, 59-60

Defender. See Windows Defender
defragmentation of disks, 193
Defragmenter, 133
Dehelean, Dorin, 124
deleting
　files permanently, 37
　history (Internet Explorer 7), 301
　restore points, 207
　temporary files, 191-192
　user accounts, 103
Deltree, Paul, 201
Denny, Mitch, 265
Deny permission, 196
DEP (Data Execution Prevention), 129
desktop admin, job description, 102
desktop heap, increasing size of, 300
detecting network sniffers, 252
DevCon, 61
device conflicts, resolving, 61
device drivers. See drivers
Device Installation settings (Group Policy), 330-331
Device Manager applet, 60-61
dfMCE equipment, Windows Media Center support for, 313
diagnostics. See troubleshooting

dialog box launchers, 211
digital identities, CardSpace, 159-161
Dilmagani, Nima, 58
Directory Services Restore Mode (Advanced Boot Options), 289
Disable Automatic Restart on System Failure (Advanced Boot Options), 289
Disable Driver Signature Enforcement (Advanced Boot Options), 289
disabling
　Activity Reporting, 85
　Administrator Approval Mode, 150-151
　elevated mode when installing applications, 151
　Hibernation mode, 90-91
　Mini Toolbar, 212
　Parental Controls, 85
　Protected Mode (Internet Explorer), 153
　services, 35
　SuperFetch, 287
　UAC (User Access Control), 150
　Welcome Center, 10
　Windows Feedback, 334
　Windows Sidebar, 25
Disk Cleanup, 133, 191-192
　Hibernation mode, disabling, 90
Disk counters (Performance Monitor), 276

Disk Management, 185
  basic disks
    converting to dynamic, 188-189
    creating partitions, 190
  disks, moving between systems, 189-190
  dynamic disks, creating volumes, 190
  remote disk administration, 187
Diskpart utility, 32, 188, 291
  commands, 295
disks
  basic disks, 186
    converting to dynamic, 188-189
    creating partitions, 190
  dynamic disks, 186
    creating volumes, 190
  hybrid drives, 205
  moving between systems, 189-190
  preventative maintenance
    compression, 192
    defragmentation, 193
    Disk Cleanup, 191-192
    error-checking, 192-193
  ReadyDrive, 205
  terminology, 186-188
Display Calibration Wizard, 80
display language, changing, 72
distribution, preparing documents for, 214-215
Dixon, Ian, 313
Document Inspector (Word 2007), 215
documents. *See also* files
  building blocks, 217-218
  Document Inspector (Word 2007), 215
  Full Screen Reading view (Word 2007), 216-217
  preparing for distribution, 214-215
  saving as PDF or XPS, 213-214
  translation tools, 218-219
dollar sign ($), hidden folder shares, 124-125
domain isolation (Windows Firewall), 174
Domain network category, 238
domains, joining, 127
down-down-across method for permissions, 198
downloading Windows Desktop Search 3.0, 48
DPI settings, 22-23
dragging to fill cells, 226
Driver Verifier, 61
drivers
  installing with DevCon, 61
  rolling back, 61
drives. *See* disks
Drop My Rights, 154
DskProbe, 189
dual booting, 31-32
  removing Windows Vista from, 32-33
Dugan, D. David, 278
Duggan, Timothy, 4, 200
dump files, creating, 279-280
DVD Maker. *See* Windows DVD Maker
DVDs, AutoPlay applet, 58
Dvorak keyboard, 72
dynamic disks, 186
  converting basic to, 188-189
  creating volumes, 190

E

EasyBCD, 30-31
Echo's Voice, 228-229
editing
  boot process, 28-31
  environment variables, 106-108
  Media Center-recorded TV shows in Windows Movie Maker, 310

user accounts, 105–108
  advanced settings, 108–109
Effective Permissions tool, 197
EFI (Extensible Firmware Interface), 27
EFS (Encrypting File System), 199–201
  BitLocker versus, 202
EFS password recovery tool, 201
EFSDump, 201
EFSInfo, 201
elevated mode, 140, 147–148
  installing applications, disabling, 151
elevating Command Prompt to Administrator, 19–21
elevation prompts, changing, 151
email messages, converting for Windows Mail, 304. *See also* Windows Mail
.eml file extension, 302
Enable Boot Logging (Advanced Boot Options), 288
Enable Low-resolution Video (640×480) (Advanced Boot Options), 288
enabling
  Activity Reporting, 85
  Aurora boot screen, 16–17

natural language search, 45–46
Parental Controls, 85
encrypting offline files, 83
Encrypting File System (EFS), 199–201
  BitLocker versus, 202
encryption
  BitLocker, 201–202
    articles on, 204
    disadvantages, 204
    installing, 202–203
    recovery keys, 204
  reset passwords and, 105
environment variables, editing, 106–108
erasing. *See* removing
error checking disks, 192–193
Error Reporting settings (Group Policy), 334–335
error reports (Corporate Error Reporting), 268, 270
errors in offline files, resolving, 84–85
Euro Currency tools, 223
Event IDs in Event Viewer, 119
Event Logs, 334
Event Viewer, 116
  custom views, creating, 117–118
  subscriptions in, 119
  Task Scheduler and, 117
  XML in, 118–119
Excel 2007
  add-ins, 223
  additional resources, 227

Analysis ToolPak (ATP), 222–223
conditional formatting, 226–227
dragging to fill cells, 226
naming ranges, 222
new features, 220–221
sharing workbooks, 224–226
SmartArt, 224
Exceptions tab (Windows Firewall), 171–172
excluding applications from Windows Defender scans, 163
expanding Control Panel from Start menu, 52–53
explicit permissions, 197
exporting
  contacts, 305
  Task Scheduler tasks, 114
extended partitions, 186
extending Active Directory schema, 334
Extensible Firmware Interface (EFI), 27

F

FAT (File Allocation Table), 182
fault tolerance, 187
FEK (file encryption key), 199
File Allocation Table (FAT), 182
file and registry virtualization, 149–150
file associations, Default Programs applet, 59–60

348 file encryption key

file encryption key (FEK), 199
File List Headings, 43
   filtering by, 46-47
file permissions, folder permissions versus, 195
file synchronization. *See* synchronization
file systems
   FAT (File Allocation Table), 182
   NTFS (New Technology File System), 182
   operational overview, 181-182
   transactional NTFS, 184-185
   WinFS, 181-184
file type, searches by, 44
Filemon, 280
files. *See also* documents
   adding metadata to, 49-50
   blue files, 192
   deleting permanently, 37
   restoring Previous Versions, 205-208
   searches. *See* searches
   selecting with check boxes, 42-43
   sharing, 120-121
      folder sharing, 122-126
      in Public Folder, 121-122
      removing metadata before, 50

filling cells by dragging, 226
filtering by file list headings, 46-47. *See also* searches
Finkelstein, Ellen, 230
Firefox, startup web pages, 115
firewall profiles, 238
firewalls
   Advanced Firewall settings (Group Policy), 331
   stateful firewalls, 170
   testing, 179
   Windows Firewall, 169-170
      advanced settings, 174-178
      Advanced tab, 172-173
      connection security rules, 179
      Exceptions tab, 171-172
      General tab, 170-171
      inbound/outbound rules, 178-179
      new features, 173-174
      third-party firewalls versus, 180
      Windows Meeting Space changes, 254
Flash memory in hybrid drives, 205
Flassner, Paul, 184
flicks, 67-68

folder display, adding metadata to, 49
Folder Options applet, 62-65
folder permissions, file permissions versus, 195
Folder Redirection, 106
folders
   for Control Panel applets, creating, 55-56
   copying from user accounts, 103
   restoring Previous Versions, 205-208
   sharing, 122-124, 126
   views for, 62, 64
font size, DPI settings, 22-23
formatting, conditional formatting in Excel 2007, 226-227
Frost, Gabe, 4, 237, 244-245
Full Screen Reading view (Word 2007), 216-217
Fulton, Scott M., 8
function discovery, 245

G

gadgets, 24
   creating, 25-26
   Windows Contacts as, 305
Gainer, David, 4, 226-227
galleries, 211

game definition file (GDF), 87
games, ratings, 87
Gao, Wenfeng, 149
GDF (game definition file), 87
Geneen, Harold S., 270
General tab
  System Configuration tool, 34
  Windows Firewall, 170–171
Google, spreadsheet sharing feature, 225–226
GPLogView, 336
GPMC (Group Policy Management Console), 320
GPOVault, 335
Gralla, Preston, 235, 239
graphical user interface. *See* user interface
graphics, changing boot screen graphic, 16–17
Greal, Nathan, 276
Gregg, Ryan, 231
Grey, Tim, 3
Group Policy, 319–320
  ADMX files, 321–323, 325–326
    central store, 324–325
    converting ADM files to, 324
  Advanced Firewall settings, 331

Device Installation settings, 330–331
management tools for, 335–337
Multiple Local Group Policy Objects (MLGPO), 327–329
Network Location Awareness (NLA), 326–327
number of settings, 320–321
Power Management settings, 92–93, 330
Printer Configuration settings, 332
Printer Driver Installation settings, 332
Problem Reports and Solutions, 268
refreshing, 326
Tablet PC settings, 333
User Account Control settings, 333
Windows Defender settings, 164, 332
Windows Error Reporting settings, 334–335
Windows Sidebar settings, 25
Wireless Networking settings, 333–334
Group Policy Administration Suites, 337
Group Policy Management Console (GPMC), 320
grouping applets, 52
GUI. *See* user interface

H

Hal.dll file, 27
Hanold, Rich, 312
Hardmeier, Sandi, 300–301
hardware
  Device Manager applet, 60–61
  installing, Add Hardware applet, 56–58
Hardware tab (System window), 128
Heidelberg, Jakob H., 5, 325
Henry, John, 248
Hermans, Dave, 57, 61
Hermes, 101
heuristic, defined, 285
Hibernation mode, 89
  disabling, 90–91
  resuming from, 28
Hicks, Jon, 2, 12
hidden folder shares, 124–125
hiding Notification Area items, 21
history, deleting in Internet Explorer 7, 301
Holmes, Chris, 3, 16, 23
home pages, multiple home pages in Internet Explorer 7, 299
Home view (Control Panel), 52
Hostname (command-line tool), 251
HOSTS file, modifying, 140

Howard, Michael, 3, 136, 154
hybrid drives, 205

I

icacls command, 139-140
iCalendar standard, 305
iCalShare, 306
ICMP blocking (Windows Firewall), 174
icons, resizing, 17
.ics file extension, 305
identity management (CardSpace), 159-161
IE7. *See* Internet Explorer 7
imagex tool, 291
imaging. *See* boot CDs
IMAPSize, 304
implicit permissions, 197
importing
   contacts, 305
   Task Scheduler tasks, 114
inbound rules (Windows Firewall), 178-179
increasing
   number of tabs in Internet Explorer 7, 300
   size of desktop heap, 300
Indexed Locations dialog box, 81

Indexing Options applet, 80-81
   advanced options, 81-82
   Modify button, 81
InfoCard. *See* CardSpace
Information Rights Management (IRM), 214
inheritance of permissions, 197
installation disc, running Memory Diagnostics tool from, 282
installing
   applications, disabling elevated mode, 151
   BitLocker, 202-203
   color profiles, 79
   devices, blocking, 330-331
   drivers with DevCon, 61
   hardware, Add Hardware applet, 56-58
   loopback adapter, 57-58
   printer drivers, 332
integrity ratings, 138-139
   ACLs (Access Control Lists) versus, 141
interface. *See* user interface
Internet Assistant VBA, 223

Internet Explorer 7 (IE7), 297
   multiple home pages, 299
   new features, 300-301
   Quick Tabs feature, 298
   security, 153
      ActiveX controls, 158
      add-ons, 157-158
      phishing filter, 154-157
      Protected Mode, 153-154
      URL validation, 158
   tab groups, 299
   tabs, increasing number of, 300
Internet searches, 48
Internet usage, Parental Controls applet, 85-88
ipconfig command, 251
iPods, URGE service and, 312
IPSec, 174
IPv6, 241-244
IRM (Information Rights Management), 214
iSCSI Initiator applet, 65-66

J

Jelen, Bill, 4, 221, 224, 227
Jetico Personal Firewall, 180

meetings **351**

job descriptions, desktop admin, 102
John Walkenbach's Favorite Excel 2007 Tips & Tricks (Walkenbach), 220
joining domains, 127
Junk Mail Filter in Windows Mail, 302-303

K

Kellett, John, 4, 274
Kelly, Bob, 4, 235, 249
Kenney, Kristan, 16
Kernel Transaction Manager (KTM), 184
keyboard layouts, changing, 72
keyboard shortcuts. *See* shortcut keys
Kim, Danny, 320, 326, 330
Krol, Rich, 88
KTM (Kernel Transaction Manager), 184

L

Langa, Fred, 186
Language Bar, 73
Language Interface Pack (LIP), 73
Lanier, Chris, 305, 313
Last Known Good Configuration (Advanced Boot Options), 288
Law, Eric, 300

Lee, Eric, 255
legacy applications, file and registry virtualization, 149-150
Likes, Bryant, 4
Link Layer Topology Discovery (LLTD), 237
LIP (Language Interface Pack), 73
listening (speech recognition), starting, 94
Live Icons, 42
LLTD (Link Layer Topology Discovery), 237
Lobato, Rodrigo, 304
Lobo, Lester, 316
local policies
    accessing, 320
    Multiple Local Group Policy Objects (MLGPO), 327-329
locations, printer configurations based on, 332
log files, CLFS (Common Log File System) API, 185. *See also* Event Viewer
logging in/out, shortcut keys, 12
Logical Disk: % Free Space counter (Performance Monitor), 276
logon scripts, 108
Lookup Wizard, 223
loopback adapter, installing, 57-58

M

Mail. *See* Windows Mail
Malicious Software Removal Tool (MSRT), 167-169
management tools for Group Policy, 335-337
manual wireless connections, 240
mapping network drives, 125-126
Mar-Elia, Darren, 5, 321, 336
Markoff, John, 270
MBR (Master Boot Record), 26, 186
MCE Test File, 314
MCECustomizer, 314
MCESync, 313
McFedries, Paul, 5, 240, 248
Media Center. *See* Windows Media Center
Media Center-recorded TV shows, editing in Windows Movie Maker, 310
Media Player. *See* Windows Media Player
media sharing, WMC (Windows Media Connect), 246
    setting up, 247-248
    WMPNSS (Windows Media Player Network Sharing Services), 246-247
meetings. *See* Windows Meeting Space

Melber, Derek, 5, 324, 326, 330, 335

memory
  as cache, 286
  desktop heap, increasing size of, 300
  ReadyBoost, 284-285
  SuperFetch, 285-287
  virtual memory, configuring, 129-130

Memory counters (Performance Monitor), 275

Memory Diagnostics tool, 281-284

memory dumps, configuring, 131

menus, classic menus in Windows Explorer, 41

Mercury, 101

message store, converting for Windows Mail, 304

metadata, 49
  adding
    to files, 49-50
    to folder display, 49
  removing, 50
  Windows Photo Gallery, 309

Micdrosoft Photosynth, 309

Microsoft Vista Unveiled (McFedries), 248

Minasi, Mark, 3, 202

Mini Toolbar, 212

mirrored volumes, 187

Mitchell, Bradley, 242

MLGPO (Multiple Local Group Policy Objects), 327-329

MMC console, creating, 109

MMCSS (Multimedia Class Scheduler Service), 312

Model Talker, 76

Morriale, Adriana, 232

Moskowitz, Jeremy, 5, 331-332, 334

motherboards, RAID on, 188

movies. *See* Windows Movie Maker

moving disks between systems, 189-190

MSCONFIG Cleanup tool, 37. *See also* System Configuration tool

MSRT (Malicious Software Removal Tool), 167-169

MTV URGE service, 311

MUI (Multilingual User Interface Pack), 73

Multimedia Class Scheduler Service (MMCSS), 312

multiple calendars in Windows Calendar, 306

multiple home pages (Internet Explorer 7), 299

Multiple Local Group Policy Objects (MLGPO), 327-329

multiple time zones, viewing, 21

music files. *See* Windows Media Player

N

naming ranges (Excel 2007), 222

NAP (Network Access Protection), 142, 174

natural language search, enabling, 45-46

NCSI (Network Connectivity Status Indicator), 234-235

NDF (Network Diagnostics Framework), 249-250

Nerenberg, Daniel, 4

net use command, 126

net user command, creating user accounts, 104-105

NetMeeting. *See* Windows Meeting Space

netsh command, 235

Network Access Protection (NAP), 142, 174

Network and Sharing Center, 233-234
  customizing network settings, 238-239
  NCSI (Network Connectivity Status Indicator), 234-235
  network map, 235-237

network categories, 238
Network Connectivity Status
   Indicator (NCSI), 234-235
Network Diagnostics
   Framework (NDF),
   249-250
Network Diagnostics Tool,
   248-251
Network Discovery, 125
network drives, mapping,
   125-126
Network Explorer,
   function discovery, 245
Network Location
   Awareness (NLA),
   326-327
network map, 235-237
network settings,
   customizing, 238-239
network sharing in
   Windows Media
   Player 11, 311
network sniffers,
   detecting, 252
networks
   function discovery, 245
   Network and Sharing
      Center, 233-234
      customizing
         network settings,
         238-239
      NCSI (Network
         Connectivity Status
         Indicator), 234-235
      network map,
         235-237
   Network Diagnostics Tool,
      248-251

troubleshooting,
   command-line tools for,
   251-253
Windows Meeting Space,
   253
   People Near Me con-
      figuration, 253-254
   starting, 254-257
wireless networking
   ad-hoc connections,
      241-244
   automatic
      connections, 239
   manual
      connections, 240
   WCN (Windows
      Connect Now), 244
   WMC (Windows Media
      Connect), 246
      setting up, 247-248
      WMPNSS (Windows
         Media Player
         Network Sharing
         Services), 246-247
new features
   Excel 2007, 220-221
   Internet Explorer 7,
      300-301
   Outlook 2007, 230-231
   PowerPoint 2007, 228
   Windows Firewall,
      173-174
   Windows Mail, 301-303
New Technology File
   System (NTFS), 182
Next Venture Partners, 300
NJ Star, 219
NLA (Network Location
   Awareness), 326-327

No Add Ons mode (Internet
   Explorer), 157
Notification Area, hiding
   items in, 21
nslookup command, 252
NTFS (New Technology File
   System), 182
   permissions, 193-194
      cumulative
         permissions, 196-197
      settings, 194-196
      share permissions
         and, 197-199
      transactional NTFS,
         184-185
Ntldr file, 26-27
Ntoskrnl.exe file, 27

O

O'Conner, Chris, 43
O'Neil, James, 5, 295
Office 2007
   compatibility, 225
   Excel 2007
      add-ins, 223
      additional resources,
         227
      Analysis ToolPak
         (ATP), 222-223
      conditional formatting,
         226-227
      dragging to fill
         cells, 226
      naming ranges, 222
      new features, 220-221
      sharing workbooks,
         224-226
      SmartArt, 224

Outlook 2007
　Calendar tips, 232
　color-coding in, 231-232
　new features, 230-231
　Vista sidebar gadgets, 231
PowerPoint 2007
　additional resources, 229-230
　new features, 228
　themes, 229
removing metadata, 50
speech recognition in, 97
user interface, 209-210
　customizing, 211-212
　Mini Toolbar, 212
　terminology, 210-211
Word 2007, 213
　as blog editor, 219-220
　building blocks, 217-218
　Document Inspector, 215
　Full Screen Reading view, 216-217
　preparing documents for distribution, 214-215
　saving documents as PDF or XPS, 213-214
　translation tools, 218-219

Office button, 210
Offline Files applet, 75, 82-83
　performance improvements, 84
　resolving errors/conflicts, 84-85
　opening System window, 126-127
operating systems, file systems and, 181
OS boot loader, 28
OsCDimg tool, 291
outbound rules (Windows Firewall), 178-179
Outlook 2007
　Calendar tips, 232
　color-coding in, 231-232
　new features, 230-231
　Vista sidebar gadgets, 231
Outlook Express. See Windows Mail
Outlook Tasks gadget, 231
Outlook Upcoming Appointments gadget, 231

P

pagefile. See virtual memory
Pages/sec counter (Performance Monitor), 275

Parental Controls applet, 85-88
partitions, 186
　configuring for dual booting, 32
　creating, 190
password reset disks, creating, 105
passwords
　backing up, 106
　resetting, encryption and, 105
　restoring, 106
patches. See updates
Patel, Parveen, 5
Patrick, Steven, 28
PCA (Program Compatibility Assistant), 147
PDF
　saving documents as, 213-214
　XPS versus, 213
Peers, Nick, 289
PEImg tool, 291
Pen and Input Devices applet, 67-68
People Near Me, configuring, 253-254
per-application volume control, 316-317
performance
　baseline, 270
　data collector sets, 276-277
　　for system diagnostics reports, 277-278
　Offline Files applet, 84

Performance Monitor, 273-274
  baselines, *274-275*
  bottlenecks, *274-275*
  counters, *275-276*
Process Monitor, 280
ReadyBoost, 284-285
Reliability Monitor, 271-272
Resource Monitor, 272-273
SuperFetch, 285-287
System Information tool, 278
Task Manager, 278-280
Windows Explorer, improving, 15-16
Windows Media Player, 312
performance logs, 277
Performance Monitor, 273-274
  baselines, 274-275
  bottlenecks, 274-275
  counters, 275-276
Performance section (Advanced tab of System window), 128-129
permissions
  file permissions, folder permissions versus, 195
  NTFS permissions, 193-194
    cumulative permissions, 196-197
    settings, 194-196
    share permissions and, 197-199
  sharing folders, 123

Phillips, Josh, 3, 20
Phishing Filter
  Internet Explorer, 154-157
  Windows Mail, 302
Photo Gallery. *See* Windows Photo Gallery
Photo Story 3.0, 309
photos, tagging, 308
Photosynth, 309
Physical/Logical Disk: % Disk Time counter (Performance Monitor), 276
Physical/Logical Disk: Disk Queue Length counter (Performance Monitor), 276
Pietroforte, Michael, 320
ping command, 174, 251
Pirillo, Chris, 97, 231
podcasts in Windows Media Player, 312
PolicyMaker, 335
portable document format. *See* PDF
ports for printers, 70
Posey, Brien M., 4, 74, 198, 243
Power Management settings (Group Policy), 92-93, 330
Power Options applet
  comparison of options, 89-90
  configuring, 91-92
  Hibernation mode, disabling, 90-91
  Sleep Mode, shortcuts for, 91

Power Users group, 143
PowerPoint 2007
  additional resources, 229-230
  new features, 228
  themes, 229
Pratley, Chris, 269
Prefetch folder, clearing, 287
preparing documents for distribution, 214-215
preventative maintenance (on disks)
  compression, 192
  defragmentation, 193
  Disk Cleanup, 191-192
  error-checking, 192-193
Preview Pane in Windows Explorer, 41
Previous Versions, 205-208
primary partitions, 186
Pringle, Craig, 333
print jobs
  managing, 69
  rendering, location for, 70
Print Management, 133
print servers, property settings, 69-71
print settings (Internet Explorer 7), 300
Print Spooler, 69
Printer Configuration settings (Group Policy), 332
Printer Driver Installation settings (Group Policy), 332
printers, sharing, 70
Printers applet, 68-71
priority of printers, 71

Private network category, 239
privileges, tracking with UAC, 145–148
Problem Reports and Solutions, 267–269
Process Monitor, 166, 280
Processor counters (Performance Monitor), 275
Processor Queue Length counter (Performance Monitor), 276
Processor Scheduling (System window), 128
profiles
  color profiles
    installing, 79
    in Windows Photo Gallery, 78
  Folder Redirection, 106
  roaming profiles, 106
  storage location, 106
  UNC (Universal Naming Convention) paths, 108
Program Compatibility Assistant (PCA), 147
promqry command, 252
properties, searching by, 44–45
property settings of print servers, 69–71
Protected Mode (Internet Explorer), 153–154
Public Folder, sharing files, 121–122
public key cryptography, EFS (Encrypting File System), 199–201
  BitLocker versus, 202
Public network category, 238
publishing calendars, 307

Q

Quick Access toolbar, customizing, 211–212
Quick Tabs feature (Internet Explorer 7), 298
QWERTY keyboard, 72

R

RADAR (Resource Exhaustion Detection and Recovery), 281
RAID, on motherboards, 188
RAID 1 volumes, 187
RAID 5 volumes, 188
Rains, Tim, 252
ranges, naming (Excel 2007), 222
ratings for games, 87
Reading Layout. See Full Screen Reading view (Word 2007)
ReadyBoost, 284–285
ReadyDrive, 205
recorded TV shows, editing in Windows Movie Maker, 310
recovery. See system recovery
recovery keys
  backing up, 199–200
  BitLocker, 204
refreshing Group Policy, 326
Regional and Language Options applet, 72–74
Registry, damage to, 289
Registry keys, Windows Mail settings, 304
Regmon, 280
Reiter, Dena, 16
Reliability Monitor, 271–272
relog command, 277
Remote Assistance, 132
Remote Desktop, 132
remote disk administration, 187
Remote tab (System window), 132
removable media devices, blocking, 330–331
Remove Properties dialog box, 50
removing
  metadata, 50
  spyware, 37
  Windows Vista from dual booting, 32–33
rendering print jobs, location for, 70
Repair tool, 248
replication, SYSVOL folder, 324

security   357

resetting passwords, encryption and, 105
resizing icons, 17
resolving offline file errors/conflicts, 84-85
Resource Exhaustion Detection and Recovery (RADAR), 281
Resource Kits, 133
Resource Monitor, 272-273
restore points, 205
 creating, 131-132
 deleting, 207
restoring
 files/folders (Previous Versions), 205-208
 usernames/passwords, 106
 Windows Mail backups, 304
resuming from hibernation mode, 28
return-to-libc attacks, 137
ribbons, 210
 contextual nature of, 211
right-click menus, Shift button and, 37-39
roaming profiles, 106
Robocopy, 112
rolling back drivers, 61
rootkits, 137
rows, number of (Excel 2007), 221
RSS feeds (Internet Explorer 7), 301

Run command, adding to Start menu, 18
running
 applets as commands, 53-55
 Memory Diagnostics tool, 282
Russinovich, Mark, 133, 139, 166, 280

S

Safe Mode (Advanced Boot Options), 120, 288
Safe Mode with Command Prompt (Advanced Boot Options), 288
Safe Mode with Networking (Advanced Boot Options), 288
SAN (storage area network), 65
SAPI (Speech Application Programming Interface), 76
saved searches, 40-41
Savill, John, 9
saving documents as PDF or XPS, 213-214
sc.exe command, 119-120
scheduling tasks. *See* Task Scheduler
Schinder, Deb, 143, 256
schtasks.exe command, 114
screen captures with Snipping Tool, 317-318
scripting Task Scheduler, 114

SDL (Security Development Lifecycle), 136
Search bar (Internet Explorer 7), 300
Search Folder, settings for, 64-65
searches, 43-44. *See also* filtering; metadata
 advanced options, 47-48
 Control Panel searches, 48
 by file list headings, 46-47
 Indexing Options applet, 80-81
  advanced options, 81-82
  Modify button, 81
 Internet searches, 48
 natural language search, enabling, 45-46
 saved searches, 40-41
 tips for, 44-45
 in Windows Contacts, 305
 in Windows Mail, 302
 in Windows Media Player 11, 311
 in WinFS, 183
sectors, 182
security, 135. *See also* encryption; Group Policy
 Access Control Lists (ACLs), integrity ratings versus, 141
 address space layout randomization (ASLR), 137
 authentication, 141
 AutoRuns, 166-167
 CardSpace, 159-161
 data protection, 142

hidden folder shares,
    124–125
HOSTS file,
    modifying, 140
Internet Explorer, 153
    ActiveX controls,
        158
    add-ons, 157–158
    phishing filter,
        154–157
    Protected Mode,
        153–154
    URL validation, 158
Malicious Software
    Removal Tool
    (MSRT), 167–169
network access
    protection, 142
printers, 70
Security Development
    Lifecycle (SDL), 136
Trustworthy
    Computing Initiative
    (TWC), 136
User Access Control
    (UAC), 142–144
    audit process
        tracking and
        audit privilege use
        settings, 148–149
    configuring,
        150–152
    disabling, 150
    file and registry
        virtualization,
        149–150
    privilege tracking,
        145–148

Windows Defender,
    161–162
    advanced options,
        163
    application
        exclusion, 163
    command-line
        parameters, 163
    Group Policies
        and, 164
    Software Explorer,
        164–165
    SpyNet, 162
Windows File
    Protection (WFP), 139
Windows Firewall,
    169–170
    advanced settings,
        174–178
    Advanced tab,
        172–173
    connection security
        rules, 179
    Exceptions tab,
        171–172
    General tab,
        170–171
    inbound/outbound
        rules, 178–179
    new features,
        173–174
    third-party firewalls
        versus, 180
Windows Integrity
    Control (WIC),
    138–139
Windows Meeting
    Space, 257

Windows Resource
    Protection (WRP),
    139–140
Windows Service
    Hardening (WSH),
    137–138
security audits, 179
Security Development
    Lifecycle (SDL), 136
*The Security
    Development Lifecycle*
    (Howard), 136
Security Space, 179
selecting files with check
    boxes, 42–43
server isolation
    (Windows Firewall), 174
services, managing,
    119–120
Services tab
    System Configuration
        tool, 35
    Task Manager, 280
setx command,
    configuring environ-
    ment variables, 107
shadow copies. *See*
    Volume Shadow Copy
share permissions,
    NTFS permissions and,
    197–199
Shared Folders (in
    Computer Management
    console), 123–124

sharing. *See also* networks
  calendars, 306
  files, 120-121
    folder sharing, 122-124, 126
    in Public Folder, 121-122
    removing metadata before, 50
  printers, 70
  spreadsheets/workbooks, 224-226
  in Windows Media Player, 311
Shields, Greg, 235
Shift button, right-click menus and, 37-39
shims, 148
shortcut keys, 10
  creating, 13-14
  logging in/out, 12
  tools for, 14
  Windows key shortcuts, 11-12
shortcuts for Sleep Mode, 91
shoulder surfing, 240
SHRINK, 32
sidebar gadgets. *See also* Windows Sidebar
  for Outlook 2007, 231
  Windows Contacts as, 305
SideShow. *See* Windows SideShow
Signature Verification Tool, 61

simple volumes, 187
SLD (Slow Link Detection), 326
Sleep Mode, 89-90
  shortcuts for, 91
Slow Link Detection (SLD), 326
slowing animations, 23-24
SmartArt in Excel 2007, 224
Sneath, Tim, 20, 112
sniffers, detecting, 252
Snipping Tool, 317-318
Software Explorer, 164-165
Solomon, David, 4, 280, 312
Solver add-in, 223
sorting by color in Excel 2007, 221
source systems, configuring for subscriptions, 119
spanned volumes, 187
Special Edition Using Microsoft Office 2007 (Bott), 213
Speech Application Programming Interface (SAPI), 76
Speech Recognition applet, 93-94
  advanced options, 96-97
  listening, starting, 94
  Speech Reference Card, 95
  Speech Tutorial, 95-96

starting, 94
  Voice Recognition Training, 96
Speech Reference Card, 95
Speech Tutorial, 95-96
Speicher, Stephen, 313
spell checking in Windows Mail, 303
spool folder, changing location of, 71
spreadsheets, sharing, 224-226
SpyNet, 162
spyware
  AutoRuns, 166-167
  removing, 37
  Windows Defender, 161-162
    advanced options, 163
    application exclusion, 163
    command-line parameters, 163
    Group Policies and, 164
    Software Explorer, 164-165
    SpyNet, 162
Squire, Patrick, 236
SRT (Startup Repair Tool), 282-284
SRVCHECK.EXE utility, 199
Stability Index, 271
stacking in Windows Media Player, 312
Stahl, Annik, 231
Stand By mode, 89

360 standard user access tokens

standard user access tokens, 145, 147
Standard User Analyzer, 148
standard users
 accounts, 102
 elevation prompts, changing, 151
 privileges of, 142-143
Start menu
 configuring, 17-19
 expanding Control Panel from, 52-53
 Run command, adding to, 18
Start Windows Normally (Advanced Boot Options), 289
starting. *See also* startup
 listening (speech recognition), 94
 Speech Recognition, 94
 Windows Meeting Space, 254-257
startup. *See also* starting
 Firefox startup web pages, 115
 Safe Mode, 120
 Welcome Center, 8-9
  customizing, 9-10
  disabling, 10
Startup and Recovery section (Advanced tab of System window), 130-131
Startup Repair Tool (SRT), 282-284
Startup tab (System Configuration tool), 35-36

stateful firewalls, 170
stopping Resource Monitor, 272
storage area network (SAN), 65
storage solutions, iSCSI Initiator applet, 65-66
Stratton, Terri, 3, 98
streaming media support, 246
striped volumes, 187
subscribing to calendars, 307
subscriptions in Event Viewer, 119
SuperFetch, 285-287
Swinford, Echo, 4, 229
Sync Center applet, 74-75
synchronization
 Offline Files applet, 82-83
 performance improvements, 84
 resolving errors/ conflicts, 84-85
 Sync Center applet, 74-75
SyncToy, 75
Sysinternals, 133, 167
System Configuration tool, 33
 Boot tab, 34-35
 General tab, 34
 MSCONFIG Cleanup tool, 37
 Services tab, 35
 Startup tab, 35-36
 Tools tab, 36

system diagnostics reports, data collector sets for, 277-278
System Health Report, 277
System Information tool, 264-266, 278
system locale, changing, 73
System log, 334
System Protection tab (System window), 131-132
system rating, 264-266
system recovery, 288
 Advanced Boot Options, 288-289
 from "blue screen of death," 131
 WinPE, 290-296
 WinRE, 289-290
System Recovery Options, 282
System Stability Chart, 271
System window
 Advanced tab, 128
 Performance section, 128-129
 Startup and Recovery section, 130-131
 User Profiles section, 130
 virtual memory, 129-130
 Computer Name tab, 127-128
 Hardware tab, 128
 opening, 126-127

Remote tab, 132
System Protection tab, 131-132
SYSVOL folder, replication, 324
Szpuszta, Mario, 5, 292

T

tab groups (Internet Explorer 7), 299
tablet devices, Pen and Input Devices applet, 67-68
Tablet Input Panel (TIP), 98
Tablet PC Settings applet, 97-99, 333
tabs, 211
  Internet Explorer 7
    increasing number of, 300
    Quick Tabs feature, 298
    tab groups, 299
tagging photos, 308
tags in searches, 44-45. *See also* metadata
takeown command, 140
Task Manager, 278-280
Task Scheduler, 111
  AT command, 114
  Event Viewer and, 117
  importing/exporting tasks, 114
  scheduling tasks, 112-113

schtasks.exe command, 114
scripting, 114
tips for, 115-116
triggers and actions, 112
tasks, Vista sidebar gadgets, 231
temporary files
  deleting, 191-192
  in Windows DVD Maker, 316
temporary offline files, 83
terminology for Office 2007 user interface, 210-211
testing firewalls, 179
Text to Speech applet, 75-76
themes
  custom themes, creating in Windows DVD Maker, 314
  PowerPoint 2007, 229
third-party firewalls, Windows Firewall versus, 180
Thomas, Guy, 276
Thurrott, Paul, 204
time limits on Parental Controls, 86
time settings in Task Scheduler, 113
time zones, viewing multiple, 21

TIP (Tablet Input Panel), 98
tools. *See also* applets
  in Computer Management console, 109-110
  for shortcut keys, 14
Tools tab (System Configuration tool), 36
tracert command, 252
training, Voice Recognition Training, 96
transactional NTFS, 184-185
translation tools (Word 2007), 218-219
Trenbeath, Brian, 87
triggers in Task Scheduler, 112
troubleshooting networks
  command-line tools, 251-253
  Network Diagnostics Tool, 248-251
Trustworthy Computing Initiative (TWC), 136
Tulloch, Mitch, 4, 192, 242, 260, 279, 330
turning on. *See* enabling
TV shows, editing recorded shows in Windows Movie Maker, 310
TWC (Trustworthy Computing Initiative), 136

U

UAC (User Account Control), 142-144
  audit process tracking and audit privilege use settings, 148-149
  configuring, 150-152
  disabling, 150
  elevating Command Prompt to Administrator, 19-21
  file and registry virtualization, 149-150
  privilege tracking, 145-148
  shortcut keys, creating, 13-14
UI. *See* user interface
unbootable, forcing Vista to, 283
UNC (Universal Naming Convention) paths, 108
Understanding IPv6 (Davies), 241
uninstalling disks, 190
Universal Naming Convention (UNC) paths, 108
Universal Plug and Play (UPnP), 246
updates, Windows Update applet, 76-77
Upgrade Advisor, 57
UPnP (Universal Plug and Play), 246
URGE service, 311

URLs
  character sets in, 156
  validation, 158
USB devices, ReadyBoost, 284-285
USB keys, creating bootable keys, 295-296
User Account Control (UAC), 142-144
  audit process tracking and audit privilege use settings, 148-149
  configuring, 150-152
  disabling, 150
  elevating Command Prompt to Administrator, 19-21
  file and registry virtualization, 149-150
  Group Policy settings, 333
  privilege tracking, 145-148
  shortcut keys, creating, 13-14
user accounts, 102
  advanced settings, 108-109
  copying folders from, 103
  creating, 102-105
  deleting, 103
  editing, 105-108
User Accounts applet, 105-109
user interface
  Office 2007, 209-210
  customizing, 211-212

  Mini Toolbar, 212
  terminology, 210-211
  Windows Explorer interface options, 39-40
user profiles. *See* profiles
User Profiles section (Advanced tab of System window), 130
usernames, backing up/restoring, 106
utilities. *See* applets

V

validation of URLs, 158
VHD files. *See* Virtual PC; Virtual Server
viewing multiple time zones, 21
views
  custom views for Event Viewer, creating, 117-118
  for folders, 62, 64
Virtual Folders. *See* saved searches
virtual memory
  configuring, 129-130
  RADAR, 281
Virtual PC, accessing backups, 261-263
Virtual Server, accessing backups, 261-263
virtualization. *See* file and registry virtualization
Vista. *See* Windows Vista

visual effects, performance issues, 128
Voice Recognition Training, 96
volume control, per-application volume control, 316-317
Volume Shadow Copy, 205
volumes, 187
  creating, 190
vssadmin.exe command-line tool, 207

W

WAIK (Windows Automated Installation Kit), 9
Walkenbach, John, 4, 220, 227
Watts, David, 195
WCN (Windows Connect Now), 244
WCS (Windows Color Management), 78-80
Web browsers. See Internet Explorer 7
web pages, Firefox startup web pages, 115
web proxies, NCSI and, 235
Web sites, allowing/blocking, 87-88
Welcome Center, 8-9
  customizing, 9-10
  disabling, 10
Wettern, Joern, 204
WFP (Windows File Protection), 139

White, Nick, 277
WIC (Windows Integrity Control), 138-139
  ACLs (Access Control Lists) versus, 141
Williams, Mark, 336
Willis, Will, 195
Windows AIK (Windows Automated Installation Kit), 9, 290
  creating WinPE boot CD, 292-295
Windows Backup. See Backup and Restore Center
Windows Boot Manager, 27
Windows Calendar, 305-307
Windows Color Management (WCS), 78-80
Windows Connect Now (WCN), 244
Windows Contacts, 304-305
Windows Defender, 161-162
  advanced options, 163
  application exclusion, 163
  command-line parameters, 163
  Group Policies and, 164, 332
  Software Explorer, 164-165
  SpyNet, 162
Windows Desktop Search 3.0, downloading, 48

Windows DVD Maker, 314-316
Windows Error Reporting settings (Group Policy), 334-335. See also Problem Reports and Solutions
Windows Experience Index, 264-266
Windows Explorer
  classic menus, 41
  interface options, 39-40
  Live Icons, 42
  performance, improving, 15-16
  Preview Pane, 41
  saved searches, 40-41
  selecting files with check boxes, 42-43
Windows Feedback, disabling, 334
Windows File Protection (WFP), 139
Windows Firewall, 169-170
  advanced settings, 174-178
  Advanced tab, 172-173
  connection security rules, 179
  Exceptions tab, 171-172
  General tab, 170-171
  inbound/outbound rules, 178-179
  new features, 173-174
  third-party firewalls versus, 180

Windows Integrity Control (WIC), 138-139
  ACLs (Access Control Lists) versus, 141
Windows key shortcuts, 11-12
Windows Mail, 301
  backing up, 303-304
  converting email messages for, 304
  new features, 301-303
Windows Media Center, 313-314
Windows Media Connect (WMC), 246
  setting up, 247-248
  WMPNSS (Windows Media Player Network Sharing Services), 246-247
Windows Media Player, 310-313
  media sharing and, 248
Windows Media Player Network Sharing Services (WMPNSS), 246-247
Windows Meeting Space, 253
  People Near Me configuration, 253-254
  starting, 254-257
Windows Movie Maker (WMM), 310
Windows PE, 32
Windows Photo Gallery, 307-309
  color management in, 78
Windows Pre-installation Environment (WinPE), 290-296
Windows Rally Development Kit, 237
Windows Recovery Environment (WinRE), 289-290
Windows Resource Protection (WRP), 139-140
Windows Service Hardening (WSH), 137-138
Windows Sidebar, 24
  disabling, 25
  gadgets, 24
    creating, 25-26
Windows SideShow applet, 76
Windows System Assessment Tool (WinSAT), 266-267
Windows Update applet, 76-77
Windows Update Driver Settings dialog box, 128
Windows Vista
  boot process, 27-28
    editing, 28-31
  dual booting with Windows XP, 31-32
  forcing to be unbootable, 283
  removing from dual booting, 32-33
Windows Vista Resource Kit, 133
Windows XP
  boot process, 26-27
  dual booting with Windows Vista, 31-32
WinFS, 181-184
WinKey, 14
WinPE (Windows Pre-installation Environment), 290-296
WinRE (Windows Recovery Environment), 289-290
winresume.exe file, 28
WinSAT (Windows System Assessment Tool), 266-267
wireless networking
  ad-hoc connections, 241-244
  automatic connections, 239
  manual connections, 240
  WCN (Windows Connect Now), 244
Wireless Networking settings (Group Policy), 333-334
wireless routers, configuring, 244
WMC (Windows Media Connect), 246
  setting up, 247-248
  WMPNSS (Windows Media Player Network Sharing Services), 246-247

WMM (Windows Movie Maker), 310
WMPNSS (Windows Media Player Network Sharing Services), 246-247
WMS. *See* Windows Meeting Space
Word 2007, 213
   as blog editor, 219-220
   building blocks, 217-218
   Document Inspector, 215
   Full Screen Reading view, 216-217
   preparing documents for distribution, 214-215
   saving documents as PDF or XPS, 213-214
   translation tools, 218-219
workbooks, sharing, 224-226
Wright, Alan, 3, 191, 207
WRP (Windows Resource Protection), 139-140
WSH (Windows Service Hardening), 137-138
Wu, Richard, 199

X-Z

XML
   ADMX files, 323
   in Event Viewer, 118-119
XP. *See* Windows XP
XPS (XML Paper Specification)
   PDF versus, 213-214
   saving documents as, 213-214

Yegulalp, Serdar, 109

Zheng, Long, 3, 22-23, 33
ZoneAlarm Pro, 180
zoom feature (Internet Explorer 7), 301

Safari
BOOKS ONLINE
ENABLED

THIS BOOK IS SAFARI ENABLED

INCLUDES FREE 45-DAY ACCESS TO THE ONLINE EDITION

The Safari® Enabled icon on the cover of your favorite technology book means the book is available through Safari Bookshelf. When you buy this book, you get free access to the online edition for 45 days.

Safari Bookshelf is an electronic reference library that lets you easily search thousands of technical books, find code samples, download chapters, and access technical information whenever and wherever you need it.

TO GAIN 45-DAY SAFARI ENABLED ACCESS TO THIS BOOK:

- Go to **http://www.quepublishing.com/safarienabled**
- Complete the brief registration form
- Enter the coupon code found in the front of this book on the "Copyright" page

If you have difficulty registering on Safari Bookshelf or accessing the online edition, please e-mail customer-service@safaribooksonline.com.

Short on time and need information fast... take a shortcut

Short Cuts are short, concise PDF documents on cutting-edge new technology that shows great promise, or an existing technology that has reached the "tipping point" and is about to take off.

Written by industry experts and bestselling authors, Short Cuts are published with you in mind—getting you the technical information you need now.

There are more than 50 Short Cuts published—here are just a few samples

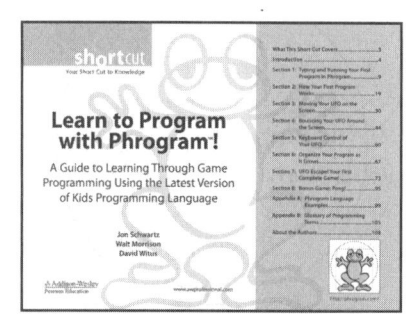

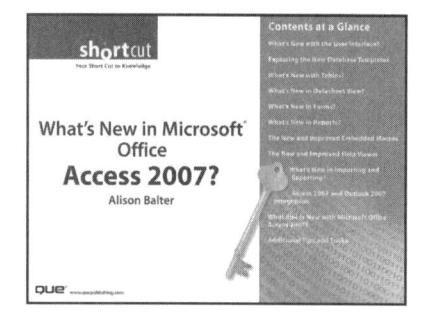

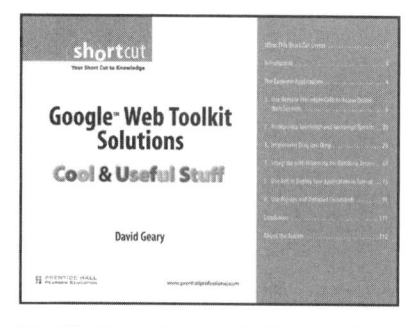

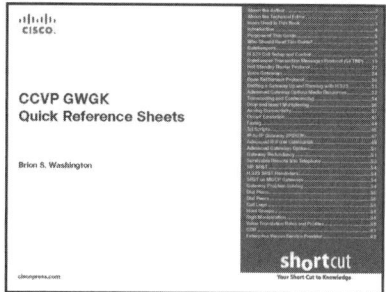

View Titles Available and Purchase Short Cuts at
www.informit.com/shortcut

Addison Wesley · Cisco Press · EXAM CRAM · IBM Press

Que · Prentice Hall · SAMS

GET TO WORK WITH BUSINESS SOLUTIONS

Let's face it, when it comes to working with software in your job, you only have time to learn enough to get things going. The time may come, however, when you have to push the limits of Microsoft Excel, Access, and other Office applications to complete more sophisticated tasks. You probably have even less time to learn new software skills now than you did before, and you certainly don't want to read multiple books just to learn how to complete a specific task. Sound familiar? We have a solution.

The **Business Solutions** series was created to provide professionals like you books focused on a specific use or application of a software program. You won't find general software information here, only details on specific software features and functions that help you perform complex tasks related to your particular productivity use. You don't need to be a programmer or a power user to become more proficient with your software. You just need some motivation and a **Business Solutions** book, written by authors who are experienced practitioners of the specific solution presented.

LOOK FOR THESE BOOKS AT YOUR FAVORITE BOOKSTORE
OR VISIT www.quepublishing.com

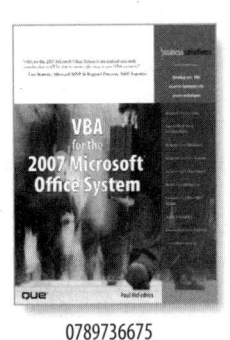

0789736675	0789736012	0789736829	0789736683
VBA for the 2007 Microsoft® Office System	Pivot Table Data Crunching for Microsoft® Office Excel® 2007	VBA and Macros for Microsoft® Office Excel® 2007	Formulas and Functions with Microsoft® Office Excel® 2007

0789736608	0789736101	0789736667	0789736691
Microsoft® Office Access 2007 for Power Users	Charts and Graphs for Microsoft® Office Excel® 2007	Tricks of the Microsoft® Office 2007 Gurus	Microsoft® Office Access 2007 Forms, Reports, and Queries

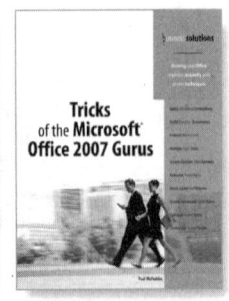

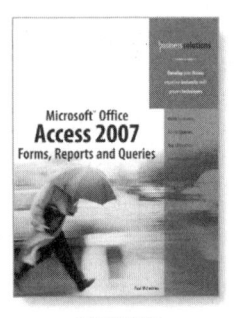

Don't wait any longer. Stop solving software problems and start focusing on business.
Get a book in the **Business Solutions** series today!